DISASTER VICTIM IDENTIFICATION

The Practitioner's Guide

DISASTER VICTIM IDENTIFICATION

The Practitioner's Guide

Edited by

PROFESSOR SUE BLACK

Director
Centre for Anatomy and Human Identification
University of Dundee

GRAHAM WALKER

Formerly UK DVI Commander
Metropolitan Police Service

LUCINA HACKMAN

DVI Programme Co-ordinator
Centre for Anatomy and Human Identification
University of Dundee

CLIVE BROOKS

Uniform Operational Support
Disaster Management Team
National Policing Improvement Agency

DUNDEE UNIVERSITY PRESS
2010

First published in Great Britain in 2010 by
Dundee University Press
University of Dundee
Dundee DD1 4HN

www.dup.dundee.ac.uk

ISBN 978 1 84586 036 3

No natural forests were destroyed to make this product;
only farmed timber was used and replanted.

British Library Cataloguing-in-Publication Data
A catalogue record for this book is available on request from the British Library

Typeset by Waverley Typesetters, Warham, Norfolk
Printed and bound by Bell & Bain Ltd, Glasgow

CONTENTS

FOREWORD

At Dundee University we have been privileged to train the National UK DVI Team and this book represents the basis of the theoretical component which was available to officers via the Virtual Learning Environment (VLE). The trouble with a book is that it is a snapshot in time and so it can very quickly become out of date. The information contained in this book was true at the time of training and should be viewed in that light and with all necessary caveats, as legislation, practices, contracts etc do not remain static and unchanging.

The text is designed to be an *aide-mémoire* for the UK students who have attended the advanced training course at Dundee. First and foremost, it is designed to be a text for nationally trained UK DVI officers who may be asked to respond to mass fatality events in a capacity that may not be fully aligned with their own in-force operational competencies. Therefore the text must reflect the wide spectrum of knowledge that may be necessary to function in this eventuality. Flexibility and adaptability are the key words for DVI and so officers cannot and must not be trained to respond to a specific type of disaster but must retain the interoperability to cope with any disaster, no matter when it happens, irrespective of where it happens and regardless of how it happens. It is a tall order to design a training course that fulfils all of these requirements and it is essential therefore that we keep the other two adjectives of DVI at the fore of our minds – pragmatism and compromise. Of course, there will be disagreements over procedures and policies adopted in this text, but they have been agreed by our partners in this project – ACPO DVI, NPIA and CIFA.

In this day of global internet access, it is essential that the deployed officer be able to access resources and for this reason the text concentrates heavily on web-based information referencing which can be readily downloaded to computers and hand-held devices from anywhere in the world. This text is not designed to be an academic, scholarly text – it is designed solely to assist the trained and deployed UK DVI officer.

We would like to thank all of those individuals, police forces, organisations and governmental offices who have willingly and selflessly granted their expertise towards creating this book. It has drawn heavily on the experiences of those who have responded to disasters in the past and who have personal experience of identifying the victims of disasters on home soil and overseas.

The introduction to the text is written by retired ACC Graham Sunderland who played a vital role in the creation of the UK DVI Team. His vision, fuelled by the unstoppable commitment of Graham Walker (the first UK DVI Commander), was sufficiently compelling to make the dream a reality. At Dundee University we are inordinately proud to have been a very small part of the UK DVI project and to have been instrumental in assisting our country to create this vitally important national capability that is a sad reflection of the needs placed upon us all by the unstable global society of today.

PROFESSOR SUE BLACK
OBE, BSc, PhD, DSc, FRSE, FRAI, HFRCPSG

LUCINA HACKMAN
RNMH, BSc, MSc

INTRODUCTION

There can be no doubt that the trauma of a mass fatality incident affects the nation as a whole and has a profound effect on all those involved in the aftermath. At a time when emergency resources are stretched, and the public demand efficient professionalism, the need for a quick and effective response from experienced personnel is of paramount importance.

The expeditious identification of the victims of such incidents has been and always will be a priority for all concerned. The families of the deceased require answers, the public need reassurance and the investigators and the Coroner (the Procurator Fiscal in Scotland) must be serviced with an effective and forensically aware recovery service.

In July 2005 the Association of Chief Police Officers (ACPO) Emergency Procedures (EP) Portfolio was invited by the Home Office to join a project board charged with the creation of a National Disaster Victim Identification Team (NDVIT), the scale and remit of which were at that time undetermined. The project board was established to ensure that everyone's needs and expectations were fully taken into account.

With the assistance of a small team of experienced professionals, working closely with the Home Office and within the parameters set by the Government's Capabilities Programme, an interim NDVIT was established by December 2005.

By identifying trained and experienced specialists throughout the UK and formalising their membership within a national team, it will be easier to develop DVI operations while significantly improving the response and resilience of all forces to mass fatality disasters both in the UK and abroad.

UK DVI is a joint initiative between the Home Office and the Foreign and Commonwealth Office of the UK Government.

In April 2006 an NDVIT Development Officer was appointed along with an NDVIT Co-ordinator. The Home Office is funding both posts. Since January 2006 the DVI Steering Group has worked hard, developing a number of work streams including agreement of a UK DVI Strategy and a Memorandum of Understanding (MOU) with the Foreign and Commonwealth Office (FCO), and an agreement with the Centre for International Forensic Assistance (CIFA) to provide medical, scientific and technical forensic expertise, as well as close liaison with training providers both within and outwith the police family. A prominent part of this work has resulted in the formation of a comprehensive training programme developed in consultation with Centrex (now NPIA), CIFA and the University of Dundee.

The overall aim in delivering the training package is for the police services of England, Wales, Scotland and Northern Ireland to provide an appropriate, effective and professional DVI contribution as part of the overall response to a mass fatality incident, either in the UK or, when requested by HM Government, overseas. This will involve the collection, examination and analysis of ante-mortem and post-mortem evidence. In effect this means the recovery of deceased victims and their remains, mortuary operations and subsequent analysis and comparison of ante- and post-mortem data to support the final identification process, including submissions to the Identification Commissioner.

The Centre for Anatomy and Human Identification within the University of Dundee's College of Life Sciences tendered successfully and has been awarded the contract to train police officers from all over the UK. Once trained, individuals will form part of the new UK DVI response capability and can be deployed to help identify victims of mass fatalities anywhere in the world. The contract is the first of its kind in the UK and was awarded to a team led by Professor Sue Black, Head of Anatomy and Forensic Anthropology at the University of Dundee. Professor Black and her team have extensive experience in DVI following deployments to incidents all over the world, including Kosovo, Iraq, Sierra Leone, Sri Lanka, Egypt and Thailand.

The training will provide practical techniques in human identification and demonstrate how to employ these skills when the UK DVI Team is deployed to mass fatalities either within the UK or overseas following the death of UK nationals. Recent incidents including the Bali bombings, the Asian tsunami, the Sharm-el-Sheikh bombing, the Bahrain boat disaster and the London bombings on 7 July 2005 are all examples of situations where the UK DVI Team might be deployed to use the skills they acquire on this course.

GRAHAM SUNDERLAND
ACPO DVI Lead
Assistant Chief Constable (Ops)
Cumbria Constabulary
April 2007

LIST OF CONTRIBUTORS

JEREMY BELL
Consular Crisis Group
Foreign and Commonwealth Office

MATTHEW BIRD
Public Order Unit
(formerly) Home Office

SUE BLACK (Prof)
Director
Centre for Anatomy and Human Identification
University of Dundee

TOM BLACK
Executive Director
Centre for International Forensic Assistance

NICK BRACKEN (Det Ch Supt)
Metropolitan Police Service

CLIVE BROOKS
Uniform Operational Support
Disaster Management Team
National Policing Improvement Agency

LAURA BURFORD
Uniform Operational Support
Disaster Management Team
National Policing Improvement Agency

EILEEN CAHILL-CANNING (Dr)
Occupational Physician
Metropolitan Police Service

DAVID COLLINS
Trainer
National Policing Improvement Agency

MIKE CONWAY
Mortuary and Post Mortem Examination Services
Chesterfield Royal Hospital

TONY CULLEN (Dr)
RAF Consultant Pathologist (deceased)

CHRISTOPHER DORRIES
HM Coroner
South Yorkshire

CARMIN DOW
Scenes of Crime Officer
Scottish Police Support Agency
Scenes Examination Branch

MICK FREE (Supt)
Metropolitan Police Service (retired)

LUCINA HACKMAN
DVI Programme Co-ordinator
Centre for Anatomy and Human Identification
University of Dundee

JAMES HARDY (Col)
RAF Dentist and Forensic Odontologist

IAN HILL (Dr)
RAF Forensic Pathologist (retired)

KRIS IRVING
Project Manager
KBR Contracts

ANDREW MACDONALD
Forensic Scientist
Cellmark Forensic Services

CHRIS MAGUIRE (Dr)
Senior Biologist
Forensic Science Services

MARGOT McBRIDE (Dr)
Programme Manager
Radiography Postgraduate Programmes
University of Dundee

DUNCAN McGARRY
National Family Liaison Advisor
National Policing Improvement Agency

WOLFRAM MEIER-AUGENSTEIN (Dr)
Senior Lecturer
Scottish Crop Research Institute/University of Dundee

GILLIAN MIDDLEMISS (DI)
Crime Operations Department
Police Service of Northern Ireland

ALAN MOSS
Anatomical Pathology Technologist

MARK OLIVER (DCI)
Senior Investigating Officer/Senior Identification Manager
Humberside Police

JOHN ROBSON
Dentist and Forensic Odontologist

GUY N RUTTY (Prof)
Head of East Midlands Forensic Pathology Unit
University of Leicester

CHRISTOPHER RYNN (Dr)
Centre for Anatomy and Human Identification
University of Dundee

GRAHAM SUNDERLAND (ACC)
UK DVI–Association of Chief Police Officers lead
Cumbria Police (retired)

GRANT THOMSON
Scenes of Crime Officer
Scottish Police Support Agency
Scenes Examination Branch

DICK VENABLES
DVI Consultant
South Yorkshire Police (retired)

GRAHAM WALKER
Formerly UK DVI Commander
Metropolitan Police Service (retired)

HOWARD WAY (DI)
Metropolitan Police Service

CAROLINE WILKINSON (Dr)
Facial Anthropologist
Centre for Anatomy and Human Identification
University of Dundee

LIST OF ABBREVIATIONS

AAIB	Air Accidents Investigation Branch
AAPT	Association of Anatomical Pathology Technologists
ABFA	American Board of Forensic Anthropology
ACPO	Association of Chief Police Officers
ACPO(S)	Association of Chief Police Officers (Scotland)
AFIS	Automated Fingerprint Identification System
AFR	Association of Forensic Radiographers
AHU	Air handling unit
AM	Ante mortem
AP	Anterior–posterior
APT	Anatomical pathology technologist
BAFM	British Association of Forensic Medicine
BAFO	British Association of Forensic Odontology
BAHID	British Association for Human Identification
BCU	Basic Command Unit
BEVAPS	European Office for Wine, Alcohol and Spirit Drinks
BHU	Body holding unit
BNOs	British Nationals (Overseas)
BOCs	British Overseas citizens
BOTCs	British Overseas Territories citizens
BPPs	British protected persons
BSs	British subjects
CB	Casualty Bureau
CBRN	Chemical, biological, radiological or nuclear
CCB	Central casualty bureau
CCG	Consular Crisis Group
CCS	Civil Contingencies Secretariat
CCTV	Closed-circuit television
CF	Compact Flash
CIBSE	Chartered Institution of Building Services Engineers
CIFA	Centre for International Forensic Assistance

CLM	Crisis Liaison Manager
CLO	Consular Liaison Officer
COSHH	Control of substances hazardous to health
CPD	Continuing Professional Development
CR	Computed Radiography
CRFP	Council for the Registration of Forensic Practitioners
CRO	Criminal Records Office
CSC	Crime Scene Co-ordinator
CSI	Crime Scene Investigator
CSM	Crime Scene Manager
CT	Computed Tomography
CTPD	Counter Terrorist Policy Department
DI	Designated Individual
DNA	Deoxyribonucleic acid
DNG	Digital negative
DoH	Department of Health
DRL	Dose reference level
DSLR	Digital Single Lens Reflex
DVI	Disaster Victim Identification
ERT	Emergency Response Team
FA	Forensic anthropologist
FAC	Family Assistance Centre
FCO	Foreign and Commonwealth Office
FCU	Fan coil unit
FLA	Family Liaison Adviser
FLC	Family Liaison Co-ordinator
FLO	Family Liaison Officer
FME	Forensic Medical Examiner
GLP	Good laboratory practice
HAA	Holding/audit area
HEI	Higher educational institution
HMIC	Her Majesty's Inspector of Constabulary
HOLMES	Home Office Large Major Enquiry System
HPA	Health Protection Agency
HPC	Health Professions Council
HSE	Health and Safety Executive
HTA	Human Tissue Authority
HVAC	High Voltage Alternating Current

ICC	International Criminal Court
ICD	Implantable cardioverter defibrillator
ICPO	International Criminal Police Organization
ICRP	International Commission on Radiological Protection
Interpol	International Criminal Police Organization
IR(ME)R 2000	Ionising Radiation (Medical Exposure) Regulations 2000
IRMS	Isotope ratio mass spectrometry
IRR 1999	Ionising Radiation Regulations 1999
ISO	International Standards Organization
IVC	Initial visual check
JRC	European Commission's Joint Research Centre
KBR	Kellogg, Brown and Root
KSF	Knowledge Skills Framework
LAPDS	Lighting and Power Distribution System
LAT	Lateral
LH	Licence Holder
MAG	Marchioness Action Group
MAIB	Marine Accident Investigation Branch
MDAT	Major Disaster Advisory Team
MHOR	Manual Handling Operations Regulations
MIR	Major Incident Room
MIRSAP	Major Incident Room Standard Administrative Procedures
Misper	Missing person
MNI	Minimum number of individuals
MOU	Memorandum of Understanding
MPR	Multi-planar reformation
MPS	Metropolitan Police Service
MRI	Magnetic Resonance Imaging
MSCT	Multiple-slice Computed Tomography
NAI	Non-accidental injury
NCB	National Central Bureau
NDVIT	National Disaster Victim Identification Team
NEMA	National Emergency Mortuary Arrangements
NHS	National Health Service
NMAT	National Mutual Aid Telephony System
NPIA	National Policing Improvement Agency
NRPB	National Radiological Protection Board

OCC	Operations Command Centre
PACE	Police and Criminal Evidence Act 1984
PCR	Polymerase chain reaction
PEP	Post-exposure prophylaxis
PFA	Police Forensic Adviser
PM	Post mortem
PNICC	Police National Information and Co-ordination Centre
PNN	Police national network
PolSA	Police Search Adviser
PolSC	Police Search Co-ordinator
PPE	Personal protective equipment
PTSD	Post-Traumatic Stress Disorder
RAIB	Rail Accident Investigation Branch
RDT	Rapid Deployment Team
RIPH	Royal Institute of Public Health
RIPHH	Royal Institute of Public Health and Hygiene
RNI	Radionuclide Imaging
SD	Secure Digital
SERM	Scene Evidence Recovery Manager
SIM	Senior Identification Manager
SIO	Senior Investigating Officer
SO15	Special Operations 15 (anti-terrorist branch)
SOCO	Scenes of Crime Officer
SOPs	Standard operating procedures
SoR	Society of Radiographers
SPF	Sun protection factor
SpHA	Special health authority
SSD	Shaded surface display
STR	Short tandem repeats
TMJ	Temporo–mandibular joint
UN	United Nations
URN	Unique reference number
US	Ultrasound
VPF	Victim profile form
VPTL	Victim Property Team Leader
VRTL	Victim Recovery Team Leader
WORM	Write Once, Read Many
WHO	World Health Organization

CHAPTER 1

UK Disaster Victim Identification (DVI)

1.1 ESTABLISHING THE UK NATIONAL DVI TEAM

"Show me the manner in which a nation cares for its dead and I will measure with mathematical exactness, the tender mercies of its people, their respect for the law of the land and their loyalty to high ideals."

William Gladstone (1871)

The practice of identifying victims of disaster is not new. Indeed, it is, and has been, central to homicide investigation throughout the last century. It was the recognition that the world was becoming a smaller place, and that citizens of any country could be involved in fatal incidents, collectively or individually, that identified a need for common identification standards and operating procedures internationally (see Table 1.1).

Interpol[1] has been the vehicle for this commonality, establishing a working party in 1980 to devise a Disaster Victim Identification (DVI) form. This was followed in 1986 by a sub-committee of police officers and forensic practitioners which has become the Interpol Standing Committee on DVI. Over 40 countries are members of the Standing Committee and over 180 countries are signatories to the principles of DVI. In addition to the Standing Committee, a Steering Group has been established. This is composed of experts in their field and aims to develop and enhance practice and make recommendations to the Standing Committee for their consideration. The UK currently has two representatives on the Steering Group.

While this work was progressing, the tragic consequences of the collision between the pleasure boat *Marchioness*[2] and the dredger *Bowbelle* on the Thames, on 20 August 1989, were eventually to reshape* DVI practices for the United Kingdom.

---

* Fifty-one people lost their lives as a result of the collision and its aftermath. Some of their bodies were recovered from the wreck of the *Marchioness* and some from the River Thames. It was of course necessary to identify them. In the course of the identification process, the hands of a number of the deceased were removed. When the relatives subsequently discovered that had happened they were naturally very distressed and pressed for a public inquiry into the circumstances in which that occurred and into identification procedures for the future.

UK Rail/Air/Boat Disasters (FATALITIES)	Terrorist Incidents in the UK (FATALITIES)	Other DVI Incidents Worldwide (FATALITIES)
Hillsborough (1989) (96)	British troops shoot rioters (1971) (28)	Oklahoma bombing (1995) (168)
Marchioness (1989) (31)	Civil rights protest (1972) (13)	World Trade Center (2001) (2,000)
Paddington rail crash (1999) (31)	IRA bomb (1972) (6)	Bali (2002) (202)
Hatfield rail crash (2000) (4)	Coach bombing (1973) (11)	Asian tsunami (2004) (approx 280,000)
Selby rail crash (2001) (10)	Car bombs (1974) (23)	Sharm-el-Sheikh (2005) (64)
Nocton rail crash (2002) (1)	Bomb in Birmingham pub (1974) (19)	Hurricane Katrina (2005) (approx 2,000)
Potters Bar rail crash (2002) (7)	Ambush N Ireland (1976) (10)	
Pershore rail crash (2003) (3)	London bombs (1982) (8)	
Romney rail crash (2003) (1)	Harrods bomb (1983) (6)	
Tebay rail crash (2004) (4)	Enniskillen bomb (1987) (11)	
Ufton Nervet rail crash (2004) (7)	Lockerbie (1988) (270)	
Helpringham rail crash (2004) (2)	Kent barracks (1989) (10)	
Romney rail crash (2005) (1)	Omagh bombing (1998) (27)	
Copmanthorpe rail crash 2006 (1)	London bombings (2005) (56)	
Grayrigg rail crash (2007) (1)		
Swainsthorpe rail crash (2007) (1)		

Table 1.1   Examples of some UK and international disasters which have elicited DVI responses

It was some 10 years after the tragedy that a public inquiry was conducted by Lord Justice Clarke. His 2001 report, "Public inquiry into the identification of victims following Major Transport Accidents",[3] complete with 36 recommendations, is central to the manner with which we undertake DVI today. That report is essential reading for UK DVI practitioners.

In making oral representations on the penultimate day of the inquiry Charles Haddon-Cave, QC, who represented the Marchioness Action Group (MAG), said this:

"The care with which our dead are treated is a mark of how civilised a society we are. Much goes on for understandable reasons behind closed doors. For this reason there is a special responsibility placed on those entrusted with this work and the authorities who supervise it to ensure that the bodies of the dead are treated with the utmost care and respect. That is what bereaved and loved ones are entitled to expect and what society at large demands."

Clarke LJ said:

> "I entirely agree with those sentiments. Respect for the dead and for the relatives of those who have died, especially where the death has been unexpected, is indeed the mark of a civilised society and should be the touchstone against which each question [that] arises should be determined."[3]

Practitioners should know that in this world of openness and freedom of information it is not only sufficient to have care and respect for the dead and relatives of the deceased, but this care and respect must be visibly apparent to the watching world. The terms "relatives" or "families", apply to parents, siblings, children, partners, guardians and others who have had a direct and close relationship with the victim.

The Clarke Report[3] is a wide-reaching and balanced document. The recommendations, most of which have been implemented or superseded, acknowledge the need for a multi-disciplinary approach to DVI.

Perhaps the most significant recommendation for UK DVI is Recommendation 10, "support for the proposal to appoint a Senior Identification Manager (SIM)".[3] The SIM is a named senior police officer who has overall responsibility for the identification process. The SIM is the link between the senior investigating officer, the Coroner and, together with Family Liaison Officers (FLOs), forges the crucial link between the identification process and the families.

Clarke LJ responded in detail to a specific incident, providing recommendations to one nation state, whereas Interpol had met with member countries earlier, to consider the global position. Resolution AGN/65/Res/13, adopted in 1996,[4] was the outcome, in which the language used was necessarily more persuasive and less directive than the Clarke Report[3] (see next section in this chapter). Specifically, Interpol called upon member countries to establish DVI teams comprising police officers, forensic pathologists and forensic odontologists or, at the very least, to appoint liaison officers responsible for DVI. In addition, they needed to ensure that such teams or officers are recognised as their country's central contact point when their own citizens are involved in a disaster, or when another member country asks for assistance. The resolution made further calls upon member countries to work together, planning and co-operating closely, to provide a rapid response to international incidents.

In some countries, this call was heeded. The Nordic countries were already collaborating well. In the Southern Hemisphere, Australia and New Zealand showed a similar level of co-operation, but in the rest of the world there was no response to the call. The UK fell into the latter category, although work was being undertaken.

- In response to events of the 1980s, the ACPO Council approved the formation of the Major Disaster Advisory Team (MDAT), consisting of individuals with specific experience who had managed aspects of major disasters, including mass fatalities.

- The Metropolitan Police produced a document entitled "The Identification of the Deceased following Mass Disaster" (the "Identification Manual") in 1994.
- It also produced a National Working Party report to the Home Secretary, entitled "Dealing with Fatalities During Disaster".
- Relationships between Coroners/Fiscals, pathologists, odontologists and other related experts were forged during homicide inquiries, where the focus was concentrated on "who did it" and "why". This resulted in transferable skills, but often by accident rather than design.

Family Liaison Officers had yet to be formally established, but body recovery/ mortuary practice as a trained skill was being developed by South Yorkshire and Metropolitan Police. While both deserve recognition, it is symptomatic of that period that they were responding to local events (the Hillsborough[5] and *Marchioness* disasters[2]) while other forces chose not to expend resources, in the hope that a comparable tragedy would not happen to them. A notable exception to this was Hertfordshire Constabulary, who engaged with South Yorkshire to train staff in body recovery and identification. Subsequent events caused all three to respond to tragedies in or near their force areas.

In 1997, the Metropolitan Police were called to respond to the Southall rail crash.[6] Two years later, they were again in action, at Ladbroke Grove.[7] In both events, the recovery and identification processes were carried out with increasing effectiveness, although the processes were not without criticism. Lessons were learned and Ladbroke Grove[7] was managed in a manner very recognisable today. At the instigation of Chief Superintendent Barry Webb, FLOs were deployed and the identification process was owned and managed by an individual senior police officer, the forerunner of the SIM.

In 2000, Hertfordshire Constabulary dealt with the Hatfield rail crash.[8] Was it fortunate that it had prepared, or a lesson for all? Less than 2 years later, the Hertfordshire team was in action again, following the Potters Bar rail crash.[9] This was a graphic demonstration of the shrinking world in which we live. Five different nationalities from three different continents comprised the seven fatalities from a train that was travelling between King's Cross and King's Lynn on a Friday lunchtime. This highlighted the importance of standardised, internationally agreed operating procedures.

In the time period between the Hatfield and Potters Bar crashes was the Selby train crash.[10] Although this occurred in North Yorkshire, the South Yorkshire team was on hand to provide the expertise needed for body recovery and temporary mortuary processes. At all three incidents, officers from MDAT provided guidance and advice. With the rapid periodicity of these incidents, the media understandably focused on the safety, or perceived danger, of rail travel, coupled with an ancillary debate about the politics of funding. Police activity in terms of DVI did not come under great scrutiny. Indeed, when measured against earlier incidents, it was recognised that valuable lessons had been learned and applied. When issues did occur it was largely about the timing of the release of information being passed to families.

Ruth Harrison undertook an analysis of the support requested by bereaved families and survivors in the immediate aftermath of the Ladbroke Grove incident.[3] She described, when giving evidence to the subsequent inquiry, that the Ladbroke Grove crash was a quantum leap in terms of use of FLOs. The importance of sharing, where possible, information with families cannot be overstated. It is listed in this manner as the first of four overriding principles identified by Clarke LJ as "the provision of honest and as far as possible, accurate information at all times and at every stage".[3]

The Clarke Report gradually had an impact around the country, senior police officers were being trained in the role of the SIM.[3] Forces examined their capabilities and, as a consequence, trained both body recovery and mortuary teams. Awareness training for FLOs was provided and mutual aid arrangements for call taking, via casualty bureaux, were put in place. However, the capability assessment by Her Majesty's Inspector of Constabulary (HMIC) describes these as piecemeal, varying from force to force, with no national strategy. Meanwhile, incidents requiring DVI continued to occur on the homeland: 58 Chinese illegal immigrants were found suffocated in a lorry container following a channel crossing[11] and 21 Chinese died in the tragedy at Morecambe Bay while cockle picking.[12] It was, however, international events that were to focus attention and ultimately create legislation which would drive the formation of a planned response.

The graphic events of 11 September 2001[13] were played out on television worldwide. The manner in which nearly 3,000 people lost their lives, in the heart of the world's superpower, created a sense of vulnerability. The subsequent identification process, relying mainly on DNA, was to teach many lessons. Gene Codes, an international software firm specialising in bioinformatics software for DNA sequence analysis, developed mass fatality identification system software (M-FISys), to deal with a large volume of minute and degraded samples, making difficult identifications possible.[14] HM Government has since purchased a licence for this software. It is interesting to note that many aspects of British family liaison practice were adopted in the US, with Duncan McGarry, UK national adviser, to the fore. His publication, *Police Family Liaison*, expands on this situation, among other practical examples where the FLO has proved invaluable.[15]

In October 2002, a suicide bomber detonated an explosive device in a Bali[16] nightclub. Many survivors took a natural escape route, only to be confronted by a larger secondary device which was secreted in a vehicle. Most of the 202 victims were Australian, but 38 Indonesians, 26 Britons, 9 Swedes, 7 Americans, 6 Germans and 4 Dutch nationals also lost their lives. In all, citizens from 21 countries were killed in the blasts. In Bali, 60 per cent of the identifications were made through dental matching.[17] There was a perception, supported understandably by some in the UK, post-*Marchioness* disaster, that of the three

5

main primary identifiers – DNA, dental and fingerprints – the latter was reducing in significance (the danger of this assumption would manifest itself later). While there is a common understanding that visual identification alone is unsound in mass fatality incidents, this was borne out when, of the 18 visual identifications made pre-DVI in Bali, one in two were found to be incorrect.

Having lived in readiness for attack from those involved in the Irish troubles, the threat at home was now perceived to be from Al Qaeda and associated Islamic radical groups. The wider world remains a troubled place, with any number of disenchanted groups resorting to violent attacks in support of their cause. The ongoing terrorist threat led to some significant changes in the approach to DVI taken by the UK. In January 2004, the Home Office established a section to lead on the cross-Government Mass Fatalities Workstream, part of the Cabinet Office Capabilities Programme.[18] The Mass Fatalities Section works with stakeholders (eg local business continuity, emergency planners and emergency services) to assess what is required to respond effectively to an incident resulting in a large number of fatalities. The Civil Contingencies Act 2004[19] received Royal Assent in November 2004. Existing legislation, the Civil Defence Act 1948,[20] which focused on war or attack by a foreign power, was repealed in its entirety. The Civil Contingencies legislation is much broader and allows for the threat of terrorism, as well as taking into account other events which might seriously damage human welfare in the United Kingdom.

The 2004 Act[19] imposes a series of duties on local bodies in England, Wales, Scotland and Northern Ireland (to be known as "Category 1 responders"). These duties include the duty to assess the risk of an emergency occurring and to maintain plans for the purposes of responding to an emergency. The range of Category 1 responders is broader than the range of local bodies which were subject to the previous legislation. It includes groups related to health, the Environment Agency and the Secretary of State, in so far as his functions pertain to the response to maritime and coastal emergencies. Police are also Category 1 responders.

The 2004 Act[19] cites "emergency": areas that would satisfy that definition include terrorist attack, disruption of fuel supplies, contamination of land with a chemical matter and an epidemic, should they reach the required level of seriousness. Clearly, a mass fatality incident, whatever the cause, falls within that definition.

Further, Category 1 responders are required to:

- assess the risk of emergencies occurring and use this to inform contingency planning;
- put in place emergency plans;
- put in place business continuity management arrangements;
- put in place arrangements to make information available to the public about civil protection matters, and to maintain arrangements to warn, inform and advise the public in the event of an emergency;

- share information with other local responders to enhance co-ordination;
- co-operate with other local responders to enhance efficiency;
- provide advice and assistance to businesses and voluntary organisations about business continuity.

It is now a statutory duty of local and regional authorities to work together in planning and preparing for emergencies. To achieve this, local and regional resilience forums[21] were established, and most of these developed working groups to identify and action areas for attention. In terms of DVI this tended to manifest itself in examining the provision of resilience mortuary facilities. It has been acknowledged that, in the event of a mass fatality incident, there will probably be factors which preclude the use of an existing hospital or public mortuary. These may include impact on daily business; accommodation of several teams working simultaneously; generation of numerous body bags; abnormal normal storage capacity requirements; and the need for added security and viewing facilities for the bereaved.

Most areas had a plan of sorts – many based on use of military sites – but, as previously mentioned, these plans had not been well maintained. Many plans were not fit for purpose and had never been tested or exercised, although, on balance, there were a few beacons of excellence. The Civil Contingencies Act 2004[19] therefore prompted a flurry of activity, as emergency plans and business continuity now needed executable plans. In turn, the examination of temporary mortuary arrangements prompted a question for the police: in the event of temporary mortuary activation, could they support the operation with trained and competent body recovery and mortuary practitioners?

While that question was being pondered, a natural disaster in South-East Asia was to result in the largest ever sustained UK policing operation, accelerating DVI developments in an unprecedented manner. At two minutes to eight on the morning of 26 December 2004, the second biggest earthquake in recorded history occurred under the Indian Ocean. It generated a tsunami[22] that ripped across the seas, killing almost 300,000 people. As the UK woke, six hours behind in time, the enormity of the situation was only just beginning to become apparent.

We now know that the tsunami claimed the lives of 151 British citizens, or people who had close links to the UK. During a 14-month period over a thousand police and forensic staff were deployed to the theatre of operations, which for the UK was Sri Lanka and Thailand. While Banda Ache suffered the greatest loss of life, UK official interest and endeavour were confined to Sri Lanka and Thailand, as that is where our citizens lost their lives. A further 2,000 staff were deployed in Operation Bracknell, the UK side of the investigation.[23]

The initial response by British authorities has been criticised in various reports as being too slow, and this is confirmed in the most recent published report. Carried out by the National Audit Office, assisted by the Zito Trust,[24] it reviews the experience of UK nationals affected by the Indian Ocean tsunami: 116 people directly involved or affected were interviewed, and their experiences analysed[24, 25] to provide lessons for the improvement of future responses.

The scenario that presented itself was among the worst imaginable in terms of DVI: an open situation, where there was no assistance in the form of a passenger manifest or employee payroll, added to the fact that many of the victims were in beachwear, and therefore carrying no putative identification such as credit cards, driving licences or photo identification. In addition, such was the destructive power of the tsunami that much of the holiday accommodation had been destroyed, taking with it personal effects and other potential intelligence sources.

It was policy, at that time, for the Metropolitan Police to respond on behalf of the Foreign Office to spontaneous incidents requiring UK policing overseas. While the need for DVI practices to be instigated was immediately clear, there were significant political hurdles to be overcome. Credit is due to the officers, directed by Detective Superintendent John McBrayne, who played their part in the delicate international negotiations. In addition to Thai nationals, 32 other nations had lost citizens, and there was little or no chance of preliminary indication from intelligence at the scene as to the nationality of the victims. The Thai Government was prepared to allow the international community to operate in its country, but the question was "how?". With the prevailing conditions, time was critical, with heat and humidity leading to accelerated degradation of the bodies.

In the UK, as in many other countries, a DVI team was on standby, ready to respond. What constituted a DVI team at that time? In reality, the team is composed according to the situation presented. It may also be influenced by resource availability, local practice and the DVI Commander's previous experience. The UK team in this instance, consisting of fingerprint and crime scene investigators, a pathologist, a forensic odontologist and experienced body recovery and mortuary operatives, was dispatched 6 days after the event.

Body recovery and storage in chilled containers was imperative. In light of the numbers involved, that task was a priority. It is accepted now, having managed that process initially, that time would have been well spent agreeing procedures in respect of staffing requirements. Two factors combined to prevent that logical step; first, it was difficult to communicate the cumulative effect† of the climate, working conditions and volume of deceased facing those in the initial deployments.† Despite fatigue quickly setting in, everyone remained task focused. Having set a tremendous pace, with good reason, there was little will to stand back, take stock and reorganise. The tempo had been set and somehow

---

† "Fatigue is a major issue in this type of work. Team members will always tend to push themselves to the point where they can no longer function efficiently. This is when mistakes are made. It is up to wiser heads to enforce full meal breaks and rest days, even if the team wants to continue working. Occupational health and safety concerns are real, and need genuine commitment by managers. In DVI we talk about the different groups of victims. The first group is the dead and injured; the second group is the families, especially those of the dead. There is a third group of potential victims – the rescuers and DVI workers."[17]

was maintained. The situation was similar across the board internationally, not confined to the UK. As a result, we have moved on, in that, alongside UK DVI, independent pragmatic occupational health practitioners will now be deployed immediately, and appropriate tiers of management will be in place. The second factor was governmental pressure. This was universal, in that the politicians had a very human desire to demonstrate to their public that things were being done. It would have been unacceptable for them to report that teams were sitting around debating management issues, with a possible outcome being that, for example, the British contingent would be coming home, only to travel out again perhaps some weeks later.

There is a further caveat, in that differing standards of examination are practised internationally. As discussed, the outcome of the *Marchioness* inquiry has massively influenced practice for UK pathology in a DVI scenario.[3] Coroners, pathologists and SIMs are extremely sensitive to the degree of intrusive investigation which should be practised.

In a paper to Interpol Standing Committee 2005, "Ethics in DVI", I argued that where the identity of the deceased cannot be known, the standard of examination should be commensurate with the most sensitive of the possible countries of origin. While this found favour, it must be remembered that in a scenario where we request admission, rather than being invited to operate, such admission is only at the behest of the host country. Negotiation as to working practices may be sensitive and prolonged. In every case, therefore, support from those who understand local culture is imperative. This will normally be the domain of the Foreign and Commonwealth Office.[26]

While the International teams commenced their work, an inquiry of unprecedented size was mounted in the UK, to determine which of our citizens had lost their lives. At the peak, there were over 20,000 possible nominals on the system. While the Metropolitan Police were commanding the incident, officers from all over the UK were engaged in the intelligence-gathering operation, either to remove those not involved from the enquiry, or to gather ante-mortem information for matching and identification.[23]

I referred earlier to a perception that fingerprints were falling behind DNA and odontology as identifiers. Poor communication between theatre and Gold Command UK allowed the myth to develop that decomposition was so advanced that the opportunity to harvest fingerprints would be minimal. FLOs were briefed accordingly.

Not unreasonably, that message was communicated in differing ways to families. When the misunderstanding was cleared up, return visits were made, causing confusion and in some cases doubt in the ability and outcome of the process. It was to be some months later that the real damage of this manifested for one family. Their daughter was identified by fingerprints and repatriated. Following the funeral, the mother recalled hearing that fingerprinting was unlikely and unreliable. She became convinced that her daughter's identification was flawed, possibly as part of a campaign by officials to get the situation cleared up "by hook or by crook". Although everything possible was done to reassure the family, the incident compounded their trauma, and was a chastening experience for the officers involved. Had we been able to take that time following the initial recovery, this might have been avoided. What we must do now is prepare for every eventuality in advance, keeping an open mind as to how the next incident may present itself.

The first step along that path is the formation of a National UK DVI team, trained and regularly exercised. The enormity of the 2004 tsunami and its tragic consequences, together with strong representation from professionals who had predicted the need for such a team, persuaded Ministers, in February 2005, to announce their sponsorship for UK DVI. Home Office Mass Fatalities were tasked with leading the project.[18]

It is acknowledged by Interpol DVI steering group that teams should be police led, but bring together practitioners from relevant scientific and governmental bodies. Throughout Operation Bracknell, the Centre for International Forensic Assistance (CIFA)[27] acted as agents for the supply of forensic practitioners.

Significantly, the Metropolitan Police realised that, despite their resources totalling almost a quarter of UK policing, the operation would soon overwhelm them. Agreement was reached that Operation Bracknell[23] would become national. Officers from 41 forces, including the police services of Northern Ireland, Scotland and Wales, served at times, either at home or overseas.

Despite the absence of a prescribed DVI team, British policing was to receive an accolade, as officers were appointed to significant command positions in the international operation.

As the work on Operation Bracknell approached a steady state, attention turned to forming UK DVI. That attention was soon to be diverted in July 2005,[28] when 52 people were murdered by four suicide bombers while using public transport in London. With their skills honed by practice, the core teams of Bracknell were redeployed to facilitate the identification and reconciliation of the victims.

Two weeks later, a thwarted attempt to cause further death and destruction stretched resources wafer thin in London. There was to be no respite, as within 2 days, three explosions killed 88 people in Sharm-el-Sheikh,[29] Egypt, including 11 UK citizens.

A request for assistance was made by the Foreign Office. The Metropolitan Police, understandably, reported that it would not be able to respond. England's second largest force, West Midlands Police, stepped up to lead the DVI process. Despite the unprecedented demands on practitioners, work progressed on the formation of a national team. An interim strategy for UK DVI was agreed by ACPO in October 2005. The vision statement reads:

"The Police Service within England, Wales, Scotland and Northern Ireland will provide an appropriate, effective and professional DVI Contribution as part of the overall response to a mass fatality incident, either in the UK; or when requested by HM Government, overseas."[30]

10

Significantly, for the first time, UK DVI was represented at ACPO, the portfolio holder being Assistant Chief Constable Graham Sunderland.

The strategy called for a development team to be in place by January 2006, which Detective Superintendent Graham Walker, then Gold Commander for Operation Bracknell, was asked to lead.

Home Office Mass Fatalities sponsored the project,[18] with CIFA[27] as contracted partners for the provision of forensic assistance. The posts of DVI Commander, responsible for development of UK DVI, and UK DVI Co-ordinator were formally established as of 1 April 2006. Chief Inspector Mick Free from ACPO emergency planning advised the team, and collectively they produced the Police Service Disaster Victim Identification Team Strategy, accepted by ACPO in October 2006.

Key to the strategy is proportionality, in order to maintain a local and regional response. Every force in the UK has agreed to provide staff, in accordance with their establishment, to be trained to a higher standard in DVI. These will form the cadre of officers available for immediate deployment to a national or international incident. The objectives for guidance, advice and procedures as stated in the strategy document are as follows. Scotland has also agreed to this guidance.

1.1   This policy is the agreed ACPO position in respect of the police disaster victim identification (DVI) arrangements for the response to a mass fatality incident within England, Wales and Northern Ireland. It reflects developments since the Interim ACPO DVI Strategy was agreed in October 2005; and contains new enhanced arrangements to significantly increase both national and local/regional capability and capacity in this area.

1.2   It draws together and provides clear direction to all the elements of the DVI process, some of which have previously been developed separately. These are:
  • Victim recovery
  • Mortuary operations
  • Casualty Bureau
  • Ante-mortem collection by FLOs
  • Forensic Matching

1.3   The policy outlined below demonstrates a strong commitment by ACPO to provide a robust response to civil emergencies in the UK; meet the requirements of the Civil Contingencies Act 2004, in respect of providing: trained and exercised staff in key areas, together with a risk assessed approach to emergency planning. In addition, these arrangements also will significantly contribute to "protective services" at a regional level and the "Preparation" strand of the UK Counter Terrorist Strategy, and the support to the Foreign and Commonwealth Office (FCO), in response to international incidents.

11

1.4   Overall Aim:

The Police Service within England, Wales and Northern Ireland will provide an appropriate, effective and professional response to a mass fatality incident in the United Kingdom; or when requested by HM Government overseas.

Section 2 – Objectives

2.1   In order to achieve the overall aim this Policy contains seven objectives.

2.2   Objective 1: Ensuring on a force/regional basis there is sufficient trained DVI staff to respond to a mass fatality incident, commensurate with local/regional risk assessment.

2.3   Objective 2: Establishing a specialist national police DVI team that is managed and co-ordinated by ACPO, that has a capacity and capability commensurate with the national risk assessment.

2.4   Objective 3: All deployments of the national police DVI cadre being undertaken by the National DVI Co-ordinator on behalf of Gold.

2.5   Objective 4: Implementing a national standard and capability in respect of Casualty Bureau; utilising national mutual aid telephony (NMAT) and Casweb.

2.6   Objective 5: Implementing a national standard and capability for Police Family Liaison Officers to respond to a disaster.

2.7   Objective 6: Establishing three forensic identification centres (commensurate with the national risk assessment) and implementing a forensic identification strategy.

2.8   Objective 7: The ACPO Chief of Staff, in liaison with the Foreign and Commonwealth Office (FCO), co-ordinating and arranging the Service's support to the FCO in respect of overseas incidents.

Section 3 – Guidance, Advice and Procedures

3.1   Objective 1: Ensuring on a force/regional basis there is sufficient trained DVI staff to respond to a mass fatality incident, commensurate with local/regional risk assessment.

3.2   Overall responsibility for co-ordinating regional police DVI arrangements rests with regional ACPO Emergency Procedures Portfolio, representatives. Central co-ordination and support to these activities is provided by the ACPO DVI Group within the Emergency Procedures Portfolio. These arrangements should include:

    i. Senior Identification Managers (SIMs), including designated Regional SIM FLO Managers (see objective 5 below).

    ii. Victim Recovery and Mortuary Teams

    iii. Casualty Bureau staff

    iv. Family Liaison Officers

    v. Specialist Forensic Support, including fingerprints, specialists photographers

3.3   Objective 2: Establishing a specialist national police DVI team that is managed and co-ordinated by ACPO, that has a capacity and capability commensurate with the national risk assessment.

3.4   A selected, specialist police DVI cadre, totalling 450 police officers and staff will be selected. Members of this cadre will primarily be concerned with "victim recovery", "post mortem" and "forensic retrieval/matching" areas of work. Representation from forces/regions will be on a proportionate basis.

3.5   Officers selected to form part of this cadre:

    i. Have their Chief Constables standing authority to deploy either within the UK or overseas, when requested by the National DVI Co-ordinator on behalf of Gold (subject to non-negotiable commitments, eg court/discipline hearings).

    ii. Will provide evidence of appropriate inoculations and personal insurance for overseas deployment as advised by the National DVI Co-ordinator.

    iii. Will undertake an annual "in force" Occupational Health Assessment as to their suitability to perform this type of work (both physically and mentally).

    iv. Where appropriate, be willing and be suitable, to be trained for CBRN response in the context of a mass fatality incident.

    v. Will be supplied by their own force with personal protective uniform (including boots, hard hat and outer clothing). (Additional specialist clothing and corporate items of uniform will be provided by the Home Office).

    vi. Will undergo an initial training course, plus supplementary training as necessary.

    vii. Will take part in a national DVI exercise at least once in every three years.

3.6   Objective 3: All deployments of the national police DVI cadre being undertaken by the National DVI Co-ordinator on behalf of Gold.

3.7   The role of the National DVI Co-ordinator is outlined in the Interim DVI Strategy. This officer will maintain the National DVI Database, which will include details of individuals who form part of the national DVI cadre.

3.8   The National DVI Co-ordinator is part of PNICC and will deploy specialist DVI resources only when requested by the Police Gold Commander.

3.9   In addition, the National DVI Development Officer (see Interim DVI Strategy) will be available to advise both Gold, local DVI management and where appropriate the FCO in respect of all DVI matters, both in the planning and operational phase.

3.10 Objective 4: Implementing a national standard and capability in respect of Casualty Bureau; utilising national mutual aid telephony (NMAT) and Casweb.

3.11 Events have demonstrated that extreme demands are likely to be made on Casualty Bureau, particularly in the initial stages of the incident. In order to ensure a robust response all forces should:

    i. As a proportion of the overall regional response, provide sufficient trained Casualty Bureau staff, including call takers, commensurate with local/regional/national risk assessment.

    ii. Endeavour to maintain up-to-date Holmes 2 Casualty Bureau "software" and sufficient readily usable "hardware".

    iii. Follow a policy of "direct input" onto the Holmes 2 system by call takers.

    iv. Consider implementing a national call taking response through PNICC, prior to opening Casualty Bureau.

    v. Make use of the "Rad" call answering system to ensure the most appropriate response to the wide range of queries likely to be received.

3.12 Objective 5: Implementing a national standard and capability for Police Family Liaison Officers to respond to a disaster.

3.13 Police Family Liaison Officers (FLOs) play a crucial role in the response to a mass fatality incident and the identification of the dead. Their primary responsibilities, as part of an identification and investigation strategy set by the Senior Investigating Officer (SIO) and the Senior Identification Manager (SIM) are to:

    i. Thoroughly investigate the circumstances surrounding those determined by the (SIM) to be "highly likely" to be missing in the incident.

    ii. Undertake any other investigation as required by the SIO/SIM.

    iii. Complete the Interpol DVI (missing persons) Form.

    iv. Ensure the collection and transmission of the most appropriate ante-mortem material to effect a rapid identification of recovered victims (with appropriate forensic advice and support).

    v. Provide an initial point of contact for families as part of a wider multi agency response.

3.14 A mass fatality incident, either in the UK, or affecting British citizens overseas, is likely to impact across the UK in terms of the residential location of those involved and their families. In order to ensure a co-ordinated, consistent national approach the following arrangements should be put into place:

    i. The SIM and SIO will set the national strategy for the deployment of FLOs in response to a mass fatality incident.

    ii. Requirements for FLO deployments will be routed to PNICC.

    iii. PNICC will contact a pre-determined, regional FLO Co-ordinator, who will be responsible for arranging the deployment.

    iv. All regional FLO arrangements will be the responsibility of a designated Regional SIM.

3.15 Objective 6: Establishing three forensic identification centres (commensurate with the national risk assessment) and implementing a forensic identification strategy.

3.16 The Home Office is currently supporting ACPO in the provision of three Forensic Identification Centres. These Centres will incorporate specialist personnel and software to facilitate the forensic matching process. These Centres will be located within MPS, West Midlands and West Yorkshire Police Areas.

3.17 Recent events have demonstrated that the accurate and timely identification of disaster victims will be greatly enhanced by implementing a forensic identification strategy to support the SIM, together with the appointment of an overall forensic co-ordinator and forensic advisors for the key areas of the process. These procedures are outlined in the ACPO Forensic Identification Strategy.

    i. Each of the above forces will be responsible for maintaining the infrastructure for the Centre and ensuring it can be operational in a timely fashion.

    ii. The Centres will be available to all forces in the UK as a national resource.

    iii. In the event of mass fatality incident a Forensic Co-ordinator should be appointed who will, on behalf of the SIM, manage the overall forensic response, including the collection of samples and forensic matching. A Forensic Manager should be appointed for each Centre that is opened. This individual, will co-ordinate activities within the Centre and report direct to the overall Forensic Co-ordinator.

    iv. Arrangements for staffing the Centre will be developed as part of the regional DVI plan, supported by \national resources as required.

3.18 Objective 7: The ACPO Chief of Staff, in liaison with the Foreign and Commonwealth Office (FCO), co-ordinating and arranging the Service's support to the FCO in respect of overseas incidents.

3.19   Standing arrangements have been agreed at Chief Constables Council for UK police assistance to international incidents. (Attached at Appendix.)

3.20   In the event of the FCO requesting assistance from the UK Police the ACPO Chief of Staff (or nominee) will contact the "on call force/region".

3.21   The President of ACPO retains the ability to nominate any force to take the lead in respect of a particular incident, if he/she feels that a specific force is better placed than the scheduled lead region/force to respond to the incident in question. For example, an incident in France affecting the channel might result in a South Coast force being asked to take the lead. Equally, the scale and nature of an incident might lend itself to a single large force with special skills taking the lead [eg MPS, PSNI]. However, such nominations will be the exception and there is a clear expectation that the scheduled lead region/force will act on behalf of ACPO in support of the FCO.

1.2   UK RESPONSE TO INTERNATIONAL DVI INCIDENTS

1.2.1   Deaths of non-British citizens in the UK

The United Kingdom is party to the Vienna Convention on Consular Relations.[31] Within this (Art 37), and similarly in bilateral consular conventions, there is a legal obligation to inform the relevant consular authorities of the death of one of their nationals on UK territory. This does not apply to citizens of Australia, New Zealand or Canada.

The Foreign and Commonwealth Office (FCO) encourages overseas governments to inform UK authorities of the death or serious injury of a British national within 24 hours. The FCO is expected to extend a similar courtesy to foreign nationals or Commonwealth citizens killed or seriously injured in the UK.[26]

On an individual basis, in the UK it is common practice for the police to inform the next-of-kin of an overseas national of the death of their relative. The police will encourage the next-of-kin to pass on this information to the relevant consular office in the Foreign or Commonwealth mission. If requested by the next-of-kin, the police take on the role of informing the consular office. It is important to remember that the families are not obligated to inform the consular office. Refusals are usually caused by the deceased being a political refugee or a political asylum seeker. In this situation, the Police Press Office and the FCO Press Office should be briefed accordingly.

In the event of a mass casualty incident in the UK, involving death or injury to foreign nationals or Commonwealth citizens, the Metropolitan Police Service (Diplomatic Protection Group) is responsible for informing foreign and Commonwealth missions in London if any of their nationals are known to have been affected.

1.3   INTERNATIONAL ASSISTANCE

1.3.1   UK National DVI Team and international co-operation/assistance through Interpol

UK DVI Team

The UK established a National DVI Team in January 2006. This interim team was composed of police officers and staff from a number of pre-identified forces. As training and exercises progress the team will come to be sourced from all UK police forces on a proportional basis. UK-DVI non-police forensic experts will continue to be deployed by CIFA.

The team is centrally co-ordinated under the ACPO President's Chief of Staff and a National DVI Co-ordinator within the Police National Information and Co-ordination Centre (PNICC). The National DVI Co-ordinator will, in consultation with the ACPO Presidents, PNICC Chief of Staff and Gold Command, deploy specialist DVI resources overseas as required. However, before this can happen the FCO must make a request for the National DVI Team to be deployed. At the same time they will work to receive assurances from the host government regarding the work the team will undertake and the terms under which they will work.

Initial assessment

It is strongly recommended that a DVI assessor is deployed prior to mobilisation of significant DVI resources. In the UK, the involvement of the DVI assessor would be decided by Gold Command. In a situation overseas the UK DVI assessor would be mobilised following discussion with UK DVI and the FCO. Specialist DVI advice and assessment is available through the National DVI Co-ordinator, who will liaise closely with the ACPO Presidents and PNICC Chief of Staff. No resources will be deployed overseas (a) unless specifically requested by the FCO and (b) until after an initial risk assessment and briefing. National Central Bureau (NCB), London must be advised of all such deployments.

International support for incident in UK

The Interpol DVI Resolution[4] recommends that facilities be extended to DVI personnel from countries whose nationals are involved in a disaster, to enable them to attend and act as liaison officers and/or observers to the identification process.

Official DVI personnel from other countries attending an incident in the UK could provide invaluable assistance in the identification process. It is important that any such international response is effectively co-ordinated. The Gold Commander, in consultation with the FCO, the Senior Investigating Officer (SIO) and the SIM should agree the arrangements in respect of this.

Interpol HQ assistance

Interpol Headquarters, Lyons, France maintains a 24/7 Command Centre.[1] In the event of a mass fatality incident occurring in any member country, including the UK, it will be able to take steps to co-ordinate the international response. It is recommended that early liaison be made with Interpol HQ (through NCB London) to ensure the most appropriate response. Interpol can also obtain the assistance of experienced international DVI specialists if required.

Interpol forms and quality control

Interpol recommends the use of the Interpol DVI forms[1] for the collection and transmission of both ante-mortem and post-mortem data. The ACPO Forensic DVI Strategy provides a structure for the collection and transmission of ante-mortem data collected within the UK. It is recommended that this system be established in any event involving mass fatalities of British nationals overseas, in addition to domestic incidents. It is vital that ante-mortem data, including the Interpol AM forms, are subject to a system of quality control and independent review prior to submission overseas.

REFERENCES

1 Interpol website [online]. Available at: http://www.interpol.int/default.asp. [Accessed: 12.11.2007.]

2 "Marchioness disaster" (17 August 2008), Wikipedia, The Free Encyclopedia [online]. Available at: http://en.wikipedia.org/w/index.php?title=Marchioness_disaster&oldid=232424979. [Accessed: 12.11.2007.]

3 Lord Justice Clark, "Public Inquiry into the Identification of Victims following Major Transport Disasters" (2001) [online]. Available at: http://www.marchioness-nsi.org.uk/index.htm. [Accessed: 12.11.2007.]

4 Interpol Resolution AGN/65/Res/13 (1996) [online]. Available at: https://www.interpol.int/Public/ICPO/GeneralAssembly/Agn65/Resolutions/AGN65RES13.asp. [Accessed: 12.09.2008.]

5 BBC, On This Day (15 April 1995) Hillsborough Disaster [online]. Available at: http://news.bbc.co.uk/onthisday/hi/dates/stories/april/15/newsid_2491000/2491195.stm. [Accessed: 12.11.2007.]

6 BBC, On This Day (19 September 1997) Southall Rail Crash [online]. Available at: http://news.bbc.co.uk/onthisday/hi/dates/stories/september/19/newsid_2524000/2524283.stm. [Accessed: 12.11.2007.]

7 Rt Hon Lord Cullen, "The Ladbroke Grove Rail Inquiry" (2001) [online]. Available at: http://www.pixunlimited.co.uk/pdf/news/transport/ladbrokegrove.pdf. [Accessed: 12.11.2007.]

8 BBC, On This Day (17 October 2000) Hatfield Rail Crash [online]. Available at: http://news.bbc.co.uk/onthisday/hi/dates/stories/october/17/newsid_2491000/2491425.stm. [Accessed: 12.11.2007.]

9 BBC News (10 May 2002), "Seven dead in Potters Bar crash" [online]. Available at: http://news.bbc.co.uk/1/hi/england/1979677.stm. [Accessed: 12.11.2007.]

10 BBC News (6 January 2003), "Selby driver jailed for five years" [online]. Available at: http://news.bbc.co.uk/1/hi/in_depth/uk/2001/selby_train_crash/default.stm. [Accessed: 12.11.2007.]

11 BBC News (19 June 2000), "58 Dead in Port Lorry" [online]. Available at: http://news.bbc.co.uk/1/hi/uk/796791.stm. [Accessed: 10.11.2007.]

12 BBC News (6 February 2004), "Tide kills 18 cockle pickers" [online]. Available at: http://news.bbc.co.uk/1/hi/england/lancashire/3464203.stm. [Accessed: 12.11.2007.]

13 "September 11 attacks" (14 October 2008), Wikipedia, The Free Encyclopedia [online]. Available at: http://en.wikipedia.org/w/index.php?title=September_11_attacks&oldid=245120718. [Accessed: 12.11.2007.]

14 Gene Codes Forensics, Inc, "The Mass Fatality Identification System (M-FISys)" [online]. Available at: http://www.genecodesforensics.com/software/. [Accessed: 14.10.08.]

15 D McGarry and K Smith, Police Family Liaison (forthcoming, Oxford University Press, Oxford).

16 "2002 Bali bombings" (13 October 2008), Wikipedia, The Free Encyclopedia [online]. Available at: http://en.wikipedia.org/w/index.php?title=2002_Bali_bombings&oldid=245036109. [Accessed: 12.11.2007.]

17 R Lain, C Griffiths and JMN Hilton, "Forensic Dental and Medical Response to the Bali Bombing" (2003) 179(7) Medical Journal of Australia 362–365. Available from: http://www.mja.com.au/public/issues/1061003/lai10499_fm.html.

18 Home Office website: "Responding to a terrorist incident" [online]. Available at: http://security.homeoffice.gov.uk/responding-terrorist-incident/managing-consequences/dealing-with-fatalities/. [Accessed: 14.09.08.]

19 Civil Contingencies Act 2004 (c 36) (HMSO, London) [online]. Available at: http://www.opsi.gov.uk/acts/acts2004/pdf/ukpga_20040036_en.pdf. [Accessed: 27.02.2008.]

20 Civil Defence Act 1948 (c 5) (HMSO, London) [online]. Available at: http://www.opsi.gov.uk/acts/acts1948/pdf/ukpga_19480005_en.pdf. [Accessed: 14.09.08.]

21 UK Resilience website [online]. Available at: http://www.ukresilience.info/. [Accessed: 12.11.2007.]

22 The Guardian, "Tsunami disaster in Thailand" [online]. Available at: http://www.guardian.co.uk/gall/0,,1380680,00.html. [Accessed: 12.11.2007.]

23 Specialist Crime Directorate, 24 May 2006, "Operation Bracknell-UK police service response to the South East Asian tsunami" [online]. Available at: http://www.met.police.uk/foi/pdfs/other_information/corporate/operation_bracknell.pdf. [Accessed: 12.11.2007.]

24 Review by the National Audit Office, assisted by the Zito Trust, "Review of the Experiences of United Kingdom Nationals Affected by the Indian Ocean Tsunami" (November 2006) [online]. Available at: http://www.zitotrust.co.uk/. [Accessed: 12.11.2007.]

25 National Audit Office website [online]. Available at: www.nao.org.uk. [Accessed: 12.11.2007.]

26 Foreign and Commonwealth Office website [online]. Available at: http://www.fco.gov.uk/en/. [Accessed: 14.08.08.]

27 CIFA website [online]. Available at: http://www.cifa.ac/login.html. [Accessed: 12.11.2007.]

28 BBC, On This Day (7 July 2005), "2005: Bomb Attacks on London" [online]. Available at: http://news.bbc.co.uk/onthisday/hi/dates/stories/july/7/newsid_4942000/4942238.stm. [Accessed: 12.11.2007.]

29 BBC News (23 July 2005), "Toll climbs in Egyptian attacks" [online]. Available at: http://news.bbc.co.uk/1/hi/world/middle_east/4709491.stm. [Accessed: 12.11.2007.]

30 G Sunderland, "Police Service Disaster Victim Identification (DVI) Team Strategy" (2006), Association of Chief Police Officers of England, Wales and Northern Ireland, London.

31 United Nations, Vienna Convention on Consular Relations 1963 [online]. Available at: http://untreaty.un.org/ilc/texts/instruments/english/conventions/9_2_1963.pdf. [Accessed: 12.11.2007.]

CHAPTER 2

The Role of the Home Office

2.1 INTRODUCTION

The work of the Mass Fatalities Workstream, which leads on the development of UK DVI within national government, sits within the overarching framework of the Government's strategy for countering international terrorism. Specifically, this process is concerned with the preparatory work that can be done to diminish the impact of terrorist attacks on the UK population and is therefore part of the PREPARE strand of the Government's strategy. The work is governed by the legislative framework of the Civil Contingencies Act 2004.[1]

The Mass Fatalities Section of the Home Office has no operational role in the mass fatalities response other than that connected with the deployment of its assets. The role of the workstream is to enable organisations with a responsibility for response to a fatalities incident to scale up that response to the level outlined in the national resilience planning assumptions. The workstream has focused on:

- the production of national guidance; and
- a programme of central assistance to local responders, comprising:
  - personnel (UK DVI);
  - infrastructure (emergency mortuary structures); and
  - equipment.

2.2 THE GOVERNMENT'S STRATEGY FOR COUNTERING INTERNATIONAL TERRORISM

The United Kingdom faces a continuing threat from extremists who believe that they can advance their aims by committing acts of terrorism here in the UK and against our citizens and interests abroad. To combat this threat, the Government has developed a counter-terrorism strategy and set up programmes and plans to give effect to it.

Since early 2003, the UK has had a long-term strategy for countering international terrorism. Its aim is "to reduce the risk from international terrorism, so that people can go about their daily lives freely and with confidence".[2]

Developing and delivering this counter-terrorism strategy involves and depends on partnerships with and between the police and emergency services, local authorities and devolved administrations, and with the private, voluntary and charitable sectors.

The strategy is divided into four strands – the "four Ps":

- **PREVENT**: aiming to prevent terrorism by tackling the radicalisation of individuals;
- **PURSUE**: aiming to reduce the terrorist threat by pursuing terrorists and those who sponsor them, and disrupting terrorists and their operations;
- **PROTECT**: aiming to reduce the vulnerability of the UK itself and UK interests overseas; and
- **PREPARE**: aiming to improve UK resilience to cope with terrorist attack and other major disruptive challenges. The key elements are:
  - identifying the potential risks the UK faces from terrorism and assessing their impact;
  - building the necessary capabilities to respond to any attacks; and
  - regularly and honestly evaluating and testing our preparedness, for example by frequently exercising to improve our response to incidents and learning lessons from incidents that do take place.

2.2.1 Identifying and assessing risks

The Civil Contingencies Secretariat (CCS)[3] in the Cabinet Office was created in July 2001 to lead assessment of the consequences for the UK of potential emergencies, whether caused by terrorism or other factors. This risk assessment process forms the basis for decisions about emergency preparedness, including investment decisions. A wide range of organisations contributes to this systematic and all-inclusive approach to risk analysis, so as to reflect the UK situation at national, regional and local levels. In particular at the local level, the conduct and publication of local risk assessments are now formal duties under the Civil Contingencies Act 2004.[1] Given the vast range of potential emergency scenarios and their consequences, it is neither practical nor prudent to plan for every scenario. Instead, planning seeks to build generic capabilities and plans which are capable of being drawn upon in response to a wide range of events.

2.2.2 Building capabilities

The cross-government Capabilities Programme[4] is the core framework through which the Government is seeking to build resilience across all parts of the United Kingdom. "Capability" is a military term which includes: personnel; equipment; training; plans; doctrine; legislation; and infrastructure. Many elements of the response to a natural or man-made disaster require a similar capability to those of a terrorist attack. The scope of the programme therefore extends to the full range of contingencies likely to face the UK in a 5-year time frame.

The Capabilities Programme consists of 18 capability "workstreams",[4] one of which is the Mass Fatalities Workstream. Another which is relevant to UK DVI is the Humanitarian Assistance Workstream led by the Department for Culture, Media and Sport.

Each workstream is the responsibility of a designated lead department. Within each lead department, a designated individual is responsible for the management of a programme of work set out in a delivery plan. Within the Cabinet Office, the programme director reports quarterly to a committee chaired by the head of CCS. Ministerial oversight of the programme is exercised through the Ministerial Committee on UK Resilience, chaired by the Home Secretary.

The leaders of the functional workstreams have responsibility for developing capability at the national (UK) level. The Regional Resilience Teams in each of the Government Offices for the Regions[5] are responsible for co-ordinating activity at the local (local authority or police force) area, and for communications between workstream leaders at the national level and local authorities and first responders.

Responsibilities at the local level have been formalised through the provisions of the Civil Contingencies Act 2004,[1] and through regulations and guidance issued after the Act passed into law. "Emergency Preparedness"[6] is the statutory Cabinet Office guidance that supports Part 1 of the Civil Contingencies Act 2004.[1] It explains local responder duties and provides good practice advice for fulfilling requirements. This is the platform on which Regional Mass Fatalities Plans and their Welsh equivalents should seek to build.

2.2.3 Evaluating and testing preparedness

The Capabilities Programme[4] has no defined end-point or outcome. An important part of the work is continually to identify, challenge and monitor the current levels of resilience in each of the areas covered by the workstreams. This enables Ministers to decide what level of resilience they wish to achieve and then to plan and, if necessary, to allocate additional resources to achieve that increased level of resilience. Testing and exercising make an important contribution to this assessment. The Mass Fatalities Section contributes to regular readiness assessments which are put to the cross-government Senior Official Committee.

2.3 THE MASS FATALITIES WORKSTREAM

Local communities face a wide range of hazards and threats – for example, acts of terrorism or severe weather – all of which could result in large-scale fatalities. The Civil Contingencies Act 2004[1] established a clear framework of roles and responsibilities for local emergency responders. In particular, the Act requires those at the core of emergency planning and response (ie Category 1 responders such as local authorities and the emergency services) to assess the risk of emergencies and to use these assessments to inform their local emergency planning work, including the production of a mass fatalities plan. A lot of resources and expertise exist locally and co-ordination of these should be the first step towards meeting the broad capability requirements for a mass fatalities response. Multi-agency working holds the key to planning for the required response to dealing with mass fatalities.

The Mass Fatalities Workstream[7] was established in January 2004. In May of that year, the Home Office published the first edition of "Guidance on Dealing with Fatalities in Emergencies".[8] (NB: – The first edition of this guidance was superseded by interim guidance, which was circulated on a restricted basis during the Summer of 2005. The interim guidance will itself be superseded by a published second edition of the guidance during 2007.) For the first time, this guidance captured the diverse requirements likely to be needed to manage fatalities in emergencies. It built on knowledge and expertise within the emergency planning and response community. The major output of this work has been the development of plans drawn up by the Regional Resilience Forums[9] in England, and their Welsh counterparts. These plans effectively detail and will, in emergencies, deliver the multi-agency mass fatalities response. However, guidance alone could not achieve the desired changes and so the Mass Fatalities Section has been driving forward work to provide central assistance to support local plans and responders.

In January 2004, the Mass Fatalities Section commissioned a capability analysis, ie a study of the ability of local responders in England and Wales to respond to incidents resulting in a large number of fatalities. In December 2004 the study reported limitations in the local readiness to respond. These limitations were mainly related to responders' ability to "scale up" their capabilities to the level needed to respond to such an incident.

2.3.1 The Central Assistance Programme

As a result of the capability analysis and its identification of gaps in local readiness, since December 2004 the Mass Fatalities Section has worked closely with stakeholders to develop a programme of central assistance. This work was given additional impetus by the Indian Ocean tsunami on 26 December 2004 and its aftermath.

The Home Office programme of central assistance is geared towards providing resources when local and regional capability is likely to be overwhelmed. Mechanisms for delivery of central assistance in an operational setting are set out in Regional and Welsh Mass Fatality Plans[10, 11] which take into account the needs of their local areas in light of their local risk assessment. The Home Office document "Supplementing Local Response Options",[12] sets out for local strategists and decision-makers the resources which are available to them in the response to an incident resulting in large numbers of deaths; ways of accessing them; and the costs.

Priority has been given to delivering three vital elements of the central assistance framework. During 2005 the Home Office worked with stakeholders to develop specifications and arrangements for delivering:

- a National Disaster Victim Identification Team (UK DVI);
- National Emergency Mortuary Arrangements (NEMA); and
- stockpiles of essential mortuary equipment.

The programme of central assistance is now established. However, its development is an ongoing process of continuous learning and improvement. The Home Office, in partnership with key stakeholders, is seeking to build on existing and evolving knowledge of good practice, including the lessons identified from responses to incidents such as the Indian Ocean tsunami, and the bombings on 7 July 2005 in London.

2.3.2 The development of UK DVI

In relation to the provision of personnel, the main findings of the capability analysis were that although pockets of excellence in DVI response had been built up at local area level, there was neither consistency in the response nor a critical mass of staff who could be deployed to an incident resulting in large-scale fatalities. As a result, the same organisations were approached time and again to provide the response to such incidents. Moreover, the experience gained in the response to individual incidents was not consolidated and was built upon only haphazardly. This was partly because there was no formally established mechanism for the national co-ordination of the DVI response, whether in relation to deployment to an incident or to the maintenance of a central core of expertise.

On 22 July 2005, a meeting was held at the Home Office with representatives from policing organisations and of the civilian forensic professions' representative bodies, at which proposals for the establishment of a national Disaster Victim Identification team were discussed and agreed. Since that meeting, UK DVI has been established with the central aim of enhancing the local DVI response through the provision of national mechanisms to:

- co-ordinate appropriately trained and experienced police and forensic personnel both operationally and in response to events; and
- provide a national understanding of requirements and standards in the development stages.

A UK DVI Management Team has been established by ACPO which is funded by a grant from the Home Office and other members of the UK DVI Sponsorship Board. The team is made up of the UK DVI Development Officer and the UK DVI Co-ordinator. The Home Office has also entered into a contract with the

25

Centre for International Forensic Assistance (CIFA)[13] for the development of the civilian arm of the UK DVI Team.

The Home Office has established the UK DVI Sponsorship Board to oversee the operational activities and future development of UK DVI. The Board's members include the UK DVI Sponsors (those Government departments and devolved administrations which co-fund the UK DVI initiative), ACPO[14] and ACPOS,[15] and CIFA.[13] The Board provides accountability for the funding devoted to the development of UK DVI by Ministers and, ultimately, Parliament.

The UK DVI Stakeholder Forum, which reports to the Sponsorship Board, is made up of the bodies whose members form UK DVI. It therefore provides a different form of accountability by validating the development that is given priority and taken forward by the UK DVI Management Team and CIFA and by reflecting the views of the experts back to the Board. To some extent it will also drive the work of UK DVI by identifying areas of weakness which need to be addressed and strengths which should be built upon.

2.4   THE CONTAMINATED FATALITIES WORKSTREAM

A separate but closely-related workstream in the Home Office deals with the handling of contaminated fatalities. This workstream is establishing a capability to deal safely with fatalities which may have been contaminated following a CBRN (chemical, biological, radiological or nuclear) incident.[16] Work is currently ongoing, and recruitment and training of a specialist cadre of personnel to undertake this work is under way. The provision of personnel to such incidents will be through UK DVI, as with a conventional incident.

2.5   NATIONAL EMERGENCY MORTUARY ARRANGEMENTS (NEMA)

Summary of proposed configuration options

The NEMA facility is currently configured to be deployed in two formats.

Full 600-casualty configuration

The full facility is separated into two main elements: the initial 24-hour-deployed receiving and storage area and the 72-hour sustainment area.

Initial 24-hour element: receiving and storage area
- Perimeter fence (covered from view).
- Temporary roadway and walkway.
- Three receiving areas.
- Three storage areas.

- Three autopsy areas (two process channels each).
- Fluoroscopy area.
- Radiography area.

72-hour element: sustainment area

- Counter-Terrorist Office.
- Operational Office.
- Embalming area.
- Encoffining area.
- Equipment store.
- Catering tent.
- Staff changing area.
- Family viewing area.

300-casualty configuration

Two 300-fatality facilities are available and are formed from a revised initial 24-hour element and the standard 72-hour package. The revised 24-hour package is listed below:

Initial 24-hour element

- Perimeter fence (covered from view).
- Temporary roadway and walkway.
- Three receiving areas.
- Two storage areas.
- Two autopsy areas (two process channels each).
- Fluoroscopy area.
- Radiography area.

The 72-hour element will remain the same as that detailed above.

Detailed descriptions of proposed solution

It is not intended that the solution should include staffing of the mortuary, or specialist equipment and consumables. However, it should include:

- operation of an all-hours on-call service for deployment of the emergency mortuary anywhere in the United Kingdom within 24 hours of being called upon;
- the required structures;
- transport of the structures to the site, construction, including connection of equipment to, eg, power/water supply; and decommissioning;

27

- all equipment to ensure that building is fit for purpose (eg generators, sinks, power management, air purification equipment, water and waste management, frozen storage etc);
- management of any sub-contractors; and
- logistics around delivery and collection.

The contract with the Home Office would be to guarantee availability of the facilities at 24 hours' notice. Activation costs incurred when the facilities are actually deployed and hired will fall to the local authority where the incident has occurred, which would take responsibility for activating the mortuary arrangements.

Introduction

Kellogg, Brown and Root (KBR) understands the key requirements for the National Emergency Mortuary Arrangement (NEMA) contract and has, throughout the rigorous procurement and design process, been diligent in ensuring that the equipment offered to the Authority meets all of the standards and legislation required by the ITT (invitation to tender). The following provides an overview of the technical equipment that will be used to provide the mortuary infrastructure.

Proposed structures

The KBR accommodation solution is provided by a range of temporary structures that conform to European and American Standards for Stability and Fire Safety and meet all UK requirements for structures of this type in terms of properties and structural strength. The walls are manufactured from the highest quality PVC with white rigid wall panels and aluminum entrance doors. All structures will be fitted with an integral cassette flooring and have access for disabled persons.

These structures have been selected as they offer a working height of 3 m which allows sufficient room for large items such as ISO (International Standards Organization) containers to be located and operated within the structures. This not only provides an all-weather working environment but also provides shrouding for activities being undertaken in the more sensitive areas. For the family viewing area, NEMA provides an environment that is sympathetic to its role: internally the structure walls will be fabric lined to soften the appearance and provide appropriate surroundings.

Within the structure the autopsy area is divided into two lanes with five partitioned bays in each. There is a bay for each of the following processes: fingerprinting, autopsy, anthropology, odontology and primary reconstruction. Fluoroscopy and radiography areas have established safe working areas of 3 m around them. The fluoroscopy area is 5 m × 10 m and the radiography area is 6.5 m × 10 m.

28

Receiving and storage areas have hard flooring and access into both areas is through a roller shutter door. Each combined storage and receiving area has the storage capacity for 200 bodies which would be stored in a mixture of reefers (frozen or chilled) and transpacks which provide chilled storage.

Equipment for these areas is stored in pods which are currently housed in five locations around the country which are mainly military. It is the responsibility of the local authority to mobilise this equipment for use in the temporary mortuary.

Flooring

NEMA will have two types of flooring finishes within the structures. For the family viewing area a hard-wearing carpet will be used and in all other areas KBR will provide low-slip vinyl flooring which is easy to clean, waterproof and chemical resistant.

Power generation

NEMA will be supplied with six 500kVA diesel-fuelled generators with a combined output that greatly exceeds the mortuary's peak power demand. These generators will be mounted and will have control equipment which will allow them to be synchronised to operate as a pair, enabling them to provide uninterrupted electrical supply 24 hours a day. As these generators will need to be sited within the perimeter fence, close to the mortuary where personnel will be working, they are super-silenced to 75dba which is well below the requirement specified in the ITT. Three generators will be deployed within 24 hours of activation of the mortuary, with the remaining three arriving on-site within 72 hours. Each generator will be connected to a bulk tank and have a day fuel tank of its own.

Lighting and power distribution

The KBR solution uses a Lighting and Power Distribution System (LAPDS) which is designed specifically to provide primary and sub-system power distribution. The system interfaces directly with the power generation equipment, providing primary distribution to smaller localised distribution equipment which feeds the lighting and final power equipment. This is a straightforward, easily understood design which cascades power down from the power source, be it generator or mains supply, to interface units. Each area has been provided with sufficient power outlets to ensure that it can fulfil its designated purpose. Power outlets in "wet" areas are waterproof.

Generators will be strategically placed on site close to areas of high consumption such as the autopsy structure. This will not only reduce cable lengths, which minimises power loss, but also will assist in keeping the site clear of cables. Particular care has been taken to ensure that power cables do not cross any of the trackway that will be used by vehicles operating within the mortuary site.

The primary distribution systems require no routine maintenance, only periodic inspection and testing in accordance with the requirements of BS 7671. All other components are designed to give long service and are able to withstand multiple deployments. The system has very few consumable components, except items such as, lighting lamps and tubes; spares will be included in the spares pack that will be provided to support every mortuary deployment.

Lighting is provided throughout the facility to the level specified in the CIBSE (Chartered Institution of Building Services Engineers) guidelines and the overall solution is based on a BS EN 60309-2 standard, enabling it to fully interface with the existing LAPDS and a whole range of bespoke BS EN 60309-2 distribution and lighting systems.

HVAC (high voltage alternating current)

To provide adequate heating and cooling for the overall system NEMA will be provided with a range of HVAC units. The disposition and use of these systems will vary according to the prevailing climatic conditions and while it is likely that not all would be required at the same time, they will be installed as part of the initial site set-up.

The HVAC equipment supplied is designed to meet the peak requirement in hot and cold climatic conditions within the UK, providing temperature control as well as air purification which is achieved by fitting units serving "wet" areas with carbon filters. These filters provide a level of air purification that exceeds that required for a mortuary environment and have an in-service life of 6 months. On long deployments, replacement of filters will be undertaken by KBR personnel using spares held in the consumables spares pack. Within the working areas, air distribution will be achieved using plenums mounted at high level. While this is acceptable within a technical working environment, for the family viewing area and offices, less obtrusive Fan Coil Units (FCUs) will be employed to deliver air directly to the location.

ISO container storage

Chilled bodies will be held in Body Holding Units (BHUs) (Figure 2.1) which are able to hold 17 bodies and are capable of maintaining temperatures down to +2°C. They are fitted with a galvanised steel racking system comprising four sets of 8ft long × 4 tier high shelves that are fully demountable for easy adjustment and cleaning, with shelves set to heights within the operating range of the standard mortuary trolley.

Frozen bodies will be held in ISO refrigeration containers (reefers) which will be fitted with the same galvanised steel racking/surfaces as the BHU to allow, with a trolley, 17 bodies to be stored. Each container is capable of maintaining a temperature down to −20°C and if required may be deployed forward to the

Figure 2.1   Body Holding Unit

incident scene to provide a temporary storage and transportation facility. These ISO containers have the ability to operate at higher temperatures which allows them to be used to hold chilled bodies if required. All refrigeration equipment complies with the Montréal protocol and all the AHUs (air handling units) use coolant gas that is monopropylene "food safe".

Fire alarm system

To minimise the installation time for the fire alarm system, NEMA will be provided with smoke detectors and alarm sounders.

The system is an integrated package which is optimised for rapid deployment and installation and will enable an alarm system to be installed at an early stage in any deployment.

Fresh water supply

Fresh water will be available in most areas from mains water, however, to allow fresh water to be available on site immediately, a 2,000-litre break tank has been provided to allow distribution until connection occurs to the mains supply. Water distribution throughout the site will be by means of poly-pipe that uses press-fit-type connectors to allow rapid construction.

To further speed the installation, pipework will be pre-assembled ready for deployment in 10-metre lengths with all connectors in place. Assembly on site will only require that the site arrangement be assessed to identify any adaptations needed to the basic design before connecting the lengths together to create the required layout.

31

Waste water

KBR views management of waste water as a vital factor in providing a robust mortuary facility and recognises that, at each site, access to suitable sewers and the local topography will have a significant impact on disposal of waste water. Without detailed prior knowledge of the layout of each potential deployment site it is impossible to calculate what is required and how long it will take to connect into the main sewerage system. To allow for any eventuality, NEMA will be provided with 14 secondary waste water tanks to serve individual areas and one main waste water tank, as stand-alone facilities until connection to a sewer is made. The secondary tanks are float operated pumping points which will be located adjacent to the unit they are serving. As the water level in the tank increases, the float switch will be activated and the pump will operate, transporting the contents to the main waste tank where it will be stored until removal from site by either discharging to a sewer or a tanker. The system incorporates sufficient waste water pipework to allow connection to the mains sewerage system up to 50 m from the mortuary facility. The one exception to this is the embalming area that will have a separate waste tank due to the toxic nature of the chemicals used in the embalming process. As with the fresh water system, the waste water will be connected using poly-pipe with press fit type connectors, with pre-assembled pipework.

Toilet and shower facilities

KBR will supply self-contained toilet and shower blocks that will be placed in both wet and dry areas. Within the first 24 hours one block of eight toilets will be deployed onto site followed by two more within 72 hours.

The toilets are of a low waste recirculating type that uses minimal water to transport the waste into a holding tank which can then be emptied by tanker or, when connected, discharged into the main sewerage system.

From initial deployment, KBR will also provide four stand-alone portable site toilets. These will be retained on site and the contract maintained for the duration of the deployment. They will be available for use by visiting drivers and tradesmen.

Tower lighting

To enable 24-hour round-the-clock construction of the mortuary, NEMA will be provided with self-powered tower lights, each with four 1,000-watt bulbs. Following construction, these lights will be used to provide safety and security lighting within the mortuary site.

Pathway and roadway

The site will be served by a network of temporary roads and paths, the demands for each being very different. While pathways will only be used by pedestrians and will employ easy to fit non-slip interlocking tiles, the roadways will need to be able to cope with constant use from heavy vehicles delivering and removing material from the site. To meet this demand the roadway, which will be among the first of all items laid on site, will be provided by 3-metre-wide lightweight aluminium hard standing trackway, suitable for any vehicle.

Fencing

It has been recognised that there is the need for fencing to keep the site secure and private. For this NEMA will be supplied with 2-metre-high screened fencing around the perimeter of the site.

To give enhanced privacy to the family viewing area, there will be additional fencing separating this facility from the main working area, which will have its own entrance and exit.

REFERENCES

1 Civil Contingencies Act 2004 (c36) (HMSO, London) [online]. Available at: http://www.opsi.gov.uk/acts/acts2004/pdf/ukpga_20040036_en.pdf. [Accessed: 27.02.2008.]

2 Countering International Terrorism: The United Kingdom's Strategy (HMSO, 2006) [online]. Available at: http://security.homeoffice.gov.uk/news-publications/publication search/general/Contest-Strategy?view=Binary. [Accessed: 14.05.08.]

3 The Civil Contingencies Secretariat [online]. Available at: http://www.ukresilience.info/ccs.aspx. [Accessed: 12/11/2007.]

4 The Capabilities Programme [online]. Available: at http://www.ukresilience.info/preparedness/ukgovernment/capabilities.aspx. [Accessed: 14.05.2008.]

5 The Government Offices for the Regions [online]. Available at: http://www.gos.gov.uk/national/. [Accessed: 12.11.2007.]

6 Emergency Preparedness [online]. Available at: http://www.ukresilience.info/upload/assets/www.ukresilience.info/emergprepfinal.pdf. [Accessed: 12.11.2007.]

7 The Mass Fatalities Workstream [online]. Available at: http://security.homeoffice.gov.uk/responding-terrorist-incident/managing-consequences/dealing-with-fatalities/. [Accessed: 13.11.2007.]

8 "Guidance on Dealing with Fatalities in Emergencies" (1st ed, 2004) [online]. Available at: http://www.ukresilience.info/upload/assets/www.ukresilience.info/fatalities.pdf. [Accessed: 12.11.2007.]

9 Regional Resilience Forums [online]. Available at: http://www.ukresilience.info/preparedness/englishregions.aspx. [Accessed: 14.05.2008.]

10 London Mass Fatality Plan [online]. Available at: http://www.londonprepared.gov.uk/londonsplans/emergencyplans/massfatality.jsp. [Accessed: 14.05.2008.]

11 Welsh Mass Fatality Plan [online]. Available at: http://wales.gov.uk/resilience/wales-resilience/?lang=en. [Accessed: 14.05.2008.]

12 Home Office Security, "Responding to a Terrorist Incident" [online]. Available at: http://security.homeoffice.gov.uk/responding-terrorist-incident/national-response/. [Accessed: 14.05.2008.]

13 Centre for International Forensic Assistance (CIFA) [online]. Available at: ttp://www.cifa.ac/login.html. [Accessed: 14.05.2008.]

14 Association of Chief Police Officers (ACPO) [online]. Available at: http://www.acpo.police.uk/. [Accessed: 14.05.2008.]

15 Association of Chief Police Officers (ACPOS) [online]. Available at: http://www.acpos.police.uk/. [Accessed: 14.05.2008.]

16 UK Resilience, "Chemical, Biological, Radiological or Nuclear (CBRN) Emergencies" [online]. Available at: http://www.ukresilience.info/emergencies/cbrn.aspx. [Accessed: 14.05.2008.]

CHAPTER 3

The Foreign and Commonwealth Office

3.1 INTRODUCTION

The Foreign and Commonwealth Office (FCO)[1] is the Government department responsible for the United Kingdom's international relations, working for UK interests throughout the world. One of its core policy responsibilities is to support UK nationals overseas in normal times and in times of crisis. This work is led by the FCO's Consular Directorate and delivered through the FCO's network of diplomatic missions (Embassies, High Commissions and Consulates) around the world.

Assistance for UK nationals includes:

*   issuing passports;
*   providing travel advice;
*   considering whether to intervene where it appears they have not received fair treatment under local law (whether as victims, suspects or sentenced prisoners) or their human rights have not been respected;
*   planning for and managing evacuations in the event of conflict, terrorism, civil disturbances or natural disasters;
*   providing information on who best to contact to help trace missing persons;
*   identifying the dead and helping to facilitate repatriation or local burial/ cremation;
*   and providing guidance and support for bereaved relatives and survivors.

All of this assistance – and much else besides – is important for the prosperity of the UK and for the security of its citizens at home and abroad.

As a matter of policy, the FCO seeks to assist all UK nationals (including British Overseas Territories citizens (BOTCs), British Overseas citizens (BOCs), British Nationals (Overseas) (BNOs), British subjects (BSs) and British protected persons (BPPs) – some of whom have no automatic right to enter or to live in the United Kingdom). It may also provide assistance to Commonwealth nationals and EU citizens where their own country has no diplomatic representation. However, the FCO has no statutory regulations governing the consular assistance it provides overseas. All consular assistance is a matter of policy, currently set out in the *Guide to Consular Services*.[1]

The Consular Crisis Group (CCG),[2] a department in the FCO's Consular Directorate in London, provides policy advice to Ministers on emergency planning and preparations. It liaises with FCO missions on civil contingency and emergency plans to help ensure that workable and flexible plans are in place around the world. CCG is based in the FCO's Crisis Centre in the main building in King Charles Street, London.

When a consular crisis occurs, such as an evacuation, a terrorist incident, a large-scale non-terrorist incident or a natural disaster, CCG takes the lead in deciding the best way to provide fast and effective consular assistance to UK nationals overseas who have been affected by the incident. This response may include expanding CCG to an integrated FCO crisis team; activating an Emergency Response Team to handle telephone calls from members of the public; despatching a Rapid Deployment Team (RDT);[1] evacuating UK nationals (including, where appropriate, with UK military assistance) or seeking the assistance of another Government. If the incident is a mass casualty event potentially involving a number of UK nationals, CCG may request the deployment of UK DVI officers overseas to the incident by activating its element of the UK DVI Protocol.

In the event of a terrorist incident, or of a kidnap/hostage-taking overseas involving UK nationals, the FCO's Counter Terrorist Policy Department (CTPD) takes the strategic lead on the crime in action elements, working closely with the National Co-ordinator of Terrorist Investigation and with the MPS Special and Anti-Terrorist Branches or with the Hostage and Crisis Negotiations Unit. However, CCG still retains operational responsibility for the consular aspects of Her Majesty's Governmental response.

As part of the response, CCG may deploy a Rapid Deployment Team to the scene of the incident. An RDT contains specially selected and trained FCO staff, the majority of whom are consular officers, but it also includes a press officer and a technical officer. It might also include other specialists (psychological support, medical assessment, police (DVI/counter-terrorism)). See section 3.4 for more details.

Because of the potential for intense media interest and consequential parliamentary concerns, it is essential that the response by everyone involved, at every stage, is highly professional and strictly in accordance with FCO regulations and instructions.

3.2 HOW THE FCO RESPONDS TO A CONSULAR CRISIS OVERSEAS

Following an incident, CCG will establish contact with the UK diplomatic mission in the country concerned, to ascertain the likelihood/extent of UK fatalities. The mission, in consultation with local authorities, will make a swift initial assessment of the situation, taking into consideration the following points:

- What is the initial assessment of the total number of victims?
- What is the initial assessment of the number of UK victims?
- Does the incident involve circumstances which necessitate particular skills not available within the region?
- Is it necessary to seek to activate the UK DVI team?
- What staff resources are required?

Depending on the volume of telephone calls received from members of the public about the incident, CCG will consider activating an Emergency Response Team (ERT)[3] of up to 30 FCO officers to handle initial telephone calls from members of the public who believe a relative or friend might be involved in the incident. The ERT will collect, record and disseminate information about UK nationals and other eligible persons. CCG will also consider deploying an RDT to the incident to assist the nearest diplomatic mission.

The relationship between the FCO and the police is a vital part of the UK's crisis response and is governed by a Memorandum of Understanding (MOU) between the police (Association of Chief Police Officers: ACPO) and the FCO which sets out the FCO policy regarding assistance to an international incident and the UK police service response to any request for assistance. The police fulfil a number of crucial roles at the request of the FCO: extra telephone call-handling capacity, Family Liaison Officers (FLOs)[4] to deal with bereaved families in the UK and provision of DVI experts overseas.[5]

3.3 FCO/POLICE CO-OPERATION

Under the terms of the FCO/ACPO MOU, every month one police force, or more than one force representing a region of the country, acts as lead for response to international incidents if requested by the FCO. In the event of a crisis, CCG will contact the Senior Identification Manager (SIM) of the lead or regional force on duty at that time. The lead force may be asked to provide:

- **Casualty Bureau support for call handling**: in the event that the ERT can no longer sustain a call centre within the FCO, the lead force will set up a Casualty Bureau to assume that responsibility. If necessary, the National Mutual Aid Telephony System (NMAT) can also be activated by the Police National Information and Co-ordination Centre (PNICC).
- **Family Liaison Co-ordinator (FLC)**: the lead force will act as FLC and will arrange for deployment of FLOs as necessary. FLOs will not be sent overseas under FCO funding.

In the event of a crisis requiring DVI specialisms, the FCO will activate, through the UK DVI team, the Protocol in place among the Home Office,[6] the Northern Ireland Office,[7] the Scottish Executive,[8] the FCO, the ACPO[9] and ACPOS

(Association of Chief Police Officers in Scotland)[10] which sets out the conditions under which the UK National DVI team will be deployed in the UK and overseas. Usually a DVI assessor will be deployed with the RDT and a small DVI team will follow on if necessary. All travel and accommodation arrangements will be handled by CCG. The FCO approves all deployments in consultation with key police representatives in a Gold Group meeting chaired by the FCO. The terms are set out in the Protocol which also covers:

- The process for requesting and authorising the deployment of UK DVI officers overseas as part of an RDT.
- The respective roles and responsibilities of the FCO and DVI officers deployed.
- Terms and conditions for deployment of DVI officers overseas.
- Overseas deployment instructions.
- Funding implications (the FCO contributes to the continuing development of the UK DVI Unit).
- Overall governance of the UK DVI Unit.

CCG may deploy a Crisis Liaison Manager (CLM) to be embedded with the lead or regional police force during the incident, especially if a DVI assessor/team has been deployed with the RDT and where there are FLO requirements in the UK or the police have set up call handling for the incident. The CLM will act as liaison between the FCO and the police, ensuring the smooth and accurate flow of information. The CLM will be involved in all meetings and briefings (especially at Gold and Silver level) if applicable.

On arrival in the country concerned, the UK DVI assessor or team will scope the incident and make a recommendation to Gold Group on the size, composition and, eventually, the likely duration of the DVI deployment. Gold Group may authorise the deployment of a full UK DVI team, commensurate with the need.

The primary aim of the DVI assessor will usually be to determine whether the local authorities in the country are likely to be overwhelmed by the incident and therefore unable to carry out victim identification effectively to UK coronial requirements.

The UK DVI Commander will arrange for the deployment of the agreed UK DVI team. The Gold Group will monitor the situation evolving at the crisis site, consulting the British Ambassador[11] or High Commissioner,[12] the RDT and the deployed UK DVI Commander, and determine the continued size and composition of the deployed UK DVI team and when it should be withdrawn back to the UK. Co-ordination in the UK will be through CCG and the UK DVI co-ordinator.

Once overseas, all members of a UK DVI team will come under the command and control of the FCO. They will take instructions from and report to either the British Ambassador or the High Commissioner or whomsoever is appointed by them.

It is important that UK DVI team members do not communicate directly or independently with the press – either UK or foreign – when on overseas deployment (or after returning from an overseas deployment) without the express authorisation of the FCO. Where technical language or information of a scientific nature is required, members of the UK DVI team will be included in press briefings, either formal or informal.

All salaries and other costs that would normally fall to the UK police for officers serving with the UK DVI Unit will fall to the FCO while team members are deployed overseas. This includes all costs arising from the deployment agreed by Gold Group as set out in the MOU (eg travel, accommodation and food). The FCO will also meet the salaries and deployment costs of civilian UK DVI team members deployed overseas with any UK DVI team. Numbers to be deployed will be agreed with the FCO when deployment is authorised.

3.4   RAPID DEPLOYMENT TEAMS (RDTs)

CCG manages the RDTs. When British nationals are involved in a large-scale emergency overseas, an RDT may be deployed as part of our overall consular response. RDTs vary in size (anything from 2 to 40 people) depending on the size of the incident and the likely number of UK nationals involved. The FCO has RDTs based in London, Hong Kong and the USA (the latter two can respond to incidents in Asia or the Americas more quickly than the London team).

The RDT provides trained support to the British Ambassador or High Commissioner and his or her consular team, to ensure that UK victims and other eligible persons and their families receive the highest possible level of consular service in the shortest possible time. Like other officials, the RDT reports to the Ambassador or High Commissioner, personally or through a nominated deputy, and takes direction from him or her. The RDT also helps to enable links with the local authorities and emergency services and ensures efficient co-operation with other British agencies that may be called to the scene. An RDT will have a variety of communications equipment at its disposal, including internationally enabled mobile telephones, satellite telephones based on several networks and two-way radios.

The FCO aims to deploy an RDT within 24 hours from the time that CCG declares a crisis. Team members are rostered for deployment at 2 hours' notice, although, in practice, because of the time it takes to obtain visas and secure seats on scheduled aircraft or to charter a plane, deployment time is more likely to be between 4 and 6 hours.

Each team is built around a core of experienced FCO staff, most with consular experience overseas and some who work within the Consular Directorate in London, all of whom have had RDT training. The team will usually include a trained press officer, either sent with the team or provided by the local Mission. Other team members can include staff of the British Red Cross Society[13] and of

International SOS[14] (providing medical and/or psychological support staff) and representatives of other relevant Government departments. In addition, where warranted by circumstances, the RDT can include a DVI assessor or team and (for terrorist incidents) FCO officers from CTPD and police officers from SO15. These members would not necessarily be on 2 hours' notice for deployment but would be deployed as soon as is practicable.

It is crucial, when overseas, to be aware of the importance of national sovereignty, ie the UK police do not have an automatic right to conduct investigations in other countries unless invited to do so by those countries. This is irrespective of the nationality of those involved. Even when such permission has been granted, sensitivities must still be observed and the team should proceed with caution, taking advice from the RDT Team Leader.

In 2006, the FCO deployed RDTs on ten separate occasions to deal with a variety of situations including a coup in Fiji (using our Hong Kong-based team);[15] bombings in Egypt[16] and Turkey;[17] and coach crashes in Seville[18] and Jeddah.[19] In 2007 we deployed teams to the Democratic Republic of Congo (civil unrest);[20] to Cameroon (plane crash);[21] to the Dominican Republic (health scare);[22] and to Thailand (Phuket plane crash).[23] A DVI team was deployed with the RDT once in 2006 and twice at the time of writing in 2007.

While families in the UK are assigned an FLO, any family travelling to the incident site will have a Consular Liaison Officer (CLO) from the RDT appointed to them. The CLO ensures that the family are kept up to date on the situation, provides full consular assistance and remains the family's main point of contact while they remain in the country. Although the DVI assessor or team can play an important role in helping to explain the DVI process to families, they should not become the normal point of contact with families: that duty should always remain with the CLO.

3.5 REPATRIATION AND CORONIAL ISSUES

The FCO is not responsible for the repatriation of bodies or mortal remains of UK nationals who die overseas. This is the responsibility of the next-of-kin. Repatriation of any bodies or mortal remains is usually handled through insurance companies whose local agents will deal with relevant national funeral directors and companies. RDT members will help facilitate this process with the families but will not lead it.

The Coroners system[24] in the UK is very decentralised. Therefore CCG will normally make contact with the Coroner who has jurisdiction over the bodies at the port of arrival. This is almost always the West London Coroner responsible for Heathrow (since this is where most deceased arrive). CCG will brief the Coroner on the potential requirements (numbers, repatriation arrangements, any details about geographical locations of the families in the UK) and ascertain if he or she is content to take on the co-ordinating role with other Coroners. Following one mass casualty incident, Coroners advise that it is quicker and more efficient for one Coroner to open the inquest on all victims and then transfer them to another district for burial or cremation. However, this responsibility will not always fall to the West London Coroner, even though this is the point of reception. The receiving Coroner will liaise with other UK Coroners to negotiate the transfer of jurisdiction for the handling of inquests.

REFERENCES

1 Foreign and Commonwealth Office website [online]. Available at: http://www.fco.gov.uk/en. [Accessed: 12.2.2007.]

2 Consular Crisis Group [online]. Available at: http://www.ukresilience.info/response/recovery_guidance/humanitarian_aspects/nationals_resident.aspx. [Accessed: 12.12.2007.]

3 Emergency Response Team [online]. Available at: http://www.4ni.co.uk/news.asp?id-46296. [Accessed: 12.12.2007.]

4 Family Liaison Officer (FLO) [online]. Available at: http://www.acpo.police.uk/asp/policies/Data/family_liaison_strategy/doc. [Accessed: 12.12.2007.]

5 CIFA [online]. Available at: http://www.cifa.ac/login.html. [Accessed: 12.12.2007.]

6 Home Office website [online]. Available at: http://www.homeoffice.gov.uk/. [Accessed: 12.12.2007.]

7 Northern Ireland Office website [online]. Available at: http://www.nio.gov.uk/. [Accessed: 12.12.2007.]

8 Scottish Government website [online]. Available at: http://www.scotland.gov.uk/Home. [Accessed: 13.11.2007.]

9 Association of Chief Police Officers of England, Wales and Northern Ireland (ACPO) website [online]. Available at: http://www.acpo.police.uk/. [Accessed: 12.12.2007.]

10 Association of Chief Police Officers in Scotland (ACPOS) website [online]. Available at: http://www.acpos.police.uk/. Last accessed: 12.12.2007.]

11 Wikipedia, *List of Ambassadors from the United Kingdom to Portugal* [online]. Available at: http://.en.wikipedia.org/wiki/List_of_Ambassadors_from_the_United_Kingdom_to_Portugal. [Accessed: 12.12.2007.]

12 Wikipedia, *High Commissioner* [online]. Available at: http://en.wikipedia.org/wiki/High_Commissioner. [Accessed: 12.12.2007.]

13 British Red Cross home page [online]. Available at: http://www.redcross.org.uk/index.asp?id=39992. [Accessed: 12.12.2007.]

14 International SOS [online]. Available at: http://www.internationalsos.com/en/index.htm?CFID=14861085&CFTOKEN=94234619. Last accessed: 12.12.2007.]

15 BBC News Online, Tuesday 5 December 2006, "Fiji military coup is denounced" [online]. Available at: http://news.bbc.co.uk/2/hi/asia-pacific/6210464.stm. [Accessed: 12.12.2007.]

16 CNN News Online, Tuesday 25 April 2006, "Three bombs rip through Egypt resort". [online]. Available at: http://www.cnn.com/2006/WORLD/meast/04/24/egypt.blasts/index.html. [Accessed: 12.12.2007.]

17 BBC News Online, Saturday 22 November 2003, "'Total chaos' of Istanbul bombing" [online]. Available at: http://news.bbc.co.uk/2/hi/europe/5292122.stm. [Accessed: 12.12.2007.]

18 Mail Online, 6 September 2006, "British tourists injured in Spanish coach crash" [online]. Available at: http://www.dailymail.co.uk/news/article–403989/British-tourists-injured-Spanish-coach crash.html. [Accessed: 12.12.2007.]

19 BBC News Online, Sunday 10 December 2006, "Third Briton died in Jeddah crash" [online]. Available at: http://news.bbc.co.uk/1/hi/world/middle_east/6164337.stm. [Accessed: 12.12.2007.]

20 Australian Government, Department of Foreign Affairs and Trade. Civil unrest in the Democratic Republic of Congo [online]. Available at: http://www.smartraveller.gov.au/zw-cgi/view.Advice/Democratic_Republic_of_the_Congo.   [Accessed: 12.12.2007.]

21 Telegraph Online, 5 May 2007, "Britons feared dead in Cameroon plane crash". Plane crash in Cameroon: Available at: http://www.telegraph.co.uk/news/main.jhtml?xml=/news/2007/05/05/wkenya205.xml. [Accessed: 12.12.2007.]

22 Travel Weekly, 8 August 2007, "FTO investigates Dominican Republic health scare" [online]. Available at: http://www.travelweekly.co.uk/Articles/2007/08/08/24834/fto-investigates-dominican-republic-health-scare-08-aug.html. [Accessed: 12.12.2007.]

23 BBC News Online, 16 September 2007, "Scores killed in Thai plane crash" [online]. Available at: http://news.bbc.co.uk/2/his/asia-pacific/6997381.stm.   [Accessed: 12.12.2007.]

24 The Coroners' Society of England and Wales [online]. Available at: http://www.coronersociety.org.uk/. [Accessed: 12.12.2007.]

CHAPTER 4

The Coroner

4.1 INTRODUCTION

The Clarke Report (more properly known as the Report of the Public Inquiry into the Identification of Victims Following Major Transport Accidents – Report of Lord Justice Clarke) underlines the importance of mutual understanding among those involved in disaster victim identification:

> "It is vital that each Agency knows, not only what its role will be in the event of a disaster producing numerous fatalities, but also the role of each of the other organizations involved."[1]

This chapter will give the reader some understanding of the role of the Coroner in a mass fatality incident. This includes a brief explanation of the relevant law (which does not distinguish between one death or 500) with particular reference to the identification of victims and difficulties arising from tissue retention. There is specific mention of the Clarke Inquiry[1] and the relationship between the Coroner and the Senior Identification Manager (SIM).

At the time of writing, the Government's further proposals on Coroner reform[2] remain unclear. A draft Coroners Bill published in 2006 was widely criticised but it is currently understood that a re-worked version of the Bill is to be published late in 2007, with the intention that this is laid before Parliament when an opportunity arises. However, it is not thought that any of the proposals in this Bill will have a significant impact on the information set out below.

4.2 THE CORONER

In looking at the role of the Coroner in disaster victim identification, it must be stressed that while there are inevitable differences between dealing with a mass fatality situation and the more common sudden or unnatural deaths over which the Coroner takes jurisdiction, the basic law remains exactly the same. Our starting point is therefore a clear understanding of the general law relating to a Coroner's inquiry.

The ancient origins of the office of Coroner lead to many misconceptions and misunderstandings. A very significant proportion of the general public do not appreciate the difference between the Coroner and a pathologist. Indeed, this itself might be an important point for a SIM to ensure that relatives understand. The Coroner is best described as "an independent judicial officer with a statutory responsibility to enquire into the cause and circumstances of any unexpected or unnatural death". This includes a specific responsibility for the identification of the deceased.

Myths abound as to the specific powers of the Coroner but the reality is best defined as follows:

1. A statutory requirement to inquire into the cause and circumstances of deaths falling within the criteria set out in s 8 of the Coroners Act 1988 ("CA 1988").[3] In simple terms, this means that:
   - the body is lying within the Coroner's district; *and*
   - there is reasonable cause to suspect a violent or unnatural death, a sudden death of unknown cause or that the death has occurred in prison.

   Note that there is no specific requirement that the death arose within the Coroner's jurisdiction – merely that the body is now present within his or her district. Thus, a death occurring abroad where the body is repatriated for funeral will fall within the Coroner's remit.
2. A statutory responsibility to establish the identity of the deceased and how, when and where the death occurred (s 11(5) CA 1988).[3]
3. A right to take lawful possession[4] and control of the body from the time that the death is reported until enquiries are complete, although a body will commonly be released as soon as practicable.

   Note the basic principle at common law is that there is no property in a body, that is to say a body cannot be owned or be regarded as the property of another.[5]

   However, the right to take possession of the body is a different concept. Clarke summarised this, and the paramount role that the Coroner has with identification by statute:

   > "So far as identification is concerned the legal position is that when the police are dealing with a suspicious death they work on behalf of the coroner because it is he who has both the responsibility for identification and the right to possession of the body until his coronial functions have been fulfilled."[1]
4. Authority to remove the body from the place of death to a suitable mortuary (s 22 CA 1988[3]). On the face of it this is relatively straightforward but in fact there is a difficulty that remains unresolved despite many approaches by Coroners to the Government seeking urgent action to amend the law. This anomaly is discussed further at section 4.4 below.
5. Sole authority to order an autopsy examination (note that the terminology of "autopsy" or "post-mortem examination' is entirely interchangeable:

the writer tends to use the former for brevity and simplicity). The Coroner has power to direct that an autopsy be performed by a registered medical practitioner under both ss 19 and 20 CA 1988.[3] However, only the power within s 20[3] would be relevant to a mass fatality situation. This power to direct (even against the wishes of the family) is almost uniquely vested in the Coroner: it is not possessed by the police (despite their own statutory responsibilities to investigate criminal aspects of a death), or by the deceased's own doctor.

6. The power under s 20[3] extends to the Coroner directing that special examinations be made. These are often referred to as the "ologies" and include examinations such as bacteriology, neuropathology and toxicology. Histology (the study of tissue samples under a microscope) is in a slightly different position as it may be regarded as part of the routine of a well-performed autopsy, but there is little doubt that extensive or specialised histology would fall within s 20.[3]

7. Power to direct the retention of tissue samples. Rule 9 of the Coroners Rules 1984,[6] as amended ("CR 1984") requires a pathologist to preserve "material" which bears upon the cause of death or the identification of the deceased for such period as the Coroner thinks fit. There is a specific procedure required by the Coroners (Amendment) Rules 2005 ("CAR 2005")[7] which is described below.

4.3   JURISDICTION ISSUES

Before a Coroner may take responsibility in a case, the body has to fall properly within his or her jurisdiction. The basic law (s 8 CA 1988[3]) is set out above but in the mass fatalities scenario there are a number of issues which may arise.

4.3.1   Body parts

First, in terms of body parts, what amounts to a "body" over which the Coroner may take jurisdiction? The normal answer is that the material found must be incompatible with life, that is to say there is no prospect that the person thought to be dead is actually alive, if somewhat hampered by the absence of the body part in question. But in a disaster this approach may have to be re-evaluated as the context of a find becomes all important.

For example, a collection of body parts from one person, not of themselves incompatible with life, found in most situations provides little proof of death but if found at the scene of an air crash or in the rubble of a collapsed skyscraper then the situation would be entirely different. Much would then depend upon whether the "victim" was known to be a passenger on the aircraft or an occupant of the building. In such a case, the parts might be regarded as a "body" if that were all that were ultimately recovered.

If the find were of one small body part such as a finger, an alternative course might be to apply to the Secretary of State under s 15 CA 1988[3] for permission to hold an inquest in the absence of a body, using the finger as evidence of death (as to which, see section 4.3.2). This possibly avoids artificial concepts of a "body", but the promptness of decision may be an issue.

4.3.2   No body recovered

If no body tissues at all are recovered from a person thought to have died at an incident, the Coroner can make application to the Secretary of State under s 15 CA 1988[3] to hold an inquest in the absence of a body. The Coroner will have to satisfy the Secretary of State that the death occurred in or near his or her jurisdiction in such circumstances that an inquest ought to be held and that the body has been destroyed or cannot be recovered. This is plainly useful in the equivalent of a World Trade Center situation but:

- there would have to be a high level of proof that the missing person was actually dead;
- this power can only be used where the death has occurred within the Coroner's jurisdiction so it would not apply to a death abroad of someone who ordinarily lived within the Coroner's jurisdiction;
- the Secretary of State may decline to order an inquest, even if there is certainty that a death has occurred to the point of a murder conviction, if he or she does not consider it desirable to do so (s 15(2) CA 1988):[3] see also *R* v *Weatherhead*.[8]

4.3.3   Deaths abroad

Where a fatality has occurred abroad and a body is to be repatriated to England or Wales, it would ordinarily come under the jurisdiction of the Coroner in whose area the funeral was to take place. The wording of s 8 CA 1988[3] (see above) means that the Coroner must hold an investigation and, if necessary, an inquest, just as if the death had occurred locally. However, in recent years there has been a tendency to keep multiple fatality cases together by treating the point of entry into the country (ie airport or seaport) as the trigger for jurisdiction. There is a separate section at the end of this chapter on the practical difficulties of dealing with deaths abroad.

4.4   MOVEMENT OF BODIES

4.4.1   Removal of body to a mortuary outside the jurisdiction

The power within s 22(1) CA 1988[3] allows the Coroner to order the removal of a body to a mortuary within his or her district or within an adjoining district of another Coroner. Movement to another district may be advantageous because of either better mortuary services or centralising facilities in a multiple fatality incident spread over two or more jurisdictions.

However, the word "adjoining" has a clear meaning restricting the removal to a jurisdiction which physically touches the original Coroner's territory. While there would seem to be nothing to prevent the body being removed further afield, it is clear that this would mean that the body was now lying in the jurisdiction of another Coroner. The saving provision in s 22(3)[3] could not apply – that removal of a body under this section does not affect the powers and duties of the original Coroner nor confer power on the Coroner to whose district the body is moved. Thus, jurisdiction is lost to the new Coroner – with the cost implications for him or her referred to below.

This whole concept of limited territorial jurisdiction is an anachronism but the clear fact remains that it is the current law. Beyond "adjoining" jurisdictions, there is no provision for Coroner A to agree with Coroner B that a body can be moved to B's jurisdiction but will still be dealt with by A. This can plainly lead to a difficulty where a mass fatality mortuary is established some distance from the scene of the incident.

4.4.2 Deaths in multiple jurisdictions

Problems can also arise where there are connected incidents in separate places or one incident (such as an aircraft exploding in flight) which scatters bodies over two or more jurisdictions. The basic situation is that the bodies will be dealt with by the Coroner for the jurisdiction in which they lie.

However, under s 14 CA 1988[3] one Coroner may request another to take jurisdiction over a body that would ordinarily fall to him or her to deal with (note that if the body has been moved to an adjoining district for autopsy under the s 22 power referred to above, it cannot be the subject of a s 14 transfer until moved back – as that section requires the body to be lying within the district). The body does not need to be moved for a s 14 transfer to be accomplished, although the inquest proceedings have to be held in the new district. In the absence of agreement the Secretary of State may be asked to make a ruling under s 14(2) CA 1988.[3]

There is a problem of an intensely practical nature with s 14. All the costs of dealing with the body, even those already expended, transfer to the receiving jurisdiction and there is no power under current coronial legislation for this to be varied by agreement. In mass fatality situations this could have a very significant financial impact on the local authority for the receiving jurisdiction.

There is, of course, nothing to stop the two Coroners working closely together and agreeing to adopt common policies while each retains jurisdiction over the bodies from his or her own area. There is no provision in coronial legislation for a "lead coroner" to be appointed, although this phrase is often bandied around. If the two jurisdictions are physically adjoining it would be possible for the bodies to be moved to a common mortuary facility while each Coroner maintained his or her own cases (see above).

4.5   AUTOPSIES

Under s 20 CA 1988,[3] the Coroner may order that an autopsy be performed to gather evidence for the inquest and for special examinations such as neuropathology or toxicology to be undertaken. Although this is not a matter requiring consent from the relatives, a number of obligations fall upon the Coroner – particularly with regard to any tissue retention.

Most provisions of the Human Tissue Act 2004 ("HTA 2004")[9] do not apply to a Coroner's autopsy, although requirements do affect the place where the autopsy is carried out. Nonetheless, there is an expectation that Coroners will follow the related Code of Practice (number 3 of several) on post-mortem examinations at paras 27–34.[10] In simple terms this means that:

- the next-of-kin will be told that there is to be an autopsy and the reasons for this will be explained sensitively before it is carried out – obviously, this cannot be followed if either the next-of-kin cannot be identified at that stage or the autopsy must be performed urgently for investigative reasons;
- the nature and purpose of the examination, together with the procedures to be followed, will be explained if requested – in such detail as the next-of-kin requires;
- the time and place of the examination will be notified, together with the opportunity for the family to have a medically qualified observer present (by rule 8, the medical observer must not interfere with the examination);
- there will be complete disclosure of any tissue retention – as to which, see below;
- the next-of-kin will be told that they are entitled to a copy of the autopsy report, and when it is likely to be available. Again, this will be difficult in certain phases of a major criminal inquiry. The Codes do not take account of this but must presumably be read with some regard to security of information where genuinely necessary in a major case.

The Coroners (Amendment) Rules 2005 ("CAR 2005")[7] brought a legislative requirement in respect of notification of tissue retention to families. In short:

- the pathologist must tell the Coroner of the exact intended retention of "material" (as to the definition of which, see below) and how long this will need to be kept. This would be a detailed list, eg two blocks from the heart; six blocks from the lung etc. The pathologist must justify the need for retention;
- the Coroner will then authorise (if appropriate) the specific retention and set the period for which the material may be retained. However, note that the

Coroner's power to authorise retention ends when his or her coronial function ceases. For the purpose of this text, this is likely to be when an inquest is concluded or a formal decision is made that there will be no inquest because of Crown Court proceedings or a judicial inquiry (s 17A CA 1988,[3] as amended);

- the pathologist must keep a record of any tissue retention and disposal. The autopsy report must declare the retention;
- the Coroner *must* tell the next-of-kin of the retention and seek their wishes as to disposal once the material can be returned. The choices of disposal are:
  - delaying the funeral until the material can be returned to the body;
  - a separate later return of the material. There is now provision in the cremation regulations for a later cremation of this material should the family so wish, although there can be practical difficulties because of the minimal amounts involved. There is little difficulty with burying the returned material in the grave as this is not to the same depth as the coffin. Note that Coroners would not generally agree to meeting the cost of this later burial/cremation under normal circumstances;
  - retention by the pathologist "for research or other purposes". In some areas this might be subdivided into the prospect that the material will be held by the pathologist for a certain length of time as part of the deceased's medical records which would not allow general research but would allow further investigation on that particular death;
  - respectful disposal by the pathologist. Note that this usually amounts to an incineration which may not be recognised as "respectful" by some faiths.

CAR 2005[7] do not define "material" but refer to material retained by a pathologist bearing upon the cause of death or identification, which presumably includes anything so retained. However, in simple terms, "material" is now very widely defined by s 53 Human Tissue Act 2004 ("HTA 2004")[9] as anything which consists of or includes human cells.

Some issues arise where "material" is retained at autopsy for investigative purposes rather than the Coroner's concerns of cause or identification and thus do not fall within either the Coroner's remit or CAR 2005.[7] Material held for a current police investigation is exempt from HTA 2004[9] although it is said that an "appropriate disposal" in accordance with the relatives' wishes would be best practice once the authority of the police to hold the material has come to an end. This is a complex topic, outside the scope of this text. The reader is directed to comprehensive guidance "Legal issues in forensic pathology and tissue retention" prepared by Dr Jeff Adams at the Forensic Science & Policy Unit of the Home Office in discussion with ACPO, the Coroners Society and the Human Tissue Authority. A further document "Human Tissue Act 2004 Briefing for Forensic Pathologists"[11] (also prepared by Dr Adams) is available on the Home Office website.

4.6   DIFFERENCES WITH A MASS FATALITY INCIDENT

Thus far, this chapter has proceeded on the basis that the relevant law applies to any unnatural or unknown cause of death, whether mass fatality incident or not. However, the reality is that dealing with 80 bodies from a disaster scenario is substantially different to the same number of cases arising over the space of a week in a busy Coroner's jurisdiction:

- bodies may have been subject to trauma and/or fragmentation, leading to difficulties of identification;
- there may be massive pressure from relatives and the media;
- the incident will almost certainly be a major crime;
- the circumstances may be such that the investigators do not necessarily know what they are looking for in the early stages.

The harsh truth is that the Coroner, the police and the other authorities involved will be trying to establish a working system for dealing with the bodies in circumstances that may initially be approaching near chaos. This will effectively mean subjugating the immediate interests of individual bereaved into a "system" at a time when their need for personal treatment is at its utmost. This will inevitably require the very highest level of skill from the SIM.

4.7   THE ROLE OF THE CORONER

The role of the Coroner in a mass fatality incident was originally described in a briefing document for the Cabinet Office (prepared by Michael Burgess, HM Coroner for Surrey and Coroner to the Royal Household) as:

- In consultation with the relevant council and police, to initiate the establishment of the emergency mortuary.
- To authorise the removal of bodies of victims.
- To appoint a supervising pathologist and authorise the examination of bodies to find a cause of death.
- To chair the Identification Commission and take reasonable steps to identify the deceased.
- To organise the collection of data concerning those whose bodies may be irrecoverable but who were believed to be victims of the event.
- To liaise and co-operate with other Coroners who may also have bodies of victims arising from the same event.
- To authorise the disposal of those bodies after appropriate examination and documentation is complete – to those who are lawfully entitled.
- At all times, to liaise with the relevant emergency services and Government departments.

This list remains valid guidance following Clarke[1] and renewed Government advice on dealing with mass fatalities.

4.8   EARLY DECISIONS – THE STRATEGIC GROUP

On notification of a multiple deaths incident, the Coroner will be concerned to decide whether a mass fatality mortuary is necessary. This will depend on a number of factors, including the scale of existing facilities, the nature of the disaster and the degree of disruption to the victims. It is almost impossible to set a hard and fast rule about what number of deaths would require special measures ahead of the actual incident.

Although this decision rests with the Coroner, he or she will need guidance from a number of sources. At a minimum this is likely to be the SIO (Senior Investigating Officer), the SIM, the supervising pathologist, the local authority mortuary manager and the local authority executive who will be responsible for providing the facility on behalf of the Coroner. This "strategic group" should meet as early as possible. Although this may be easier said than done, it is a matter of priority at that stage. Once the basics have been decided there is likely to be need for a further meeting, perhaps with the contractors providing the mortuary structure, in order to finalise more detailed plans.

It is clear that there should be robust contact arrangements for this group (including deputies). At least some of the planning can be done in advance so that the choices are of previously discussed alternatives rather than starting with a blank sheet of paper. There must be familiarity with the existing national arrangements for an emergency mortuary structure and equipment (NEMA).

4.9   THE MORTUARY OPERATION

Although the Coroner has an overall responsibility for matters affecting the recovered victims, he or she will recognise that the mortuary is also a major part of the evidence-gathering operation for a significant crime.

The Coroner's interest at this stage is primarily with identification and establishing the cause of death. Identification matters are dealt with below (see section 4.12) but some comment on the extent of examination to be authorised is appropriate. On this point both the Coroner and the SIM will seek the advice of the supervising pathologist, a senior forensic pathologist, probably identified well in advance, who will lead the medical side of the mortuary operation on behalf of both the police and the Coroner. Choice of the supervising pathologist rests with the Coroner but might reasonably be the subject of discussion with the potential SIO and SIM.

The SIM and the Coroner will be concerned to establish identity and cause of death to an agreed standard of proof. In practical terms this is likely to be "beyond reasonable doubt" if such can be achieved (see section 4.12 for further comment on this). However, at the same time they will wish to cause further minimum disruption to the victims' bodies. In some mass fatality situations it will be necessary to order a full post-mortem examination; in others it may not if the cause of death is self-evident or can be ascertained without a full examination. These issues will differ from case to case but it suffices here to note that there is little place for *automatic* recourse to a full autopsy of every victim, let alone unnecessary disruption to jaws, fingers or hands etc.

4.10   EXPECTATIONS OF THE RELATIVES

From the Coroner's point of view, it might reasonably be anticipated that the bereaved will have certain expectations:

- That they will only need to give detailed information about their relative on one occasion rather than being asked the same questions repeatedly by different people.
- That the body will be recovered immediately, particularly if lying in a public place.
- That this will include the recovery of all fragments, no matter how many or how small.
- That there will be prompt identification of each and every body or body part.
- That the body will be released as soon as identified.
- That systems for recovery, identification and release will be better than normal rather than worse.

Clarke[1] says that a number of questions by families can be foreseen:

"Most people who are bereaved as a result of a disaster have no idea what to expect. It is often their first experience of sudden death. They tend to want general information about the following matters, no doubt among many others.

- where the body will be taken once it has been found?
- what happens to a body at a mortuary?
- how the identification process will work?
- the role of the Coroner and the police?
- what is a post mortem, when will it take place and why?
- what rights they have regarding the body, the PM and viewing?
- when the body will be released?"

The writer would respectfully suggest that the following questions might equally be anticipated, some rather more pointedly:

- Why are the bodies being left *in situ* for so long before recovery?
- Why are you using a tent for a mortuary?
- Why is the identification process taking so long?
- Why am I being discouraged from viewing the body?
- If I have been dissuaded from viewing for myself, how do I really know that the identification is correct?
- Why is there a delay in releasing the body to me?

The Coroner will be reliant upon the SIM to ensure that appropriate and correct answers are being given to all of these questions, preferably before they are even asked.

Delay in identification will be a contentious matter and merits special mention here. While there is good reason for a methodical approach, and sometimes an operational need to prioritise particular aspects of the mortuary work, it is inevitable that the media and relatives will question any apparent delay. Comparisons will be made with foreign jurisdictions that identified twice as many victims in half the time. Whether those identifications subsequently proved correct is unlikely to receive much mention.

Experience now suggests that this issue needs careful media handling right from the start. It may not be practicable to manage the public expectation fully but there should be clear explanation of exactly what stage the process is at and when identifications are likely, with as full an explanation as the investigative circumstances permit.

4.11   INFORMATION TO FAMILIES

Information is sometimes described as "a cheap commodity" or "something that costs nothing to give but is priceless to receive". In modern society, the probability is that failure to give proper information will be perceived as "covering up" or hiding dreadful facts. This is particularly so where the Coroner and the police are taking unusual measures that are not easily understood by the bereaved.

The writer has always considered the words of Dr Jim Swire, father of a Lockerbie victim, to give a lead on communicating with families:

"What we wanted was information about exactly how and why people died, why we were being dissuaded from viewing the crash site, how the identification process worked and why we were not being allowed to see the bodies. This would have helped far more than counsellors telling us how we should feel."

Clarke[1] also reminds us that:

"Even if there is no information to give, families should be informed that this is the case and the reason for it."

4.12   THE IDENTIFICATION COMMISSION

The Commission will be chaired by the Coroner, for he or she has ultimate responsibility under statute (s 11(5) CA 1988[3]) for identification of the bodies. Although the ultimate identification decision will be made within the inquest proceedings, the practical situation is that the Coroner must be satisfied at the time of the Identification Commission.

The question arises as to the standard of proof necessary. With a small number of exceptions not relevant here, the facts found at inquest are established "on the balance of probabilities" rather than "beyond reasonable doubt". It could be argued at a theoretical level that the identity of a mass fatality victim need only be established on the balance of probabilities but the reader is unlikely to take much persuading that this would be a disastrous approach! The reality is that any such identification needs to be beyond reasonable doubt unless and until such proves impossible. Any deviation from this standard needs to be carefully discussed, particularly with the potential victim's family.

Methods of identification fall outside the remit of this chapter. However, it is clear that the Identification Commission must work by an agreed method and to an agreed standard. Criteria should be established for the use of particular methods of identification. Agreement should be reached on the acceptable primary methods of identification (likely to be fingerprints, odontology and sometimes DNA) and whether one primary identifier is regarded as sufficient. It may be agreed that one primary method plus one or more secondary methods (eg jewellery, marks and scars etc) will be accepted.

Whatever the methodology, it is essential that there is clear agreement on standardisation of approach unless and until such time as some flexibility is necessary to move forward. If this proves to be the case it must always be discussed between the SIM and the Coroner before proceeding.

4.13   VIEWING

It is immediately necessary to distinguish between:

- "social viewing" where the bereaved are allowed to be with a body that has already been positively identified by scientific or other means; and
- "visual identification" where relatives are being asked to view a body for the purpose of identification.

Social viewing may be very common and can create many practical difficulties. Visual identification is most unlikely to have any place at all.

Clarke[1] gave a clear and emphatic lead on permitting social viewing:

"The importance of viewing the body for the grieving process should be emphasised to coroners and their staff. While the coroner or the coroner's officers may have reservations about the wisdom of viewing the remains of the deceased where there has been disfigurement by trauma, dismemberment, decomposition or mutilation, they should be reminded that the members of the family must never be prevented from viewing the remains."

Accepting that the authorities have no right to deny viewing, it is plainly incumbent on those involved to ensure that relatives are making a fully informed decision when they consider viewing a mutilated, fragmented or decomposed victim. There must always be a clear explanation of the state of the body and the circumstances in which the actual viewing will be made. This may extend to a "health warning" or perhaps in extreme cases the signing of a disclaimer.

Steps can be taken to minimise the impact of viewing a burnt or mutilated body. Mortuary technicians are generally extremely experienced at dealing with this situation and it is often wise to seek their advice.

While photographs may assist relatives in their decision on viewing, they can also be a source of contention, as can video of body recovery from the scene. It is not unknown for the bereaved to request access to such material. It is difficult to suggest any hard and fast rule, as circumstances will vary, and what cannot be released at an early stage may be subject to disclosure later. Nonetheless, it is respectfully suggested that the starting point (subject to an informed decision by the family and health warnings etc) is asking whether there is a real operational reason for refusal rather than imposing one's own standards and beliefs.

Both the Coroner and the SIM should also take care as to how they communicate any thoughts about the appropriateness of viewing. What starts as an intention that the bereaved can view, but only after a warning, may be translated several stages down the chain as a prohibition. Clarke[1] referred to this in relation to *Marchioness* families being told that they could not view their loved ones:

"It is likely that the coroner's officers and police liaison officers, acting from the best of motives, namely to avoid distress to relatives, sought to dissuade from viewing those relatives that expressed a wish to view. it is quite possible that such officers used language which suggested that viewing was prohibited rather than ill-advised to achieve what they thought best, namely that a loving parent would not be distressed by the sight of their child's decomposing body."

4.14 RELEASE OF THE BODY

The question of who is lawfully entitled to take possession of a body following release can be immensely difficult. The general rule is that an executor carries first entitlement, but where there is no will there may be a number of people with competing claims to be administrator of the estate. Unlike an executor, none of the potential administrators have any legal rights until the grant of letters of administration is obtained.

Family disputes, including relatives denying rights to "common law partners" are familiar ground for Coroners, but where there is a real dispute as to who is entitled to receive the body it is a matter for the civil courts rather than the Coroner to decide.

4.15   THE CORONER AND THE SIM

The Coroner and the SIM should not be meeting for the first time on the occasion of the incident. Some mutual understanding and broad planning are essential. The opportunity should be taken to work together on exercises, whether practical or table-top.

Clarke regarded the role of the SIM (*inter alia*) as creating a link between the Coroner and the police. The Coroner will view the SIM as a trusted adviser with specialist knowledge of the subject. The SIM will also effectively be the facilitator for the Coroner who has no resources to take forward agreed actions. The Coroner will expect constant communication to and from the SIM. Ideally, this is a relationship of the utmost trust, for the reality is that the SIM and the Coroner "sink or swim" together. There should be common aims moving towards established outcomes, with agreed contingency plans.

However, it is also fair to say that the SIM is entitled to have expectations of the Coroner which would include ready availability, clear and concise instructions (with goal posts that only move when unavoidable) and that the Coroner will be a team player so far as his/her legal position allows.

The Coroner, the SIM, the supervising pathologist and the SIO should be working together as a team, albeit each with a significantly different role. They will together have in mind the implications of Article 8 of the European Convention on Human Rights[12] which provides for the right to private and family life. Case law makes it clear that the right to grieve (and thus for prompt return of the body) is an intimate part of private life, requiring particularly serious reason before interference could be justified.[13]

They will also be working together to agree the minimum that reasonably needs to be done to the recovered victims, consistent with certain identification and the preservation or securing of evidence. Together they must devise a strategy to deal with:

- the recovery process;
- transport and storage;
- medical issues;
- identification.

All of this requires a balance between a methodical and fail-safe system, proper expediency and the expectations of the bereaved. This strategy must also take account of the need to preserve and secure evidence for the criminal aspects of the investigation.

4.16 DIFFICULTIES WITH BODIES RETURNED FROM ABROAD

Basic issues of jurisdiction on deaths abroad are dealt with in section 4.3.3. As referred to there, the Coroner will take jurisdiction over a body repatriated to his or her district in exactly the same manner as if the death had occurred locally. However, the similarity ends almost at that point.

Dealing with bodies where the identification process has been "completed' abroad can actually be far more difficult than starting from scratch with an incident at home. Sadly, history shows that there is no place whatsoever for assumptions that foreign authorities have been effective in their identification procedures.

A number of specific difficulties arise with multiple deaths in foreign jurisdictions:

- Local staff may be inexperienced or working to lower standards, so the reliability of the initial identification process may be in question.
- Political expedience may have led to an early site clearance, possibly with a rather different attitude to small remains than is likely in the UK.
- Any foreign autopsy may be to different standards. It is not uncommon that many or all of the internal organs will have been removed, leading to significant difficulties for any examination in this country.
- There may be difficulty where a "body" has been repatriated but subsequently remains are recovered and returned, unexpectedly or otherwise.
- The Coroner does not have any legal status until such time as a body is actually returned, thus any visit to the foreign disaster scene or domestic preparation to receive the bodies is effectively made on an informal basis.

But, as with any such death, the bereaved will have expectations, and the SIM may well be dealing with families who have already been frustrated and deeply upset by events and attitudes entirely outside his or her control.

ACKNOWLEDGEMENTS

I am grateful to Mr Michael Burgess (HM Coroner for Surrey and Coroner for the Royal Household) and Ms Debbie Large (Senior Lecturer at Teesside University) for their helpful comments on the first draft of this chapter.

REFERENCES

1 Lord Justice Clarke, "Public Inquiry into the Identification of Victims following Major Transport Disasters" (2001) [online]. Available at: http://www.marchioness-nsi.org.uk. [Accessed: 13.11.2007.]

2   Coroner Reform: The Government's Draft Bill (2006) Improving death investigation in England and Wales [online]. Available at: http://www.dca.gov.uk/legist/coroners_draft.pdf. [Accessed: 13.11.2007.]

3   Coroners Act 1988 (c 13) (HMSO, London) [online]. Available at: http://www.opsi.gov.uk/acts/acts1988/pdf/ukpga_19880013_en.pdf. [Accessed: 13.11.2007.]

4   *R* v *Bristol Coroner, ex parte Kerr* [1974] 2 All ER 719.

5   *Dobson* v *North Tyneside Health Authority* [1996] 4 All ER 474.

6   King's College London, Coroners' Law Resource [online]. Available at: http://www.kcl.ac.uk/depsta/law/research/coroners/1984rules.html. [Accessed: 27.11.2007.]

7   Coroners (Amendment) Rules 2005 (SI 2005/420) (HMSO, London) [online]. Available at: ttp://www.opsi.gov.uk/si/si2005/20050420.htm. [Accessed: 13.11.2007.]

8   *R* v *Weatherhead* [1996] 160 JP 627.

9   Human Tissue Act 2004 (c 30) (HMSO, London) [online]. Available at: http://www.opsi.gov.uk/acts/acts2004/20040030.htm. [Accessed: 13.11.2007.]

10 Human Tissue Authority, "Code of Practice – Post Mortem Examination" (2006) [online]. Available at: http://www.hta.gov.uk/_db/_documents/2006-07-04_Approved_by_Parliament_-_Code_of_Practice_3_-_Post_Mortem.pdf. [Accessed: 13.11.2007.]

11 Human Tissue Act 2004 (c 30) Briefing for Forensic Practitioners (HMSO, London) [online]. Available at: http://www.homeoffice.gov.uk/documents/human-tissue-act-briefing?view=Binary. [Accessed: 13.11.2007.]

12 Article 8 ECHR [online]. Available at: http://www.hri.org/docs/ECHR50.html#C.Art8. [Accessed: 13.11.2007.]

13 *Dudgeon* v *UK* (1982) 4 EHRR 149 at para 52.

CHAPTER 5

The Centre for International Forensic Assistance (CIFA)

5.1 INTRODUCTION

The last quarter of a century has confirmed unequivocally that, although war crimes, crimes against humanity, mass fatalities and terrorist attacks are permanent features of our time, forensic assistance in the UK has struggled to keep pace with humanitarian or judicial demands, and successive UK Governments have, until recently, failed to address the need for long-term investment in a permanent DVI response facility. It is an acknowledged fact that the sporadic and largely unpredictable occurrence of these incidents places an enormous burden on Government resources to provide even basic deployment capabilities on a multi-disciplinary scale; therefore it was essential that a cost-effective and viable solution be identified and implemented.

After the 1996 Interpol meeting in Antalya,[1] all member countries (including the UK) were advised to establish DVI teams consisting of police officers, forensic pathologists and forensic odontologists or, failing that, at least appoint a police officer to take responsibility for DVI matters and be a first point of contact. Interpol[2] further recommended that approved Interpol DVI forms[3] be used without exception, and that all member countries should take steps to meet regularly to discuss DVI and enhance the levels of co-operation and exchange of information at an international level. Those Interpol recommendations[2] could in no way have been considered exhaustive, they merely sought to form a sound basis for each member country to pursue best practice in the establishment of a DVI capability within its own prevailing legal framework.

In line with Interpol recommendations and current practice in many countries around the world, it was logical that the police should become the backbone of any DVI capability to be developed in the UK. In the case of the most recent major international disaster – the tsunami in south east Asia – the Police National Information and Co-ordination Centre (PNICC) was activated early (together with the National Casualty Bureau (or NCB), whose main role is to co-ordinate the efforts made to locate injured or deceased UK citizens) and maintained a pivotal role during the year following the disaster. In addition, a strategic-level, multi-agency Gold Group was set up by the police and led eventually by a senior Metropolitan Police Service (MPS) officer, DAC John Yates. The co-ordination of all activities of Operation Bracknell was undertaken between Association of Chief Police Officers (ACPO),[4] the MPS[5] and the Foreign and Commonwealth Office (FCO):[6] the department that led the UK Government's response to the disaster.

Once there were opportunities to consider what lessons could be learned from the tsunami[7] and the London bombings of 2005,[8] the British Government realised that any established DVI framework in the UK should be created with the ability to serve more than one master, ie for use in both domestic and overseas incidents, creating a more cost-efficient service. For domestic purposes, DVI teams will work with the police, Coroners/Procurators Fiscal, local authorities and the devolved administrations around the country, and be backed ultimately by the authority of ACPO[4] and the Home Office.[9] Alternatively, DVI teams may need to be deployed overseas in support of an FCO response or initiative, as was the case in recent years with the 2004 Asian tsunami (Figure 5.1),[7] Kosovo, Bahrain (Figure 5.2),[10,11] Sharm el Sheikh (Figures 5.3 and 5.4)[12,13] and Iraq.

Figure 5.1   CIFA personnel were deployed in response to the Asian tsunami

5.2   THE RECENT APPROACH TO DVI IN THE UK

In the past, incidents dealt with by the UK tended to have been managed in isolation, with forensic teams being assembled and deployed as and when required, on a tribunal- or case-specific basis. Once the immediate need for forensic assistance passed, the operational capabilities of a UK forensic team generally reverted to pre-incident levels, resulting in a loss (or at best an erosion) of accumulated knowledge, experience and contacts until the next situation arose which demanded their resurrection. The management and economic inefficiencies of such a pattern

Figure 5.2   Mortuary in Bahrain

of response are manifest. With the scale of recent terrorist threats and global disasters, it was timely for the British Government to examine both the domestic and overseas provision of forensic services and standards of practice, to ensure that future demands on the UK Government for such services are appropriately and professionally fulfilled. A structured, centralised and permanent UK DVI capability (founded on the lessons of previous deployments), which maintains the capability for rapid national and international deployment on both large and small scales, is both an extremely powerful humanitarian tool for identification of the deceased and an equally vital judicial tool for the procurement of incontrovertible evidence to facilitate successful prosecutions.

Figure 5.3   The information centre at the Marriott Hotel in Sharm-el-Sheikh

Figure 5.4   Sharm-el-Sheikh victims were processed by CIFA staff

5.3   DVI IN OTHER COUNTRIES

Although there is no single universal protocol to determine the response to any disaster or terrorist attack, the most common feature underpinning the emergency DVI response of most other countries is that their law enforcement agencies are central to their integrated emergency management framework. Domestic emergencies will generally also involve hospitals, the fire brigade, ambulance service, local authorities and coastguard, etc, whereas overseas emergencies (where the citizens of that country are involved) will often necessitate the involvement and co-operation of the military and Interpol.[14] In Switzerland, Germany, Israel and Spain, for example, the requests for DVI response teams are managed through federal and regional police or military commanders, and they deploy according to their own emergency response models. The scale and composition of the DVI response is usually determined by a permanent Team Leader or police-appointed DVI Commander.

There are dozens of countries around the world which, as members of Interpol, have worked hard to establish DVI teams after the ICPO (International Criminal Police Organization) – Interpol meeting held in Antalya in 1996,[1] though a number of countries have been working towards DVI capability since recommendations to that effect were made by Interpol at their meeting in Manila in 1980.[15]

5.4   A BRIEF HISTORY OF CIFA

The need for an organisation such as CIFA was recognised after direct experience was gained with the various British forensic teams involved in war crimes investigations in Rwanda and the Balkans, and in conflicts such as Sierra Leone, Iraq and East Timor. The managers of successive British forensic teams over the years were undoubtedly aware of the vast accumulation of forensic experience inherent in our colleagues, but few seemed conscious of the need for central organisation and co-ordination of such a vital asset, or the requirements needed to develop and maintain professional standards.

CIFA was deployed to Kosovo in 2002 in a humanitarian follow-up programme on cessation of the UNICTY investigations. CIFA has the flexibility to operate large and small team deployments and the following table compares the differences and similarities between two very different large and rolling deployments.

	Kosovo	Thailand
Nature of the deployment	War crimes	Natural disaster
Overarching authority	United Nations	Thai Government
National authority	UN War Crimes of FCO	FCO
Legal remit	Prosecutorial	Non-prosecutorial
Principal police remit	Investigative	Family Liaison and ID
Security	Military protection (UNMIK)	Safe environment
Quality of facilities	Poor to reasonable	Excellent
Living conditions	Reasonable	Excellent
Pathology requirement	Important	Largely not required
Odontology requirement	None	Important
Anthropology requirement	Important	Largely not required
Radiography requirement	Fluoroscopy	Dental radiography
DNA analysis	Limited	Important
Fingerprint requirement	None	Important
Identification success	Low	High

Table 5.1   Comparison of the needs of CIFA involvement in Kosovo and Thailand

As a result, CIFA was created in 2001 with the co-operation and financial support of the FCO.[6] It was housed originally within a major Scottish university. Since that time, CIFA has evolved into an independent, multidisciplinary, international forensic organisation offering an extensive array of professional services utilising an equally wide range of experts from around the world. The organisation is now managed by a Directorate of individuals highly experienced in the fields of logistics, mission management and deployment, evidentiary procedures and educational provision (see Table 5.1).

Given the organisational complexities of any university, it proved difficult for CIFA to develop into the required flexible organisation. Therefore, in 2003, with the continued funding and support from the FCO,[6] CIFA became an independent legal entity with greatly enhanced operational flexibility, a more rapid response capability and a customised support structure. CIFA continues to be a not-for-profit organisation, though now with clearly defined Articles of Association, without shareholders and limited by guarantee. None of the five Directors draws any salary from CIFA, but are instead remunerated only for specific services rendered. Currently, the five Directors of CIFA are as follows:

- **Professor Sue Black**: one of the worlds' leading forensic anthropologists, and Head of the Centre for Anatomy and Human Identification at the University of Dundee. She is a founder of the British Association for Human Identification (BAHID), co-founder of CIFA and was speciality assessor for her discipline for the Council for the Registration of Forensic Practitioners.

- **Dr Dick Shepherd**: one of the leading Home Office forensic pathologists in the UK, and immediate past President of the British Association of Forensic Medicine (BAFM). Dr Shepherd has considerable experience of DVI deployments all over the world and was a key figure in the investigation into the Bali bombings.

- **Dr John Robson**: a forensic odontologist with over 40 years' experience, and immediate past President of the British Association of Forensic Odontologists (BAFO). Dr Robson has more recent DVI deployment and management experience than almost any other forensic odontologist in the UK and took a lead role in the identification processes following the Asian tsunami.

- **Assistant Chief Constable Steve Watts**: ACC Watts is responsible for Special Operations in Hampshire Constabulary, and his appointment to CIFA was expressly approved by ACPO in 2003. He has over 30 years' experience as a serving officer, and assumed overall command as the SIO for UK forensic investigations in Kosovo throughout 2000.

- **Tom Black**: originally an anatomist, Mr Black re-trained in a firm of chartered accountants and has nearly 25 years' finance and business management experience, nearly 20 of which have been at senior management level. He is the administrative and operational single point of contact (+44 (0)1569 760022, tom.black@cifa.ac).

5.5 CIFA'S CAPABILITIES

The Directors of CIFA believe that the organisation offers the UK Government an effective, proven and cost-efficient service through its existing forensic database, with plans to develop a stand-alone UK DVI database of non-police forensic experts. While it may be obvious that UK DVI must be led by the police and/or the Coroner/Procurator Fiscal, it must be recognised that the diverse multidisciplinary nature of non-police forensic personnel requires an appropriately subtle and understated management style.

The forensic practitioners on the UK DVI/CIFA database are nearly all civilians, often with varying responsibilities to patients, students, employers and other institutions, which may sometimes preclude rapid deployment. Therefore it is essential that the database available to UK DVI is maintained and developed to facilitate the swift assembly of appropriate teams with the ability to provide the scope for long-term rolling programmes, such as those provided in 2005 to Thailand[7] and Sri Lanka[16] following the tsunami. CIFA's organisational structure is designed both to support and to deliver the best from this core resource, ie an unrivalled international database of experienced professionals with forensic medical, scientific and technical expertise. Practitioners on the database are widely recognised as invaluable professionals of the highest integrity and professional standing who willingly offer their services for the investigations of mass fatalities, war crimes or human rights abuses.

CIFA operates a policy of low-key discretion and professional responsibility. It does not advertise through brochures, nor does it issue press releases concerning its work. Its Standard Terms and Conditions together with its mission contracts bind approved members of CIFA with a confidentiality undertaking and code of conduct. Any material breach of confidentiality or actions which bring CIFA, or the organisation/Government department that commissioned the deployment, into disrepute would necessitate removal from our database and negate all future undertakings with UK DVI and CIFA. CIFA does not require exclusivity from its members, who are free to work with other organisations.

Within its own network of strategic alliances, CIFA strives to create and maintain complementary and symbiotic relationships with a variety of key organisations (for example ACPO,[4] the UN,[17] the ICC,[18] Interpol,[14] various branches of the British military,[19] the Home Office,[9] the FCO,[6] various suppliers, logistics specialists, universities, body recovery agents, repatriation and funereal services and several professional forensic associations such as BAFO,[20] BAFM,[21] BAHID,[22] the Association of Forensic Radiographers (AFR),[23] the Association of Anatomical Pathology Technologists (AAPT)[24] etc). CIFA is able to work and align with these groups to offer a co-ordinated "one-stop" forensic capability to support and supply any non-police medical, technical and scientific requirements.

5.6   THE CIFA DATABASE

The heart of CIFA's capability is a comprehensive database of forensic professionals with international experience of DVI deployments, as well as search and recovery techniques, police procedures, evidence conservation, post-mortem interpretation and general identification of the deceased. The database currently comprises several hundred practitioners of confirmed competence from over 35 countries representing more than 33 different disciplines and these experts have provided their professional assistance in deployment to over 27 different countries (see Tables 5.2, 5.3 and 5.4).

Argentina	Greece	Peru
Australia	Holland	Philippines
Austria	India	Poland
Belgium	Ireland	Portugal
Brazil	Italy	South Africa
Canada	Jordan	Spain
Chile	Kosovo	Sri Lanka
Colombia	Lithuania	Sweden
Czech Republic	Malaysia	Turkey
Denmark	Mexico	United Kingdom
France	New Zealand	United States
Germany	Norway	

Table 5.2   Examples of countries currently represented on the CIFA database

Personnel registered on the CIFA database must evidence their suitability, qualifications and experience by submission of a detailed application form and two professional references (based broadly on the accepted practice of the Council for the Registration of Forensic Practitioners[25] (CRFP – originally a Home Office initiative)). CIFA considers the application and the two nominated referees are asked to provide references as necessary. Once approved, CIFA may then assign

Forensic pathology	Forensic anthropology	Forensic archaeology
DNA testing	Facial anthropology	Forensic odontology
Mortuary technology	Forensic radiography	Body recovery
Fingerprinting	Forensic podiatry	Forensic palynology
Forensic entomology	Forensic artistry	Forensic animation
Embalming	Interpreters	International law
Crime scene management	Exhibits	Environmental profiling
Torture victim analysis	Police photography	Ballistics
Fire investigation	Military and security advisers	IT and database management
Document analysis	EOD	Logistical support
Toxicology	Police surgeons	Specialist search and recovery

Table 5.3   Examples of some of the disciplines registered on the CIFA database

Argentina	Greece	Philippines
Bali	Grenada	Romania
Bosnia	Guatemala	Rwanda
Cambodia	Iraq	Saudi Arabia
Chile	Israel	Sierra Leone
Congo	Kazakhstan	South Africa
Cyprus	Kosovo	Sri Lanka
East Timor	Nepal	Thailand
El Salvador	Peru	United Arab Emirates
Plus many other locations around the world.		

Table 5.4   Examples of countries where CIFA experts have provided assistance

the member to either "full operational" or "provisional" status, depending upon suitability, qualifications and relevant experience. "Full operational" membership indicates that the new member is deemed suitably qualified and experienced to be deployed under conditions where no supervision is required for them to carry out their duties. Such experts are also asked to provide a description of their particular area of expertise so that a more refined indication of capabilities can be identified, for example identification from juvenile remains, experience of aviation disasters etc.

A "provisional" status indicates that the new member is not considered to have sufficient experience to operate independently, and may require mentoring until such time as they are able to work unsupervised through additional experience or training. This category of membership is important for the training of inexperienced personnel to allow them to develop "best practice" approaches through direct involvement in multi-disciplinary experiences that offer exposure to situations that they might be unlikely to encounter otherwise. For example, in the year after the Asian tsunami, this approach allowed CIFA effectively to treble the available pool of seasoned forensic odontologists for UK DVI by providing a solid platform for training, experience and personal development.

This policy also helps to ensure that inappropriately qualified or inexperienced personnel are not placed prematurely in positions unsuited to their temperament or current abilities, thereby helping to safeguard evidential and operational standards as well as protecting the wellbeing of the practitioner. Practitioners who clearly fail to meet required standards may be reassigned or removed from the database. This removes unsuitable practitioners from the forensic arena, thereby ensuring that high international standards are encouraged and maintained.

The centralisation and amalgamation of human resources has the distinct advantage of giving flexibility of choice which allows for the optimisation of UK DVI team dynamics. For example, teams may be constructed on the basis of geographical location, cultural or religious composition and even sex. While it may not be "politically correct" to admit to such selection, it is unavoidable and essential when placing DVI teams into sensitive and politically fragile areas of the world, in order to ensure maximum co-operation and minimal intrusion. For example, in 1999, 2000 and 2002, the involvement of a Serbian pathologist in Kosovo would have been equally as inappropriate and unacceptable as the deployment of an Albanian pathologist to Belgrade. The ability to draw from a large database ensures that the most appropriate personnel can be selected and that the team deployed will be operationally viable, effective and cost-efficient. Such "cherry picking" of personnel requires extensive and detailed knowledge of forensic practitioners and a constantly evolving database and, to that end, CIFA Directors maintain regular personal contact with large numbers of operatives on the CIFA database.

On many occasions since CIFA's inception, it has proven vital to have members based locally where teams have been deployed. They may speak the language, have some official local standing or simply know key individuals (for example, medical examiners, Coroners, Police Commissioners etc) whose general or specific influence and counsel can be accessed to make the DVI team deployment more effective and to help avoid conflict.

Similarly, having access to the right kind of forensic expertise for a huge range of possible scenarios can be crucial to the success of a DVI team operating either at home or far from the UK. For example, having a prominent local pathologist and an odontologist as CIFA members once helped resolve a difficult and unexpected conflict with local authorities by overcoming local legal and procedural requirements of which CIFA had previously been unaware.

5.7 CIFA BASE FACILITIES

CIFA maintains the finance, administration and logistical capabilities necessary to facilitate and support all types of forensic deployments for UK DVI. This includes the sourcing of practitioners and some of their specialist equipment, co-ordinating their transportation and accommodation, storage of their reports and evidence, mission payments, contracts, visa assistance, medical and life insurance provision, government and diplomatic liaison, budgeting and production of final mission accounts etc. This support facility underpins the flexibility of the organisation which can respond rapidly to changing environments, offering the "24/7" support required when personnel are deployed. Maintenance of the "home team" is also essential for servicing and developing the database, organising and managing deployments, and for helping to co-ordinate and implement training programmes while still attending to all the statutory obligations incumbent on the Directors of the organisation.

The reliability of this facility is not in question: during 2005, CIFA deployed nearly 40 teams of forensic experts to Sri Lanka[16] and Thailand,[7] attending to all of their transport, accommodation and communications needs. This approach ensures that the forensic practitioner is free from all other organisational concerns and can concentrate on the professional requirements of his or her deployment. Each team had access to a CIFA mobile telephone, allowing voice and SMS contact to be maintained with family members at home. CIFA personnel were available by telephone or e-mail on a "24/7" basis for the entirety of the deployments, in case any difficulties were encountered that could not be dealt with by the onsite DVI Team Leader.

It should also be noted that when CIFA's mission records were audited by the Metropolitan Police[5] on behalf of the Foreign Office[6] for the tsunami work undertaken by CIFA in 2005/06, every penny of the £1million+ of taxpayers' funds was documented and accounted for. Furthermore, not one single item of expenditure warranted a challenge or query from the Government over the propriety of CIFA's management of this large-scale, prolonged DVI deployment. This is a record of which the Directorate is justifiably proud.

5.8 THE ONGOING ROLE OF CIFA IN UK DVI

In the Spring of 2006, CIFA entered into a contract with the Home Office[9] to be the sole providers of non-police forensic personnel to the UK DVI Team and to create, for the long term, a database of experts upon which the UK DVI could draw, should a team be activated. (Note: at the time of writing this chapter this information was accurate.)

In addition to the provision of personnel, CIFA provides all ancillary support necessary to get the right experts to the right place at the right time and then home again when the job is done. CIFA will participate in regular desktop and live exercises with the police, Coroners/Procurators Fiscal, the Home Office[9] and local authorities to ensure that all aspects of the call-out mechanism operate smoothly and as expected.

In the event of a mass fatality or other event where the UK DVI Team is to be activated, the call-out process will most probably cascade as shown in Figure 5.6.

There is a common misconception regarding the extent to which UK DVI/ CIFA becomes involved in the event of a mass fatality in the UK. In line with the core concepts of the Home Office Central Assistance programme,[9] UK DVI is intended to supplement and not to replace the local response capability. An invitation for the UK DVI Team to contribute to investigation of an incident in England and Wales will be made ultimately at the discretion of a Coroner, though taking cognisance of any recommendations made by the police, the local authority, the lead pathologist and any agreed regional or local Mass Fatalities Plan.

In Scotland, the Procurator Fiscal oversees the co-ordination of the response to a mass fatality in much the same way as the Coroner does in England and

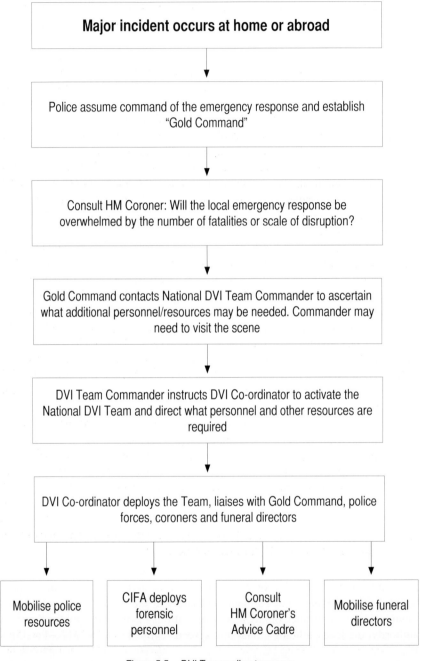

Figure 5.5   DVI Team call-out process

Wales, in Northern Ireland this area of responsibility is co-ordinated by the Northern Ireland Office. In each case, UK DVI/CIFA will only supply non-police forensic personnel as required and authorised by these individuals or organisations.

Where an incident has occurred overseas, and it is thought that UK subjects may be among the deceased, UK DVI will deploy only when requested to do so by the FCO.[6] In addition to whatever assistance can be rendered by the FCO[6] from the British Embassy or Consulate nearest to the incident, the FCO[6] will also dispatch its own rapid deployment team of officials to feed back information to UK DVI in preparation for its deployment, and to work alongside UK DVI forensic experts once they have arrived in the affected country.

CIFA contributes only a small part of the UK DVI capability: although this contribution is multi-disciplinary in nature, it must be borne in mind that UK DVI as a whole is multi-agency in nature and involves (from a police perspective) casualty bureau, family assistance, victim identification, mortuary management and body recovery.

CIFA has been tasked by the Home Office[9] and the UK DVI Sponsorship Board (the multi-agency group which has management oversight of UK DVI) to ensure that membership levels for all key non-police forensic disciplines are maximised by the Spring of 2008. CIFA will work with UK DVI management to establish a joint training model to help the specialists better to appreciate their own contributions within the context of a DVI deployment as a whole, and this commenced with the forensic anthropologists in April of 2007 under the auspices of BAHID.[22] It is anticipated that UK DVI exercises will commence in late 2007 and continue through 2008 to ensure all aspects of the UK DVI call-out arrangements can be tested thoroughly in order to identify any apparent weaknesses.

In association with the National Policing Improvement Agency (NPIA)[26] and the University of Dundee,[27] CIFA has agreed to support the police training programme for the UK National Team by the provision of experienced practitioners from its database, ensuring that the officers are being instructed by only the most operationally experienced medical, scientific and technical personnel. CIFA has therefore nominated key personnel to contribute to the development of the educational resource that will form the basis for the development of national standards of operation that could well serve to influence a commonality of international standards in DVI through Interpol.

REFERENCES

1 ICPO–Interpol, General Assembly, 65th Session, Anatalya, 23–29 October 1996, Resolution No AGN/65/RES/13 [online]. Available at: http://www.interpol.int/Public/ICPO/GeneralAssembly/Agn65/Resolutions/AGN65RES13.asp. [Accessed: 14.05.2008.]

2 Interpol website, "Disaster Victim Identification Guidelines" (2008) [online]. Available at: http://www.interpol.int!Public/DisasterVictim/default.asp. [Accessed: 15.05.2008.]

3 Interpol DVI forms [online]. Available at: http://www.interpol.intIPublic/ DisasterVictirn/Forms/Default.asp. [Accessed: 15.05.2008.]

4 Association of Chief Police Officers (ACPO) website [online]. Available at: http:// www.acpo. police.uk/. [Accessed: 12.05.2008.]

5 Metropolitan Police Service (MPS) website [online]. Available at: http://www.met. police. uk/. [Accessed: 15.05.2008.]

6 British Foreign and Commonwealth Office (FCO) website [online]. Available at: http://www.fco.gov.uk/en/. [Accessed: 15.05.2008.]

7 Thailand Tsunami website [online]. Available at: http://www.thailandtsunami.com/. [Accessed: 18.10.2007.]

8 BBC News, "7 July report highlights failings" [online]. Available at: http://news.bbc. co.uk/l/hi/in_depth/uk/2005/london_explosions/default.stm. [Accessed 15.05.2008.]

9 British Home Office (HO) website [online]. Available at: http://www.mod.uk/ defenceinternet/home. [Accessed: 15.05.2008.]

10 C Faraj, K Flower and B Starr, "At least 57 die in Bahrain boat disaster", CNN. com (31 March 2006) [online]. Available at: http://edition.cnn.com/2006/WORLD/ meast/03/31/bahrain.accident/index.html?eref=sites. [Accessed 18.10.2007.]

11 BBC News (2 April 2006), "Bahrain boat 'was not licensed'" [online]. Available at: http//news.bbc.co.uk/1/hi/world/middle_east/4868932.stm. [Accessed: 18.10.2007.]

12 BBC News (23 July 2005), "Toll climbs in Egyptian attacks" [online]. Available at: http://news.bbc.co.uk/l/hi/world/middle_east/4709491.strn. [Accessed 18.10.2007.]

13 A Damon, A Goodman, A Van Marsh and J Vause, "Bombs kill scores in Egyptian resort town", CNN.com (25 July 2005) [online]. Available at: http://edition.cnn.com/2005/ WORLD/meast/07/23/egypt.explosions/index.html. [Accessed: 18.10.2007.]

14 Interpol website [online]. Available at: http://www.interpol.int/. [Accessed: 15.05.2008.]

15 Interpol 49th General Assembly Session, Manila, 1980 [online]. Available at: http://www.interpol.int/public/DisasterVictim/Guide/appendices.asp.   [Accessed: 18.05.2008.]

16 Asian Human Rights Commission, Press Release AHRC-PL-01-2005 [online]. Available   at: http://www.ahrchk.net/pr/mainfile.php/2005mr/117/.   [Accessed: 18.10.2007.]

17 United Nations (UN) website [online]. Available at: http://www.un.org/. [Accessed: 15.05.2008.]

18 International Criminal Court (ICC) website [online]. Available at: http://www.icc-cpi. int/. [Accessed: 15.05.2008.]

19 UK Ministry of Defence website [online]. Available at: http://www.mod.uk/ defenceinternet/home. [Accessed: 15.05.2008.]

20 British Association for Forensic Odontology (BAFO) website [online]. Available at: http//www.bafo.org.uk/. [Accessed: 15.05.2008.]

21 British Association in Forensic Medicine (BAFM) website [online]. Available at: ttp://www.bafm.org/. [Accessed: 15.05.2008.]

22 British Association for Human Identification (BAHID) website [online]. Available at: http://www.bahid.org/. [Accessed: 15.05.2008.]

23 Association of Forensic Radiographers (AFR) website [online]. Available at: http://www.afr.org.uk/. [Accessed: 15.05.2008.]

24 Association of Anatomical Pathology Technology (AAPT) website [online]. Available at: http://www.aaptuk.org/aapt_council.htm. [Accessed: 15.05.2008.]

25 Council for the Registration of Forensic Practitioners (CRFP) website [online]. Available at: http://www.crfp.org.uk/. [Accessed: 15.05.2008.]

26 National Policing Improvement Agency (NPIA) website [online]. Available at: http://www.npia.police.uk/. [Accessed: 15.05.2008.]

27 University of Dundee website [online]. Available at: http://www.dundee.ac.uk/. [Accessed: 14.05.2008.]

CHAPTER 6

The Senior Identification Manager (SIM)

6.1 INTRODUCTION

The Senior Identification Manager (SIM) is a police senior investigator and leader, responsible for the entirety of the identification process.

The SIM employs different disciplines in incident-specific sequence and degrees to ensure the deceased are:

- recovered in a dignified manner which ensures integrity of identification and forensic evidence;
- identified as speedily as possible using ethical means, with families kept informed throughout the process.

In order to achieve these objectives the SIM must work in partnership with:

- those commanding the incident;
- investigators, to meet their evidential requirements;
- coronial authorities, to meet legal requirements and identification standards.

It is the responsibility of the state following mass fatality incidents to answer the questions:

- who was responsible? (criminal culpability);
- who died?;
- how can we prevent further incidents?

The identification process is only one element in an inter-dependent state response to mass fatalities. Senior Identification Managers must work together with those leading the other constituent parts to attain the highest standards alluded to by William Gladstone in 1871:

> "Show me the manner in which a nation cares for its dead and I will measure, with mathematical exactness, the tender mercies of its people, their respect for the law of the land and their loyalty to high ideals."

75

6.2 MASS FATALITIES

A mass fatality incident is defined, by those who organise the response to them, as "any incident where the number of fatalities is greater than normal local arrangements can manage".[1]

Public authorities, in dealing with fatalities, need to be integrated with all aspects of the response to, and recovery from, such situations and incidents. Organisations need to work in collaboration with others on key activities.

The response to a mass fatality incident will require special arrangements to be implemented at a local, regional or national level, depending on the capabilities and capacity at each level and the scale and the complexity of the emergency.

The police co-ordinate all the activities of the responding agencies at and around the scene of an emergency.

Such incidents are regarded as crimes until or unless a decision is made to the contrary.

Strategic priorities are set according to the incident, for example:

- to save life and deal with those injured;
- to preserve public health and public safety;
- the investigation of criminal offences;
- the safe recovery and identification of the deceased;
- minimise disruption to the public;
- reassurance of the public;
- return to normality.

The investigation of a mass fatality incident will require key figures working closely together, and in fact each share interlinking and often joint roles and responsibilities:

Who was responsible?

- The Senior Investigating Officer (SIO) leads the investigation.

Who died?

- The Coroner or Procurator Fiscal ultimately is responsible for the identification of the dead.
- The Senior Identification Manager (SIM) leads the police arrangements to identify the dead.

How can we prevent further such incidents?

- The Health and Safety Executive,[2] Air Accident Investigation Branch,[3] Marine Accidents Investigation Branch[4] and Rail Accident Investigation Branch[5] have investigatory responsibilities, primarily to establish the circumstances and causes of the incident, to ensure that safety action is taken to prevent that accident happening again.

Mass fatalities will result in a combination of legal proceedings:

- criminal hearings at Crown Courts to determine criminal culpability, eg murder, manslaughter, corporate manslaughter, death by dangerous driving;
- inquests at Coroners Courts to establish who died, the cause and circumstances;
- public inquiries – commissioned by the Government.

It is the responsibility of the police to anticipate and service the requirements for all three proceedings.

The preventive measures recommended by the Coroner and public inquiries reduce greatly the likelihood of further such disasters.

It is, however, the initial actions carried out in the glare of publicity which will determine the success of the state's response, and the confidence of the public, including most importantly the family and friends of those who died.

In the case of intentional acts to kill, the SIO has the dual challenge of investigating the mass fatality incident, while leading the dynamic response to identify and stop those planning any further atrocities.

The preparations carried out by the Coroner, police, local authorities and other agencies, working together under governmental emergency planning arrangements, enable the inevitable chaotic circumstances following an incident to be brought to order more quickly.

6.3 THE NATURE OF MASS FATALITY INCIDENTS – A MATTER OF SCALE

Those making the initial response to an incident should be guided by the following principles which underpin all major investigations:

Five Building Block Principles

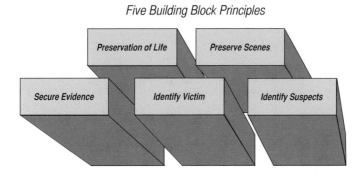

Figure 6.1   The five Building Block Principles underpinning the response to all disasters

The fact that the principles are adopted as a matter of course in standard major investigations (eg by SIOs leading murder enquiries) enables experienced investigators to make sense of the apparent added complexity of mass fatality incidents – the difference tends to be a matter of scale and balance between the different building blocks.

The investigators are performing tasks that they do as a matter of course in their normal profession. By applying the well-defined and understood Five Building Block Principles (Figure 6.1) adopted on conventional cases, investigators are able to bring order and structure to mass fatality investigations.

- The preservation of life – this is the first responsibility for those initially deployed to the scene.
- Preserve scenes – identify, secure and protect.
- Secure evidence – focused questioning of witnesses to identify and secure material.
- Identify victims – instigate actions to lead to their early identification.
- Identify and arrest suspects – a priority.

6.3.1   Closed or open incidents

Mass fatalities may be generally categorised as closed or open incidents or indeed can be a variable combination of both.[6]

Closed incidents

Closed incidents are where the identity of mass fatalities is known, prior to the actual matching of information before death (ante mortem) with the information recovered from their bodies (post mortem).

In a closed incident, the ante-mortem information can be gathered more efficiently and more quickly compared with that gathered from the deceased. The process of matching is more straightforward, as the SIM is matching a specific number of missing individuals with the same number of dead from the incident.

An example of a closed incident is the Russian nuclear-powered submarine K-141 *Kursk* which foundered on the bed of the Barents Sea on 12 August 2000. The identity of the 118 crew was known – any bodies recovered could be matched with confidence against the ante-mortem pool.[7]

A further example is the helicopter crash off Peterhead on 1 April 2009. The details of the workers and crew were known.[8]

Once an incident is identified as closed, the issue for the SIM is the ease with which the bodies can be recovered to compare against the ante-mortem inventory. Once recovered, the issue is the quality of the ante-mortem and post-mortem information for comparison.

For instance, only some of the *Kursk* crew could be recovered in 2000, and the remainder in 2001. Of those bodies recovered, at least three could not be identified due to major explosive disruption to their bodies.

Open incidents

Open incidents are where the identities of the casualties are not known prior to any matching procedures.

Such an incident will usually attract a much larger list of missing persons than bodies recovered. Furthermore, any list of persons missing may not include all of the dead.

The challenge therefore is to reduce the missing person list as quickly as possible by enquiries to eliminate those reported missing as being alive. Those still reported missing are more likely to be involved in the incident; higher-quality ante-mortem information is produced about these persons and compared with the post-mortem information.

Enquiries resulting from the post-mortem information may lead to the identification of those not reported as missing – eg property found on the body, DNA/fingerprint or medical characteristics which suggests further persons to be considered for ante-mortem harvest.

Identification from an open list therefore relies upon exact matching from a large and probably incomplete ante-mortem inventory against post-mortem records.

The nature of the disaster usually indicates the complexity of the ante-mortem collection task. An incident at a school, for example, will usually involve victims from a small geographical area, eg the Aberfan disaster – ante-mortem collection becoming a comparatively straightforward task.[9] A transport accident near a capital city will usually involve victims from around the world – requiring global ante-mortem collection enquiries, eg Potters Bar.[10]

Again, the ease with which the bodies can be recovered, and their available physical features for comparison (eg disruption), are important factors as to whether identification can take place.

The Ladbroke Grove train crash on 5 October 1999,[11] an example of an open incident, cost 31 lives, including 2 New Zealanders, 1 South African, 1 Norwegian, 1 Sri Lankan, 1 American and 1 Korean.

Mixed incidents

These may be regarded as a combination of closed and open incidents.

Pan Am Flight 103, flying from Germany to the US, exploded over the Scottish town of Lockerbie. All 258 passengers and crew on board were killed, as were 12 residents of the town.[12]

This mass fatality terrorist attack was therefore a complex mix of known and unknown victims.

79

Ante-mortem information was required from predominantly the US and Germany – little from the UK.

6.4 INVESTIGATION, PREVENTION AND IDENTIFICATION

The comparative scale of investigation, identification and prevention differs among mass fatality incidents.

In general terms the investigative imperatives are greatest with intentional acts to kill or injure – where the need to save life from further planned attacks is paramount. The investigative requirements in a man-made disaster or accident are usually complex and lengthy. In a natural disaster the investigation is likely to be outweighed by the needs for prevention and identification.

The investigation requires the identity of any victims to be resolved and evidence retrieved from them.

The prevention requirements can be carried out in different ways – transport safety measures; building and stadium design; public order and crowd control training; industrial safety measures; and education.

Prevention requires to know "how" the victims died and how to stop further deaths.

The identification requirements run parallel to both investigation and prevention.

The scale of the identification task will be determined by:

- number of dead;
- recovery location, accessibility and risks;
- disruption and disfigurement of the dead;
- forensic and property scene requirements;
- availability of missing person information;
- quality of ante-mortem information;
- quality of post-mortem information;
- trained personnel.

6.5 THE REQUIREMENT TO IDENTIFY THE DECEASED

There are several drivers for the requirement to identify the dead and investigators must be aware of both the legal and humanitarian reasons.

> "The importance first, of honest, accurate information being given to families as early and regularly as possible and at all times thereafter and secondly if accurate information cannot be given, of the families being told why not."
>
> Rec 33 Clarke Report[13]

- *Statutory requirement*

  Eg s 11(5) Coroners Act 1988: the responsibility to establish the identity of the deceased and how, when and where the death occurred.[14]

- *Interpol resolution*

  Resolution AGN/65/Res/13 October 1996 recognises "that for legal, religious, cultural and other reasons, human beings have the right not to lose their identities after death, and that the identification of disaster victims is often of vital importance for police investigations".[15]

- *Judicial recommendations*

  Eg "Public Inquiry into the Identification of Victims following Major Transport Accidents": report of Lord Justice Clarke 2001.[13]

- *Duty to the victims and their families*

  As evidenced throughout successive mass fatality investigations.

- *Crime investigation*

  Requirement to identify victims and suspects to prove criminal culpability.

6.6 CORPORATE MANSLAUGHTER

New legislation increases the investigation element for all mass disasters.

The Corporate Manslaughter Act of 2007,[16] which came into effect on 4 April 2008, enables the prosecution of companies, organisations and government bodies to face criminal proceedings if they are found to have caused death due to their corporate health and safety failings. Previous requirements to identify the "controlling mind" within an organisation have been removed.

This enables a wider application of criminal culpability to mass fatality incidents:

- natural disasters – what should have been done to prevent this?
- man-made disasters/accidents – who was negligent?
- intentional acts – what should have been done by the authorities to prevent this?

6.7 PREPARING FOR THE WORST – LEARNING FROM THE PAST

The planning for mass fatality incidents will inevitably be coloured by the most recent emergency with which the authorities have dealt.

In order to avoid planning for just the last disaster it is necessary to examine different, and often recent, mass fatality incidents to help us plan for the unexpected – in other words, to assist in threat and risk assessment. Once risks are identified, steps can be made to mitigate the risks and organise resources for their occurrence.

The differing types of disaster emphasise different elements of investigation, identification and prevention. The balance of the elements will always be incident specific.

The early agreements, and continued working relationships between the leaders – particularly the SIO, Coroner and SIM – are essential.

It is worthwhile therefore to consider the different nature of disasters and to consider the different challenges which face the leaders. See Table 6.1 for a non-exhaustive list of disasters:

Natural

Volcano	Montserrat, 25 June 1997, an overseas UK territory where, following the eruption, the authorities were blamed for failing to carry out adequate evacuation and preventing deaths
Flood	South-East Asian tsunami, 26 December 2004, where 33,000 died in Sri Lanka alone.
Hurricane	Hurrican Katrina, 29 August 2005, affected America's Gulf Coast, particularly New Orleans, where at least 1,500 died.
Earthquake	Italy, 6 April 2009, centred on the medieval town of L'Aquila.
Landslide/Avalanche	China, May 2008.

Man-made Disaster-Accident

Fire	Bradford City FC, 11 May 1985, 56 people died when the wooden main stand caught light, probably from a discarded match or cigarette- the stand having previously been identified as a safety risk. The report by Lord Justice Taylor led to major reforms in stadium security.
Air	Manchester Airport crash, 22 August 1985. 55 people died when a plane burst into flames during take off-many people died on board from inhaling toxic fumes.
Boat	*Herald of Free Enterprise*, 6 March 1987 outside Zeebruge. Over 190 passengers died when the bow doors were left open and the boat flooded and sank.
Fire Underground	Kings Cross Underground, 18 November 1987, 31 people were killed when the underground station caught on fire, probably due to a discarded match or cigarette. Body 115 was not identified until January 2004 as rough sleeper Alexander Fallon.

Man-made Disaster-Accident

Airplane	Concorde crash, Paris, 25 July 2000, killing 113 people – due to runway debris puncturing the plane's tyre.
Train Crash	Selby, 28 February 2001. 10 people died after a Land-Rover driver fell asleep at the wheel, left the road and struck a train on the East Coast mainline. The driver was convicted of 10 counts of death by dangerous driving.
Train Crash	Potters Bar train crash, 10 May 2002 – 7 passengers were killed when a train derailed.
Helicopter	North-east Scotland, near Peterhead, 1 April 2009. 16 died when the helicopter returning with oil workers crashed into the sea.
Crushing	Hillsborough, 15 April 1989. 96 Liverpool supporters died in the central standing area when a gate was opened by police, leading to a fatal crush – private prosecutions launched against the police commanders were discontinued by the Director of Public Prosecutions.
Stampede/crushing	Rajashan, Indian, 30 September 2008, at least 147 were killed at a Hindu temple – one of several similar incidents.
Gas or Chemical Leak	Bhopal Gas Tragedy, 3 December 1984. Toxic gas was released at Union Carbide pesticide plant approximately 8,000 died within 2 weeks. The UK has identified COMAH (Control of Major Accident Hazards regulations) sites to limit risk.

Intentional Act to Injure or Kill

War Crimes	Kosova, Balkans 1999 – SO13 in 1999 and the British Forensic Team in 2000. DNA comparisons continue to this day.
Chemical, Biological, Radiological or Nuclear (CBRN)	Japanese Tokyo subway, 20 March 1995. Sarin gas attack by domestic terrorists killed 12.
Explosions	New York Twin Towers, 11 September 2001; London Transport Bombings, 7 July 2005.
Arson	Bush fires in Australia, 7 February 2009, more than 200 people were killed when bush fires were deliberately started. Described as murder by Prime Minister Kevin Rudd.

Table 6.1   A list of recent disasters and some of their causes

6.8 THE NATIONAL PLANNING ASSUMPTIONS

The UK Government has carried out national threat assessments which inform Mass Fatality National Planning Assumptions – Emergency Planning.

For DVI purposes this includes the requirement to plan for large volumes of mass fatalities in multiple locations. The assumptions consider mass fatality incidents resulting from natural, man-made and intentional acts to kill, including Chemical, Biological, Radiological and Nuclear (CBRN) incidents.

The UK DVI National Strategy details arrangements for:

- Victim Recovery;
- Mortuary Operations;
- Casualty Bureau'
- Ante-mortem Collection by Family Liaison Officers;
- Forensic Matching.

The strategy places the responsibility for mass fatality incidents to be catered for at the following levels:

- force;
- regional;
- national;
- international.

6.8.1 Force

Forces must be resilient for DVI incidents occurring within their own force. Each has at least one SIM – selected from Detective Chief Inspector or Detective Superintendent SIOs (differs among forces) having attended NPIA (National Policing Improvement Agency) SIM training.

The force lead SIM is responsible for ensuring that all DVI elements are in place within their force area.

6.8.2 Regional

Regions provide extra capacity above that which forces can be expected to provide. The point at which regional assistance would be required differs according to the capacity and capability of individual forces.

Regional arrangements differ throughout the country, with some police forces collaborating to form a purely regional team, while other regions have forces agreeing assistance on a mutual aid basis.

The intention is that each region has a UK DVI Commander appointed to form a conduit between UK DVI and the region.

Each region contributes a proportionate number of staff towards the UK DVI Team. A proportionate number of SIMs within the region are selected for the advanced UK DVI course – and are referred to as UK DVI SIMs.

6.8.3   National and international

National and international capacity is created by drawing upon UK DVI staff throughout the UK, all of whom attended the UK DVI advanced training, including the UK DVI SIMs.

UK DVI SIMs may be deployed nationally or internationally.

A small number of UK DVI SIMs are nominated as UK DVI Commanders – an internationally recognised term.

These are Detective Superintendents (or DCIs nominated as Acting Detective Superintendents for UK DVI purposes with significant operational DVI experience) with additional training, such as joint Counter Terrorism training.

Their role is:

- To act as regional liaison for UK DVI.
- To carry out the role of assessor in the event of an international deployment.
- To act as adviser to Gold Command in the event of national or international deploy-ments.
- To carry out the role of SIM for a national or international deployment where their additional training and experience makes them the most suitable person to be appointed to carry out the task.

A proportion of the UK DVI team is CBRN trained – and staff form the national CBRN DVI response, including international collaboration arrangements. Some UK DVI Commanders are CBRN trained, and may perform the role of SIM or Silver Commander in a CBRN DVI incident.

6.9   THE ORIGIN OF THE SENIOR IDENTIFICATION MANAGER ROLE

The sinking of the *Marchioness* was the genesis for the role of the SIM.

A series of disasters struck the UK during the 1980s, each bringing its own investigative challenges, but the collision between the party boat *Marchioness* and the sea dredger *Bowbelle* had repercussions which resonate to this day.[13]

As an example, the Bradford City Football Ground fire of 11 May 1985 during the last match of the season, filmed on live television, had substantial investigation and identification demands. The main stand, filled with spectators, caught alight, probably as a result of a discarded match or cigarette, setting fire to accumulated rubbish underneath the old wooden stand: 56 died and 52 deceased were recovered from the stand.[17]

The SIO, Detective Superintendent Kevin Cooper, had overall responsibility for the investigation, and allocated the majority of investigative resources and efforts into tracing an offender. The investigation regarded the identification of the dead as a lesser task, the SIO recording his identification responsibilities as "to assist the Uniform Branch, as necessary, with regards to lines of enquiry relevant to the identification of deceased persons".

Superintendent Rand, untrained in the role, was only appointed on day 2, to identify the bodies already removed from the scene by ill-equipped officers. Rand was allocated far less resources to identify the dead.

The Committee of Inquiry into Crowd Safety and Control at Sports Grounds Interim and Final Reports, by Mr Justice Popplewell,[18] also considered the Heysel riots and made far-reaching recommendations for stadium safety and policing.

The *Marchioness* investigation stands apart from Bradford and other disasters others because, in the words of Lord Justice Clarke:[13]

> "The principal lessons which can be learned from this and other major disasters is the importance of respecting the dead and their relatives, of acting with sensitivity throughout and of ensuring that (save where a compelling public interest requires otherwise) full, honest and accurate information is given to relatives at every stage."

The *Marchioness*, with 130 people aboard, was struck by the *Bowbelle* at 01.46am on 20 August 1989. The pleasure boat sank almost immediately. Fifty-one people died, 41 were rescued, and the remainder self-rescued from the scene.

The Metropolitan Police co-ordinated the *Marchioness* scene with skill and professionalism, using the Gold/Silver/Bronze Command structure – the Gold Commander declaring the incident as a crime investigation. Liaison with other agencies and emergency services was well co-ordinated. The Criminal Investigation structure was:

Silver	Detective Superintendent	Senior Investigating Officer
Bronze	Detective Chief Inspector	Relative Liaison Officers
Bronze	Detective Inspector	Scene Management
Bronze	Detective Inspector	Mortuary Team
Bronze	Detective Inspector	Major Incident Room, Enquiry Team

The criminal investigation moved along well-practised lines, and the captain was prosecuted.

The identification process was managed by:

- Central Casualty Bureau;
- mortuary work;
- the same Major Incident Room as the investigation;
- Relative Liaison Team with dual responsibility for obtaining evidence for identification and to provide support to the bereaved relatives.

Apart from visual identification, the Coroner's identification criteria placed substantial emphasis on fingerprint evidence which, if there was no match against National (fingerprint) Identification Bureau records, was one of the criteria needed in conjunction with others to make a positive identification. The police held the belief that the requirements for dental identification would be difficult, yet 19 victims were eventually identified by dental comparison in conjunction with clothing or jewellery.

The Mortuary Bronze was of the opinion that the later bodies recovered from the river were not suitable for visual identification. Twenty-five of the bodies had the hands removed within the mortuary and submitted to the laboratory for special treatment to recover satisfactory fingerprints, yet only four victims were identified by this method. There were no satisfactory records detailing the decision-making process or agreements between the SIO, Mortuary Bronze or Coroner. In later years, in the absence of records, the parties involved could not agree on who had authorised the removal of the hands.[13]

This process was not unusual to achieve identifications of single, badly decomposed bodies removed from the Thames, who were then identified against police fingerprint records. The method proved to be unsuitable in the *Marchioness* investigation. The necessity to remove the hands was not considered on a case-by-case basis, when other less disruptive forms of identification were likely to be successful in the near future. The removal of the hands has also achieved infamy because the hands were not, in every case, reunited with the bodies prior to family viewings. Families and Relative Liaison Officers had been unaware of the process. In fact, body parts from the victims of the *Marchioness* were found at the mortuary years after. The process, widely publicised as gruesome and unnecessary, was regarded as evidence of the lack of importance placed by the authorities on identifying the dead, coupled with a lack of respect for the deceased themselves.

Furthermore, police dissuaded families from carrying out viewings of the bodies because it was believed that to do so would add to their distress.

Families lost trust in the authorities, including the Police and Coroner. The families believed that they had not been told the truth about the process of the identifications; many believed that the bodies of the bereaved had not been treated with respect; they were unable to gain adequate information or gain adequate representation rights in later proceedings. Two family representative groups were formed, and their strong public representations were a driver for improvement.

The concerns that the families had are of particular importance to SIMs:

- the removal of the hands for identification purposes at a time when identification by non-invasive means was likely in the near future;
- the failure of anyone in authority to inform the relatives that the hands had been removed;
- the refusal to allow the relatives to view the bodies;
- in some cases, the return of the body without the hands;

- the failure thereafter to return the hands to the body;
- in one case the disposal of hands which were discovered much later without informing the relatives and without their authority;
- the issue of inaccurate and insensitive interim death certificates;
- a lack of detailed information available to families;
- a lack of overall co-ordination of the identification procedures.

In 1992, partly as a result of concerns expressed by the families who lost loved ones in the *Marchioness* disaster, the Metropolitan Police Service set up a working group, in 1994 produced a document "The Identification of the Deceased Following Mass Disaster"[19] and was the first group to suggest the formation of an Identification Commission chaired by a Coroner.

In March 2000, Detective Chief Superintendent Barry Webb, Head of the Metropolitan Murder Review Group, and a founder member of the Major Disaster Advisory Team (MDAT), produced a review report of the Ladbroke Grove rail crash of 5 October 1999. In 2000 he also reviewed the *Marchioness* incident.

His main recommendations related to:

- Casualty Bureau – the formation of a pro-active unit to make call-backs to ascertain whether reported missing persons have since been traced by families.
- Family Liaison – FLO arrangements, viewing arrangements and family-to-police working relationships.
- Senior Identification Manager – the creation of a new post to have overall responsibility for the identification process, representing the police on the Identification Commission, allowing the SIO to focus upon investigating the cause of the disaster.

DCS Webb's reviews were presented to the "Public Inquiry into the Identification of Victims following Major Transport Accidents" – report of Lord Justice Clarke, published March 2001.[13]

The Clarke Report had the following terms of reference:

1. To consider and to report on procedures to establish the identity of the victims of the collision between the *Bowbelle* and the *Marchioness*.
2. To review and to report on the procedures currently followed when establishing the identity of victims following similar accidents.
3. In the interests of minimising distress to the families of the victims:
    (a) To advise on what additional procedures should be followed, if any, when the need to identify victims arises following similar incidents;
    and
    (b) To consider and advise on procedures for the notification and involvement of the next-of-kin in cases when it is necessary to establish the identity of such victims.

Lord Justice Clarke made 36 main recommendations, including supporting the recommendations by DCS Webb.

The recommendations included:[13]

- *Recommendation 3*

  The regulation of removal of human material from the deceased, including for identification purposes.

- *Recommendation 5*

  "The methods used for establishing the identity of the deceased should, wherever possible, avoid any unnecessary invasive procedures or disfigurement or mutilation and that body parts should not be removed for the purposes of identification except where it is necessary to do so as a last resort. The position is somewhat different in the case of samples taken for DNA purposes."

  Note that this recommendation did not exclude the removal of body parts, including hands, but that such action should be necessary and not carried out as a matter of course – but with the express permission of the Coroner.

  The principle of unnecessary invasive procedure is now a key matter for discussion between the SIO, the SIM and the Coroner, and requires continual review as the identification process takes place. As an example, one of the first considerations is whether any internal examination is required, where an autopsy is for identification purposes only in a mass fatality incident, and the cause of death can be determined without such examination.

- *Recommendation 8*

  Coroners and their staff should meet with families or groups to explain procedures, and keep relatives informed.

- *Recommendation 9*

  Endorsing DCS Webb's 21 recommendations regarding amendments to the ACPO Manual, dealing with:
  - Casualty Bureau.
  - Documentation processes in the mortuary.
  - Family liaison role including FLO viewing guidelines.

- *Recommendation 10*

  "In particular I support the proposal to appoint a Senior Identification Manager (SIM) namely a senior police officer to have overall responsibility for the identification process."

- *Recommendation 14*

  Clear procedures between the Coroner, Police, local authority, mortuary and the pathologists, setting out clear procedures for the custody and release of bodies and body parts.

- *Recommendation 17*

  "Those responsible for the management and running of mortuaries must ensure that strict procedures are followed and that all procedures are documented from the time a body or body parts arrive at the mortuary until the time a body is identified and released for burial."

- *Recommendations 21–22*

  Placing responsibility on the Home Office for national contingency planning including Local Authorities. Emergency services to work together in emergencies.

- *Recommendations 23–24*

  That the Identification Commission should be chaired by the Coroner, or in their absence, for the Coroner and Incident Commander to decide who should take the chair. The SIM should be a member.

- *Recommendations 25–30*

  Advice on viewing – stressing the right for relatives to view the body, unrestricted, and preparatory guidance for FLO and mortuary staff.

  The emphasis is on providing information in advance to relatives, such as the state of the body, photographs and mortuary layout, that viewing is at the family's own discretion, but they should be aware of available support services.

- *Recommendation 33*

  "I stress again the importance first of honest accurate information being given to families as early and regularly as possible and at all times thereafter and secondly if accurate information cannot be given, of the families being told why not. If FLOs do not already receive it, I recommend that they be given appropriate training in this regard."

The general principles that should be kept in mind throughout the identification process after a major disaster are:

- provision of honest and, as far as possible, accurate information at all times and at every stage;
- respect for the deceased and the bereaved;
- a sympathetic and caring approach throughout; and
- the avoidance of mistaken identification.

The role of Senior Identification Manager, distinct to the role of Senior Investigating Officer, was therefore firmly established within the UK once the Clarke Report was published.

Not only were the procedural lessons learned and incorporated from the *Marchioness* investigation within the SIM role; the special care and respect that the victims and their families deserve place a special responsibility on the SIM and are the touchstones against which operational decision-making should be determined.

Charles Haddon-Cave QC, representing the Marchioness Action Group at the inquiry, said:[13]

> "The care with which our dead are treated is a mark of how civilised a society we are. Much goes on for understandable reasons behind closed doors. For this reason there is a special responsibility placed on those entrusted with this work and the authorities who supervise it to ensure that bodies of the dead are treated with the utmost care and respect. That is what bereaved and loved ones are entitled to expect and what society at large demands."

6.10   DISTINCTION BETWEEN THE SENIOR IDENTIFICATION MANAGER AND THE SENIOR INVESTIGATING OFFICER

It is important to acknowledge that the SIO is the officer in charge of the investigation. Their investigations may bring together a large group of professionals into a temporary team. This usually involves staff from within the police service and specialists from outside. In complex cases it is possible for hundreds of people to have some level of professional involvement in the investigation.

The SIM role is purposely of the same rank and authority as the SIO: to ensure the needs of the dead are given the weight they deserve – equal to that of the investigation. The SIM creates a bridge between the Coroner and his/her staff on the one hand and the police on the other and, together with the FLOs, forges a crucial link between the police, the bereaved and survivors.

The SIO must address the strategic priorities of saving life and investigating criminal offences. In the case of outstanding suspects in incidents involving intentional acts to kill, the greatest imperative will be to trace outstanding offenders, who may be intent on committing further acts of atrocity.

Indeed, in the case of a terrorist incident, the SIO may be simultaneously conducting a Major Covert Terrorist Investigation, as well as the overt attack which has resulted in the mass fatality. The SIO will be, in partnership with the Security Service, engaged in a high-pressure and all-consuming mobile investigation, probably involving multiple locations and multiple subjects, often with international partners.

The identity of any persons carrying out the attack and their associates is vital information for the SIO, and this will create an imperative to locate and examine any potential suspects who may also have died in the attack, probably in advance of the recovery of innocent victims.

In order to prove the case, a detailed forensic examination of the scene, suspects and at least some victims is likely to be required.

In the case of a transport disaster the scene evidence indicating how the accident occurred, required for prosecution and prevention of further incidents, is the core upon which the SIO and other agencies will build their case.

The Clarke Report[13] ensures that the needs of the victims are always represented, and that a substantial area of work may be taken from the SIO, and carried out with equal skill, equal authority and appropriate resources. The priority order of body recovery must be addressed by the SIM, to ensure that speedy recovery can be made of bodies without hindering the evidential requirements. Body recovery rationale must be considered in detail: broad single scene body recovery strategy is not sufficient and must be divided on a sector-by-sector basis and within that sector on a body-by-body basis.

The SIM should be an accredited Senior Investigating Officer, with additional SIM training, in order that the requirements of the SIO can be properly anticipated by the SIM.

The SIM and SIO must work closely with each other to ensure that their priorities are met, and objectives aligned (see Table 6.2). Although the SIM concentrates on identification, the evidential requirements for the SIO must be considered, and the SIO given the opportunity of taking total responsibility for some of the areas normally associated with the SIM through the formation of joint strategies – eg recovery of believed suspects, or placing investigative requirements on the SIM's work.

The SIM

- relieves the SIO of the responsibility for the identification process
- provides the link to the SIO with regard to the investigation process
- ensures the agreed forensic strategy is implemented regarding:
  - scenes
  - bodies
  - mortuary

- provides the link to families for the investigation
- ensures the agreed witness strategy is implemented
- shares intelligence regarding:
  - witnesses
  - families
  - scene
  - suspects

- agrees strategies regarding:
  - scene – forensic and Scene Evidence Recovery Manager (SERM)
  - mortuary – forensic
  - exhibits
  - witnesses – forensic, key and significant
  - families
  - media.

TERMS OF REFERENCE BETWEEN SIO AND SIM

	SIM	SIO	Comment and Instruction
MISSING PERSONS and PUBLIC INFORMATION			
Establish Casualty Bureau Questions			
Establish Casualty Bureau Misper/Involvement grading			
Establish Call avoidance strategy			
Appoint Hospital liaison co-ordinator			
Establish question and data collection strategy from hospitals			
Establish question and data collection strategy from temporary survivors reception centres etc			
Establish question and data collection strategy from family reception centres etc			
ANTE-MORTEM DATA and FAMILY MATTERS			
Initial FLO deployment in relation to Ante-mortem harvest			
Strategy of Ante-mortem harvest			
Initial point of contact for information to families			
BODY RECOVERY and SCENE EXAMINATION			
Management of the inner cordon			
Dignified and effective recovery of bodies and human remains			
Recovery of personal property which may aid identification			
Co-ordinate recovery of other items of evidence			
POST MORTEM and IDENTIFICATION			
Negotiate mortuary location			
Establish Mortuary team			
Establish ID Commission			
Establish strategy for PM to determine cause of death			
Establish strategy for PM to establish identity			
Agree DNA examination, retention and disposal policy			
Preparation of inquest file			
Notification to Next-of-Kin when identification is made			
	Print Name		**Signature**
Gold Commander			
Senior Identification Manager			
Senior Investigating Officer			
Operation Name			**Date**

This document is the basis of agreeing the roles and responsibilities between the Senior Investigating Officer and Senior Identification Manager. Any change and other agreements must be subject to a policy log entry.

Table 6.2   The terms of reference between the SIM and the SIO

The success of the partnership between the SIO and SIM will be determined by their early agreements, forged very shortly after they are both appointed. They will be reviewed as the investigation progresses.

Standard terms of reference may be drawn up in an *aide memoire* by the SIM, in order to allow the SIO to place investigative requirements upon the areas of SIM responsibility, initially in the areas of:

- missing persons and public information;
- ante-mortem data and family matters;
- body recovery and scene examination;
- post-mortem data and identification.

6.11   COMMAND STRUCTURE IN MASS FATALITY INCIDENTS

The management arrangements must establish a clear command structure at the earliest opportunity and enable emergency services, specialist investigators, local authorities, public health and coronial representatives to bring about order to the initial chaos following a mass fatality.

The Gold/Silver/Bronze command structure is likely to be used:

- *Gold – Strategic*
  Establishing strategic objectives and overall management framework, ensuring long-term resources and expertise.

- *Silver – Tactical*
  Determining priorities in obtaining and allocating resources, planning and co-ordinating overall response.

- *Bronze – Operational*
  The "doers", managing front-line operations.

SIMs and SIOs attend Gold Strategic meetings, and their roles require them to interact with strategic partners.

The incident will have a nominated Silver Commander, who will have the responsibility of co-ordinating the response – and meeting the needs of the SIO and SIM.

It is an incident-specific decision as to whether the SIO and SIM are nominated as Silver Investigation and Silver Identification (this would be a structure acknowledging multiple silvers) or whether they act alongside nominated Silver Commanders, and are referred to by their titles of SIO and SIM.

The Command structure must enable the SIM to have managerial responsibility for:

- Casualty Bureau/documentation teams (reception centres/hospitals);
- family liaison and ante-mortem collection;

- the SERM and body recovery;
- the Mortuary Manager and post mortem;
- reconciliation (matching) – working to the Identification Commission.

6.12   THE DVI PROCESS

Disaster victim identification is a process that can be applied to a single case or mass fatality incidents.

The process is to bring together ante-mortem information with post-mortem information, to make a positive identification by scientifically acceptable means.

The standards to which the positive identification will be made will be determined by the Coroner: nevertheless, accepted standards have been developed which will usually meet the requirements for mass fatality incidents.

The quality of information collected and recorded is a key factor in comparing ante-mortem and post-mortem information. A logical approach is to record ante-mortem and post-mortem information in a format that enables easy comparison between the two, concentrating on those information areas which are likely to result in a positive reconciliation.

The collection of ante-mortem information requires police to obtain detailed information about those people highly likely to be involved in the incident and forward this information to the matching centre. It follows that police everywhere would benefit from access to a commonly available and understood format that can be easily transferred and compared with post-mortem information.

The Interpol DVI forms[20] ante mortem and post mortem:

- are available on the internet;
- are agreed by Interpol member police forces throughout the world;
- are available in all Interpol languages (English, French, Arabic and Spanish);
- contain all likely comparison points;
- are structured for easy comparison;
- are compatible with computer comparison software (Plassdata).

Although other DVI forms have been produced, the Interpol forms have been successfully tested internationally, and are familiar to practitioners. The Interpol forms should be used as a matter of course.

It must be accepted that some of the descriptive elements within the Interpol forms are so subjective that no realistic comparison is likely to follow from them. The advantages of international co-operation by using Interpol standardised forms, available throughout the world, far outweigh the complaints that the forms are difficult to complete.

- Police in countries or places from which people have been reported missing record the ante-mortem information on **Interpol yellow ante-mortem forms**.
- Post-mortem data is collected by DVI teams working in mortuaries and who record the information on **Interpol pink post-mortem forms**.

The forms are used at the matching centre to compare the ante-mortem and the post-mortem information. Once likely matches are indicated by comparison of the forms, the supporting physical evidence is compared by experts to decide whether the identification criteria can be met.

- Once a reconciliation is made, the match is recorded in an **Interpol Victim Identification Report**.

The success of the DVI process depends on the comparison factors being present in both ante-mortem and post-mortem information.

Victims of large-scale disasters are identified on the basis of an assessment of multiple factors. The degree to which bodies are damaged, the time bodies have been left exposed and the associated changes in the condition of bodies influence the nature and quality of post-mortem data, and the applicability of specific methods of identification.

- Where ante-mortem information is not collected, a match cannot be made with a body.

Even where ante-mortem information has been collected, the reliability of the source information, and the speed with which a comprehensive collection of physical evidence can take place will determine whether the information can be compared with the available physical evidence from the mortuary.

As an example of the comparison process: if fingerprint detail is only available from the right thumb of a victim in the mortuary, comparison will only be possible if the ante-mortem collection of latent fingerprints includes the right thumbprint.

Mass fatality incidents tend to produce a large number of reported missing persons. The collection of ante-mortem information will take a substantial amount of time, during which additional information about particular nominals will be included, while newly reported missing persons are added to the list, and others are found (removed from the list).

Stability can be achieved with the post-mortem pool of information if recovery of all the dead takes place and if all disciplines are used at quality initial examinations – a "right first time" policy. As the number of reported missing persons becomes equivalent to the number of dead, the matching exercise becomes easier.

The quality control of ante-mortem and post-mortem data collection is vital to achieve rapid and accurate identifications.

The DVI process requires identifications to be made by:

- positive comparison; or
- a series of eliminations.

The high-volume comparison between a changing ante-mortem information pool, and post-mortem information pool must be a continually recorded process, with elimination criteria being set by the SIM to aid the comparisons.

As positive comparisons have been made of the dead using standard comparison criteria, there is likely to be a residual number of problematic cases. Additional post-mortem examination will usually identify evidence that can be compared with detailed additional ante-mortem investigation.

DVI is not achieved alone by:

- body recovery;
- mortuary management;
- ante-mortem data;
- post-mortem data

but by successfully combining many disciplines and information sources.

The SIM must devote sufficient resources to each task at the right time, to collect appropriate information for the particular incident. The order and depth to which each task is completed require professional judgement by the SIM.

6.13 POLICY FILES

One of the most important aspects of managing the identification process is the systematic recording of the SIM's policies. SIMs should use the policy file to record critical policy decisions. It is the definitive record upon which they rely when subsequently asked to account for decisions at:

- the Identification Commission;
- the Crown Court;
- Coroner inquests;
- other judicial proceedings;
- public inquiries;
- reviews.

The policy file should be used to document the progress of the investigation.

The SIM must adopt a disciplined approach to planning the identification process and this should be recorded in the policy file. In particular, the SIM should concentrate on strategic and operational priorities.

6.14   IDENTIFICATION CRITERIA

Following any fatality, the responsibility for establishing the identity of the deceased, cause, location and time of death rests with the Coroner. When dealing with fatalities in an emergency this is likely to be agreed in consultation with the SIM and expert members of the Identification Commission.

The standard of proof required by UK Coroners is that of "the balance of probabilities", but in order to avoid mistaken identity in mass fatalities the higher standard of "beyond reasonable doubt" is vital.

The SIO's views should also be taken into account, as to prove a homicide, the higher standard is likely to be required.

Even in a mass fatality, there may be occasion, where the lower standard is used; however, the greatest efforts must be made to avoid mistaken identity. The lower standard is likely to be employed when all the set identification criteria methods have been exhausted for all remaining unidentified bodies.

The method by which "beyond reasonable doubt" is achieved is by the setting of identification criteria. The setting of these must be incident specific – considering whether the criteria are likely to achieve the objectives of meeting the standard of proof.

Internationally accepted criteria are:

Primary

- Fingerprints;
- Dental comparison (Odontology);
- DNA;
- Unique medical condition.

Secondary

- Marks;
- Scars;
- Tattoos;
- Medical deformity/condition;
- Jewellery;
- Property;
- Documents;
- Clothing;
- Physical appearance.

Assistance

- Photograph (visual);
- Body location.

The confirmation of one primary identification criterion is likely to be sufficient for a positive identification, if no exclusionary factors are present (information that suggests to the contrary). Any primary identification criterion alone is usually sufficient to meet the standard of "beyond reasonable doubt".

Other primary, secondary or even assistance criteria may also be present at the time that the single primary identification criterion is met, and may be used as supporting criteria. It is important, however, that the identification is not delayed while waiting for additional criteria.

A combination of more than one secondary criterion may be sufficient to meet the standard of beyond reasonable doubt, again if no exclusionary factors are present.

In practice, while further unidentified bodies remain, secondary criteria are not likely to be used, when the realistic prospect of primary criteria being achieved remains. The greater the number and individuality of the secondary criteria present, the greater the likelihood of the Identification Commission agreeing an identification from secondary criteria at an early stage.

Visual identification has proved unreliable for mass fatality incidents and should not be regarded as being sufficient to meet the higher standard of proof required.

Visual identification may be relied upon in single cases coming before a Coroner outside mass fatality incidents, when there is less likelihood of mistaken identity. Even then, where there is the possibility of mistaken identity, Coroners will err on the side of caution. In fact, cases at Coroners' Courts usually have secondary and assistance criteria as supporting evidence.

There are many examples of mistaken visual identification in mass fatality incidents.

Visual identification was relied upon following the Luxor, Egypt, tourist massacre of 17 November 1997, where 63 people, 59 of them tourists from seven different nationalities, were killed by an Islamic group disguised as members of the security forces.[21] Two victims were mistakenly identified as British, and repatriated to the UK. It was not until a ring was removed from a victim in the mortuary at the UK, and the inscription examined, that the mistake was realised. Odontological comparison confirmed the mistake.

As in the Luxor case, one mistaken identification will lead to the possible mis-identification of a second victim.

Despite the high standards of competence achieved once full DVI systems are in operation, the greatest chance of mistaken identity usually happens immediately following a mass disaster. Particularly where mass fatalities take place in undeveloped countries, where visual identification is the norm, the risk is that victims will be mistakenly identified visually, and bodies released prior to DVI control.

Following the tsunami in Sri Lanka, prior to the Identification Commission being established, and DVI standards being applied, one victim was mistakenly identified visually as a British woman, and repatriated to the UK. The woman was in fact Swiss. The British missing person was identified later using appropriate criteria. The family of the Swiss woman had to endure the double tragedy of their daughter dying in the tragedy, and being transported incorrectly to the UK.

Where bodies are identified without the criteria being correctly applied, there remains the chance that such an identification is incorrect. The SIM must set a policy still to obtain ante-mortem and if possible post-mortem information from such victims, to compare with other unidentified victims.

The SIM must ensure that the integrity of the DVI process is maintained. In order to maintain the confidence of the international community for that, and every other, mass fatality disaster, every effort must be made to avoid such mistakes.

6.15   THE PRIMARY IDENTIFIERS

6.15.1   Fingerprints

Fingerprints, palm prints and footprints (plantars) present excellent opportunities for conclusive scientific matching. The prerequisites for the identification of victims on the basis of fingerprints is the availability of viable ante-mortem and post-mortem prints, and the expertise of those involved in collection and comparison. Fingerprint comparisons in mass disasters will rarely have the luxury of a full set of AM prints to compare against a full set of PM prints.

As all police forces have fingerprint resources, then there is the potential for fingerprint experts to take post-mortem fingerprints, and carry out comparisons in theatre. Ante-mortem fingerprint collection can also be performed by police anywhere. Fingerprints may be transferred electronically to the matching units.

The SIM must consider whether fingerprints are going to be a likely comparison source following the disaster. If the hands of the dead are in a condition capable of being fingerprinted then an ante-mortem recovery plan can be devised. There are more limited opportunities to recover ante-mortem palm prints and plantars, and therefore the SIM must decide if it is an appropriate allocation of resources to take them. Such a decision must be balanced against the availability of such samples through deterioration in individual cases at a later stage should the need arise.

The skills and expertise of those taking the post-mortem prints must be considered by the SIM, who must ensure that the most competent staff in possession of the most up-to-date techniques are selected. Fingerprint experts in the UK are increasingly less likely to take fingerprints by manual methods in the normal course of their duties. Often, Crime Scene Investigators take prints in the mortuary for standard cases, and the experts purely concentrate on computer-based comparison work.

The SIM should liaise with the Mortuary Manager as to the order of post-mortem examination – care should be taken that the hands are not damaged by clothing stripping – it may in some circumstances be appropriate to take fingerprint evidence at the start of the process.

New electronic transfer technology may allow fingerprint scanning at the scene. Similarly, the SIM should consider conventional fingerprinting at the scene if there is a likelihood of damage being caused during the transfer, or if ante-mortem information is already available for rapid matching.

The SIM should be open minded about the possibility of fingerprint evidence being available – in previous mass fatalities incorrect assumptions have been made that post-mortem prints would be irretrievable.

When recovery is delayed, then ideally the SIM would be in possession of the ante-mortem fingerprint evidence prior to post mortems taking place.

Ante-mortem fingerprint evidence is available from several sources. The SIM should consider opportunities in theatre, eg hotel rooms, vehicles, and work locations.

The FLO should assist in the search of a victim's address and assist the CSI with details of the victim's lifestyle, which will identify those places best targeted for latent print collection.

Focused searching at a location for latent prints when in possession of a post-mortem fingerprint set should be carried out by fingerprint experts, who can assess the quality of retrieved prints at a scene, and make instant initial judgements as to the likelihood of a match.

The availability of reference print AM evidence varies from country to country.

The SIM should consider the following possibilities:

- police, prison and immigration records;
- national identification and travel documentation;
- finger, hand and plantar prints are regularly taken from the military and aircrews;
- biometric systems – eg school register systems.

Latent print recovery should be considered at:

- homes;
- temporary locations, eg hotels;
- work locations;
- vehicles.

At those locations, recovery should be considered from areas specific to the victim:

- magazines, books and personal papers including travel paperwork;
- photographs;
- toys, paintings and musical instruments;
- electrical items, batteries and CDs/DVDs;
- bathroom floors and wall surfaces.

In instances where there are insufficient points of comparison to produce a positive identification, partial fingerprints may prove useful for elimination ie comparison with AM or PM prints cannot be those of the missing person or body.

6.15.2   Dental comparison (odontology)

The swift and comprehensive collection of ante-mortem dental information is likely to be the key to producing the quickest identifications in a mass fatality incident.

In a closed or mixed incident every effort should be made to obtain the dental records at the earliest possibility, ideally before the post-mortem process begins. The distinctive quality of some dental work allows forensic odontologists to recognise potential matches rapidly.

The SIM must ensure that all possible locations are investigated by the FLO to produce the most accurate and most up-to-date record of the missing person's teeth. Unfortunately, dental records, unlike medical records, are not collated at one place, but remain with the original practitioners. Many people, for instance, have NHS work (charted), private treatment (uncharted) as well as hospital treatment. Photographs are very useful, and forensic odontologists may make positive identifications by mapping ante-mortem photographs onto those taken in the mortuary. The ante-mortem harvest may identify dental samples also suitable for DNA (see below). A search against the name and date of birth of a deceased can be undertaken through contacting the Business Services Authority (formerly Dental Practice Board) at Eastbourne. This database may hold a record of the last NHS dentist attended by the deceased in England and Wales. Similar facilities occur in Edinburgh for Scotland and Belfast for Northern Ireland.

Dentistry is a particularly useful eliminator, even where the configuration of the teeth does not allow sufficient uniqueness to produce a positive identification. Logic allows simple conclusions when direct comparisons are made in the matching process – ie a tooth missing ante mortem but present post mortem means the two examples cannot be the same person. Odontologists can age childrens' teeth accurately, helping to assist in elimination.

Accurate comparisons rely on comparing accurate ante-mortem records against accurately charted post-mortem records. The possibility of further dental work or changes having taken place since the last ante-mortem records were obtained, and damage or teeth being lost in the mass fatality, are complicating factors. Inaccurate charting of dental ante-mortem information is not uncommon.

The value of odontology reduces when dealing with a post-mortem population that has experienced relatively little dental work (children), little or no charting (undeveloped countries) or the standard of dental health increases to the extent that fewer points of comparison exist.

Forensic odontologists achieve speedy identifications as their examinations can all be carried out in theatre without further specialist processes – with the assistance of photography and mobile radiography. They should be used to quality control the ante-mortem collection, carry out the post-mortem examinations and X-rays, and then form an integral part of the matching process. They are persuasive members of an Identification Commission.

6.15.3 DNA

The use of DNA in the investigation of mass fatalities is more complex than the use of the first two primary identifiers.

The process involves laboratory production of a profile from ante-mortem samples, also the laboratory production of a profile from post-mortem samples, and the comparison by a DNA expert.

DNA use is therefore comparatively slow and expensive and, as the costs, will fall upon the Coroner, the SIM must consider DNA submissions in consultation with the Coroner, and on a case-by-case basis.

It is, however, often the only reliable option to reunite non-identifiable body parts with each other, where bodies are disrupted.

Where, as in the case of bodies recovered in the Maldives following the tsunami, only torsos were recovered, odontology and fingerprint disciplines were redundant. In the case of children, where odontology is of lesser value, and fingerprints will be reliant upon tracing comparison latent fingerprints, DNA may provide the solution.

Its worth is, of course, renowned in the examination of skeletal remains, the Balkans war crime exhumations being subject of continued examinations to this day.

Different forensic suppliers have shown different success rates with the production of post-mortem DNA profiles. The SIM should ensure that the correct forensic supplier is identified, and consulted about which PM sample is likely to have the highest profile production percentage. Such a decision will depend on the type of incident and particular laboratory. SIMs should be mindful of the principle of avoiding unnecessary invasive procedures – eg the removal of mid-shaft thighbone causes extensive disruption.

SIMs should also ensure that in the case of international collaborations, a co-ordinated forensic strategy is adopted, to ensure that AM and PM profiles are produced in the same format, suitable for direct comparison and interpretation with associated information sharing protocols. The packaging, storage and transportation of AM and PM samples is crucial to ensure integrity of the samples and process.

Ante-mortem collection

Reference DNA

Reference DNA samples are the most reliable and straightforward to be used for AM DNA profile production as they can be safely attributed to the victim.

103

Sources include:

- national DNA database (s 64 of PACE 1984);
- hospital records (samples are kept on record, including from biopsies);
- Guthrie test – newborn baby blood sample.

Surrogate DNA

Profiles are produced from items believed to bear the victim's DNA. The SIM must ensure that FLOs are briefed to think laterally to find examples of surrogate DNA, and aim to identify items which will solely bear the DNA of the victim. As there is never certainty that the sample is from the victim (eg multi-use of toothbrushes), several samples should be taken to reduce the chances of a mistake being made.

Sources include:

- toothbrush;
- hairbrush;
- razor;
- musical instruments;
- footwear/gloves.

Elimination DNA samples may be required to rule out siblings or other parties.

Familial DNA

This is a complex procedure, requiring the production and interpretation of DNA profiles from buccal swabs taken from parents, children and siblings to compare with PM DNA samples.

Biological parents may not be available or known (adoption); indeed, the fact of adoption may not be known by surviving members of a family.

As in the *Marchioness* investigation, the FLO must consider the possibility that the biological father of the victim may not be known within the remaining family members – presenting difficult communications with the family. One estimate is that 10 per cent of us have a different biological father than we think.

FLOs should prepare family trees and ensure that samples are taken from all the immediate family – which, due to the spread of families, may require international collaboration.

Where more than one family member is believed to be a casualty, great care should be taken to ensure that same-sex siblings are not the subject of mistaken identity through the use of familial DNA measures. Where more than one person has died, and a family member has been identified by criteria other than DNA, their sample may be used to contribute to the familial DNA samples to identify the remaining family members.

DNA post-mortem collection

- blood sample;
- deep thigh muscle swab;
- deep thigh muscle sample;
- teeth (molar);
- rib;
- mid-shaft thighbone (bone marrow).

In the case of teeth removal, dental charting and X-ray should take place prior to teeth removal. Single-rooted front teeth should be avoided if at all possible.

Unique medical condition

Since the 1980s, most medical appliances and implants bear unique serial numbers. One reason for this has been the need to attribute blame for medical negligence litigation. Hospitals record the details of serial numbers within patient records and, in order to prove the identification, the continuity of the implant to the patient should be proved. Manufacturer records may also be examined to trace the hospital or clinic to which a particular device was issued.

Typical unique physical matches include:

- knee or hip joints with unique serial numbers;
- breast implants with unique serial numbers;
- heart pacemakers.

It may be possible to prove the unique physical match by other means, including a combination of secondary factors.

As an example, a combination of an incomplete DNA profile, with older non-serial numbered surgical implants or matching X-rays showing fractures or pinned joints may be sufficient to amount to a unique physical match.

6.16 THE SIM'S CO-ORDINATION ROLE

The SIM's role can be divided into four main areas (see Figure 6.2). It is the combination of these roles to varying degrees and the timing that each element employ that will determine the success of the SIM's approach:

- missing person and public information;
- body and property recovery;
- ante-mortem harvest and family liaison;
- post-mortem process.

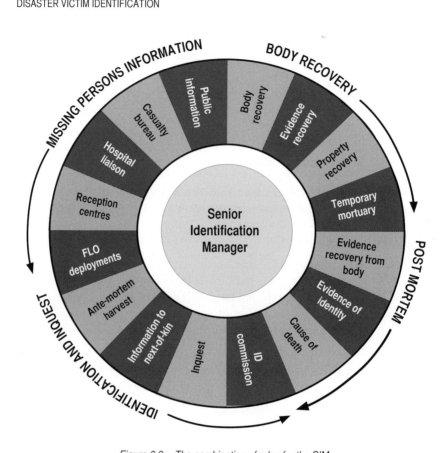

Figure 6.2   The combination of roles for the SIM

6.17   MISSING PERSONS AND PUBLIC INFORMATION

The SIM must ensure that an accurate picture of the incident is provided to the media at an early stage, including preparing the public for a single emergency line (Casualty Bureau). The exact location and details of the incident, including timings and destinations if a transport incident, should be given so as to reassure the public. This will reduce the volume, but increase the quality, of calls that are received.

There will be a public information thirst for progress of the identification from incident through to inquest.

The SIM should accept that high levels of coverage will be transmitted by the 24/7 media. A balance must be achieved between giving regular, open and general explanations of the progress to the public while providing honest, accurate information to families as early and regularly as possible via FLOs.

The SIM should be regarded as the single source of information about the number of dead and progress from recovery through to identifications. As such the SIM and Coroner must agree with the media lead at Gold meetings the timings of information releases which will meet the needs of the national media. Co-ordination by the media lead with central government media will ensure there is a consistent and clear line.

All media forms should be utilised, including the internet, which will avoid unnecessary calls from the public once the Casualty Bureau is opened.

The SIM must plan the call avoidance strategy with the Casualty Bureau Manager. Although Casualty Bureau can now accommodate the highest volume of calls, too high a volume will create a major problem in the accurate assessment and grading of missing persons. Often it is sensible to delay the opening of Casualty Bureau until the picture becomes clear. In general terms the objective is to receive higher quality, but fewer, calls once Casualty Bureau is activated. This will be achieved when more information can be given to the public, since they are then given a greater opportunity to establish whether their family members are actually involved.

The SIM's aim is to have the Casualty Bureau list reduced as quickly as possible to match the number of bodies recovered from the scene.

The SIM will be responsible for creating a list of questions for the Casualty Bureau call-takers to ask callers in order to assist with the grading of missing persons (Mispers). These questions are bespoke to the incident and will be designed to grade the missing persons into groups from "highly likely to be involved", "known to be in the locality/on board/at the event" etc, through to "Misper not involved". This narrowing of the group of potential victims by the use of questions is probably one of the main roles of the SIM as the grading "highly likely to be involved" is used to target the collection of ante-mortem data by the FLOs. Any identification relies not just on the collection of post-mortem information, but in having a high standard of relevant ante-mortem data with which to compare.

Documentation teams are despatched to locations where casualties and survivors are located, for instance hospitals and survivor reception centres.

It is the responsibility of the documentation teams to ascertain the details of these people and transfer the information to the Casualty Bureau. Where possible the SIM, Casualty Bureau manager and Documentation Team leaders should meet to ensure that there is a common recognised information picture prior to deployment.

The General Messaging Unit and Collation Unit within the Casualty Bureau, distinct from the Call-taking Unit, match duplicate entries, record the details of survivors as well as enabling the SIM to set parameters to cancel missing persons as found.

6.18   BODY AND PROPERTY RECOVERY

The SIM is responsible for the recovery of the bodies and property at the scene of the incident. The Scene Evidence Recovery Manager (SERM) will supervise the body and property recovery team leaders and will be responsible to the SIM and the SIO.

Following terrorist explosive attacks the scene will be managed by a Bomb Scene Manager, rather than a SERM.

The recovery operations will be carried out in accordance with a strategy prepared by the SIM in consultation with the SIO and taking into consideration any forensic strategy.

The SIM must ensure that, despite the mechanical nature of body and evidence recovery, a respectful methodology is achieved. The SIM must aim to reduce the actuality and impression that unrecovered victims are lying exposed and unprotected, and ensure that a compassionate and respectful approach is taken. The bodies of the dead must never appear to be treated by the authorities as mere evidential items.

The SIM will make decisions about whether an initial visual check of the dead should be carried out at the scene in order to obtain early information that could assist in identifying the victim – putative identifiers, such as ID cards or wallets. The SIM, while ensuring that the integrity of the overall DVI process is maintained, must always look for opportunities to gain fast-track information to make early identifications. This includes fingerprinting, photography of identification documents and forwarding the information to an intelligence cell within the Casualty Bureau. Slavish adherence to process may hinder speedy identification.

The SIM must aim to gain information from the recovery phase at the earliest opportunity which will support the elevation of a reported person to the status of a Grade 1 missing person "highly likely to be involved", triggering FLO activation.

During the recovery period the SIM will decide with the Coroner on what, in that incident, amounts to a body part, and what amounts to remaining or "residual material".

Residual material will not be subject to the DVI process and will be treated effectively as clinical waste – but disposed of by respectful cremation arrangements through the Coroner. The level of disruption will be a determining factor, but in previous incidents a criterion has been set whereby anything below 5 cm cubed that is not a body part capable of aiding identification (eg a finger) could be treated as such.

Body parts not treated as residual will be available for reuniting with other body parts – usually via DNA profiling and comparison.

Following terrorist attacks, SIMs should take great steps to separate the bodies and body parts of those committing the atrocities from innocent victims of the attacks. This principle applies from recovery, through identification to disposal.

6.19 POST-MORTEM PROCESS

The SIM will ensure the following:

- That a mortuary in England and Wales and Northern Ireland is licensed in accordance with the Human Tissue Act 2004[22] and that an appropriate designated individual is identified. This is not the case for Scotland which is covered by differing legislation.
- Liaise with the Coroner/Procurator Fiscal and agree the identification criteria.
- Decide what documentation is to be used in the mortuary, eg Interpol DVI forms, including body movement registers.
- Provide the mortuary teams to carry out the tasks of stripping and searching the bodies, recording information on the agreed forms, photography and fingerprinting of the victims, the correct seizure procedures, packaging and continuity of exhibits, assisting the pathologist and other forensic or medical personnel where necessary.
- That the relevant risk assessments are carried out and updated as needed.

6.20 THE SIM WITHIN THE CBRN ENVIRONMENT

The UK provides a national DVI response to Chemical, Biological, Radiological and Nuclear (CBRN) incidents. International collaboration agreements are in place.

For many years it was assumed that DVI would be impossible within the CBRN environment and yet the principles of recovery, post mortem through to body release, have been exercised and can be operated in reality.

Members of the UK DVI Team form the response together with odontologists, pathologists and APTs.

It is important that those performing the role of SIM following a CBRN incident are fully trained in CBRN DVI. Each incident will require substantial modifications to standard practices to achieve the principles as set out in the Clarke Report,[13] while complying with the restrictions of working within the CBRN environment.

6.21 THE SIM ABROAD – TEAM LEADER

The SIM abroad operates with support from the UK, and on behalf of the Foreign and Commonwealth Office. DVI operations abroad will involve co-operation with the local authorities, often other nationalities, Interpol and the military.

The SIM can only work with the consent of the local government and must attempt to maintain international DVI standards while working within local legal and cultural considerations.

An assessment of the disaster by a DVI Commander would involve the following considerations:

- Nature of the disaster
- Numbers of victims
- Level of disruption
- What means of identification will be employed (primary and secondary)?
- Who is to be identified – all or some victims?
- Who has primacy for the identification?
  - Local
  - Interpol
  - Separate international collaboration
- Legal considerations
- What specialists are required?
  - Pathologists
  - APTs
  - Odontologists
  - CSIs
  - Anthropologists
  - Fingerprint experts
  - DNA experts
- Interpreters
- Forensic matching capacity in theatre
- Logistics
  - Risk assessment
  - Proposed operating site
  - Office accommodation
  - Mortuary facilities
  - Transport availability
  - Welfare considerations for the team
  - Food
  - Water
  - Sanitation
  - Shelter
  - Availability of medical facilities
  - Personal inoculation requirements
- Equipment availability
- IT requirements

- Time difference – UK support arrangements
- Costs
- Environmental profile
  - Extreme terrain
  - Mountainous
  - Poor access to theatre of operation
  - High-density population
  - Extreme damage to infrastructure
  - Liable to earthquakes or aftershocks
  - Extreme heat
  - Extreme cold
  - Other geological hazards
  - War zone
  - Local unrest
  - Cultural awareness
  - Road and rail networks
  - Telephone landlines
  - Airports and landing strips
  - Mobile telephony
  - Internet access
- International DVI resources in theatre
- Military assistance requirements, eg security and bomb disposal.

The extent of international collaboration, or indeed access to assist with the DVI process, is likely to depend on the existing DVI capacity, and the development of the nation. This will vary from the SIM only providing ante-mortem information, to commanding an international collaboration.

The SIM's role must be to encourage the DVI standards to be those of the affected country with the highest domestic standards – Interpol standards are suitable. Even European countries have differing views over the level of invasive procedures considered acceptable for identification.

Ante-mortem opportunities are likely to be available in theatre – and local police resources or those from the DVI team may meet the need. Victims living or working abroad, those with dual nationalities, or elimination ante-mortem requirements will present family members and locations for forensic and background ante-mortem collection to the SIM.

There will be inevitable family liaison requirements abroad – possibly without the assistance of trained officers

Exhumation may be required – mass grave deposit sites will pose particular recovery difficulties.

Consider the various burial or repatriation options available following a death abroad:

- cremation in theatre, followed by burial or retention of ashes;
- burial in theatre;
- return of the body;
- return of the ashes.

The SIM abroad not only has operational commitments but, as the team leader, has managerial and welfare responsibilities without the ready support provided by the standard police infrastructure.

The political demands are significant – the formation of the Identification Commission and negotiating with ambassadorial representatives to agree common goals and guidance are standard requirements of the job.

Personnel requirements will form a major part of the SIM's work abroad, including local pay arrangements.

Procedures to deal with the unidentified will present the SIM with differing considerations, from property retention to burial of marked bodies in marked graves to allow later recovery if necessary.

The author of this section is a UK DVI Commander. This is a relatively new discipline I want to acknowledge that much of the source material is inevitably gained from fellow SIMs, DVI colleagues, material assimilated from training, from public sources and organisations, eg the Clarke Report and Interpol. I claim no additional rights to any of this material, which is written with the sole intention of improving and informing the UK's DVI response.

REFERENCES

1 D Alexander, *Principles of Emergency Planning and Management*. (Terra Publishing, Harpenden, 2002).

2 Health and Safety Executive Website [online]. Available at: http://www.hse.gov.uk/index.htm. [Accessed: 28.09.09.]

3 Air Accident Investigation Branch (AAIB) website [online]. Available at: http://www.aaib.gov.uk/home/index.cfm. [Accessed: 28.09.09.]

4 Marine Accident Investigation Branch (MAIB) website [online]. Available at: http://www.maib.gov.uk/home/index.cfm. [Accessed: 28.09.09.]

5 Rail Accident Investigation Branch (RAIB) website [online]. Available at: http://www.raib.gov.uk/home/index.cfm. [Accessed: 28.09.09.]

6 Interpol *"New DVI Guide"* Interpol website [online]. Available at: http://www.interpol.int/Public/DisasterVictim/Guide.asp. [Accessed: 28.09.09.]

7 Russialink, K-141 KYPCK The Russian Atomic Submarine Kursk website [online]. Available at: http://www.russialink.org.uk/kursk/. [Accessed: 28.09.09.]

8 S Carrell (3 April 2009) *Seabed search for bodies after North Sea helicopter crash*. Guardian.co.uk [online]. Available at: http://www.guardian.co.uk/uk/2009/apr/03/scotland-helicopter-crash-victims. [Accessed: 28.09.09.]

9 I McLean and M Johnes, *Aberfan: Government and Disasters*. (Welsh Academic Press, 2000).

10 HSE Potters Bar Investigation Board (May 2003) *Train Derailment at Potters Bar 10 May 2002* [online]. Available at: http://www.rail-reg.gov.uk/upload/pdf/incident-pottersbar-may03progrep.pdf. [Accessed: 28.09.09.]

11 The Rt Hon Lord Cullen (2000) *The Ladbroke Grove Rail Inquiry, Part 1 Report*. HSE (Health and Safety Commission [online]. Available at: http://www.pixunlimited. co.uk/pdf/news/transport/ladbrokegrove.pdf. [Accessed: 28.09.09.]

12 "Pan Am Flight 103", *Wikipedia* [online]. Available at: http://en.wikipedia.org/w/index.php?title=Pan_Am_Flight_103&oldid=316283306. [Accessed 28.09.09.]

13 Clarke, Anthony Lord Justice, 23 March 2001, *Great Britain Inquiry into the Identification of Victims following Major Transport Accidents. Cm 5012*. TSO (The Stationery Office). Available from: http://www.tsoshop.co.uk/bookstore.asp?FO=115 9966&Action=Book&ProductID=9780101501224&From=SearchResults.

14 Coroners Act 1988 (c 13) (HMSO, London) [online]. Available at: http://www.opsi. gov.uk/Acts/acts1988/pdf/ukpga_19880013_en.pdf. [Accessed: 28.09.09.]

15 Interpol Resolution AGN/65/res/13 (1996) [online]. Available at: https://www. interpol.int/Public/ICPO/GeneralAssembly/Agn65/Resolutions/AGN65RES13.asp. [Accessed: 28.09.09.]

16 Corporate Manslaughter and Corporate Homicide Act 2007 (c 19) (HMSO, London) [online]. Available at: http://www.uk-legislation.hmso.gov.uk/acts/acts2007/pdf/ ukpga_20070019_en.pdf. [Accessed: 28.09.09.]

17 P Firth, *Four Minutes to Hell: The Story of the Bradford City Fire*. (Paul Firth, Liverpool, 2005).

18 Popplewell, Mr Justice, July 1985, *Committee of Inquiry into Crowd Safety and Control at Sports Grounds* (Cmnd 9585) (HMSO, London) [online]. Available at: http://www.la84foundation.org/SportsLibrary/SportingTraditions/1986/st0202/ st0202n.pdf. [Accessed: 28.09.09.]

19 Metropolitan Police Service, TO20 Branch, New Scotland Yard, *The Identification of the Deceased Following Mass Disaster* (January 1994) [online]. Available at: http://www.dft.gov.uk/pgr/shippingports/shipping/safety/tsifinal/xg1theidentification ofth5019.pdf. [Accessed: 28.09.09.]

20 Interpol Antemortem Form, Postmortem Form, Disaster Victim Identification Report Form, Interpol website [online]. Available at: http://www.interpol.int/Public/ DisasterVictim/Forms/Default.asp. [Accessed: 20.09.09.]

21 On This Day, BBC News: 1997: *Egyptian militants kill tourists at Luxor*. BBC News website [online]. Available at: http://news.bbc.co.uk/onthisday/hi/dates/stories/ november/17/newsid_2519000/2519581.stm. [Accessed: 28.09.09.]

22 Human Tissue Act 2004 (c 30) (HMSO, London) [online]. Available at: http://www. opsi.gov.uk/ACTS/acts2004/ukpga_20040030_en_1. [Accessed: 10.06.08.]

CHAPTER 7

Casualty Bureau

7.1 INTRODUCTION

The Association of Chief Police Officers (ACPO) defined the purpose of Casualty Bureau in 2005[1] as:

"Providing an initial point of contact to receive and access data relating to persons who have, or are believed to have, been involved in an incident."

Four primary objectives underpin the purpose:

1. inform the investigation process relating to the incident;
2. trace and identify people involved in the incident;
3. reconcile missing persons reports;
4. collate accurate information for relevant parties.

7.2 BACKGROUND AND DEVELOPMENT OF CASUALTY BUREAU

At the outbreak of World War II, the Government realised that casualties resulting from air raids on London would require a procedure to ensure that details of those killed and injured could be collated. This would allow relatives or friends who enquired at police stations to be given accurate information. By the early part of 1940, arrangements had been made for the police to collect information from hospitals and mortuaries. This would consist of the names and addresses of persons killed or injured. By the end of November 1940, over 700 casualty lists covering more than 32,000 cases had been circulated, and nearly 2,000 messages had been sent to the UK police service. After the war Casualty Bureau remained very much unchanged and unused for the next decade.

In 1957 a train crash occurred in Lewisham and it became clear that the previous Casualty Bureau system, operating in the context of war, was unable to meet the requirements of peacetime. This prompted a review of Casualty Bureau arrangements. The review identified and set down the basic business processes that have evolved into the Casualty Bureau system that operates to date.

Probably the most significant development for post-war Casualty Bureau was the Paddington rail crash. Thirty-one people died and dozens were injured when a commuter service run by Thames Trains passed a red signal and collided with a Great Western express train on 5 October 1999. Lord Cullen was subsequently appointed to head the inquiry into the crash.[2] His findings revealed that a number of the bereaved were highly critical of the way in which the Casualty Bureau of the Metropolitan Police had been organised. During the first 24 hours post-incident, 3,868 calls were received from members of the public, reporting nearly 2,000 persons missing or possibly involved in the crash. As there was no passenger manifest or way of recording who was on board the trains in question, this placed a particular burden on the Casualty Bureau. In total, staff were enquiring into 5,000 reports of missing people, possible survivors and casualties of the event. All these reports were recorded on a manual card index which, because of the volume of enquiries, caused operational difficulties and delays in informing anxious friends and relatives. Additional confusion was caused by the fact that other organisations had issued different telephone numbers for the use of members of the public. Lord Cullen[2] made three noteworthy recommendations that subsequently set the scene for how data would be processed in a live operation:

"4.119 It is highly desirable that the system used in the Casualty Bureau and other police forces for the reception of information about missing persons, casualties and survivors in the event of a major incident should be computerised in order to avoid delay and distress. So far as is practicable, a person who receives a call should be able to enter the information received directly into the computer, and, to the extent appropriate, provide information from it to the caller. There should be a set procedure for the returning of a call where information cannot meantime be provided to the caller. This should include the logging of incoming and outgoing calls. It should be understood that, wherever possible, an assurance should be given that the call will be returned in the given period of time, and this assurance honoured.

4.120 Steps should be taken to extend computerisation to all police forces and to ensure that the information collated by each police force is readily available to all others. For this purpose it may be desirable, in the interest of economy and efficiency, for these facilities to be provided on call from one or more central locations.

4.121 The police service, in co-operation with the other emergency services, should use their best endeavours to ensure that, in order to avoid confusion, common telephone numbers are issued for the use of members of the public who are seeking to give or obtain information about persons who have, or may have, been involved in a major incident."

Recognising the many similarities that exist between the investigation of a major incident and a major disaster, the Home Office Large Major Enquiry System (HOLMES 2) then provided the facilities for disaster management via the Casualty Bureau operations. The system was already in use for crime investigation within the UK police service, however, additional functions required for Casualty

Bureau operations were fully integrated into the solution, with a similar corporate approach as used in the crime utilities. Following the Cullen Inquiry, the UK police service adopted full computerisation of the provision of Casualty Bureau via Holmes 2.[3]

The provision of minute-by-minute news services and entertainment through the various mediums of television (territorial, digital and satellite), radio and internet (blogs and podcasts) are some of the developments over the past 25 years that have opened up the information floodgates. Via mobile phones, computers, television screens and other technologies, expectations of instant provision of information and data have fuelled the thirst for increased knowledge; a greater sense of vulnerability has been created along with the generation of real-time expectations of instant issue resolution. This is in contrast with the expectations of the 1940s and 1950s, where many parts of society would have waited patiently for information to be brought to them via "the establishment".

This cultural change was epitomised when, on 11 September 2001, via pictures beamed across the world in real time, the world witnessed an act of terrorism that caused the collapse of the two World Trade Center Towers in New York. Casualty Bureau was activated in the UK by the Metropolitan Police and started to receive 1,000 calls an hour. The volume of calls outstripped resources and, while the rest of the UK police service had Casualty Bureaux, there were no structures or Information and Communication Technologies (ICT) facilities in place to connect them up in order to provide further capacity. Many calls from the public were abandoned before they were answered.

It became clear that Casualty Bureau would have to provide a national approach to call-taking. A technical solution was subsequently provided and implemented UK wide in the form of CasWeb. This software allowed all Casualty Bureaux to connect securely and to combine to provide mutual aid to support a host force (the force "owning" the incident).[3] A telephony system – National Mutual Aid Telephony (NMAT) – was also devised that would allow call-takers from any Casualty Bureau located in the UK to access and answer calls made to the host Casualty Bureau. All information provided to a call-taker would then be directly input via CasWeb and then automatically transferred into Holmes 2, allowing the host force to process that data accordingly.[4]

The system was put to use robustly on 7 July 2005, in London, when four suicide bombers caused 52 deaths and many casualties on three Tube trains and one bus during the morning rush hour. Some 43,000 calls were initially presented to Casualty Bureau. These calls were answered, in the first 8 hours, by 200 call-takers from within the UK police service, acting on behalf of the Metropolitan Police. Two-thirds of calls initially went unanswered. Callers were anxious about people who had potentially been involved, and they had an expectation that their enquiries would be answered. By the afternoon of the following day, the number of callers fell considerably; many later calls were cancellations of original missing persons reports. NMAT and Casweb withstood the rigours of the incident. The only issue for the police service was the capacity to receive a large number of

117

calls and resilience when processing large amounts of data. Work is ongoing in an attempt to address this by means of a reorganisation of resources and further automated technical solutions.

7.3   KEY CASUALTY BUREAU FUNCTIONS AND RESPONSIBILITIES

The Casualty Bureau, when operational following a mass casualty incident, will come under the remit of the Senior Identification Manager (SIM). It is the SIM, or their nominated Bronze Command, who will set the criteria by which calls will be taken and recorded, along with associated policy. Opening and closing times, welfare and how Casualty Bureau links in with the rest of the Disaster Victim Identification (DVI) process are included within the responsibilities assigned to the SIM role in Casualty Bureau.

A Casualty Bureau will be activated following a major incident involving deaths and/or casualties. There will also be occasions when Casualty Bureau will be activated to act as a single point of information provision, ie warning and informing the public about flooding or any other type of incident that will generate calls to the police service. It can also be used to collate information following a witness appeal, or appeal for information, by the police. In fact, where the volume of calls being received by the police is such that it is starting to affect the operational effectiveness of communications or policing functions, this will be enough to trigger a live Casualty Bureau. When this is the case and it is not dealing with death or casualties then the function may be renamed as an "information centre". The principles of how incoming intelligence is processed will remain similar to a Casualty Bureau, with the parameters of operation set by the Senior Investigating Officer (SIO) rather than the SIM.

The decision to activate a Casualty Bureau will normally be taken by Gold Command. Gold will usually make that informed decision after receiving information from Silver or Bronze Control, or the Foreign and Commonwealth Office (FCO). It will become apparent in the early stages of the incident whether a force will be able to cope by utilising its own resources or whether national mutual aid will be required in order to bolster the response.

The role of the Police National Incident Co-ordination Centre (PNICC) will be to act on behalf of the host force to secure and co-ordinate the provision of mutual aid. Mutual aid for Casualty Bureau may take the form of call-takers who will remain in their own force, taking calls on behalf of the host force, or the provision of operators for certain functions of Casualty Bureau that cannot be delivered remotely. PNICC will receive direction from the SIM or Casualty Bureau Bronze. These officers will monitor calls made to Casualty Bureau in order to ensure that sufficient resources to meet demand are made available from across the UK police service. Protocols and guidance outline how PNICC and Casualty Bureau operate together.

Bronze Command will provide information from the scene of the incident to Silver which will subsequently inform Gold on first reports of estimated deaths and/or casualties. This will also give indication of the necessity for activation of Casualty Bureau and the capacity required.

The FCO provides protection and assistance for British nationals abroad. Part of this responsibility is: tracing missing persons; identifying the dead; arranging repatriation or local internment or cremation; and providing advice and support for bereaved relatives and survivors. In the event of a mass casualty incident abroad, such as the tsunami in central Asia or the Sharm-El- Sheikh bombings in 2005, the FCO has neither the capacity nor the capability to conduct a DVI process, and so calls on UK policing to perform this role. Although the FCO does have limited call-taking facilities, there is a specified rota throughout the year during which policing regions will undertake to assist and support the FCO during a response to an incident abroad. This includes the full Casualty Bureau functions. A memorandum of understanding exists, outlining how the FCO and UK policing will work together.

Once the decision has been made to activate Casualty Bureau, the staffing levels and location will be decided by the SIM in consultation with the incident commander. A HOLMES 2 Casualty Bureau account will be created and maintained to manage information concerning persons believed to be involved in the incident. The National Policing Improvement Agency (NPIA) helpdesk will, on application from the lead force in the relevant region nominated to co-ordinate call handling, issue two telephone numbers for circulation via the media, asking enquirers to contact Casualty Bureau. One number is a freephone number for callers dialling Casualty Bureau from within the UK; the second number is a low-cost number for callers dialling from outside the UK.

The SIM will also, working with Gold Command, formulate a media strategy in relation to Casualty Bureau. That strategy will include accurate details of the incident, contact numbers for Casualty Bureau and its purpose.

Casualty Bureau comprises four core modules:

1. Incident Contact Centre (ICC);
2, Casualty Information Unit (CIU);
3. Nominals Matching Unit (NMU);
4. General Message Unit (GMU).

7.4   INCIDENT CONTACT CENTRE (ICC)

The ICC is responsible for:

- answering incoming enquiries from members of the public;
- recording details of possible missing persons; and
- recording messages for onward transmission to other areas of the identification or investigation process.

To support a call-taker in assessing the likelihood of involvement of a person reported missing, the SIM will construct a set of questions to be asked of each caller who reports a missing person. The questions will be formulated before Casualty Bureau starts taking calls, will be incident-specific, and will not number more than 10. They will be reviewable as required.

The SIM's questions underpin a grading system which the call-taker will then apply to ensure both a uniformity of response to each caller and the nature and degree of involvement a reported missing person will have in connection with the incident. The answers to the question result in the missing person being assigned a grade. The grading system is as follows:

1. **highly likely** to be involved;
2. **possibly** involved;
3. **highly unlikely** to be involved;
4. **spare**;
5. **spare**;
6. **spare**;
7. cancellation – **missing person is a casualty**;
8. cancellation – **missing person located safe and well**;
9. **not involved**.

Recorded Grade 1 missing persons are probably involved in the incident and therefore prioritisation would be given to deploying an FLO to continue investigations into their identity.

All messages received by the ICC are forwarded to the receiver (central decision-maker) who is responsible for prioritising, actioning and resolving those messages.

7.4.1   ICC work flow

See Figure 7.1.

7.5   CASUALTY INFORMATION UNIT (CIU)

The CIU will receive and process information from a variety of sources. Police documentation teams will be deployed to hospitals, mortuaries, survivor centres, evacuee centres and friends' and relatives' centres in order to gather and transmit intelligence relating to persons involved in the incident. Casualties can be divided into two categories: **identified** (those who are verbally able to identify themselves) and **unidentified** (those who cannot identify themselves as they are either unconscious or deceased).

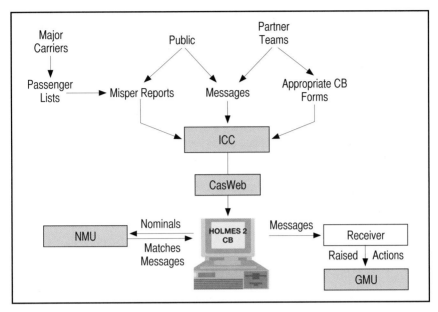

Figure 7.1   Incident Contact Centre work flow

7.5.1   CIU work flow

See Figure 7.2.

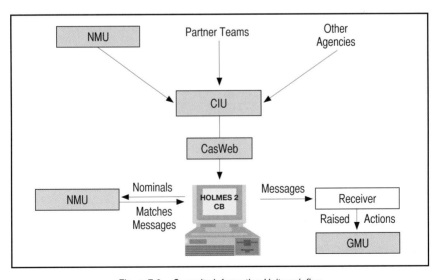

Figure 7.2   Casualty Information Unit work flow

7.6   NOMINALS MATCHING UNIT (NMU)

The NMU administers the matching of casualties, survivors and evacuees with reported missing persons. Once a match has been made, SIM and/or SIO policy will determine how and when the appropriate person or family is informed. It must always be borne in mind that any person identified as having been present at the incident, whether their status is as casualty, survivor or evacuee, may also be a significant witness or, indeed, they may also be a suspect. Any caller to the Casualty Bureau may be an associate of the suspect and so any message out of the Casualty Bureau may alert a suspect or their associate.

7.6.1   NMU work flow

See Figure 7.3.

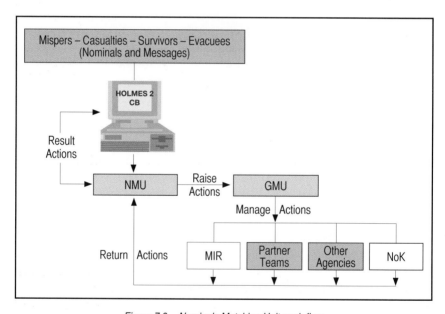

Figure 7.3   Nominals Matching Unit work flow

7.7   GENERAL MESSAGE UNIT (GMU)

The GMU is responsible for monitoring and managing all messages and actions that are part of Casualty Bureau data flow. It is also responsible for notifying next-of-kin (NOK), or the most appropriate other person, of the whereabouts of reported missing persons, in accordance with SIM/SIO policy. This unit is the interface with other functions of DVI that take place outside Casualty Bureau, eg

Major Incident Room (MIR) (where the investigation of the incident takes place), partner agencies and Family Liaison.

7.7.1 General Message Unit work flow

See Figure 7.4.

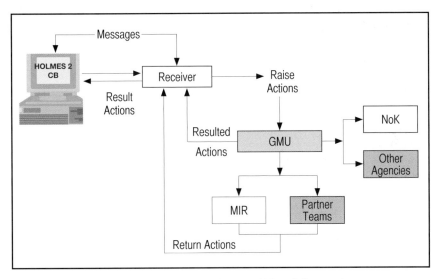

Figure 7.4   General Message Unit work flow

7.8 DATA PROCESSING

During the course of a live operation a Casualty Bureau can expect to handle large quantities of verifiable or speculative data received from a wide range of sources. Such quantities of data (eg during the 2005 London bombings the number of missing people reported reached 3,961 in one hour) require effective management to ensure that accurate and timely information is provided to the correct parties. There is also a need to comply with legislation associated with the handling and sharing of data.

All documentation, unless unrestricted, must be assigned protection under the Government Protective Marking Scheme (GPMS). Other legislation (such as the Data Protection Act 1998 (DPA);[5] the Freedom of Information Act 2000 (FOI);[6] and the Criminal Procedure and Investigations Act 1996 (CPIA)[7]) must be adhered to. Further guidance is available from ACPO[8] and from non-statutory sources.[9]

Emergency Preparedness: Guidance on Part 1 of the Civil Contingencies Act 2004[10,11] states that it is a police responsibility, when emergencies occur, to consider setting up a Casualty Bureau. Every force contributing to UK policing must be able to deploy some form of Casualty Bureau function, whether it is a self-contained end-to-end process, part of a policing regional response or in the role of host force in a response utilising national mutual aid. As with all emergency response functions, there is a clear responsibility for the police service to ensure that all staff deployed to Casualty Bureau are trained in accordance with national guidance; ongoing refresher training is provided; resilience issues are considered and addressed; and testing and exercising of all aspects of Casualty Bureau takes place at regular intervals. A fully tested and exercised business continuity plan must also exist.

REFERENCES

1 ACPO, *Guidance on Casualty Bureau Standard Administrative Procedures* (NPIA, Wyboston, 2008).

2 Lord Cullen, Health and Safety Commission, *The Ladbroke Rail Enquiry Part 1 Report* (HMSO, 2001) [online]. Available at: http://www.pixunlimited.co.uk/pdf/news/transport/ladbrokegrove.pdf. [Accessed: 12.12.2008.]

3 UNISYS, "What is HOLMES2?" [online]. Available at: http://www.holmes2.com/holmes2/whatish2/. [Accessed: 12.12.2008.]

4 NPIA, "Major Investigation and Casualty Bureau Management" [online]. Available at: http://www.npia.police.uk/en/10512.htm. [Accessed 12.12.2008.]

5 Data Protection Act 1998 (c 29) (HMSO, London) [online]. Available at: http://www.opsi.gov.uk/acts/acts1998/ukpga_19980029_en_1. [Accessed: 12.12.2008.]

6 Freedom of Information Act 2000 (c 36) (HMSO, London) [online]. Available at: http://www.opsi.gov.uk/acts/acts2000/pdf/ukpga_20000036_en.pdf. [Accessed: 12.12.2008.]

7 Criminal Procedure and Investigations Act 1996 (c 25) (HMSO, London) [online]. Available at: http://www.opsi.gov.uk/acts/acts1996/Ukpga_19960025_en_1. [Accessed: 12.12.2008.]

8 ACPO, *Guidance on the Management of Police Information* (NCPE, Wyboston, 2006).

9 HM Government, *Data Protection and Sharing – Guidance for Emergency Planners and Responder; Non statutory Guidance to Complement Emergency Preparedness and Emergency Response and Recovery* (London, 2007).

10 HM Government, *Emergency Preparedness: Guidance on Part 1 of the Civil Contingencies Act 2004, its associated Regulations and non statutory arrangements* (London, 2005).

11 Civil Contingencies Act 2004 (c 36) (HMSO, London) [online]. Available at: http://www.opsi.gov.uk/acts/acts2004/pdf/ukpga_20040036_en.pdf. [Accessed: 12.12.2008.]

CHAPTER 8

Ante-Mortem Collection

8.1 INTRODUCTION

Successful disaster victim identification depends upon matching ante-mortem (AM) forensic information with gathered post-mortem (PM) forensic information.[1] The collection of PM information data depends on the condition of the deceased,[1] and this in turn affects the AM data collection strategy. After each disaster, decisions taken must be informed by the event itself.

In the United Kingdom the responsibility for collecting AM data following a disaster rests with the civilian police service. This includes the data that is collected from the people who know most about the missing person, as well as the forensic data and material that could provide the valuable link leading to an identification. The purpose of this chapter is to outline this process and to show how the implementation of the Police Family Liaison system[2] has helped develop a quicker, more reliable way of getting AM data into a system in order to assist the work already being undertaken by body recovery, mortuary, Casualty Bureau, Major Incident Room and, ultimately, Identification Commission personnel.

8.2 POLICE FAMILY LIAISON

The relationship between the police and the community is rarely more important than in times of crisis. Families and communities look to the lead agencies for leadership, support and well-practised strategies, which will facilitate recovery.

Experience in the UK has shown that failure to respond appropriately in the immediate aftermath of an event can leave on families and communities scars that may never go away.

The role of the Family Liaison Officer (FLO) as it is recognised today can be traced to two incidents. First, the racist murder of Stephen Lawrence, a young black man, in London in 1993 brought about an organisational crisis within the police service. The resultant public inquiry[3] exposed failures in how police deal with families in the aftermath of such fatal incidents and produced six recommendations specifically related to ways in which family liaison could be improved, including the use of officers whose experience and training outfits them for this role.

The reality was that while the police had a very clear responsibility to deal with victims of burglary, assault, theft etc, their relationship with relatives after the death of a loved one was much more vague.

In these circumstances, the police investigation followed a traditional template. There was provision within this template for liaison with the dead person's family but, clearly, in the Lawrence case it had failed disastrously in a very public way and something had to be done if the police service was to improve its relationship with families and communities and prevent further harm.

Running in parallel with this process was the build-up to another public inquiry; this one involved a public transportation disaster where 51 young people had lost their lives on the pleasure cruiser *Marchioness* on the River Thames in London in 1989.

Again, it became apparent that the victims' families felt badly let down by the police liaison and although the police were able to show that they had made great efforts to improve their procedures, the public inquiry exposed these failings. Lord Justice Clarke mentions in his recommendations the need for fully trained Family Liaison Officers who would work with families.[4] Indeed, Lord Justice Clarke felt strongly enough about the needs of families that he outlined in detail the information that should be shared with families throughout the DVI process and how this should be done.

A great deal of progress has taken place in this area and the current model of Police Family Liaison has been used effectively in many major incidents, including the World Trade Center attacks, the Bali terrorist attacks, the Asian tsunami, the London bombings and other domestic disasters.

8.3   DISASTER AND POLICE FAMILY LIAISON OFFICERS

On 5 October 1999 a train crash occurred just outside Ladbroke Grove in central London. Thirty-one people died and many more were injured.

Early media reports stated that the death toll could be as high as 500. This was partly because of the devastation of the front carriages of the train.

There was unprecedented media coverage – a phenomenon which added another dimension to the recovery operation. It was very difficult to keep families apprised of genuine updates when rumours and speculation were being beamed directly into their homes via 24-hour news stations.

At this time there were no written protocols for the deployment of FLOs in mass fatality incidents, as it was not clear if this was a police investigation or a recovery following a tragic accident.

However, police body recovery experts were being used and the police casualty bureau had been opened, with an emergency number being released to worried relatives via the media.

The police service was still recovering from the Stephen Lawrence inquiry criticisms[3] and the *Marchioness* public inquiry[4] was looming, with potential for further (although historic) criticism around dealing with families. A decision was made that FLOs would be deployed for the first time to a disaster in the UK.

In the first 48 hours after the crash, 111 FLOs were deployed to families and survivors, their investigative purpose being to liaise with families who had reported loved ones missing.

The first task was to ensure that FLOs were deployed to those families who were most likely to both benefit from their presence and provide information that might lead to the positive identification of a victim of the crash. This was done through the use of the Central Casualty Bureau (CCB)[5] in conjunction with HOLMES.[6]

In the event of a disaster the CCB provides a bespoke telephone service which gives a first point of contact for family and friends of potential victims. Through the use of a series of questions designed in consultation with the Senior Identification Manager (SIM) and the Senior Investigating Officer (SIO), the Bureau will assign a series of grades to those who have been reported as missing. The information collected is compared with information which is constantly being received about survivors and those who have been taken to hospital. The result is a list of people who may have been caught up in the disaster. Any disaster, however, leads to more people being reported as "likely to have been involved" than are actually involved and therefore the information is passed through a set of filters created by the queries designed by the SIM and the SIO. A "Grade 1 Misper" therefore refers to someone who is "highly likely" to have been caught up in the event. The Casualty Bureau in the Ladbroke Grove incident had managed to put several hundred reports into the grading system via their telephone system. As a result, they had a list of identified Grade 1 Mispers, who were believed to have been on the train, had not been taken to hospital and who had not been heard from since the crash. They also had a list of Grade 2 Mispers – those who were less likely to have been involved but who still could not be ruled out, so in this case there was supporting evidence to say that they were very likely to have been on the train and had not been heard from since the crash. This grading system allows for the best and most efficient use of resources.

FLOs were deployed to all families falling within these two categories. Officers were briefed and equipped with the appropriate documentation required to obtain full descriptive details of missing loved ones.

It is a fact that, at any given time, any incident of this scale is highly likely to involve foreign nationals. Therefore it was important that the response to this incident conformed to international policing protocols[1] for the identification and repatriation of deceased citizens which would aid in ensuring that a thorough system was in place and which would avoid any errors in identification.

Difficulties in identification often follow a mass fatality incident because of the high incidence of burning, body fragmentation and decomposition.[7,8,9] As a result, the primary sources of identification must be checked and corroborated.

Dental records, DNA, fingerprints or some unique medical factors are the best and most acceptable identification means.[1] However, these involve asking families many questions involving a range of personal issues; and great understanding of both the families' tragedy and the efforts of the responding agencies is crucial. The type of information collected will be decided prior to deployment of the officers by the SIO and/or the SIM. These decisions constitute the forensic strategy which will underlie the strategic objectives of these two senior officers.

8.4 LESSONS FROM LADBROKE GROVE

A debrief of the FLOs was held a month after the Ladbroke Grove rail disaster and a range of concerns was raised by the practitioners. These fell into the following categories:

8.4.1 Operational

- There were communication problems at the outset and these improved drastically when phones and pagers were supplied to the FLOs. However, the communication between the different disciplines responding was poor; that was partly linked to the FLOs being a new aspect to the police response.
- The FLOs also had transportation problems at the beginning. While many of the responders will, of necessity, be located at or near the disaster itself, this was not so for the FLOs whose role it was to trace relatives and friends wherever they were and to gather the AM data urgently.
- There was also criticism of the team structure at the beginning and praise for the system that later evolved and which took the form of small teams with a team leader, each with their own recognised roles and responsibilities.

8.4.2 Deployment

- There were concerns about the efficiency of the call-out system for FLOs in an emergency and also the negotiation that was required with local line managers for the release of locally employed staff onto a major incident. What this actually indicated was that the training for Family Liaison had to be extended beyond just the FLOs and into those who manage, supervise and support them. Consequently, the roles of Family Liaison Co-ordinator (FLC) and Family Liaison Adviser (FLA) were developed within all forces.[2] The former is a senior manager who has, ideally, experience of the role of FLO and acts as co-ordinator, administrative supervisor and support point for all the FLOs within that specific force. The FLA is a role which can be activated in individual situations such as that of a mass disaster; this officer would work directly to advise the SIO and/or the SIM on how many FLOs to deploy, the forensic strategy that might be followed and to assist the SIO and/or the SIM in supporting and liaising with the FLOs as they undertake their work. All of these roles are fundamental to success in a major disaster investigation.

8.4.3 Training

- Some of the officers felt that the training that had previously been provided was not effective in preparing them for an incident of this nature. They were right: no provision had been made for engagement in a mass fatality incident. Although they were still dealing with only one family at a time, there was a different paper flow system with different police disciplines and external partners from anything that they had dealt with before when dealing with homicide or road death.
- Additional training was required when asking FLOs to obtain consent from families for the release of medical information and new forms had to be designed to assist with this process.
- Many of the FLOs felt that training around how they exited from a family was required. While they had been given some training, it had proved to be inadequate for this type of deployment. The journey through the criminal justice system for a family is different in mass fatality cases than it is in a homicide case.

8.4.4 Welfare

- It was recognised that support systems needed to be built in for major incidents, over and above those designed for normal business. Many FLOs had to spend periods of time away from home and that in itself brought problems about how to juggle home and business. Therefore, extra consideration had to be designed in order to keep staff safe and healthy and to allow business to run smoothly.
- It was suggested that between major incidents there should be regular "team meetings" where good practice could be exchanged and working relationships could be developed in "peace time".

8.4.5 Planning

- FLOs requested that a service policy be developed, with protocols understood by all. This was borne out of a fundamental acceptance that Family Liaison was there to stay in coping with mass fatalities and that accordingly there was a need to plan and prepare for the next time. Also, there was an acceptance that this could not be done in isolation but had to be developed alongside the other disciplines who respond to mass fatalities. In Family Liaison this would mean engaging with external agencies as well as police partners.

129

8.5 DEVELOPMENT

As the newest police discipline in mass fatalities, the AM collection team became exposed to many disasters over the next few years. The events of 11 September 2001 drew a Family Liaison response from the United Kingdom and a number of FLO teams were sent to New York in the months following that disaster. Their role was, on behalf of the UK Government, to assist the New York authorities in identifying and repatriating any UK citizens killed in the attack on the World Trade Center.

This was achieved through the collection of AM data from the affected UK families, along with any medical information, and transporting it according to international protocols to those entrusted with the identification of the dead, namely the Office of the Chief Medical Examiner in the City of New York.

8.5.1 Bali bombings

A similar protocol was applied to the terrorist attacks in Bali, Indonesia, in October 2002. In this incident the investigation was led by Indonesian and Australian law enforcement and the UK Government supported the situation by sending a UK Family Liaison/AM collection team. While the team working in Indonesia was an important part of the plan, it was part of an overall strategy that sought out potential AM information wherever it could be found. Therefore, running simultaneously in the UK, a Family Liaison team worked to gather and forward without delay any data or forensic material as it became available.

8.5.2 Asian tsunami

The events of 26 December 2004 were unprecedented across the world and unique again to the domestic police service in the UK. The UK DVI response was to send teams of appropriately trained officers to Thailand in order to assist in a truly international and multi-disciplinary response. It would be fair to say that it was some time before an effective Family Liaison/AM plan kicked in properly. Much of the early response was taken up with call handling, as UK citizens who were worried about their friends and relatives reported their concerns to the Police Casualty Bureau.

It took some time for the call handling to become manageable because of the extremely high volume of calls. Only then was a true picture formed of the location of the friends and relatives of those missing. It became clear that they were not concentrated in one area, therefore all UK police forces needed to come together to deal with the collection of AM data. From a Police Family Liaison point of view, it was clear that a regional plan was required. The Family Liaison plan was to separate into regions which were akin to the working regions applied by the Association of Chief Police Officers. This was easy to administer because these regions had existing working relationships and, from a Family Liaison perspective, the FLCs and FLAs were known to each other.

Each region then became responsible for the full investigation into each missing person, including the collection of statements, AM data, forensic exhibits etc. The collection was undertaken to the standards required in Thailand, quality assurance occurring locally before information was transported and received in London. From there it was transferred into Thailand where the UK had representation within the International Information Management Centre based in Phuket.

Lessons

The main lesson from the Family Liaison response to the tsunami flowed from the fact that, because of the sheer volume of activity, many police FLOs who had no previous training in this area had been deployed. It had never been anticipated that the domestic police would have to respond on such a scale and most forces found that they did not have the resilience in DVI-trained FLOs to cope with a disaster of this magnitude. This is an area that has now been addressed and DVI training for all FLOs is available as a national package to all forces in the UK from 2008.

Prior to this, training was available but it was not to a national standard, thereby leading to a variation in practice which in turn led to quality control issues.

8.5.3   London bombings (July 2005)

The London bombs in many ways showed how many lessons had been learned and a "joined up" approach was quick to engage. Included in this was a new development in the UK – a Family Assistance Centre (FAC) or, as it was known in London, the 7 July Humanitarian Assistance Centre.[10]

This multi-agency centre was modelled on the FAC that had been opened and run in Manhattan in the days and months following the attacks on the World Trade Center. The overall intention was to provide a "one-stop shop" for people affected by the attacks. It provided an added dimension to the Family Liaison response, in as much as FLOs were able to trace relatives and friends who were proving difficult to contact at their homes. As often happens in a disaster, relatives will make their way to where the incident occurred in order to try to find more information about what has happened. This is totally understandable and care had to be given by authorities to provide information, shelter and assistance to people when this occurred.

Unfortunately a family's need to go to the area can cause difficulties for the FLOs when it comes to contacting them in order to gather AM data. Having the capability to interview and capture data wherever the family is becomes a major step forward in making identifications more quickly without losing quality of data.

8.6   WHAT FLOs NEED TO COLLECT

The first step to collecting AM data is for the SIO and/or the SIM to decide an overarching forensic strategy. The rapid deployment of FLOs is vital but must be done in a thoughtful and planned manner. To be effective, and also to minimise the distress felt by the families, they must have an accurate remit to follow. The SIO and/or the SIM must decide guidelines for the collection of AM data, including which data to collect. These guidelines will be driven by the type of disaster and the resulting state of the remains. A disaster which has resulted in bodies being badly burned might not indicate a need for the collection of AM fingerprints, for example.

The four primary identifiers as advised by Interpol[1] are:

- DNA;
- odontology;
- fingerprints;
- unique medical conditions.

Because of a number of incidents in which visual identification was proven to be erroneous, this is not recommended in the UK as a positive means of identification.[11] However, this does not preclude the family from wishing to see the body of their loved one. According to Lord Justice Clarke's recommendations, this is a request which should be fulfilled once identities have been established.[4]

Whichever types of information the FLO is collecting, they must remain flexible. A great deal of the information that they are trying to retrieve may not be in the individual's primary abode but an assiduous look at their past medical, dental and work history often reveals invaluable information. In addition, with an increasing emphasis on the use of biometric data in security systems, these could act as a potential repository for unique identification information. This hunt therefore will involve a degree of investigation and, potentially, imagination on the part of the FLO.

8.6.1   Dental and medical records

First of all, in order to comply with international protocols it is likely that FLOs will be asked to complete the AM section of the Interpol DVI forms. The other half of these forms will be completed at the mortuary and the aim will be to find sufficient data in order that a forensic match can be made between the AM and PM forms.

Original dental records can be extremely important when trying to make an identification and therefore families will be asked to permit access to all dental records.[9,12,13] Original records, when released by dentists, can be compared against the information collected during examination of the deceased in the mortuary.

However, the collection of information can take some time to organise, so the FLO must get permission as soon as possible, along with the details of all dental practitioners. It is worth taking the time, as not only does odontology provide a robust primary identifier which may still be available for examination after decomposition has rendered DNA and fingerprints problematic, but additional information can be gleaned in the shape of gum shields or other dental work which might indicate a unique medical condition or provide the source of a DNA profile.

It must be remembered that, in the UK, dental records are not kept centrally and can exist in sites other than at the office of the primary dentist. Records can also exist in dental hospitals and emergency dentists, so all of these must be checked.

Odontologists often request photographs of the missing person. These photographs could prove to be extremely valuable to the identification process if they show a good, clear, recent picture of the missing person smiling and showing their teeth. A comprehensive understanding of what could be useful and where to find it is required by the FLO.

Medical records are also an important source of information. They may reveal the existence of unique DNA material or, failing that, unique medical conditions and the existence of images such as X-rays which might prove invaluable. The individual's general practitioner would be the place to start, and the records that they hold would indicate where other possible sources of information might be found. This information can lead to the retrieval of reference DNA, that is, DNA which is known to come directly from a named individual. Tissue biopsies or stored blood from the Guthrie test for children[14] can all speed up the collection of DNA and these would be held at local histology laboratories. Knowledge that the individual was on the blood donor register or bone marrow donor register is also invaluable information, as this can also be a supply of reference DNA. In addition, medical records will contain information about past surgical interventions which might have resulted in the placement of an implant or the removal of an organ which might narrow down the possible identification parameters, if not lead to a positive identification in themselves.

X-rays and CT or MRI scans may be a source of identifying information, especially if they are of areas of the body which might be considered unique, such as the frontal sinuses.[15,16,17] These are usually held at the hospital at which they are taken but medical notes will indicate that they have been taken and where they can be found, providing they have been retained.

Collected medical records should also include podiatry records, if they exist, as these can also be fairly specific to the individual, adding to the weight of information used in making the identification.[18]

Unique medical conditions and implants can play a role in identification.[16,19,20] Care must be taken with these, as the use of unique medical conditions relies on there being little chance that anyone else affected by the disaster will have the same condition. Implants are useful if they have an identification code which, through records, links them to the individual. Not all implants are numbered, however, and those will be of little evidential value. They may be used as an intelligence indicator, allowing intelligence gathering to become more directed.

Once gathered, all material must be recorded and preserved appropriately by the FLO, according to investigative standards.

8.6.2 DNA

While it has become increasingly high profile, DNA may not always be the best method of identification.[21] There are a number of reasons for this, not least being that, with commingling, the problems of cross-contamination loom large, for the collection of both AM and PM data.[22] DNA testing is also expensive and relatively slow. DNA may play a larger role in situations in which significant fragmentation has occurred, as it is able not just to identify remains but to allow them to be reunited.[8,23]

Because of the difficulties associated with decomposition, DNA must be recovered and stored while decisions are made about the forensic strategy.[21] One of the most useful additions to a Family Liaison Team in the aftermath of a disaster would be a Forensic Adviser. The FLOs may have to identify potential opportunities for recovering DNA and that is an area where advice from experts will be gratefully received.

Reference DNA might be available on the National DNA Database. In the event of a mass disaster this can be retrieved in the UK under s 118 of the Serious and Organised Crime Act 2005.[24] This allows for the use of DNA from the database to identify a victim.

If reference DNA can not be traced there are a number of other options to follow. First, a DNA profile can be developed using familial DNA.[8,21] If a DNA profile which is extrapolated from DNA profiles of family members is to be used to establish identity, the FLO will have to prepare a comprehensive lineage chart or "family tree" in order that the best advice is taken as to the person from whom the FLO should gather a DNA swab. This will minimise duplication of work, as well as avoid unnecessary swabbing of individuals unlikely to yield a positive result. As previously noted, assiduous checking of medical records might allow for the collection of the reference DNA of the target individual, with no need to take specimens from family members.

At all times the FLO needs to keep the family aware of the processes involved and avoid raising expectations regarding timescale.

It is also possible to explore items which the individual is believed to have used and on which they may therefore have left their DNA. Care must be taken in these situations as it is possible that others may have used the items, and therefore any DNA profile created might not be from the target individual. It might be helpful in these situations to use familial DNA, if available, to check the profile. Through this double check the reliability of the profile is established. The DNA extracted from the profile is known as a surrogate reference sample.

The following items may be gathered from the home, place of work, lockers at the gym, inside a motor vehicle etc:[8,21]

- clothing (unwashed, preferably);
- toothbrush;
- used cups or mugs;
- letters or envelopes that the missing person has sealed;
- bedding;
- telephone, especially one used exclusively by the missing person;
- skin cells trapped inside the links of a watch.

8.6.3 Fingerprints

Fingerprints are a commonly used biometric indicator of identity.[25] It should also be noted that, with the increase in the number of security systems using biometric data, the FLO should consider these as an additional source of unique information about an individual.[25]

While the use of fingerprints can be limited by the condition of the remains, their use should be considered in each circumstance. Despite initial misgivings, a significant number of identifications after the Asian tsunami were confirmed through the use of fingerprints as well as dental matches.[13]

The collection of fingerprints will follow a similar process to the DNA capture, in as much as knowing the lifestyle and routine of the missing person is highly significant to success. The Forensic Adviser can assist greatly here by explaining the type of surfaces that may yield a positive result. On any visit to the family home the FLO may even have to ask families to hand over valuable and precious items for forensic examination. It is important that they explain to the family what that process may do to the item and whether it can be returned to them later in the same state as it was given. Additionally, it is important, as with DNA, that prints are taken from something that has been handled only by the missing person. Fingerprints of all those in the family can be taken to exclude them. It is recommended that latent fingerprint retrieval is undertaken by a specialist, although they should be guided by the intelligence generated by the FLO.

Advice on the return of property and many other valuable areas for FLOs can be obtained from the website of the registered charity Disaster Action.[26] This charity is run by survivors and bereaved people from previous disasters and provides invaluable advice to responders. However, it acts primarily as a support point for people affected by the disaster and is a superb resource to which to direct relatives and friends in the aftermath of a mass fatality incident in the UK or abroad.

With fingerprints it may be necessary for the FLO to find a way of preserving them until the fingerprint expert has examined the area. Families may feel the need to tidy or dust an area in the hope that their loved one will return home safely. It is also important to ask the family and friends to identify places no one other than the missing person has touched.

8.6.4 Other supporting information

Information on clothing and jewellery must be recorded on the AM DVI forms. This will provide valuable, although not conclusive, information which could assist identification. It would be wrong to identify someone because of an item which was in their possession. They could easily have found it prior to the incident. Also, there is very little in the way of unique clothing, although it can help greatly to find out as much information as possible about what someone was wearing. Where it was purchased, as well as size, stains, rips, replacement buttons etc, can all assist when trying to make an identification. The same process should be repeated for jewellery, with particular attention paid to inscriptions bearing names and dates.

Photographs of the clothing and/or jewellery being worn should be asked for and, failing that, pictures of the same item in a catalogue can be of assistance.

Full descriptions of tattoos need to be recorded, ideally with a good, clear photograph showing them. It must be noted that in the event of a closed disaster, where there is a list of known casualties, the use of tattoos might be very relevant in establishing a suggested identity.

8.7 COLLATING THE AM DATA

In many large disasters it is often advisable that the SIM creates a submission strategy with regard to the AM data that is examined. All AM data should pass to a central area where it can be sorted, stored and accessed as needed.[27] Even a relatively small disaster with a limited number of victims can conceivably generate a large amount of AM data and a method of prioritising this data should be decided at the beginning. This would, of necessity, reflect the forensic strategy and will depend upon the nature of the disaster. If bodies are intact, for example, it might be appropriate for dental information to be fast tracked through the AM data collecting point in an attempt to provide the information to the odontologists at the earliest possible moment. As data comes in it should all go through a process of evaluation and review to ensure that it is retrieved and managed effectively. This would be done by the appropriate expert input: odontology information should be checked by an odontologist etc.[27] Again, this ensures that only relevant and useable information reaches the reconciliation team who will be undertaking the matching process.

8.8 CONCLUSION

Ultimately, the DVI process will guide FLOs into the important areas where investigation is crucial. Their investigative experience and training in the area of mass fatalities, as well as their professionalism when dealing with traumatised bereaved relatives, will add a dimension to identification and recovery. This dimension was not present in the UK prior to the Ladbroke Grove rail disaster. The coming together of disciplines in this area since 1999 has been driven by good leadership in a period which served up unprecedented challenges.

REFERENCES

1 Interpol website [online]. Available at: http://www.interpol.int/default.asp. [Accessed: 12.11.2007.]

2 ACPO Family Liaison Strategy Manual [online]. Available at: http://www.brake.org. uk/resources/downloads/ACPO%20Family%20Liaison.pdf. [Accessed: 12.11.2008.]

3 The Stephen Lawrence Inquiry. Report by Sir William MacPherson of Cluny [online]. Available at: http://www.archive.official-documents.co.uk/document/cm42/ 4262/4262.htm. [Accessed: 12.11.2008.]

4 Lord Justice Clark, "The Identification of Victims Following Major Transport Accidents" [online]. Available at: http://www.marchioness-nsi.org.uk/index.htm. [Accessed: 12.11.2007.]

5 Central Casualty Bureau [online]. Available at: http://www.met.police.uk/casualty/. [Accessed: 12.11 2008.]

6 HOLMES (Home Office Large Major Enquiry System) [online]. Available at: http:// www.holmes2.com/holmes2/index.php. [Accessed: 13.11.2008.]

7 H J Meyer, "The Kaprun cable car fire disaster – aspects of forensic organisation following a mass fatality with 155 victims" (2003) 138 *Forensic Science International* 1.

8 B Budowle, F R Bieber and A J Eisenberg, "Forensic Aspects of mass disasters: Strategic considerations for DNA-based human identification" (2005) 7 *Legal Medicine* 230.

9 R Bux, D Heidemann, M Enders and H Bratzke, "The value of examination aids in victim identification: a retrospective study of an airplane crash in Nepal in 2002" (2006) 164 *Forensic Science International* 155.

10 London Resilience, Humanitarian Assistance Centre Plan [online]. Available at: ttp://www.londonprepared.gov.uk/londonsplans/emergencyplans/hac.jsp. [Accessed: 30.11.2008.]

11 R Lain, C Griffiths and J M N Hilton, "Forensic dental and medical response to the Bali bombing" (2003) 179(7) *The Medical Journal of Australia* 362.

12 J Dumancic, Z Kaic, V Njemirovski, H Brkic and D Zecevic, "Dental Identification after Two Mass Disasters in Croatia" (2001) 42(6) *Croatian Medical Journal* 657.

13 M Petju, A Suteerayongprasert, R Thongpud and K Hassiri, "Importance of dental records for victim identification following the Indian Ocean tsunami disaster in Thailand" (2007) 121 *Public Health* 251.

14 "What is the Guthrie test and why is it done?" [online]. Available at: http://www.midwivesonline.com/parents/parents.php?id=96&tid=NEW1FATHERS. [Accessed: 13.11.2007.]

15 M Pfaeffli, P Vock, R Dirnhofer, M Braun, S A Bollinger and M J Thali, "Post-mortem radiological CT identification based on classical ante-mortem X-ray examinations" (2007) 171 *Forensic Science International* 111.

16 AZ Mundorff, G Vidoli and J Melinek, "Anthropological and Radiographic Comparison of Vertebrae for Identification of Decomposed Human Remains" (2006) 51(5) *Journal of Forensic Sciences* 1002.

17 RF da Silva, FB Prado, IGC Caputo, KL Devito, T de L Botelho and ED Junior, "The forensic importance of frontal sinus radiographs" (2009) 16(1) *Journal of Forensic and Legal Medicine* 18.

18 DM Sanger and W Vernon, "Value of a Strength Scale in Identification From Podiatry Records" (1997) 47(2) *Journal of Forensic Identification* 162.

19 EK Simpson, RA James, DA Eitzen and RW Byard, "Role of Orthopedic Implants and Bone Morphology in the Identification of Human Remains" (2007) 52(2) *Journal of Forensic Sciences* 442.

20 HD Ubelaker and CH Jacobs, "Identification of Orthopedic Device Manufacturer" (1995) 40(2) *Journal of Forensic Sciences* 168.

21 A Alonso, P Martin, C Albarran, P Garcia, L Fernandez de Simon, M J Iturralde, A Fernandez-Rodriguez, I Atienza, J Capilla, J Garcia-Hirschfeld, P Matinez, G Vallejo, O Garcia, E Garcia, P Real, D Alvarez, A Leon and M Sancho, "Challenges of DNA Profiling in Mass Disaster Investigation" (2005) 46(4) *Croatian Medical Journal* 540.

22 R Zehner, "'Foreign' DNA in tissue adherent to compact bone from tsunami victims" (2007) *Forensic Science International: Genetics* 218.

23 B Leclair, "Large-scale comparative genotyping and kinship analysis: evolution in its use for human identification in mass fatality incidents and missing persons databasing" (2004) 1261 *International Congress Series* 42.

24 Serious Organised Crime and Police Act 2005 (c 15) (HMSO, London) [online]. Available at: http://www.opsi.gov.uk/ACTS/acts2005/20050015.htm. [Accessed: 13.11.2007.]

25 K Ware, *Biometrics and Strong Authentication* (McGraw-Hill, Osborne, 2002).

26 Disaster Action website [online]. Available at: http://www.disasteraction.org.uk/. [Accessed 14.11.2008.]

27 E De Valck, "Major incident response: Collecting ante-mortem data" (2006) 159S *Forensic Science International* S15.

CHAPTER 9

Scene Evidence Recovery

9.1 SCENE MANAGEMENT

Scene management (see Figure 9.1) and site stabilisation during any mass disaster within the UK mainland will be co-ordinated by the police, as incident sites are normally treated as crime scenes. General crime scene procedures should therefore be followed. Naturally, this situation may not apply if the mass fatality incident is on foreign soil.

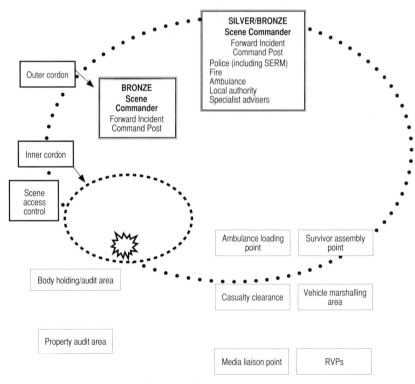

Figure 9.1   Scene management

9.2   COMMAND STRUCTURE

- *The Senior Investigating Officer (SIO)* is responsible for the overall investigation of the incident and gathering all available evidence, in conjunction with other investigative agencies where applicable.
- *The Senior Identification Manager (SIM)* is (on behalf of the Coroner or Procurator Fiscal) responsible for the identification of the deceased, which includes the recovery of victims and human remains from the scene.
- *The Scene Evidence Recovery Manager (SERM)* has overall responsibility for the recovery and recording of deceased victims, human remains and property. The appointment of the SERM will normally be made by the SIO in conjunction with the SIM. It may be considered good practice for the SERM to be an experienced SIO, trained in the role of a SIM.

Scene Evidence Recovery Teams under the command of the SERM are responsible for the recovery of victims and human remains as evidence and for identification purposes. Key personnel will be:

- DVI Recovery Co-ordinator;
- Property Recovery Co-ordinator;
- PolSA (Police Search Adviser);
- Forensic Co-ordinator;
- search trained officers.

It is likely that the police will request the support of forensic specialists and other emergency services in order to instruct and carry out duties at the site. In cases where terrorism is suspected, the SIO should be consulted prior to commencement of any aspect of scene recovery. To ensure a co-ordinated response to the recovery operation, the SERM will develop and implement a plan to remove the deceased, property and evidence from the scene for examination by appropriate investigating agencies. This will involve establishing a Scene Evidence Recovery Group composed of representatives from all of the organisations that have a part to play in this process.

The SERM should chair the Scene Evidence Recovery Group. In general, membership would include:

- Scene Evidence Recovery Manager (SERM);
- Victim Recovery Team Co-ordinator and Property Recovery Team Co-ordinator;
- Police Search Adviser (PolSA) (and Police Search Co-ordinator (PolSC) if more than one scene is under investigation);
- Police Forensic Adviser/Crime Scene Manager (PFA/CSM) (and Crime Scene Co-ordinator (CSC) if more than one scene is under investigation);

- Health and Safety Executive;[1]
- Welfare and Risk Assessment officers;
- Fire and Rescue Supervisor;
- local authority representative;
- Coroner's[2] or Procurator Fiscal's[3] representative;
- other members, as appropriate, which may include investigative bodies such as Air Accidents Investigation Branch (AAIB)[4] or the Rail Accident Investigation Branch (RAIB)[5] or the Marine Accident Investigation Branch (MAIB);[6]
- contractors or representatives from other organisations (with approval by Gold Command) providing technical or specialist equipment such as heavy lifting and cutting gear, heavy haulage etc;
- forensic pathologists;
- forensic anthropologists;
- environmental agency;
- financial and legal advisers;
- utility companies;
- construction design manager/surveyor.

Other functions of the SERM include:

- to co-ordinate the activities of all organisations deployed at the scene, taking into account such issues as natural terrain, hazards, location of human remains and prevailing weather conditions, and establish documented protocols for operating;
- to document a recovery plan, including priorities agreed with the SIO/SIM, together with a clear health and safety policy; complemented by documented risk assessment;
- to designate an audit/holding area and a property audit area;
- to be responsible for the health, safety and welfare of all staff under their command, including the provision of suitable clothing, equipment and safe systems of work.

The incident site and surrounding area must be secured (ie an inner cordon must be designated), with areas sectioned off, preventing unauthorised attendance and enabling the various elements of the wider emergency response to be conducted safely, securely and simultaneously.

Scene management specific to mass fatalities will involve deploying staff for specific duties, putting in place mechanisms for recording all activity at the site and reporting back to Gold Command on any activity undertaken. Aerial photography, 360° degree imaging and other forms of environmental scanning may be appropriate and will assist the investigation as well as the planning of the recovery phase.

Themes that will be managed throughout the response to recover and identify the deceased will include:

- the nature and scale of operations and how these influence other on-site activities;
- identification and location of resources available for deployment, including specialist advice;
- evidential recovery of the deceased and personal property;
- duties/limitations/health and safety of those deployed as part of the response;
- the removal of debris and wreckage which may be blocking access to the deceased;
- the transport of debris and wreckage from the site for further evidential sifting at a designated and secure location;
- constant communication with other responders at the site and the lead Coroner/Fiscal, to ensure that victim search and recovery is consistent with the identification criteria, such as whether an initial visual search or a cursory identification check is carried out at the scene.

9.3   SCENE STABILISATION AND CLEARANCE

The generic function of scene clearance begins as part of the initial response to the emergency as a whole and recovery will not normally begin until a full and proper risk assessment has been conducted (see below). In the first instance, the prime focus is to rescue the living and to clear access routes to and from the incident site. To assist with the immediate response, particularly to support the police on victim search and recovery of the deceased, the key objectives of site stabilisation are likely to include the following:

- rescuing trapped and injured persons;
- recovering fatalities and/or human remains;
- facilitating the criminal and other investigations;
- recovering personal, technical and other items of evidential value.

Those responsible for site clearance may be requested to create a space for a temporary Body Holding/Audit Area and Property Audit Area. These are usually at, or adjacent to, the incident site. These areas will hold bodies or property prior to them being transported to the emergency mortuary; see below for how property not associated with the body is processed.

While the police co-ordinate all activities at the scene, there may be a need for other groups to be involved. For example, an assessment of the structural stability of buildings affected in the incident would be co-ordinated by the local authority in whose area the incident occurred.

Continuity and integrity of the scene, and everything collected from it, may be critical to the process of identifying the deceased. Prevention of cross-contamination of any evidence is vital, and the advice of forensic experts will be essential throughout the process. Debris and wreckage may be removed to an off-site location for further sifting, checking and forensic examination. This may uncover further human remains or personal property that may assist with the process of identifying the deceased.

9.4 JOINT DYNAMIC RISK ASSESSMENT

No recovery activity should take place until a full risk assessment has been undertaken. It is imperative that operations are conducted safely and within existing or adapted protocols. This minimises the potential for mistakes in the early stages and undoubtedly saves time. All emergency services present at the site are involved in the initial joint risk assessment, allowing them to utilise their own appropriately skilled staff, and maintain responsibility for their own staff, unless agreed otherwise (see "SERM" below). General health and safety regulations, along with those specific to individual responder organisations, must be taken into account and kept under review throughout the response at the site. Activities need to adapt to meet the demands, conditions and circumstances of the working environment, so the risk assessment must remain dynamic. This does not, however, replace the legal requirement to record the risk assessment as, and when, appropriate.

To ensure a safe working environment, all staff deployed at the site must be fully briefed on what risks and hazards are present at the site, how these should be managed and what safety precautions are required – ie personal protective equipment or safety equipment. Briefings must cover individual as well as team responsibilities and incident reporting procedures including any "near miss". The list in Figure 9.2 is not exhaustive but it does illustrate the types of risks and hazards that may be present at any type of incident site – to be explored as part of the risk assessment and managed accordingly.

In a mass fatality incident it may be good practice for a multi-agency risk assessment team to be formed. This would be supported by personnel with expertise in areas such as local knowledge of the area and infrastructure, Occupational Health, Infection Control, Structural Stability, and Health and Safety. A lead will be established as dictated by the demands of the emergency. The personnel involved must have a certain standard of skills:

- *Health and safety advisers* should be familiar with the area in which the incident has occurred and with any risks and hazards that may exist.

- *Occupational health advisers* should be familiar with health and infection advice or regulations, trauma support and welfare assistance.

143

RISKS TO PERSONNEL DEPLOYED TO RECOVER THE DECEASED

PHYSICAL RISKS

(a) **Infection Control** – hygiene and safety at the point of entry, handling of bodies and remains, use of equipment, exit points and cross-contamination with other areas.

(b) **Manual Handling** – access to bodies, lifting and recovering heavy weights.

(c) **Physical Injury** – working in debris and confined areas, and exposure to elements such as heat, cold, smoke, dust, gas, electricity, water, fuel, explosives, and chemical, biological or radiological substances/materials

(d) **Using Personal Protective Equipment (PPE)** – must be appropriate to the activity required and the conditions of the working environment. The time staff can be operational for is likely to be restricted by the type of PPE required. Staff must be trained and briefed about how to wear and use kit.

(e) **Rest Areas** – infection and cross-contamination within operational areas will be considerations, alongside the rotation and refreshing of staff and protecting them from the media and other attention.

PSYCHOLOGICAL RISK (STRESS and TRAUMA)

(a) Staff directly or indirectly engaged with the response ie site stabilisation, recovering the deceased, transporting equipment or bodies, or security staff.

(b) Casualty and survivors still at the site – separate Initial Reception Areas should be provided for these to be treated at the site or taken to hospital, or provision made for others to evacuate the site. This will make space for the process of identifying the deceased to begin.

(c) Families and the bereaved – will want fast access to victim information. Consideration should be given to establishing a Family and Friends Assistance centre at an early stage which will act as an initial focal point of information. This may later be followed by a Humanitarian Assistance Centre to provide longer-term information and support.

LOGISTICAL CONSIDERATIONS

(a) How many people is it safe to have on site and in certain areas for operation or other duties at any given time?

(b) How will staff/others be directed around the site, ie where to go and not to go?

(c) What vehicles/equipment are required on site and how will these be manoeuvred?

(d) Where should the entry/exit points for the incident site be and is there any need to close roads and redirect traffic?

Figure 9.2   List of potential risks to be considered

144

- *The Health and Safety Executive (HSE)* will be able to provide advice to those deployed to the site responsible for carrying out risk assessments.

9.5 RECOVERING THE DECEASED

The SERM will implement the policy decided as a result of negotiations between the SIO and the SIM and after authorisation of the Coroner or Fiscal. This will include the Search and Recovery Strategy (deceased victims, property and evidence) and incorporate strategies for forensic information gathering, the identification strategy and how the investigation of the incident should be carried out. Details such as a scene examination plan outlining the proposed victim recovery prioritisation (such as the pilot at an air disaster) and decisions on the recovery of fragmented remains/residual human tissue should be considered part of this process.

Boundary limitations and search areas should be identified, including a safe route into and out of the scene. This may include temporary walkways and physical barriers for the inner cordon, such as weld-mesh fencing. Consideration should be given to creating a forensic pathway into and out of the scene. This would be searched and cleared to facilitate a common approach path. All personnel entering the area must be authorised, briefed and equipped. They should also be fully trained, although, if correctly enforced, this policy would not allow other site visitors, such as VIPs, to attend. If access is authorised to such visitors, they must be escorted by trained staff at all times.

All personnel must be logged into and out of the cordon.

A clearly defined demarcation line between the "clean" and "dirty" areas should be established and decontamination/safe undressing procedures strictly applied. Suitable disposal of PPE/contaminated equipment will also be a priority.

An emergency evacuation procedure must be established and communicated by way of the initial site briefing.

An assessment of Victim Recovery Teams, Property Recovery Teams and search resources that are available and those that may be required will be made at this stage. It is possible that scenarios and priorities will change as new information and intelligence become available. Because of this, the decision-making process of determining and prioritising scenarios must be recorded and the whole process must constantly be reassessed to ensure the appropriate use of available resources and that the best strategy is being pursued.

It must be considered that a disaster can result in victims who may be severely traumatised, disrupted and/or burned. It would be a natural response for the dead to be recovered from the incident scene as soon as resources can be deployed away from the response to rescue the living. However, if the following procedures are not followed, this may lead to vital evidence being lost or destroyed:

- The overall Incident Commander (Gold) should consider that the Coroner or Fiscal, the supervising pathologist or other investigating agency (such as the AAIB[4] or the RAIB[5]) may wish to view the deceased *in situ*. Therefore, these authorities should be consulted before recovery of the deceased commences.

- Police DVI Teams will locate, document, recover and process the bodies of the deceased, which will be held at the site until suitable emergency mortuary reception and storage facilities are able to receive them. It is vital that only trained and fully briefed officers should be tasked to carry out such duties. The briefing will include the search and recovery strategy as well as the method statement (roles, responsibilities and the actual task methodology) in order to control residual risk.

- Until a medical practitioner has pronounced life extinct and the police body labelling endorsed, bodies of the deceased should not be moved or removed. In addition, no moving of bodies or removal from the scene will take place until the police have the consent of the Coroner or Fiscal. Generally, the only exception to this will be when it is necessary to preserve the dead from destruction or loss by fire or chemicals, or to rescue or provide medical treatment for trapped survivors. If it is necessary to move the deceased, where practicable the reasons should be documented, the body and its original position marked and, if possible, photographed, and any movement of the victim should be reported to the SERM to ensure continuity of evidence.

The pronouncing of life extinct does not always have to be declared on an individual basis by a doctor, especially regarding body parts. There is provision for this aspect to be pre-authorised by agreement with the Coroner or Procurator Fiscal, and provision for this is made in the Victim Recovery Label Booklet. In either case a supervising pathologist or lead medical practitioner can be present on site to assist.

Religious and cultural customs differ considerably throughout the world and this fact must be taken into account when planning the response to disaster scenarios. Experience proves that this factor is of particular relevance when dealing with the remains of the victims.

Each religious faith[7] and ethnic culture has its own considerations when dealing with the dead. It is not possible to list the requirements and expectations of each individual denomination or persuasion in this guide, but the importance of sensitivity and understanding when dealing with all victims should never be overlooked.

Nevertheless, religious and cultural considerations, however important in their own right, cannot be allowed to compromise the legal processes to which investigating agencies may be bound by law.

Deployment of police DVI Teams is not subject to any set criteria. Each incident will be examined and considered within its own circumstances. Incidents to which these teams are likely to be deployed fall under one or more of the following four broad definitions:

1. incidents with a number of fatalities for whom victim identification will be required – or where the number of fatalities is unknown;
2. incidents of mass fatalities where victim identification will be required and where the number of fatalities is thought to be high;
3. incidents where victims have been subject to physical trauma, disfigurement, amputation or fragmentation;
4. incidents where the recovery of the deceased is likely to prove a prolonged operation, for example if there is a problem with access when carrying out the physical recovery operation.

A record should be made of:

- the process that has been adopted and why – explaining why alternatives have not been pursued;
- actions taken as part of the victim recovery process; and
- views on the outcome and effectiveness of search and victim recovery in the short, medium and long term.

The decision concerning the formation and deployment of the police DVI Teams will be influenced by consideration of:

- health and safety of staff on site and those undertaking specific duties;
- evidential requirements;
- other influencing factors, for example involvement of other statutory investigators.

Police Victim Recovery Teams will normally consist of a minimum of five trained members. The team is likely to consist of one Team Leader (scribe), two Recovery Officers and two Safety Officers. There is an option for a trained photographer to be allocated as a further member of the team but this will depend on the scale of the incident and availability of assets etc:

- The scribe will complete the ACPO Victim Label Booklet. The scribe will remain clean, avoiding contamination of themselves or the paperwork throughout the process.
- Recovery officers will recover deceased victims or fragmented human remains, videoing the process (if this is to be done), and placing bodies or remains into appropriate body bags. These are smaller for fragments and full size for whole bodies.
- Safety officers will monitor the process to ensure the safety of the recovery officers – particularly in confined spaces and among debris – and, where appropriate, may assist with removing the dead after the recording process has been completed.

A forensic photographer, crime scene investigator, search adviser, property team leader and Scene Manager may also be deployed to work alongside the police Victim Search and Recovery Teams. It must be remembered that the police train specialist officers who undertake the duties of searching for and recovering the deceased. It is vital that only trained and fully briefed officers should be tasked to carry out such duties.

Selection of officers to undertake these duties is influenced by a number of factors including:

1. personal and professional circumstances;
2. physical and mental welfare;
3. availability of volunteers;
4. organisational, departmental and Basic Command Unit (BCU) support;
5. staff, team and organisational resilience – including the ability to sustain a response over a long period of time;
6. de-selection of staff for organisational or personal reasons, and the confidentiality of any decisions.

Recovery Teams will:

- identify and plot the position of the victim or remains for inclusion on an overall plan;
- arrange for the victim or remains to be examined by a doctor and forensic/crime scene officers as soon as possible:
- ensure that photographic evidence is obtained, showing the location of the victim or remains. Best practice will be:
  - the first photograph of each recovery should be the front cover of the ACPO Booklet, detailing the URN;
  - a wide shot – showing the location of the victim or remains;
  - a mid-shot – showing the location and point of reference if possible;
  - scribe completes the "body/fragments" label of the ACPO Victim Recovery Booklet which is then attached to the victim (upper arm if possible) by a recovery officer;
  - a close-up shot of the "body/fragment" label once attached, showing the URN;
- complete the "body/fragment" section of the ACPO Victim Recovery Booklet. The first photograph of each recovery should be the front cover of the ACPO Booklet;
- complete and detach the "bag" and "scene" sections of the booklet;
- attach the "body bag" section of the label to the exterior of the bag and photograph, showing the URN;
- at the scene, fix, by a stake or other means, this scene label, with URN uppermost, in order to indicate clearly the location from which the victim

was removed (fix near to the location of the head if possible) and photograph, showing the URN;

- place the victim or remains in a body bag;
- if possible, take a photograph showing all labels (victim/fragment, bag, scene) and URN *in situ* prior to zipping up the bag;
- seal the body bag (this is an option – see section 9.6.4 Transportation);
- ensure that each photograph taken shows the numbers on the victim or remains and that the bag and the scene label all bear the same URN;
- remove the victim to the Holding/Audit Area;
- complete and detach the small tear-off section and hand to the Holding/Audit Officer.

The location of the victim or remains may be plotted or recorded by GPS at this stage. Operations may be physically and psychologically demanding. Alongside health and safety and welfare considerations, there should also be a de-selection process to protect the organisation and officers undertaking duties. Risks and hazards associated with the process of victim search and recovery of the deceased are likely to include:

1. **Lifting weights**: precautions will need to be taken for manual handling, and stretchers, trolleys and body bags must be used appropriately.
2. **Exposure to body fluids**: suitable personal protective equipment (PPE) should be worn, and supervision may be required by specialists or medics
3. **Stress and trauma**: volunteer workers can offer practical support and occupational health advisers may be required on site. Plans for follow-up support for responders should be activated and services such as appropriate debriefing made available.
4. **Searching debris and handling unknown substances**: suitable PPE should be worn, liaison with other services will be required, and it may be necessary to withdraw operations until it is safe for workers to continue.
5. **Adverse working conditions** (these may include weather, lighting etc): control measures such as suitable PPE and clothing, regular breaks and suitable refreshments. Waterproof clothing, technical support (such as artificial heat or light), and withdrawing operations until it is safe to continue are all measures which should be considered.

More preparation time is likely to be required if the incident has occurred in a confined or difficult-to-access space; specialist advice from the Fire and Rescue Service should be sought as appropriate.

The factors which may create variations in recovery time will include: difficulties in locating the deceased; the need to remove wreckage or debris; and other hazards such as chemical spills.

Recovery will be conducted under the overall supervision of the SERM and carried out as part of a carefully documented process. In the UK, this process will use ACPO Victim Recovery Label Booklets, each bearing a URN. If deployed overseas, protocols agreed in the affected country will be adhered to, generally using the B section of the Interpol DVI form.

It is generally accepted police practice that the bodies of the deceased are not searched at the scene. A systematic and detailed search will take place by trained and equipped officers in the sterile environment of the mortuary. This position is based upon many years of experience and fulfils the need to maintain strict control of the identification process which, in turn, both avoids mistaken identifications and enables the police to provide families with accurate information at all stages of the identification process. It is essential that officers dealing with potentially bereaved families have a clear purpose and accurate information and are not put in a position where families may be inadvertently misled about a possible identification. While the identification process, including the recovery aspect, will always be a priority and needs to be dealt with as speedily as possible, it is vital to maintain the integrity of the overall process and minimise any opportunities for mistakes that may undermine confidence in both the identification of victims and the process itself.

Any deviation from the standard operating procedures of obtaining identification evidence only on arrival at the mortuary will be a matter for the SIM in consultation with the SIO. Any processes used to collect "identification intelligence" prior to a deceased victim being removed to the mortuary must be very carefully managed and controlled. If conducted, their primary purpose should be seen as an intelligence tool to speed up the deployment of Police Family Liaison Officers (FLOs)[8] and the subsequent collection of ante-mortem material to assist with the identification process.

9.5.1 Initial visual check

An initial visual check (IVC) provides a quick visual overview of a deceased victim and should locate any obvious material of relevance to the identification process. An IVC may be able to offer information to the SIM which would assist in the deployment of FLOs[8] and speed up the overall identification process. An IVC is restricted to what the officer can see without moving or exploring the victim's clothing etc.

If an item providing "identification intelligence" is accessible from the IVC and is attached to the victim (for example photographic ID on a lanyard) it should *not* be removed, but photographed *in situ* and full details recorded in the Victim Recovery Booklet. A process should be in place for this information to be fast tracked to the Casualty Bureau Identification Cell.

If circumstances dictate, a policy decision may be made to continue the IVC further, for example a simple look for the first item of identification information or documentation by patting the pockets of an outer garment (see "Group 2 property" below). It does *not* consist of a search, as all items of clothing and associated property will be thoroughly and systematically removed and searched by trained officers at the mortuary. It is also important to consider the health and safety implications for using more intrusive techniques at the scene, such as sharps, blood, pathogens, toxins and fuel contaminants.

An IVC is *not* to provide proof of identification, but again may assist the SIM in the deployment of FLOs at an early stage.

If an item has been located and removed for checking, for example a passport from an outer jacket pocket, a detailed record of the document should be made in the VRI (Victim Recovery Identification) Scene Notes section of the ACPO Booklet. This should also include a full description of the original location of the item. The item should then be placed in a clear property bag and physically attached to the deceased, if possible near to the Victim Recovery Label. A photographic record of the process should be made.

Whatever strategy is employed, it is vitally important that DVRI team members are provided with a comprehensive briefing on the agreed process, prior to deployment.

The SIM, in consultation with the SIO and the SERM, will establish a protocol to ensure that any "identification intelligence" recovered from the scene is processed without delay and all necessary and appropriate action is taken. The FLO should not be deployed unless appropriately authorised and properly briefed.

9.6   DVRI PROCESS

9.6.1   Search and separate recovery

The recovery of the human remains is also an evidence recovery process which will be conducted by appropriately trained police personnel. There may be incidents involving large-scale or wide area searches (Lockerbie, for example) where simultaneous search and recovery operations may be impractical for the entire operation. It may be necessary in such circumstances to seek wider support. If a non-DVRI search team is utilised (police, military or civilian), consideration should be given to allocating a trained officer to each team, area or sector. If utilised, the team must be fully briefed and comply with the DVI recovery procedure as outlined above.

The health, safety and welfare of staff conducting this work are paramount. Staff must wear PPE as deemed necessary by the ongoing risk assessment.

Strict procedures must be adhered to, in order to ensure decontamination, removal and disposal of PPE upon leaving the designated area.

It is important to emphasise that for reasons such as safety of staff, accuracy of the identification procedure and integrity of evidence, the process of victim recovery cannot be rushed.

9.6.2   Victim Holding/Audit Area

A Victim Holding/Audit Area (HAA) should ideally be set up prior to any recovery being undertaken. A Holding Audit Team should be established and consist of four DVI trained officers. Once the deceased has been recovered, and before they are transported to the emergency mortuary, they will be held in this area. The main purpose of this facility is to provide quality assurance, ensuring that all relevant documentation is accurate and complete prior to transfer to the mortuary. Portable structures have been used for this function with success in the past.

A Holding Audit Team should be established and should consist of four DVI trained officers, at least one of whom should have experience in handling and processing exhibits. A written log of all victims and remains recovered from the scene will be maintained, ensuring that these are placed in a suitable order for transfer to the mortuary. All movements will be carefully recorded so as to maintain an audit trail for the whole process.

A record will be made in the Holding Audit Area Log of details such as sector/grid, URN of body/fragment and receiving officer.

The Victim Recovery Co-ordinator will ensure that a record is maintained for Recovery Team members, time deployed, welfare breaks etc.

If the strategy dictates use of the initial visual check option, a record will also be made including the URN assigned to the remains, full details of possible identity documents found and details of the officer receiving that information at the Casualty Bureau Identification Cell. All paperwork, including entries made in the Victim Recovery Label Booklet, will be checked at the Audit Area. The booklet will then be placed in a clear bag and will accompany the relevant body bag to the mortuary.

It will be for the police to determine – in conjunction with the Coroner/Fiscal and supervising pathologist – whether body storage in the audit area should be refrigerated. A decision will depend on the condition of the remains and the time it might take from recovery to transportation of the deceased to the emergency mortuary. Depending on the type of emergency mortuary, it may take between 24 and 48 hours to become fully operational. If a demountable structure is to be used, however, the reception and storage sections could be operational far sooner. It must be remembered that the Victim HAA is not a substitute for an emergency mortuary. It will not be used to search bodies, save in the exceptional circumstances outlined above. Medical examinations will be carried out only at the emergency mortuary.

However, a direct and secure communication link should be established between the Audit Area and the Casualty Bureau. This link can be used to provide early intelligence from the scene and may assist in the identification/investigation process.

The location of a victim HAA will be subject to variable factors – the number of dead; the location and scale of the incident itself; and the resources available.

Necessary resources include: the structure itself; equipment to configure it (such as racking); a laptop computer with printer; and digital photographic printer, and police officers to operate it and keep the facility secure. It is important for the location to be on or close to the incident site, since the task of moving the deceased will be both physically and psychologically demanding. The area should have suitable access points for vehicles collecting the deceased, and it should be screened to avoid media and public exposure.

9.6.3 Treatment of personal property

In the aftermath of an emergency, many items of personal property will be found at the site of the incident, nearby or even some distance away. Some of these may have become separated from their owners – others may still be on or with those who have died.

Property found on a body should not be removed. If an item (such as a watch) falls from the victim during the recovery process it should be placed in a separate plastic bag and then in the same body bag as the deceased. The circumstances should always be recorded in the ACPO Booklet. Mobile phones and other property of potential importance to the investigation or identification process should not be ignored or left where they may be accidentally damaged. Such items should be brought to the attention of the SERM for a policy decision on recovery.

Other property will be left *in situ* for Police Property Recovery Teams. The make-up of these teams will be determined by the circumstances and the extent to which recovery of personal property is required for evidential or identification purposes.

Personal property recovered should be documented, the position in which it was found should be plotted and the item given a URN. It may also be photographed *in situ*. Items are then temporarily stored at a Property Audit Area located near the Victim HAA before being transported to a secure location determined by the police – the emergency mortuary may be one (but not the only) option.

It is possible that personal property found could belong to: the deceased; casualties; survivors; suspects; or those attending the scene to respond to the emergency, so no assumptions should be made about ownership of property.

Personal property is important for a number of reasons. It may provide invaluable supporting evidence to the identification process, potentially locating a person in the area at the time the incident occurred. It may support the investigation process by leading to the identification of the perpetrator(s) if criminal activity is suspected. Finally, personal property will be of importance to families.

"Technical property" is that which might assist in establishing the cause of the incident. It should not be removed or disturbed without consultation with the police SERM.

Personal property will broadly fall within two groups:

153

- *Group One*: property which is readily identifiable and can be matched to an identified person whose cause of death has been confirmed by the Coroner or Fiscal. Such items include possessions with a clearly identifiable name on them, such as passports, bank or credit cards or cheque books. Other items, such as mobile phones or laptops (with contact lists or photographic/video imaging equipment) or uniquely identifiable jewellery, also fall within this group.

- *Group Two*: property which cannot immediately be allocated to an identified person whose cause of death has been confirmed by the Coroner or Fiscal. Such items include possessions that we all might carry on a day-to-day basis – books, paperwork, luggage, toys etc. Also included are those items that can only be attributed to a business or other organisation.

Ownership needs to be confirmed by a police or other appropriate authority. Efforts are likely to focus on the items classed in *Group One*. Where relevant, property recovered will be kept in secure storage either at the emergency mortuary or elsewhere – the police will determine the best location as dictated by the incident and the likely volume of property that might be recovered.

For advice concerning the return of property, see Home Office publication "Guidance On Dealing with Fatalities in Emergencies".[9]

Technical and evidential property is that which might assist the investigation in establishing the cause of the incident. As such, it should not be removed or disturbed without consultation with the police, forensic adviser and any technical specialist adviser such as AAIB,[4] RAIB[5] or MAIB.[6]

In cases of suspected terrorist attacks, the SIO must be consulted prior to commencing the victim search and recovery operation – in addition to the mortuary process.

9.6.4 Transportation

The police, in conjunction with the lead Coroner/Fiscal, will organise transport arrangements for taking the recovered deceased to the emergency mortuary. Any decisions will need to be based on risk assessment and this should identify all the hazards and suggest suitable control measures for:

1. collecting the bodies at the site;
2. the journey to the emergency mortuary;
3. reception arrangements at the emergency mortuary.

Treating the deceased with dignity and families with respect

Recent experience of emergencies has demonstrated that media coverage of events will be broadcast simultaneously as the operation is underway. Therefore, it is recommended that a secure and screened area on site and at the mortuary should be allocated for body collection and reception.

Investigation and identification requirements

Preservation of the bodies for the purposes of any criminal investigation may be the key to finding the perpetrators. Equally, if mistakes are made during the transportation of bodies this could have a major impact on the identification process. It is important to establish and maintain continuity throughout the process. Good practice dictates that deceased victims should be accompanied by the police transportation officer during any periods in transit and accurate records kept. The relevant ACPO Victim Recovery Booklet will be signed by the mortuary reception officer and the carbon copies taken out and returned to the Holding/Audit Area by the transportation officer for continuity. Consideration may be given to sealing the body bag with a uniquely numbered tamper-proof seal, prior to transportation from the scene. If this option is used, due care should be exercised as a further number will be injected into the recovery process. The procedure should be photographed and a reference made to the seal and number in the ACPO Victim Recovery Booklet. It should be noted there may also be evidential considerations that reinforce the importance of this aspect. In respect of suspected terrorist incidents all arrangements for the removal and storage of victims must also be agreed by the SIO.

The importance of a comprehensive briefing prior to deployment has been mentioned. Equally, the importance of de-briefing cannot be over-emphasised and should always be included as part of the DVRI strategy.

Prior to the conclusion of the victim recovery phase, a final sweep of the area for any remains, equipment or any other items that may have been left should be carried out. It may be of benefit to utilise the assistance of specialist police dogs trained in the detection and location of human remains.

BIBLIOGRAPHY

For more detailed information on search techniques, please refer to the ACPO guide "Practical Advice on Search Management and Procedures" (2006).

For further information, please refer to:

- Interpol DVI Manual;
- "Guidance on Dealing with Fatalities in Emergencies";[9]
- Guidance on Development of a Site Clearance Capability in England and Wales;[10]
- ACPO Emergency Procedures Manual;
- Murder Investigation Manual;
- Search Management and Procedures Manual.

REFERENCES

1 Health and Safety Executive [online]. Available at: http://www.hse.gov.uk/. [Accessed: 14.11.2007.]

2 Coroner [online]. Available at: http://www.coronersociety.org.uk/. [Accessed: 14.11.2007.]

3 Procurator Fiscal [online]. Available at: http://www.crownoffice.gov.uk/. [Accessed: 14.11.2007.]

4 Air Accident Investigation Branch website [online]. Available at: http://www.aaib.dft.gov.uk/home/index.cfm. [Accessed: 14.11.2007.]

5 Rail Accident Investigation Branch website [online]. Available at: http://www.raib.gov.uk/home/index.cfm. [Accessed: 14.11.2007.]

6 Marine Accident Investigation Branch website [online]. Available at: http://www.maib.gov.uk/home/index.cfm. [Accessed: 29.11.2007.]

7 Home Office and Cabinet Office, "The Needs of Faith Communities in Major Emergencies" (2005) (HMSO) [online]. Available at: http://security.homeoffice.gov.uk/news-publications/publication-search/guidance-disasters/faith-communities?view=Binary. [Accessed: 14.11.2007.]

8 Association of Chief Police Officers, ACPO Family Liaison Strategy (2000) [online]. Available at: hww.acpo.police.uk/asp/policies/Data/family_liaison_strategy.doc. [Accessed 21.05.2008.]

9 Home Office and Cabinet Office, "Guidance on dealing with Fatalities in Emergencies" (HMSO) [online]. Available at: http://www.ukresilience.info/upload/assets/www.ukresilience.info/fatalities.pdf. [Accessed: 14.11.2007.]

10 Office of the Deputy Prime Minister, "Guidance on Development of a Site Clearance Capability in England and Wales" (2005) (HMSO) [online]. Available at: http://www.communities.gov.uk/publications/fire/guidancedevelopment. [Accessed: 29.1.2007.]

SUGGESTED KIT AND EQUIPMENT LIST FOR DVRI TEAMS

Requirements will vary depending on a variety of factors such as the type of incident, the location and the weather.

Reference should also be made to the Health and Safety at Work Act 1974 which outlines the duties of employers and employees. It also includes Regulations relevant to DVRI, such as manual handling, safe systems of work, use of tools and any other apparatus for work. In particular, the Personal Protective Equipment Regulations 1992 includes all equipment which is intended to be worn or held by a person at work, and which protects them against one or more risks to their health and safety. The PPE Regulations include guidance on:

- the provision and suitability of equipment;
- compatibility;
- suitability assessment;

- maintenance
- accommodation/storage;
- information, instruction and training;
- correct use of PPE and reporting of defective PPE procedures.

PPE

Head protection (various types from basic safety hats to approved Fire and
    Rescue type)
Face masks (various types from dust protection to full-face respiratory
    protection)
Eye protectors/Safety goggles/glasses
Ear defenders
Disposable suits/coveralls
Disposable gloves
Heavy-duty rubber gloves
Rigger gloves
Safety gloves
Safety boots (Recommended CE Safety Standard for protection against impact,
    penetration, water absorption and static)
Safety wellingtons
Multi-purpose tool, including knife
Intrinsically safe flashlight
Wet-weather jacket and over-trousers
Identity armband or similar
Rucksack

SITE EQUIPMENT

ACPO VR Label Booklets
Interpol DVI Forms
ACPO VPF Forms

First aid/medical equipment
Decontamination equipment: buckets, bowls, footbaths, water, cleaning fluids,
    chairs, tables, matting, antiseptic wipes
Body bags (medium-weight to extra-heavy-weight with pouch for VR Label)
Disaster pouches (various sizes)
Viscera bags
Large heavy-duty plastic sheets
Bio-hazard bags
Body and property stakes/poles (metal and wood)
Stretchers

Police tape
Masking tape
Clipboards (including weather-proof type)
Compass, tape measure, ruler
Pens, marker pens, pencils, safety lamps, spray paint (various), GPS System
Digital camera
Video camera
Waste bags
Contaminated waste bags
Cordon access control kit/ID cards
Laptop computer and digital photographic printer (for use at the Holding/Audit Area)
Various tools (eg hammers, shovels, garden rakes and trowels)
Radio communications
Some forces have purpose-built trailers with generators, lighting and inflatable tents. These can be located at the cordon control and/or Body Holding/Audit Area.

DOCUMENTATION/ADMIN

Identity bracelets
Exhibit logs
Exhibit labels
Exhibit bags (various)
Policy logs
Incident/message forms

Tape, scissors, string, stapler and staples, tape measure, bulldog clips, sticky labels, plastic folders and sleeves, hole punch, envelopes (various), portable white boards, cleaners and pens.

WELFARE

- Washing facilities (with hot water).
- Shelter, ideally out of sight of scene, with food and drink.
- Adequate supplies of personal protective clothing and appropriate advice/support if required.

CHAPTER 10

The Anatomical Pathology Technologist (APT)

10.1 INTRODUCTION

Anatomical pathology technologists (APTs) are professional staff who work in mortuary/post-mortem departments throughout the UK. APTs either work in NHS Trust Hospitals or are employed by local authorities in public mortuaries.

An APT's primary role is to provide assistance to pathologists and other scientific/medical professionals in conducting post-mortem examinations. Post-mortem work is varied, depending on the facilities available and service user requirements.

The range of post mortems carried out includes:

- HM Coroner's post mortem;
- hospital post mortem;
- forensic post mortem;
- paediatric post mortem.

APTs liaise with a range of people including pathologists, doctors, police officers, funeral directors, bereaved families, transplant co-ordinators, nursing staff, trust chaplaincy and other religious faith leaders.

Other responsibilities or duties of an APT may include:

- management of the mortuary services and the post-mortem room;
- ensuring that equipment and instruments are working and kept clean, disinfected and ready for use;
- taking samples for clinical examination (for example, toxicology or histology);
- ensuring continuity in identification of deceased from hospital wards or the community;
- maintaining accurate records of valuables and property belonging to the deceased;
- ensuring that legal documentation is dealt with correctly;
- conducting viewings for families;
- enucleation of eyes for corneal grafts.[1]

159

10.2   ENTRY REQUIREMENTS

There are currently no minimum qualifications for trainee APTs, although hospitals will often look for some evidence of knowledge in science, and a range of GCSEs may be beneficial. Many trainees already have a background in working within the healthcare sector.

10.3   TRAINING

Trainees start their training with a short period of observing an experienced APT and asking questions, followed by direct involvement in work, under the supervision of pathologists and experienced APTs. During the training they will carry out practical tests, which are recorded in a practical assessment book and signed, upon satisfactory completion, by an experienced APT or consultant pathologist They are then able to attend teaching sessions on a course designed by the Royal Institute of Public Health and Hygiene (RIPHH).[2] The teaching will involve either day release or some block release time at a centre, which provides a more intensive 2-week residential course.

Topics covered include:

- Anatomy and Physiology;
- Post-Mortem Examination Techniques;
- Health and Hygiene;
- Hazards and Precautions;
- Legislation and Codes of Practice;
- Administration and Documentation.

Trainees usually finish the course within a period of 2 years. At this point they will be eligible to sit a combined written and oral examination, leading to the RIPHH Certificate in Anatomical Pathology Technology.

Once certificate qualified, APTs are encouraged to undertake a further study period of 2 years, leading to a diploma awarded by the RIPHH. This diploma enables APTs to continue their careers into advanced technical work or management.

10.4   THE FUTURE FOR APTs

APTs are currently undergoing various transformations regarding their professional status, most notably the future regulation of the profession with the Health Professions Council (HPC)[3] by 2009.

As a result of this, and to meet the requirements of the HPC, all APTs will be required to become involved with Knowledge Skills Framework (KSF), and Continuing Professional Development (CPD).

There is a professional organisation specifically for APTs: the Association of Anatomical Pathology Technologists (AAPT).[4] This organisation is supported by the Royal College of Pathologists,[5] the Institute of Biomedical Science[6] and the RIPHH.[2]

10.5 THE ROLE OF THE APT IN A MAJOR DISASTER

The following information has been compiled to assist APTs, the police and DVI teams to understand their role and interactions during the conception and running of a resilience mortuary in the event of a "major incident".

10.5.1 "Major incidents"

A "major incident" can be defined as any incident where the local facilities cannot cope with the numbers or types of victim generated by the incident.

The initiation of a resilience mortuary will be decided jointly by the Coroner, the police and the manager of the local mortuary facilities.

Once the decision is made to set up a resilience mortuary, staff for the facility will obviously have to be brought in from outside the local area. Police staff will be provided, usually by mutual aid, from other police forces throughout the UK and possibly by envoking UK DVI; non-police staff will often be provided by the Centre for International Forensic Assistance (CIFA).[7]

APTs are skilled in dealing with the deceased, in handling, preparation and reconstruction, as well as being conversant with the health and safety aspects and risks associated with the dead. Their knowledge is vital in the safe running of the mortuary, and even more so in the resilience mortuary as there will be many staff unfamiliar with the problems usually encountered there.

APTs will advise and assist in the initial layout of the temporary mortuary, which will include the marking out of demarcation areas. These are the colour-coded zones designated as "clean" (green), "transitional" (yellow), and "dirty/wet" (red) areas.

10.5.2 Police staff

During the response to the incident, the police will be tasked with the investigation of the incident and the identification of the victims. The officer in charge of the investigation – the Senior Investigating Officer (SIO) – will work alongside the Senior Identification Manager (SIM), the Coroner and the lead pathologist to ascertain who the victims are and how they came by their deaths. This will include the gathering of evidential material in an effort to conclude the investigation.

10.5.3   Mortuary admission

Every body or body part will be labelled at the scene by the Victim Recovery Identification Team, using the labels contained within the ACPO Victim Label Booklet. Each booklet and set of labels has a unique reference number (URN) which is eight digits long. One label is attached to the body/part, a scene label is left at the point of the find (towards the head end of the body), another attached to the outside of the body bag and the last label goes to the holding area/audit control point.

The booklet from which the URN is obtained also contains a scene note and a list of the recovery team, general descriptions of the body/fragment, information about the scene and a space for an instant photograph.

A rough sketch plan of where the body or part was recovered from within the sector and several free-text sections for notes are also included. The last page in the booklet is a continuity section giving an audit trail of the body movements from scene to holding area/audit control point, collection and transport from the holding area/audit control point and details of it being received in the mortuary. These are carbon copies and the back (orange) copies are returned to the audit control point and reconciled with the audit label, following delivery of the body/part to the mortuary. At the back of the booklet are pages of barcode labels which can be used for continuity and labelling of all items removed from the body/part and for all paperwork generated throughout the mortuary process.

10.5.4   Arrival at the resilience mortuary

Once the body or body part has been transported from the body holding area to the resilience mortuary, all external bag label numbers are checked with their ACPO booklets and are booked into a mortuary register log. This consists of a Word document with the following details: URN; date and time received; name and signature of person receiving, location of body/part in store; and the name, date, time and signature of the person taking the body/part into the mortuary/examination process.

The body is allocated a unique waterproof folder with a booklet of Interpol DVI forms[8] for the next stage in the process.

Once the body or part is in the system, a body movement log will be started.

10.5.5   Body movements

Throughout the mortuary process, every deceased individual is logged via an audit trail or "body movement log": this allows the police mortuary manager to know where every body is during the process. A wall log, blackboard or whiteboard is usually used as a visual aid.

This log is started on delivery of the body to the mortuary by the receiving officer. All subsequent movements of the body are entered on the log sheet; this will include entry into the post-mortem process, fluoroscopy, fingerprinting, reconstruction, viewing etc. Multiple entries will necessitate extra copies of the log; a bar-code label is attached to the bottom right-hand corner and the total number of log sheets entered at the top.

The body number must be completed at the top of the form; this is the last six digits of the ACPO victim label. The suffix of "A" or "B" is added if there is more than half of the body (A) or less than half of the body (B). Therefore all intact bodies will be suffixed with an "A", as will incidences where more than half of the remains of the individual are present. Smaller body fragments will be suffixed with a "B".

The body or body part to be transferred for examination is checked to ensure that all information is correct and is signed out of the body store by the transferring officers. The waterproof pouch containing all the necessary documentation stays with the body throughout the rest of the processes.

10.6   DVI FORMS

The police teams work to an internationally recognised system of identification paperwork: the Interpol DVI forms.[8] These are complicated, convoluted data-set forms, which can be sifted manually or by computer to match (ie be reconciled with) ante-mortem data obtained from families of the missing/deceased.

Post-mortem (PM) forms are pink in colour and sectioned: identical in format to the Ante-mortem (AM) forms, which are yellow in colour, to ease comparison.

The PM forms are laid out as follows:

1. Five preliminary pages:
    - **B0**: a checklist of operations within the mortuary (photography, finger-prints, autopsy, dental examination, samples);
    - **B**: the scene note;
    - **C1**: listing of clothing and footwear;
    - **C2**: list of personal effects;
    - **C3**: list of jewellery.

2. Four pages to give a physical description of the deceased:
    - **D1**: includes the state of the body, estimated age, height, weight, build, race and head hair type/description;
    - **D2**: description of forehead, eyebrows, eyes, nose, facial hair, ears, mouth, lips, teeth and smoking habits;
    - **D3**: description of chin, neck, hands, feet, body hair, pubic hair, specific details (including, scars, marks, tattoos, malformations and amputations) circumcision and "other peculiarities");

- **D4**: a body sketch map on which to annotate damage, burnt, decomposed, skeletonised, missing or loose body parts, scars, piercings, skin marks, tattoo marks, malformations and amputations.

3. Four forms to list details of the Autopsy

4. Four pages to give a medical history/description of the deceased:
   - **E1**: internal examination: head, chest, abdomen, other internal organs, skeleton/soft tissue and "various" (pregnancy, healed fractures, operations, artificial appliances (eg pacemaker, hip prosthesis etc);
   - **E2**: medical conclusion, sex, estimated age, a list of samples taken, "other clues to identification" and other medical findings;
   - **E3**: diagrammatic skeleton map;
   - **E4**: DNA sample and DNA profile.

5. Two forms to list a dental examination:
   - **F1**: dental findings, "in single cases", material present (jaws, fragmentary remains, single teeth, other), supplementary details;
   - **F2**: dental findings including a dental chart, specific descriptions (crowns, bridges, dentures and implants), further findings (occlusion, attrition, anomalies, smoker, periodontal status etc), X-rays, supplementary examination and estimated age.

6. Further information form:
   - **G**: used to explain data given on previous pages if there is insufficient space available on that page (cross-referenced using item number).

Familiarise yourself with a form now!

Visit the Interpol website[8]

Remember: the forms are printed out on pink paper, and so do not appear pink on screen!

10.7 ASSISTANCE FROM THE APT

As a specialist in most disciplines within the mortuary environment, the APT will be required to assist with body handling, strip and search, medical terminology, health and safety, the well being of staff, risk assessments and the post-mortem examination process.

The appointed Mortuary Facilities Manager (an experienced APT in major incident/disaster situations) and senior APTs will also be expected to take part in any meetings organised by the DVI commanders, so that any relevant information can be passed on to colleagues.

APTs may be requested to assist the pathologist, the Mortuary Facilities Manager, the radiographer, the odontologist, the anthropologist, the fingerprinting specialist and/or with reconstruction, viewings, embalming, encoffining and repatriation.

10.7.1   The APT and the Mortuary Facilities Manager

The APT will work with the appointed Mortuary Facilities Manager to ensure that:

- logistical support is maintained throughout the resilience mortuary;
- all personnel strictly adhere to all relevant health and safety legislation;
- all appropriate hygiene practices are employed (including wet/dry area discipline);
- clinical waste is properly handled, stored and disposed of;
- all parts of the mortuary are properly cleaned; and
- the mortuary facility is decommissioned properly (including all necessary cleansing and repairs are undertaken in advance).

10.7.2   The APT and the pathologist

The APT will prepare the post-mortem room prior to any examinations being carried out. This includes ensuring that:

- all clinical waste bags are in place;
- all the instruments required for the examination are laid out, ready for use;
- any electrical equipment used is working and in a good state of repair;
- sufficient disinfectants, basins, sponges and general cleaning materials are available;
- sufficient PPE is available;
- there are adequate local hand-washing facilities, with clean paper towels for drying hands.

In each autopsy area, a wall log, blackboard or whiteboard is normally used as a visible record of who is involved and which part of the examination process has been completed. The APTs will attach, maintain and update the workflow chart as and when necessary.

In the autopsy suite, the APT assists the pathologist in examining the body with the aim of discovering the cause of death:

- The APT assists the pathologist in an external examination of the body, and helps to take samples of tissue for further analysis.

- On instructions from the forensic pathologist, the APT may also be required to eviscerate the body or to carry out specialist techniques.
- After the examination the APT's responsibility is (on the authority of the Coroner) to reconstitute the body to an acceptable level, for health and safety reasons and for the family to be able to view the deceased.
- The APT is also responsible for ensuring that any samples or specimens retained are placed into the correct containers, and that adequate storage is available until they can be transported for analysis.
- All maintenance of equipment and instruments used during the post-mortem examination is the responsibility of the APT.
- The APT must be fully conversant with the potential safety hazards while working in the resilience mortuary, particularly the risks of infection from those who have been identified as having a communicable disease.

Implanted pacemakers, defibrillators and loop recorders

A variety of implanted surgical prostheses may aid the identification of a disaster victim; most have a unique serial number which can be traced back via the manufacturer to the implanting centre, and therefore possibly the deceased's medical record and identity.

Cardiac pacemakers

Implanted under the skin of the chest wall, usually on the left-hand side of the body, cardiac pacemakers come in a variety of shapes and sizes.

Standard cardiac pacemakers (see Figure 10.1) can be identified by the lettering on the casing: this is "SSI(R)", "VVI(R)", "AAI(R)", "DDD(R)", "VDD(R)" or "VDR(R)". They may have one or more wire leads going into the heart.

Defibrillator pacemakers

Larger in size than the standard cardiac pacemaker, the implantable cardioverter defibrillator (ICD) (see Figure 10.1) can pose a threat to the pathologist or the APT if the leads are cut or interrupted, as they are designed to shock an arrhythmic heart. They must be deactivated by a cardiac technician prior to removal.

These can be identified by the lettering on the casing: this is "DDDD" or "DDDCD".

They usually have four wire leads going into the heart.

Loop recorders

These are small, wireless implanted information recorders (see Figure 10.1). They are placed under the skin of the chest wall, in a similar position to cardiac and defibrillator pacemakers and monitor and record the heart rate, beat and rhythm. They pose no threat to the remover.

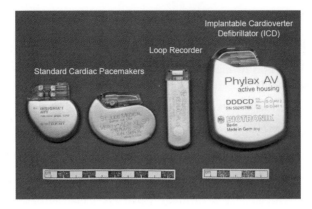

*Figure 10.1   Cardiac pacemakers, a loop recorder and an ICD, to show the
size differences among them*

Pacemakers, defibrillators and loop recorders

Each of these implants is slightly different in size and shape to the others:
defibrillators are two or three times thicker than standard pacemakers and loop
recorders.

10.7.3   The APT and the anthropologist

The anthropologist examines skeletal remains for identification purposes, or may
be requested by the pathologist to examine a particular structure during the post-
mortem examination.

The APT can assist the anthropologist by recording all matters (as directed
by the anthropologist) on the approved post-mortem documentation and passing
this information into the formal possession of the Mortuary Documentation
Officer.

APTs can also assist the anthropologist in laying out skeletal remains, or
carrying out dissection of any remaining soft tissue, and cleaning the bones for
further examination.

10.7.4   The APT and the odontologist

The odontologist may require access to the teeth for charting or radiographic
examination. Difficulties may arise if the body is in *rigor mortis*. The APT can
assist the odontologist by performing a facial dissection or jaw re-section in
a dignified and professional manner, to expose the dental structure so that the
odontologist can examine the teeth effectively.

These procedures are carried out as follows:

**Note: Authority from HM Coroner or the Procurator Fiscal must be
obtained before carrying out these procedures.**

167

Viewable bodies

Restricted opening due to *rigor mortis* may require:

- intra-oral incision of masticatory muscles, with or without fracture of the mandibular condyles;
- breaking the *rigor* with bilateral leverage of the jaws in the retro-molar regions;
- waiting until the *rigor* subsides;
- infra-mandibular dissection, with or without mandibular resection.

Removal of the larynx and tongue at autopsy may facilitate dental charting and radiographic examination. Careful dissection of the incinerated head, in particular, is required to preserve fragile tooth structure and jaws *in situ*. Ideally, radiographs should be made prior to manipulation of badly burned fragments; stabilisation of such tissue should be instituted where necessary.

Preservation of evidence

Jaw resection may be required for cases in which body parts are to be transferred, with proper authorisation, to other facilities for additional examination and testing.

Facial dissection: infra-mandibular approach

- Bilateral incisions are made across the upper anterior neck and extended to points posterior and inferior to the ears.
- The skin and underlying tissues are then reflected upward over the lower face, thereby exposing the mandible.
- The tissues can also be reflected back far enough to expose the maxilla, which better exposes the upper and lower teeth for photographic and radiographic purposes. (See Figure 10.2.)

Jaw resection: electric oscillating saw method

- The soft tissue and muscle attachments on the lateral aspect of the mandible are dissected away by incisions which extend through the muco–buccal fold to the lower border of the mandible.
- Lingual attachments are similarly incised to include the internal pterygoid attachments to the medial aspect of the rami and the masseter attachments on the lateral aspect.
- On the maxilla, facial attachments are incised high on the malar processes and superior to the anterior nasal spine.

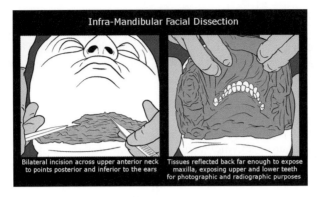

Figure 10.2   Infra-mandibular facial dissection

- Oscillating saw cuts are made high on the mandibular rami to avoid possible impacted third molars. (Alternatively, the mandible may be removed by disarticulation at the temporo-mandibular joint (TMJ).)
- Bony cuts on the maxilla are made high on the malar processes and above the anterior nasal spine to avoid the apices of the maxillary teeth.
- A surgical mallet and chisel inserted into the saw cuts in the malar processes and above the anterior nasal spine are used to complete the separation of the maxilla.
- Remaining soft tissues in the soft palate and fauces are then dissected free. (See Figure 10.3.)

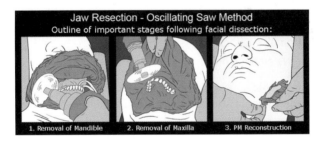

Figure 10.3   Jaw resection: oscillating saw method

Reconstruction of facial dissection and jaw resection

It is important to ensure that the maxilla and mandible are replaced *in situ* as this ensures that any future examination of the teeth is not hindered by first having to locate the dentition within the body bag.

The maxilla and the mandible can be replaced following examination. The face is then reconstructed in the normal manner as per forensic post-mortem procedure.

169

If it is impractical to suture the maxilla and mandible back into place (for example, if the body is decomposed) then they should be placed into a suitable clear plastic bag which has been clearly marked with the URN. This bag should then be attached securely to the head area, using plastic cable ties. All loose teeth should also be placed into this bag.

10.8 SUMMARY

The APT is the hub of activities within the mortuary environment. The knowledge, skills and experience of the APT will be drawn upon by all staff; their input is invaluable and vital to the safe and effective running of the resilience mortuary.

There follow details of some of the main roles of the APT:

1. involvement in strip and search of the remains;
2. health and safety responsibilities, including infection control and manual handling.

10.9 INVOLVEMENT IN STRIP AND SEARCH

One of the first activities to occur when the deceased enters the temporary mortuary is the undressing of the body. To ensure that this procedure is carried out effectively, the following procedure is recommended.

10.9.1 Training requirements

"On-the-job" training under the supervision of an experienced APT.

10.9.2 Protective clothing (PPE)

Gloves and disposable aprons must be worn when handling the deceased. Other protective clothing should also be available and used as and when required.

10.9.3 Policy

- Manual handling policy and procedure.
- Manual handling risk assessment.
- Infection control policy.

A minimum of two people should be used for the removal of clothing from the deceased.

Clothing should be removed methodically: normally starting at the top of the body and working downwards. APTs have considerable experience in this process, and will be able to demonstrate and advise on the best method.

All removed clothing is then handed to the relevant DVI officers so that it can be searched thoroughly for any belongings, and moved on to the next stage in the DVI proceedings, ie photography.

Please note: It is important that this seemingly simple task is carried out with dignity, care and respect for the deceased at all times.

10.9.4 Procedure

Remember photographs at each stage, if appropriate, with URN and scale in frame. Once the body has entered the mortuary process, the bag can be opened. The bag label URN must be checked with the body/fragment label URN and confirmed to be a match. A brief observation of the inside of the body bag should be made for any extra "non-attached" parts or loose property; these should be dealt with immediately, then:

- a cursory "pat down" of the deceased should be undertaken to identify possible hazards or property;
- pockets should be carefully inspected, using forceps, if required, to ensure that no sharp objects exist (if possible, remove hazards first: alert your team to the hazard);
- any obvious and easy way to get to property should be used, for example a wallet etc should be removed to aid a speedy identification (flag up to the Mortuary Operations Manager of an imminent potential identification, eg photo driving licence, passport etc).

Clothing should be removed "from top to toe". Remove in the following order, if present:

- hat/headwear;
- glasses (check for contact lenses or glass eye);
- earrings, nose studs/rings, lip/face piercings;
- necklaces, neck jewellery (remember to undo clasp and remove chain from behind head, holding both ends of the chain at the same time, to retain any pendant);
- upper garments should then be removed – with assistance from the APT if possible.

If no APT is present, the following technique should be used for all items of *upper* clothing:

- undo any buttons or zips on the garment;
- hold the right hand of the deceased;
- bend arm at elbow (to "break" *rigor*);
- flex arm at shoulder and extend arm away from centre of body;

- bend at elbow again and raise point of bent elbow towards the middle of the body;
- with the arm still raised, grasp the right lower edge of the top garment (towards the hip);
- pull up on the lower edge, the examiner working their fingers up the inside of the arm, towards the armpit;
- carefully work the garment edge over the point of the elbow;
- push the elbow away and the arm backwards, down the sleeve;
- remove the hand from the sleeve;
- pull the front of the garment up (if not already open, unbuttoned etc);
- pull the back of the garment up:
  - if unbuttoned/unzipped:
    - simply slide garment under the head;
    - slide garment across to the left and down the left arm and off the hand;
  - if no buttons or zip (ie pullover etc):
    - grasp the right side of the, now semi-rolled, shoulder of the garment;
    - pull over the right side of the head;
    - work hand around the neck of the garment, freeing it over the head
    - pull garment across the left shoulder, down the back and left arm and over the hand.

For *lower* clothing, including trousers, skirts etc:

- remove footwear (boots, shoes etc) but leave the socks, tights etc (this stops garments from sticking to feet);
- undo any belt or waistband
- work each side down, left and right in small steps, lifting each foot in turn to assist;
- slide garment off feet, keeping the garment over the examination table so that items from pockets etc are not strewn across floor and lost;
- remove socks/tights and underclothes.

10.10   HEALTH AND SAFETY IN THE DVI MORTUARY

10.10.1   Introduction

This section focuses on the various health and safety issues present in the DVI temporary mortuary environment.

Successful control of exposure to biological and other risks in the mortuary and post-mortem examination areas depends on having effective arrangements for managing health and safety. Therefore, all staff working in the mortuary should have knowledge and a good understanding of the following key areas related to work in the mortuary and post-mortem facilities, including:

- control of substances hazardous to health (COSHH);[9]
- manual handling;
- risk assessments;
- infection control;
- safe working practices or standard operating procedures (SOPs).

10.10.2 Infection control

During handling of the deceased, personnel may come into contact with blood, tissue, secretions and excreta and be exposed to pathogens including blood-borne viruses, bacteria, pathogenic fungi, parasites and unconventional agents associated with transmissible encephalopathies (diseases of the brain).

The most common means of transmission is direct contact via the hands. Blood-borne infections are most likely to be transmitted by direct inoculation through a sharps injury, broken skin or a mucous membrane (for example, the mouth, the eyes or the nasal cavity).

As the identity of the deceased within the resilience mortuary is unknown, it is impossible to identify those bodies possibly carrying infections.

Eating, drinking and smoking are strictly forbidden within the body storage area and post-mortem examination room in the mortuary – use designated areas only.

Universal precautions

The following precautions *must* be taken when handling all bodies or body parts:

1. Cover cuts and abrasions with a waterproof dressing.
2. *Always* wear *full PPE*, including:
   - Tyvek suit over surgical scrubs;
   - seamless, non-powdered gloves (especially if contact with blood or body fluids is anticipated, eg when handling un-bagged exhibits);
   - double gloves if directly involved in body handling;
   - safety glasses/goggles/visor, for eye protection;
   - disposable plastic apron;
   - face mask (if indicated).
3. Avoid any movement that may bring your gloved hand in contact with your bare skin.
4. Do not chew pens or tear sticky tape with your teeth.
5. Do not touch any object with contaminated gloves.
6. You *must* ensure that you wash and decontaminate your hands *immediately after* removing gloves etc and *before* handling equipment or paperwork or performing any other activity.

The deceased will be enclosed in a body bag from the scene and may be leaking, disrupted, infested or infected. If you are to handle a body contained in a body bag you *must* use the universal precautions above.

10.10.3 Manual handling

This section highlights some areas for consideration when examining moving and handling in a mortuary environment, with particular emphasis on the load, tasks undertaken, equipment in use, handlers and environmental aspects.

Introduction

The moving and handling of the deceased are daily occurrences for mortuary staff, therefore precautions are taken to ensure that this activity is carried out in a safe and risk-free manner. In the DVI temporary mortuary, the same precautions should be adopted by all staff involved with the moving and handling of bodies throughout the mortuary environment.

As part of general legislation covering health and safety in the workplace, the Manual Handling Operations Regulations (MHOR) 1992[10] (amended in 2002) set out specific measures concerning the safe manual handling and management of loads. These include a requirement to avoid the manual handling of loads wherever possible, to assess hazardous operations and to reduce any risks involved. This may be addressed through the provision of information, training and appropriate equipment, as well as an ongoing process of review.

It therefore follows that an examination of the working practices within a mortuary environment will highlight those aspects of work which present manual handling hazards. This information can then be used as a basis from which safer working practices may be established. Some suggested areas for consideration are discussed below.

The load

A detailed examination of the load to be moved is an essential element of any manual handling risk assessment. The weight, size and shape of the body can present considerable difficulties when it comes to moving and handling any person. Several qualities become apparent, which lead to even a live, co-operative person being difficult to handle. The "load" is often unstable, the weight unevenly distributed and it is not always possible to secure sufficient grip or adopt a safe posture in order to facilitate an effective transfer.

It therefore follows that the moving and handling of the deceased in a dignified manner is likely to be problematic. Again, weight is an issue because it is likely to be beyond the Health and Safety Executive (HSE) guidelines.[10] Further factors posing challenges to manual handling may also be present, and it is important to identify these so that the features of individual loads can be ascertained.

In the mortuary, bodies will differ in presentation. The nature of the load to be handled may be affected by factors such as the presence or absence of clothing or other covering, muscle rigidity or flaccidity and general skin condition or contamination, and these factors must be taken into consideration.

The time and circumstances of death will influence the general condition of a body. A recently deceased person from traumatic circumstances associated with a major incident or disaster presents a very different handling problem compared with a body that has been moved directly from a hospital ward to a hospital mortuary.

Tasks undertaken

The tasks undertaken within the DVI mortuary regarding manual handling and the moving of bodies vary, and may be influenced by the available facilities, equipment and number of staff available. Some examples are given here, considering tasks in terms of both transfers and clinical issues.

Transfers

May include moving a body between:

- surfaces of equal height, such as from one trolley to another of equal height;
- surfaces of different heights, such as from a fixed-height trolley to a lower or higher trolley;
- storage facility and examination surfaces, such as fridge racking and post-mortem examination tables;
- different rooms, such as body store to relatives' viewing room;
- mortuary and vehicle (removing the deceased from the incident site).

Clinical issues

May include:

- carrying out post-mortem examinations;
- accurate weighing of the body;
- controlling infection;
- dealing with contamination;
- cleaning and de-contamination of equipment;
- facilitating relatives' viewing;

Equipment

Clearly, the equipment used within the temporary DVI mortuary will reflect the precise environment and the tasks carried out within it. A brief list of equipment that may be used in the mortuary is given here:

- mortuary tray;
- fixed-height trolley;
- variable-height hydraulic trolley;
- body store racking system;
- post-mortem table;
- organ-weighing scales;
- body bag;
- stretcher;
- coffin;
- funeral directors' trolley.

Handlers

The roles and backgrounds of handlers who will be carrying out moving and handling tasks within the DVI mortuary will be determined by the wider context and environment in which the mortuary is situated, the number of deaths involved and the demands that are placed upon it. As with many manual handling situations, the manual handling procedures and techniques routinely used in a mortuary will be influenced by the number of personnel employed there who already have a great deal of experience in the movement and handling of the deceased. If staff have been insufficiently trained in the dangers of manual handling, it is unlikely that they will be aware of undertaking manual handling operations which could be hazardous. The tradition, policies and procedures of their own employing organisation and the industry as a whole may also give the impression that certain activities are expected of them. For example, if an employee is expected to work alone, he or she may believe that he or she is expected to carry out tasks independently. If no equipment is made available, it may be presumed that it is not needed. Custom and practice within a workplace may cause employees to establish routines and carry out activities in a way they believe to be acceptable, and any suggested change is viewed as unnecessary even if current practice is deemed to be unsafe.

Environment

As with any other area in which moving and handling of loads are necessary, the structure and layout of the DVI mortuary will impact upon the ease with which tasks can be undertaken. Basic internal structural and environmental factors such as floor space, levels and surfaces, along with doorways, ceiling heights and lighting, are important. Aspects such as low lighting levels, wet floors, tiled surfaces and frequently used doors can present hazards to the movement of bodies around the mortuary.

The DVI mortuary consists of several different rooms and areas, each with different purposes and features to consider. For example, a clinical area (such as the post-mortem examination area) is likely to have a floor covering that facilitates ease of cleaning and de-contamination, but this may also mean that it can become slippery. A post-mortem area is likely to be more spacious than a relatives' viewing room, which is often cramped and less brightly lit. The need to move the deceased between areas, such as from the storage area to the viewing room, may require movement through doorways as well as across different floor surfaces.

The areas in which bodies are received at the mortuary, and where they are later transferred, also need to be considered, particularly if there is a requirement to move bodies through security doors, or to and from vehicles. The location of parking bays, the space around them and the type of ground covering can present significant hazards to the handling of the body, in and out of vehicles.

Conclusion

It can be seen that there are many factors requiring attention when moving and handling within a mortuary environment, although these will vary significantly, depending on the severity and nature of any major incident. There is a need for any person who is involved in working within the DVI mortuary, and who is involved in the moving and handling of bodies, to apply two underlying principles, regardless of where such tasks are undertaken.

The first principle is that all moving and handling tasks should be implemented in accordance with the requirements set out in the MHOR,[10] to ensure the safety of handlers, the load and others using the working environment.

The second principle is that the dignity of the deceased should not be compromised, and thus all moving and handling tasks should be fulfilled in a professional and respectful manner at all times.

REFERENCES

1 Wikipedia, Enucleation of eyes [online]. Available at: http://en.wikipedia.org/wiki/Enucleation. [Accessed: 03.06.2008.]

2 Royal Institute of Public Health and Hygiene (RIPHH) [online]. Available at: http://www.riph.org.uk/healthinformation/. [Accessed: 03.06.08.]

3 Health Professionals Council (HPC) [online]. Available at: http://www.hpc-uk.org/. [Accessed: 03.06.08.]

4 Association of Anatomical Pathology Technologists (AAPT) website [online]. Available at: www.aaptuk.org. [Accessed: 18.10.2007.]

5 Royal College of Pathologists (RCP) website [online]. Available at: www.rcpath.org. [Accessed: 18.10.2007.]

6 Institute of Biomedical Science website [online]. Available at: www.ibms.org. [Accessed: 18.10.2007.]

7 Centre for International Forensic Assistance (CIFA) [online]. Available at: http://www.cifa.ac/about.html. [Accessed: 18.10.2007.]

8 Interpol DVI recording forms [online]. Available at: http://www.interpol.int/Public/
   DisasterVictim/PMForm.pdf. [Accessed: 18.10.2007.]
9 Health and Safety Executive, Control of Substances Hazardous to Health (COSHH)
   [online]. Available at: http://www.hse.gov.uk/coshh/. [Accessed: 18.06.08.]
10 Manual handling operations manual (MHOR) [online]. Available at: http://www.hse.
   gov.uk/pubns/manlinde.htm. [Accessed: 18.10.2007.]

CHAPTER 11

Mortuary Management

11.1 THE PURPOSE OF THE TEMPORARY MORTUARY

The purpose of the temporary mortuary facility is:

- To establish identity through careful examination of the deceased and associated property and to obtain evidence, which can be matched with data obtained by the Ante-Mortem Team working via the Identification Cell of the casualty bureau.
- To establish the precise cause of death – through the appropriate level of examination of the deceased by pathologists and other experts.
- To collect evidence of crime, not only relating to the cause of death but by examination of clothing and other exhibits recovered from the deceased, for example bomb fragments.
- To preserve and record personal effects of the deceased.
- To prepare deceased victims for release to family members, by reconstructive techniques where necessary. Embalming may be appropriate in some cases, particularly in the case of repatriation overseas.

The temporary mortuary will play an indispensable central role in the collection of evidence. The police will work within the mortuary for documentation purposes and work in close liaison with the casualty bureau Identification Cell.

The needs and concerns of the bereaved are important and should be considered at all times.

All deceased victims and human remains should be dealt with in a careful, respectful and dignified manner.

11.2 HM CORONER/PROCURATOR FISCAL'S RESPONSIBILITY

It is the responsibility of the Coroner or the Procurator Fiscal to authorise all procedures pertaining to the handling of the deceased and human remains, from the time of death to their release to the next-of-kin. This also involves making decisions in relation to their movement to or from a temporary mortuary and their examination within these premises.

It should be noted that the Coroner or Procurator Fiscal has possession of the body, but not ownership. A deceased person cannot be property.

The Coroner or Procurator Fiscal, who will primarily be involved with the identification of the deceased, must be made aware of, and give consent for, anything that happens to the remains. The Coroner or Procurator Fiscal will work closely with the pathologist, the police Senior Investigating Officer (SIO) and the Senior Identification Manager (SIM) to establish a strategy as to recovery, identification and other guidelines relating to the deceased.

Where several related incidents have occurred in different areas, the Coroners responsible for these areas may decide to elect an "incident" or "lead" Coroner or Procurator Fiscal, to ensure consistency.

It is the responsibility of the police to manage the reception of, and documentation of, the deceased at the mortuary. They will also be responsible for the evidential continuity of the bodies and any associated exhibits.

11.3   ACTIVATION OF AN EMERGENCY OR TEMPORARY MORTUARY

The term "emergency mortuary" is an alternative term for a temporary mortuary facility. The Home Office has produced instructions regarding the invocation of a large emergency mortuary. These instructions are known as the "National Emergency Mortuary Arrangements" or "NEMA" (see Chapter 2). At the outset of a mass fatality incident, the decision to activate an emergency mortuary will lie with the Coroner or Procurator Fiscal responsible for the district in which the victims are recovered.

The decision to activate the emergency mortuary is to be made in consultation with other key personnel, such as the lead pathologist, the police SIO, the SIM and any other person who is able to offer appropriate advice. This meeting will be known as a "Mass Fatality Co-ordination Group". It is chaired by the Coroner or Procurator Fiscal and will include representatives from the relevant local authority.

The criteria for establishing such a facility are not exhaustive, but general considerations will be as follows:

- the capacity of the local mortuary is potentially insufficient;
- for reasons pertaining to the incident, local facilities are in a sub-optimal location;
- the incident involves CBRN[1]/hazardous material;
- the nature of the incident suggests that essential supplies are not guaranteed (for example electricity or water);

- the number of casualties or duration of the incident or threat is unknown;
- the security of the mortuary requires a dedicated secure location;
- the duration of likely mortuary activity is such that it would seriously disrupt the continued requirement for local mortuary services.

The emergency mortuary can also deploy a storage-only option, to assist in significant capacity-shortage incidents, not caused by a specific incident.

NOTE: The decision to use an emergency mortuary rather than an existing facility will not detract from the mortuary procedures to be adopted, which apply to every mass fatality investigation.

11.4   MORTUARY MANAGEMENT

The operation of the mortuary will depend on inter-agency working. Despite the police taking the lead role in the management of the process, the success of the process depends on team work and an understanding of the roles of all the agencies represented.

There will be three roles in mortuary management:

1. **Mortuary Operations Manager**: a senior police officer responsible for all the police operations within the "wet" side of the mortuary.
2. **Mortuary Documentation Officer**: a senior police officer responsible for the overall management of the mortuary, with particular reference to the victim identification process and collection of post-mortem data.
3. **Mortuary Facilities Manager**: usually a local authority mortuary manager who will be responsible for all the non-police operations within the mortuary.

To facilitate the process, a Mortuary Management Team will be formed, which will meet at regular intervals and include the following:

- SIM (or their deputy);
- Mortuary Documentation Officer;
- Mortuary Facilities Manager;
- Mortuary Operations Manager;
- supervising forensic pathologist;
- Coroner's Officer/Procurator Fiscal;
- Ante-Mortem Co-ordinator;
- Resources Manager;
- health and safety adviser;
- specialist advisers, as required.

11.5 MORTUARY MANAGEMENT TEAM RESPONSIBILITIES

The Mortuary Management Team will meet on a regular basis.
The responsibilities of the team include:

- Day-to-day operational management of the emergency mortuary.
- Co-ordination of supplies, equipment, services and staff.
- Overall supervision of mortuary procedures.
- Briefing to family members regarding viewing arrangements. (Any such arrangements will be made through the Family Liaison Officer (FLO).)
- Liaison with the Police Press Officer, Government departments and press offices, with regard to the progress of the identification process and other relevant issues.
- It should be noted that the "Management of Information Unit" (part of the Identification Commission) is responsible for the release of information as to the number of persons and fatalities believed to be involved in the incident.
- Constantly to assess the working of the mortuary to identify and address any problems.
- To record any information which may be useful for any de-briefings.

A written record should be made of all decisions made by the Mortuary Management Team. The use of a tape-recorder to record meetings will be considered.

11.6 INDIVIDUAL MORTUARY TASKS

11.6.1 Mortuary Facilities Manager

An experienced mortuary manager appointed by the local authority or local health authority.

- Arranges operational and logistical support as required.
- With the Mortuary Operations Manager, liaises with the Local Authority Liaison Officers (and, where appropriate, the Site Liaison Officer) concerning any assistance they can give.
- Liaises with the Mortuary Operations Manager regarding general administration and welfare.
- Has responsibility for mortuary equipment.

- In consultation with the supervising pathologist, ensures that health, safety and hygiene precautions are understood and practised by all.
- Liaises with the Mortuary Operations Manager to ensure that wet/dry area rules are followed.
- Ensures the proper handling, storage and disposal of clinical waste.
- Monitors usage and stocks of personal protective equipment (PPE), stationery, office supplies and refreshments. Arranges re-supply in good time, of sufficient quality and in sufficient quantity.
- With the Mortuary Operations Manager, oversees staffing requirements.
- With the Mortuary Operations Manager, ensures that there is a qualified first-aider on site at all times.
- Supervises the cleaning of all parts of the mortuary facility.
- Arranges and supervises the closure of the mortuary ensuring that any necessary cleaning and repairs are conducted to return the site to its normal use.
- Could liaise with the Human Tissue Authority[2] to ensure that the requirements of the Human Tissue Act 2004[3] are met.

11.6.2   Senior Identification Manager (SIM)

A senior police officer trained for the role.

- The SIM has overall responsibility for all police staff involved in all aspects of the identification process.
- Assists the Coroner or Fiscal in establishing an Identification Commission.
- In consultation with the Coroner or Fiscal and the SIO, the SIM will develop a recovery strategy. This will establish when and how deceased victims and human remains are removed from the scene and taken to the mortuary. This may involve a site visit by the Coroner or Fiscal and the supervising pathologist.
- The SIM will liaise with the Mortuary Facilities Manager appointed by the local authority or health authority.
- The SIM, in consultation with the Coroner or Fiscal and the SIO, will develop an identification strategy (also known as the forensic strategy).
- The SIM (working on behalf of the Coroner or Fiscal) has overall responsibility for the identification process, creates a bridge between the Coroner or Fiscal and the police and (together with the FLO) forges a crucial link between the police, the bereaved and survivors.
- Liaises with the forensic science provider and the Coroner or Fiscal to ensure that there is a policy of random (sample) duplicate analysis of DNA to check and validate the DNA identification process if DNA is used.

11.6.3   Mortuary Documentation Officer

A police officer.

- Responsible to the SIM.
- Is a member of the Mortuary Management Team.
- Ensures that continuity is maintained in respect of each fatality.
- Assumes responsibility for all aspects of documentation in relation to the post-mortem examination of victims.
- With the authority of the SIM, supervises any visual identification with the Coroner's Officer/Fiscal.
- Collates post-mortem data of each victim into a single file.

11.6.4   Mortuary Operations Manager

A police officer.

- Responsible to the SIM.
- Is a member of the Mortuary Management Team.
- Implements the Mortuary Plan in relation to the process of obtaining/seizing and retention of evidence and personal property.
- Provides direct supervision and support to the police Mortuary Teams.
- Ensures continuity of each deceased victim or human remains for evidentiary purposes.
- Supervises the correct completion of post-mortem documentation, and ensures that it is delivered to the Mortuary Documentation Officer.
- Liaises with the Supervising Forensic Pathologist, forensic scientists, odontologist and other specialists engaged in the mortuary to ensure that the Mortuary Plan is adhered to.
- With the Mortuary Facilities Manager, liaises with the Local Authority Liaison Officers (and where appropriate the Site Liaison Officer) concerning any assistance they can give.
- Liaises with the Mortuary Facilities Manager to ensure that wet/dry area discipline is adhered to, as are health and safety risk assessments.
- With the Mortuary Facilities Manager ensures that there is a qualified first-aider on site at all times.

11.6.5   Coroner's Officer

- Responsible to the Coroner.
- Supports the Coroner in all their functions.

- In Scotland; the Procurator Fiscal would fulfil this role.
- Is a member of the Mortuary Management Team. Documents all decisions made by the Coroner, particularly in relation to:
  - the extent of the examination of the deceased;
  - the taking of specimens or samples for analysis and examination;
  - the retention of material for further examination;
  - the release of bodies and remains to the family (including any secondary remains);
  - the disposal of deceased victims and remains (where there are no family or none known to have an interest).
- The Coroner's Officer is an acknowledged expert in dealing with procedures following death. Their assistance and advice will be invaluable in a mass fatality incident.
- A "Senior Coroner's Officer" may be appointed to supervise and oversee other Coroner's Officers.

11.6.6 Ante-Mortem Co-ordinator

A police officer.

- The Ante-Mortem Co-ordinator and Team will be responsible for compiling a file for each person reported missing, or believed to have been involved and not yet identified. This is done for comparison with post-mortem data and for the information of the Coroner/Procurator Fiscal.
- The functions of the Team will be to:
  - prepare a list of missing persons believed to have been involved in the disaster;
  - establish evidence that such missing persons were likely to have been involved;
  - prepare a file for comparison purposes, using information from the Police Post Mortem Form, for presentation to the Coroner/Procurator Fiscal and deliberation by the Identification Commission, subject to identification requirements;
  - on the authority of the SIM, liaise with the Family Liaison Co-ordinator (FLC) to inform the next-of-kin when all identifications have been completed;
  - provide a point of contact for the FLC and FLOs and provide them with all possible assistance.
- The size of the Ante-Mortem Team will depend to a large extent on the number of fatalities, but the Ante-Mortem Co-ordinator and a nucleus of the team should be activated as soon as practicable to work closely with the casualty bureau.

- The Ante Mortem Co-ordinator is a member of the Mortuary Management Team, and will provide practical assistance for the identification process (for example, it may be useful to obtain trade catalogues to show relatives to assist them in describing jewellery or clothing).
- Depending on the identification policy, photographs may need to be obtained from the bereaved in order to assist in the identification process. The FLO will facilitate this.

11.6.7   Mortuary Duty Officer

A police officer.

A Police Duty Officer should be on duty at the mortuary at all times.

- Responsible to the Mortuary Operations Manager.
- Ensures the smooth running of the mortuary, particularly in the absence of the Documentation Officer, Mortuary Operations Manager and Mortuary Facilities Manager.
- Ensures that the Mortuary Plan is followed at all times.
- Liaises with the Mortuary Managers to arrange logistical and operational support within the mortuary.
- Has overall responsibly for the integrity of the site at all times (for example, security).
- Assumes responsibility for visitors to the mortuary.

11.6.8   Mortuary Loggist

Police staff.

- Responsible to the Mortuary Duty Officer.
- Controls access and egress from the site by maintaining a log of all persons who enter and leave the site.

11.6.9   Administration Assistant

- Assists other mortuary staff in the provision and completion of documentation including the taking of minutes at mortuary meetings.

11.6.10   Body Reception Officer

Police staff.

NOTE: The roles of the Body Reception Officer and the Body Storage Officer may be fulfilled by one officer or team, depending on the size and nature of the incident.

- Supervises the reception of each deceased victim or human remains, and ensures that:
  - each body bag is accompanied by a "Scene Note" from the ACPO Victim Label Booklet. This is completed at the scene and bears the matching unique reference number (URN);
  - the details of the body bag are entered into the Mortuary Reception and Post-Mortem Log/Register, and the log is appropriately maintained;
  - the details of the body/part are entered into the Individual Body/Part Movement Log, and the log is appropriately maintained;
  - personal property (unless on the body) does not come into the mortuary.

11.6.11 Body Storage Officer

Police staff.

(See note for Body Reception Officer, above.)

- Arranges with the Coroner's Officer and FLOs for victims to be viewed by the bereaved.
- Maintains and completes the Body Storage Log/Register.
- Liaises with the Viewing Supervisor regarding viewing.
- Seizes the original body bag and labels, and carries out the re-bagging process.
- Liaises with the Coroner's Officer, FLOs and the undertakers regarding the release of the body.
- Maintains the Release Log.

11.6.12 Post-Mortem Document Officer

A police officer.

- Responsible to the Mortuary Documentation Officer.
- Supervises the Post-Mortem Teams.
- Ensures that the body and personal effects are photographed before and after removal of clothing. (See also duties of photographer.)
- Records details of all items removed or taken from the body on the DVI forms.
- Ensures that property removed is handed to the Exhibits Team for recording.
- Makes any notes as directed by the pathologist.
- Passes the completed forms to the Mortuary Documentation Officer.

11.6.13   Team Exhibits Officer

A trained police Exhibits Officer.

- Responsible to the Post-Mortem Document Officer.
- Part of the Post Mortem Team.
- Receives all items of property and/or samples removed from the body by the pathologist and/or Post-Mortem Team.
- Completes a Major Incident Exhibit Register in respect of all such items, maintaining at least one register for the contents of each body bag examined.
- Completes an exhibit label for each item of property and/or sample removed from the deceased victim/human remains, securely attaching them to the appropriate packaging or container.
- Ensures that all items of property/exhibits/samples are packaged and stored in accordance with UK DVI exhibit handling policies.
- Ensures that photographs are taken of individual items of property removed from the body, including an additional instant photograph if available. The instant photograph should be firmly affixed to the outside of the packaging/container to show the contents.

11.6.14   Search Officer

Police staff.

- Responsible to the Post-Mortem Document Officer.
- Part of the Post-Mortem Team.
- Assists the pathologist and mortuary technician systematically to remove all items of clothing and property from the body or body part.
- Searches all items of clothing and property removed to establish evidence of identification.
- Provides an accurate detailed description of all items, narrating the same to the Team Exhibits Officer.
- Where appropriate, assists the Team Exhibits Officer in the packaging of items.

11.16.15   Mortuary Technician

A professional Anatomy Pathology Technologist.

- Responsible to the Supervising Forensic Pathologist.
- Prepares the deceased victim for any post-mortem examination.
- Liaises with the Mortuary Facility Manager regarding equipment requirements.

- May be part of the Post-Mortem Team.
- May assist the pathologist with the post-mortem process.

11.6.16   Lead Forensic Odontologist

- May be required to assist the SIM in providing primary identification evidence through dental examination and charting.
- Appointed by the Coroner/Procurator Fiscal.
- The Forensic Odontologist is likely to need an assistant.

11.6.17   Odontologist assistant

May be police staff.

- Responsible to the Mortuary Documentation Officer.
- Records all matters as directed by the odontologist on the approved post-mortem documentation and passes the same to the Mortuary Documentation Officer.

11.6.18   Lead Forensic Anthropologist

- The Forensic Anthropologist may be required to assist the SIM and is qualified in the identification of human remains.
- Appointed by the Coroner or Procurator Fiscal.
- The forensic anthropologist may need an assistant

11.6.19   Mortuary photographer

A police-authorised photographer.

- Responsible to the Mortuary Documentation Officer.
- Responsible for photographing deceased victims or human remains:
  - after removal from the body bag, prior to being stripped.
  - after clothing (but not jewellery) has been removed. This photograph should pay particular attention to the jewellery and should include any personal effects.
  - after all personal effects removed.
- Photographs will always include the URN.
- Take any photographs required by the pathologist or other specialists during the course of their examinations.
- Prepare photographs for production in any inquest or inquiry for identification purposes to the Identification Commission.

11.6.20 Mortuary Main Exhibits Officer

Trained police exhibits officer.

- Responsible to the Mortuary Documentation Officer.
- Records details of all property received from the Team Exhibits Officers.
- Assumes responsibility for property taken from the deceased.
- Places a copy of the property exhibit book in the body file.
- Ensures that personal effects are stored securely until disposal.
- Ensures continuity of any items identified as evidence.
- Liaises with the Exhibits Officer who may be attached to the Major Incident Room or any Scene Exhibits Officers. It will be necessary to record details of items seized and recovered on the HOLMES II Incident Database.
- Consults with the FLC concerning which items of property the relatives wish to be returned in due course.
- Liaises with FLC, the SIO and funeral directors concerning the cleaning and restoration of property.
- Disposes of property according to instructions from the SIO and the SIM.

11.6.21 Fingerprint Officer

A police-authorised officer.

- Responsible to the Mortuary Documentation Officer.
- Obtains fingerprints and/or footprints from the deceased, as directed. Ear prints have previously been used for identification purposes and may also be appropriate.
- Arranges for fingerprints to be taken for comparison purposes through liaison with Ante-Mortem Co-ordinator.
- Prepares comparisons for presentation to the Identification Commission and Coroner.

11.6.22 Stretcher bearers

- Responsible to the Body Reception Officer.
- Move bodies and body parts around the mortuary as required. This will include for examination, storage and viewing.
- Completes the Body Movement Log in respect of all such actions.

11.6.23 Resources Manager

- Reports to the Mortuary Management Team.
- May be an employee of a police force or local authority
- Assists with the supply and set-up of the disaster mortuary.
- Assists the Mortuary Managers in the supply of services and equipment.

11.6.24 First-aider

- The Mortuary Managers will arrange for a qualified first-aider to be available at the disaster mortuary at all times.
- The first-aider may be any member of the mortuary staff or from the voluntary sector.
- The first-aider will be expected to provide basic first aid to any member of the mortuary staff or any visitors to the facility.

11.6.25 Viewing Supervisor

- The Viewing Supervisor will report to the Mortuary Operations Manager.
- Will liaise with stretcher bearers to ensure that they place a deceased victim in the correct area, ready for viewing by family members.
- Will ensure that the viewing room is prepared for family members.

A non-exhaustive mortuary personnel schematic (Figure 11.1) has been prepared. Depending upon the size of the disaster, and the number of officers and support staff involved in the response, it may be that some of the roles listed above are combined.

11.7 ACPO VICTIM LABEL IDENTIFICATION NUMBER

The ACPO Victim Label includes a number of self-adhesive repeat body numbers that are required to be fixed to every document created in relation to the victim or body part. This label will also be affixed to the container or packaging for every item of personal property and sample taken from the body or body part.

11.8 MORTUARY PROCEDURES

11.8.1 Arrival and registration

In all cases of suspected terrorist incidents the Anti-Terrorist Squad Commander must be consulted before the removal of any remains or possessions and/or any investigation to establish the identification of the victims commences.

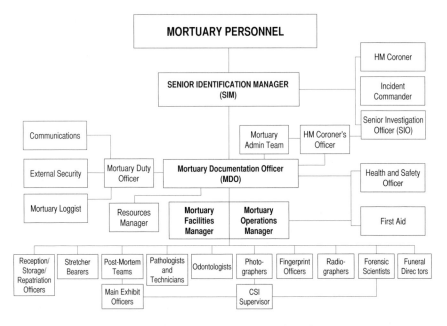

Figure 11.1   Mortuary personnel schematic

Body bags must be inspected on arrival, to ensure that the Victim Recovery Labels on the outside of the body bag correspond with the attendant paperwork received from the Scene Transport Officer.

To maintain integrity, the body bags should not be opened at this stage.

The Body Reception Team will complete any necessary documentation.

It is recommended that a Mortuary Reception Register be maintained. This register would need to record: the sequence number of the body or fragment being examined; the URN of the remains; the date and time received along with the details of the receiving officer; the details of the transporting officer; the storage location; the date and time that the examination began; and who the examining pathologist is. It can also include whether or not an ID check was carried out and by whom, and a space for comments. If a terrorist incident is suspected, consideration should be given to subjecting bodies on arrival to a radiological scan. This will ensure that there are no munitions attached to the body. A visual search for such munitions should have been made prior to the body being removed from the scene. The decision to search the body at the time of recovery will be one for the SIM in conjunction with the SIO.

In cases where a cursory identification check of the victim (see Chapter 10) has been carried out by the recovery team, personal items of property may have been checked and placed in clear property bags, which are then attached to the body (if possible) and placed in the body bag with the remains (if not). This procedure will be recorded in the text pages of the relevant ACPO Victim Label Booklet, and the item(s) will be allocated an appropriate exhibit/production number in accordance with mortuary exhibit numbering procedures, described below.

It will be for the SIM, in conjunction with the SIO, to decide on the method of examination of the victim.

The process referred to in this chapter caters for a "conveyor belt" system whereby victims are received at the mortuary and are then subjected, in turn, to the various examination processes.

In cases of either a small number/non-disrupted victims, or slow recovery process from the scene, this may be an appropriate operational method. However, it does mean that in some cases victims will be stored in the reception storage area for an unacceptable period before an examination has taken place.

There is an option to elect to pursue an examination process which, if no search intervention has taken place at the scene, requires the contents of each body bag to be searched for "Identification intelligence" upon arrival at the mortuary reception.

A cursory search should be carried out in an attempt to discover items providing clues as to the identification of the victim, for example driving licence, identity cards, mobile phones, wallet etc.

Care should be taken to note the position of the item, and due consideration be given to its location. For example, a credit card found loose in a body bag *may not* belong to the victim with which it has become associated.

In the case of search intervention at this stage, the relevant mortuary documentation would be commenced in respect of the examination of that body bag, and any items examined should be seized, appropriately labelled and packaged as per the process described below.

Please note that this is not a "full search" and once any item has been found which would give an indication as to a "*possible*" identification of the victim, then the process will be suspended and the victim returned to the storage area, pending a full examination at a later time.

The advantage of this process is that an early intervention can take place in the relatively controlled environment of the mortuary, and any findings can be documented on the appropriate mortuary forms.

Any intervention for searching should be carried out under the supervision of the pathologist and in the cases of suspected terrorist incidents, with the approval of the SO15 SIO.

11.8.2 Storage

When deceased victims or human remains are not actively being subjected to a particular mortuary process, they must be returned to the refrigerated area for safe storage.

It is recommended that a Mortuary Storage Register is maintained. This form should include: the URN of the victim; the date and time that the victim was placed in the storage area; the name of the receiving officer; the location of the remains within the storage area; whether the victim has been identified; and if so a space for their details should be provided. The form also needs to include details of any release of the remains and this should include space to record whose authority the remains are released on, the date and time of release and the details of to whom they are released.

Deceased victims should always be stored separately from each other, to minimise the potential for cross-contamination.

Efforts should be made for storage to be divided into two sections. One section of the mortuary storage area should be set aside for deceased victims *prior to* post mortem. The other side should be used for bodies *after* post mortem.

If this is not possible, the distinction can be made by different-coloured body bags or distinctive labelling.

Every effort will be made for deceased victims and human remains to be stored and handled in accordance with any religious specifications, once identification is made. This may require female victims to be stored separately from male victims. This process may not necessarily begin concurrent with the identification process, but should be put into effect once identification of the individual is made and awareness of requirements has been raised.

The FLO will advise the Mortuary Manager regarding any religious specifications for the storage of an individual body. Requests regarding religious protocol should be fulfilled unless they seriously affect the efficient running of the mortuary.

If the incident is suspected to have a terrorist origin, every effort will be made to store the human remains of persons who have been identified as suspects in a separate area to those of the deceased victims.

11.8.3 External examination and photography ("strip and search")

In cases of a terrorist incident it may be necessary for external body samples or swabs to be taken prior to examination and photography.

As each body bag is opened, the remains should be placed on the mortuary tray.

If the contents of a body bag are severely disrupted it may be necessary for the remains to be kept in the original body bag throughout the process of examination or post mortem. (See the section on re-bagging.)

A plastic "hospital" identification bracelet should be attached to an appropriate part of the victim and labelled with the appropriate ACPO Victim Label Number. This should be fastened securely and will provide a permanent identification number for the duration of the examination process in the event that the ACPO Victim Label becomes detached.

Photographs of the clothed body (front, rear and side profile) should be taken at this stage, with the label with the URN on clearly visible. An instant photograph (if the facilities are available) should also be taken and attached to the Body File.

All jewellery, wallets, documents etc should then be removed from the body and described with the details recorded on the Interpol Disaster Victim Identification (DVI) form.

Detailed descriptions of jewellery can be important, particularly if engraved with an inscription or jeweller's mark.

All property will be photographed and passed to the Team Exhibits Officer who will place the items into a property bag bearing the URN.

The Exhibits Officer will complete a property label in respect of each item of property recovered.

Each item will be given an exhibit/production number, which will be in the following format:

ACPO Victim Label Number; Exhibit Officer's initials and then a sequential number at the end:

eg 60123456/KG1

In addition, the officer will make an entry describing the property removed in an Exhibits Register. There will be at least one Exhibit Register per body bag (ie an Exhibit Register will not be used for more than one body bag).

The Team Exhibits Officer will ensure that a self-adhesive bar code label from the ACPO Victim Label Booklet for that victim or body part is affixed to every completed exhibit label.

If possible a further instant photograph will be taken of each item of property and attached to the outside of the sealed property bag (which will save the need to open and re-seal the bag to check the contents).

If the item is damaged, contaminated or bloodstained, brief details will be shown on the property label. If the item is wet or damp, it may not be appropriate for it to be sealed in a plastic bag. The Team Exhibits Officer will be trained to decide the correct way of sealing and storing such exhibits.

The body should be stripped of all clothing and the details recorded on the DVI form. This will include a full description of *every* item, including the size, make, colour etc.

The clothing and personal effects should be placed into appropriate packaging, labelled with the body number and sealed. The clothing may be stored within the mortuary until the contents are returned to family or destroyed. Clothing should be photographed before disposal. If clothing is wet or damp, it may not be appropriate for it to be sealed in a plastic bag. The Main Mortuary Exhibits Officer will be trained to decide the correct way of sealing and storing such exhibits.

The Team Exhibits Officer will pass all items recovered during examination and post mortem (along with the relevant Exhibits Register) to the Mortuary Main Exhibits Officer who will be responsible for appropriate storage.

11.8.4 Cleaning of the body and photography

The body should then be washed. However, before washing, any appropriate external body samples or swabs should be taken. This is a particular concern in the case of terrorist offences. The SIO or SIM will advise as to whether such swabs are necessary. The pathologist should be briefed about the need for samples or swabs before any examination or removal of property takes place.

After washing, a physical description will be noted on the DVI form. This will include any marks scars, malformations, amputations etc.

Documentation should be completed. The body should again be photographed (front and back), with the body number clearly visible.

11.8.5 Radiography

If radiography is required, the Supervising Forensic Pathologist will determine the most suitable time.

If available, digital radiography should be used. This obviates the need for many health and safety considerations and the results are quicker and easier to disseminate for identification purposes.

Radiography can establish features not visible to the naked eye, such as surgical appliances, pathologies, healed fractures and unique bone structure. It can also reveal items within the body, such as munitions and shrapnel.

The UK National DVI Team Co-ordinator will be able to facilitate the supply of equipment and qualified staff for radiography.

If, through radiography, items are discovered within a body or body part which may be evidence (for instance, munitions and shrapnel), this information should be documented and passed to both the pathologist and the Mortuary Documentation Officer.

Oral radiography

Provision should be made for the use of oral radiography equipment. (See Chapter 18.)

11.8.6 Fingerprints

Prints of fingers, palm, toes and feet should be taken, and details of any missing fingers and toes documented on the Interpol DVI form.

11.8.7 DNA toxicology and other intimate samples

The SIM will liaise with the forensic science provider.

The forensic science provider will advise the SIM and Coroner or Fiscal regarding the collection, profiling and matching of ante-mortem and post-mortem samples for DNA analysis. The overriding aim will be to ensure that, where appropriate, deceased victims and human remains are identified and reunited using the most suitable and effective scientific methods available. The process will be undertaken in a way that is legal, proportionate, accountable and necessary, ensuring integrity and continuity throughout.

In mass fatality incidents it should be considered whether to have scientific facilities for DNA collection and analysis at the mortuary.

The SIM may arrange with the forensic science provider to appoint a Liaison Officer within the mortuary, in line with the ACPO strategy, for the use of DNA to identify victims of mass fatality incidents.

The presiding Coroner/Procurator Fiscal will determine the acquisition of "intimate samples" by the pathologist. The details of any such samples obtained, whether for forensic examination to determine identification, or those taken for toxicology and/or histology samples, must be recorded on the Interpol DVI documentation. In addition, a separate entry for each sample taken should be made in the Exhibits Register for that victim/body part.

NOTE: It is essential that in England, Northern Ireland and Wales, all samples taken are recorded on the appropriate documentation to comply with the provisions of the Human Tissue Act 2004[3] and the Coroners Amendment Rules 2005[4] regarding seizure, examination and retention of tissue.

11.8.8 Odontology

After completion of the post mortem, and if required, an odontologist will undertake the charting of teeth and record pertinent details. Comparison will be made with the deceased's dental records, obtained with the assistance of the FLO.

If any invasive procedures are required in order to acquire dental data, the Coroner or Fiscal must be advised and give authority. If facial superimposition or reconstruction is likely to be attempted then it is imperative that appropriate facial photographs (front and both sides) are taken prior to disruption of the soft tissue of the face by the odontologist.

11.8.9 Re-bagging

After the examination process, the remains will be stored in a new, clean bag.

This is because:

- the original bag will be soiled and contaminated and may also be of significant evidential value;
- colour-coded body bags may be used to assist storage.

The Body Storage Officers will assist in re-bagging.

After the transfer of the remains to a new body bag, the old body bag will be carefully sealed, packaged and treated as an exhibit.

11.8.10   Embalming and encoffining

The embalming and encoffining of the deceased may be done by representatives from the private sector.

There are faith issues to be considered in relation to embalming. Embalming will not take place until written authority is received from the family of the victim or their representative.

Embalming may be required if a victim is to be repatriated abroad, in order to prevent further decomposition *en route*.

11.8.11   Viewing of bodies

Arrangements for viewing, either for identification or as part of the grieving process, will be made by the FLC in consultation with the Mortuary Documentation Officer and the Coroner's Officer.

A facility will be established at the mortuary site for viewing to take place. A Viewing Supervisor will liaise with FLOs and stretcher bearers to ensure that viewing of the correct person takes place.

The Viewing Supervisor will ensure that viewing facilities are suitable and clean. Religious symbols or items should be available or removed where appropriate.

11.8.12   Release of bodies to relatives

When the incident Coroner/Procurator Fiscal is satisfied that a body can be released to the next-of-kin, they will sign the appropriate form. This decision will usually be made in consultation with the SIM and/or the SIO.

Each body will be released by the Coroner/Procurator Fiscal to the family's chosen undertakers as soon as the investigation and identification process is complete for that individual.

In the event that bodies are not intact, arrangements will be made in accordance with the wishes of each family, and in consultation with their FLO. The inquest will be formally opened and a burial or cremation order issued.

198

11.9 BODIES NOT CLAIMED

The Coroner/Procurator Fiscal will decide the procedures in relation to bodies that are unclaimed. This may be the case if a next-of-kin cannot be discovered, or if a next-of-kin is identified but does not wish to claim the body.

If a body is unclaimed, the local authority will arrange for burial or cremation in accordance with any identified religion or faith.

If a next-of-kin is identified but does not wish to claim the body they will still be advised of the time, date and location of the funeral.

11.10 BODIES TO BE REPATRIATED ABROAD

When a deceased victim has to be repatriated abroad, the Coroner/Procurator Fiscal will sign an "out of England" form.

11.11 VICTIM DOCUMENTATION

The Interpol Disaster Victim Identification (DVI) forms are a standard form agreed for use by all Interpol member countries. ACPO has authorised the use of an alternative Mortuary Documentation Form – Victim Profile Forms (VPFs), however these will not be used by the National DVI Team.

NOTE: In any event, documentation completed within the "wet" area of the mortuary should be copied and sealed before leaving the mortuary. The copies will then be forwarded to the casualty bureau/DVI Identification Cell for indexing and the originals preserved in a plastic bag for health and safety reasons.

11.12 DISCLOSURE

All documentation created within the mortuary may be subject to disclosure. The Police Disclosure Officer will be attached to the Major Incident Room. The Disclosure Officer must be advised of all documentation that is created in relation to the Incident.

Consideration should be given for key members of staff to be issued with a hardback book in which to write notes including decisions/rationale etc. These books can then be submitted to the Disclosure Officer on completion.

The Mortuary Documentation Officer will liaise with the Police Disclosure Officer regarding documentation and other disclosable data created within the mortuary.

11.13   DATA PROTECTION

Copies of personal or sensitive documentation that are no longer required by the Data Protection Officer should be shredded/destroyed, particularly items which may identify the deceased.

The police will ensure that appropriate police documentation is available at the mortuary.

No person is to take any photographic image by any means within the mortuary other than an official photographer authorised by the police.

11.14   PROPERTY

Property at the mortuary will be either:

- personal property attached to the body; or
- evidence.

11.14.1   Personal property

Property and evidence will be collected and collated at the incident scene unless it is attached to, or on the body (ie clothing, jewellery, contents of pockets etc). It will not be taken to the mortuary unless it is unquestionably on or with a victim/body part.

The Body Reception Officer will ensure that personal property (unless on the body) does not come into the mortuary.

All items, whether personal property, clothing or samples (including fingerprints, DNA swabs etc), however and when ever in the process they are recovered will be handed to the Main Exhibits Officer. Before receiving any items the Main Exhibits Officer will ensure that they are labelled in the appropriate and approved manner.

The Mortuary Main Exhibits Officer will then record details of each item in the Exhibits Register specific to that victim.

Disposal of personal property

Careful consideration should be given to making a decision to clean property without first consulting family members through the FLC. Certain faiths require that all parts of a body are buried or cremated, and this may include bloodstained clothing. In addition to ascertaining the wishes of families, the SIM or the SIO should also seek advice in relation to any health and safety implications in returning potentially contaminated items to relatives.

A photograph of each item should be retained before it is returned.

11.14.2   Evidence

Evidence will be:

- items recovered following a terrorist incident;
- items required for other evidential purposes;
- medical evidence

Evidence of terrorist incidents

Following a terrorist incident it may be decided that any device or item will need to be re-constituted to provide evidence. Examples are:

- a bomb or other explosive device;
- a vehicle used for a vehicle-borne explosive device (eg car bomb);
- a vehicle involved in the incident (eg the fuselage of an aircraft).

Fragments of such items may be recovered at the mortuary and be discovered during radiography or during "strip and search" prior to post mortem.

In terrorist incidents, trained Exhibits Officers from the Police Anti-Terrorist Branch will be attached to the mortuary. The Police Anti-Terrorist Branch will be responsible for the safekeeping of all exhibits recovered following a terrorist incident.

Non-medical evidence

Items identified as evidence will be labelled and stored in accordance with the instructions shown above. Advice should be sought from the SIM/SIO before any items of evidence are cleaned.

Medical evidence

Medical evidence such as samples should be refrigerated or frozen; depending on the nature of the item. The Main Exhibits Officer will seek advice on the methods of storage from the scientific service provider.

Storage

All evidence should be stored securely. Access to stored evidence should be controlled. It is the duty of the Mortuary Operations Manager (assisted by the Mortuary Duty Officer) to ensure the security of evidence.

It may be necessary for soiled items to be refrigerated; however, the Mortuary Exhibits Officer will seek advice on the methods of storage from the scientific service provider.

201

11.15 MORTUARY EQUIPMENT

Where an emergency mortuary is activated, the appropriate local authority has a responsibility to provide the equipment required to operate the facility. However, the police will need to supply various items, such as cameras and fingerprinting kits.

Care should be taken in the "wet" area to minimise cross-contamination between each body or body part. Contamination is of particular concern in the process of collection of identification evidence.

11.16 POLICE MORTUARY STAFF

11.16.1 Recruitment and training

It can be upsetting, exhausting and stressful to work in a mortuary. No person will be expected to work in or enter the "wet" area of the mortuary without their consent.

Police officers and police staff deployed in the mortuary should be appropriately trained to work in this environment. The use of non-trained personnel in the mortuary is not recommended. The trained individual should retain the right not to work in the mortuary at any time, depending upon their wishes.

All staff should be aware of the feelings and welfare of other members of staff and report any potential problems.

All staff working in the mortuary will be required:

- to understand their role within the mortuary;
- to conduct their tasks with care, accuracy and propriety;
- not to take any photographs, videos or recordings, other than those required for official business;
- not to remove any personal items or items of equipment from the mortuary;
- to treat all personal information as confidential;
- to report honestly any problems and stress they may have to a senior officer;
- to understand their duties under:
  - Police (Health and Safety Act) 1997[5]
  - Data Protection Act (DPA) 1998[6]
  - Disclosure Rules.[7]

11.16.2 Welfare and health issues

Welfare is of paramount importance. The Police Occupational Health Department will provide support for police staff where needed. All other employing organisations will provide occupational health support for their staff. In a large facility, consideration should be given for an Occupational Health Co-ordinator.

All staff should be aware of the stress that can be caused by working in the mortuary, and should report to a manager any care concerns either experienced by themselves or apparent in others. The Facility and Operational Mortuary Managers will monitor levels of illness among staff, which can be a primary indicator of stress.

The Facility and Operational Mortuary Managers will ensure that their staff take regular breaks away from the "wet" area of the mortuary. Such breaks will be compulsory. All staff must be given the opportunity to be de-briefed and receive psychological support at the end of each working period.

There will be a dedicated first aid post at the disaster mortuary. The post will supply first aid facilities to both staff and visitors to the mortuary. Members of the voluntary sector may staff the first aid post.

Due to radiography equipment being used within the mortuary facility, special care should be taken in respect of vulnerable groups (eg pregnant women) working on site.

11.16.3   Accommodation

Facilities should be provided to accommodate police staff deployed in the mortuary. It is good practice for staff, no matter how close to the incident they live, to use local facilities in order to minimise the potential for contamination and family stress. However, some staff may prefer to commute from home.

11.16.4   Health and safety

The Police Mortuary Managers (Mortuary Documentation Officer and Mortuary Operations Manager) have a duty of care to staff deployed within the facility. It will be the responsibility of the Mortuary Documentation Officer to compile a risk assessment for such a deployment and ensure compliance of the same. The Mortuary Operations Manager will have the responsibility to enforce the content of the assessment in conjunction with other agencies managers within the "wet" area of the mortuary

11.17   VIEWING

Facilities will be made available for families to visit and view the deceased for grieving purposes, as soon as appropriate. They should not be prevented from seeing the body, but must be given appropriate advice and assistance.

It is the responsibility of the FLO to arrange viewing through the Coroner's officer/Fiscal. The FLO should accompany the family and remain with them during the viewing process, although it will be the responsibility of the police staff within the mortuary to convey the body to the viewing area and then to return it to the appropriate storage area after the viewing has taken place.

NOTE: Mortuary staff will not interface with the victims' relatives/friends at any time.

11.18 SECURITY

The Mortuary Management Team will arrange with the police and the local authority to provide security at the mortuary site. The Mortuary Duty Officer will be responsible for security of the mortuary and will work under the direction of the Mortuary Operations Manager.

ACKNOWLEDGEMENTS

Much of the work in this chapter has also been used in the Home Office document "On Dealing with Mass Disasters". The author would also like to thank Kevin Gordon, Member of the British Transport Police and London Resilience Team, for his assistance.

REFERENCES

1 Chemical, Biological, Radiological and Nuclear (CBRN). Available at: http://www. hpa.org.uk/emergency/CBRN.htm. [Accessed: 14.11.2007.]
2 Human Tissue Authority website. Available at http://www.hta.gov.uk/. [Accessed: 14.11.2007.]
3 Human Tissue Act 2004 (c 30) [online]. Available at http://www.opsi.gov.uk/ACTS/ acts2004/ukpga_20040030_en_1. [Accessed: 28.08.09.]
4 Coroners (Amendment) Rules 2005 (SI 2005/420) [online]. Available at http://www. opsi.gov.uk/SI/si2005/20050420.htm. [Accessed: 28.09.09.]
5 Police (Health and Safety) Act 1997 (c 37) [online]. Available at http://www.opsi.gov. uk/acts/acts1997/1997042.htm. [Accessed: 14.11.2007.]
6 Data Protection Act (DPA) 1998 (c 29) [online]. Available at http://www.opsi.gov.uk/ acts/acts1998/19980029.htm. [Accessed: 14.11.2007.]
7 Disclosure Rules [online]. Available at http://www.cps.gov.uk/legal/section20/ chapter_g.html. [Accessed: 14.11.2007.]

CHAPTER 12

Exhibits and Personal Effects

12.1 INTRODUCTION

The collection, packaging and storage of exhibits are vitally important aspects in the investigation of any crime or potential crime. It is important that the same care is exercised when dealing with exhibits within the DVI arena.

Those involved with handling exhibits must consider three basic factors regarding each and every item:

1. **Integrity of the exhibit**: the honesty and accountability of the exhibit must be beyond question. Exhibits must be dealt with in such a way that it can be demonstrated that no interference with or loss or addition of material could conceivably have taken place at any stage, either deliberately or accidentally.
2. **Continuity of the exhibit**: continuity means that, from the moment the evidence is found through to presentation in court, every single movement of the exhibit must be documented and accounted for.
3. **Packaging of the exhibit**: the packaging of the exhibit must preserve the integrity and continuity of the exhibit, and it must be received by the forensic scientist or court in the same condition as (or as near as possible to) that in which it was originally found.

Within the DVI arena, exhibits will be collected in order to identify the deceased, assist in establishing the cause of death and, where relevant, to provide evidence of any crime that may have been committed. In the case of a natural disaster involving mass fatalities, evidence of a crime may not be an issue.

The Senior Identification Manager (SIM), in consultation with the Senior Investigating Officer (SIO), will make decisions about the collection of exhibits. Any decisions will be passed on to the body recovery officers, search teams and mortuary teams.

In this chapter, any reference to the "victim" includes bodies or parts thereof. The victim is to be treated as an exhibit only if the DVI team is working alongside

SO15; this would not be a requirement in any other circumstances, as the ACPO Body Recovery Booklet will suffice.

This section will deal with the following:

- ante-mortem exhibits;
- post-mortem exhibits;
- personal effects;
- packaging of exhibits;
- exhibit marking;
- storage of exhibits; and
- repatriation.

12.2   ANTE-MORTEM EXHIBITS

The Family Liaison Officer (FLO) will normally collect the ante-mortem exhibits and record *extremely detailed* descriptions of the missing person, their clothing, jewellery and documents on the yellow Interpol DVI ante-mortem form. This information will usually be provided by the missing person's family.

The items to be collected by the FLO to assist in the identification process may include the following:

- **Dental records**: details of the missing person's dentist should be obtained in order that a dental chart can be provided for comparison purposes.
- **Fingerprints**: the experience and training of a Crime Scene Investigator (CSI) is useful when considering items that may bear the fingerprints of the missing person. These items must be obtained and packaged appropriately (more information on packaging and exhibiting later in this chapter).
- **DNA**: a CSI is also useful when considering items that may contain DNA of the missing person, for example hairbrushes and toothbrushes used exclusively by the missing person.
- **X-rays and medical records**: known medical conditions or surgical interventions are extremely useful in the identification process, for comparison with post-mortem observations.

The FLO and the CSI will ensure the correct storage and transfer of all exhibits, and provide a statement to the Major Incident Room (MIR) detailing their actions.

12.3   POST-MORTEM EXHIBITS

Members of the post-mortem team will be responsible for the collection, packaging and onward transmission of exhibits taken from the victims. The pink Interpol DVI post-mortem form will be completed in detail during the mortuary processes. Where extra space is required for recording, section G of the form can be utilised. An exhibit book will be completed alongside the pink Interpol form: one exhibits book per victim. The bar code from the ACPO Body Recovery Booklet pertaining to that victim will be placed on the front of the corresponding exhibits book. The exhibits book that the UK DVI National Team will utilise is the standard major incident register. The exhibits book itself will not be exhibited.

Search officers who are part of the post-mortem team will:

- ensure that photographs of the victim are taken, both clothed and unclothed, including both front and back views;
- assist the pathologist and mortuary technicians systematically to search and remove all items of clothing and property from each victim. This search will also include the body bag from which the victim was removed. This bag may need to be packaged as a site of potential evidence, in accordance with the directions of the SIO;
- ensure that photographs are taken of each item of clothing and property as they are removed;
- search all these items to establish, where possible, evidence of identification;
- provide a detailed description of each item for the documentation officer in the team;
- act as "finder" for the exhibits process – this will enhance and simplify the continuity process;
- where necessary, assist the team exhibits officer to package and exhibit the items.

The post-mortem team exhibits officer will:

- receive, seize and produce all items of property and samples removed from the body by the search officer who acts as "finder". Any samples taken by the pathologist will be exhibited as the pathologist's samples and fingerprints will be exhibited by the person taking the fingerprint;
- complete an exhibits register for each victim, working closely with the scribe who is completing the pink Interpol post-mortem form to ensure that descriptions of exhibits are recorded the same both in the exhibits book and on the Interpol form;
- package the items appropriately, in accordance with current instructions and SIO policy;
- ensure that photographs are taken of each item;
- where appropriate, ensure that an instant photograph (often a Polaroid) is taken of items that could be useful for identification purposes but cannot be

viewed easily because of the packaging material and/or health and safety considerations, for example contamination;

- hand all the exhibits and exhibits register(s) from each victim to the mortuary exhibits officer. If an item is fast tracked they will ensure that this is recorded in the exhibits book and the pink Interpol form and pass the item for fast tracking to the main exhibits officer.

The main exhibits officer will:

- record in detail all the exhibits received from the post-mortem team exhibits officer;
- assume responsibility for all exhibits taken from the victim;
- ensure continuity of all exhibits taken from the victim;
- record the movements of any exhibits in the exhibits register;
- liaise with the incident exhibits officer in the MIR;
- consult the FLO about items that the family may wish to have returned, and their wishes regarding the cleaning and restoration of items;
- dispose of property in accordance with SIO/SIM policy.

The presiding Coroner or Procurator Fiscal will agree the identification criteria. The SIM, in consultation with the SIO, will agree which exhibits are required, not only for identification purposes but also as evidence if a crime is suspected.

The identification methods are broken down into three categories:

1. Primary
    - fingerprints;
    - DNA;
    - odontology;
    - unique medical condition.

2. Secondary
    - jewellery;
    - personal effects;
    - distinctive clothing;
    - marks/scars/tattoos;
    - blood grouping;
    - physical disease.

3. Assistance only
    - visual;
    - photographic;
    - physical description;
    - body location (at time of recovery);
    - clothing.

During all aspects of the post-mortem process, detailed notes must be made of the physical description of the victim and any items of clothing, jewellery or documentation removed from them. Care should be taken to document the brand and size of clothing, in addition to the colour and type of the item.

Photographs of jewellery, clothing and documents may be useful to assist the Identification Commission in making comparisons with the ante-mortem details. Every photograph should include the unique reference number (URN) for that particular victim (see Figure 12.1).

Figure 12.1   Photograph of a personal item, with URN and scale in the picture

The exhibits strategy of the SIO/SIM regarding items removed from the victim during post mortem must be adhered to strictly. All exhibits must be marked with the URN for that particular victim.

The exhibits from each victim will be passed from the mortuary post-mortem team exhibits officer to the mortuary main exhibits officer for accounting and storage.

All officers who search for, find, package and exhibit an item of potential evidentiary value will provide statements to the MIR detailing their actions. Continuity statements will also be required from any person having any responsibility for the storage and movement of exhibits.

At the end of the post-mortem process it may be necessary to place the body in a new body bag which should be marked with the URN for that particular victim.

12.4   PERSONAL EFFECTS

Although personal effects may not be required as evidence, they may be required for assistance in the identification process. *All personal effects should be packaged and exhibited in the same way as evidential exhibits.* It must be remembered that an item may not immediately appear to be of evidential value, although it may become so at a later stage. Therefore, the evidential chain must be commenced immediately, irrespective of the anticipated outcome.

As stated previously, Polaroid photographs should be taken of items that cannot be properly viewed when packaged. This may provide assistance to the FLO when he or she visits the family.

Although personal effects may be badly contaminated by body fluids or other contaminants, it cannot be assumed that the family would want the items to be cleaned prior to their return. The FLO must ensure that the wishes of the family are passed on to the SIM and exhibits officers.

Some items may have been treated with harmful chemicals during the investigative process. There may be circumstances when items cannot be cleaned or restored, as these processes may damage the exhibit. Therefore it may not be possible to return the item to the family.

12.5   PACKAGING OF EXHIBITS

Exhibits must be packaged as per current instructions. The type of packaging will also depend on whether items are wet or bloodstained or whether an explosive device is suspected. Post-mortem teams must also ensure that the instructions of the SIO or the SIM are complied with. All exhibits will be packaged, sealed and documented within the mortuary.

When items are to be packaged in bags or boxes that permit little or no view of the item, consideration should be given to having a Polaroid photograph taken of the item prior to packaging, which should be attached to the outside of the package. This will reduce the necessity for repackaging if an item becomes important in the identification process.

The exhibits seized during a disaster are likely to be contaminated in some way by body fluids, chemicals or other contaminants, depending on the nature of the incident. Those working in the post-mortem team should wear personal protective equipment (PPE) in accordance with risk assessment recommendations.

If exhibits are to be dried prior to storage, adequate provision has to be made, with appropriate drying facilities that meet health and safety requirements. The forensic preservation of clothing should be addressed, as well as potential cross-contamination issues. Once dried, items can then be placed in paper sacks, sealed and the original packaging retained.

DNA samples should be frozen or refrigerated and those for isotopic analysis should be refrigerated.

12.6 EXHIBIT MARKING

Although exhibits will be packaged according to current guidelines, there can be some confusion regarding their marking in incidents involving mass fatalities. The recommended method of marking exhibits in these circumstances is as follows.

The Unique Victim Recovery Label Number (URN) and accompanying bar code will appear first on the label by utilising one of the self-adhesive labels from the ACPO Victim Recovery Booklet. This will be followed by the initials of the officer exhibiting the item, and then a sequential number. An example of this is:

600077/GRM1

While there is no requirement to write the six-figure number on every entry in the exhibits book, it should be indicated at the top of every page, and should always be written on exhibit bags and labels.

When processing a different victim, the exhibit number of the team's exhibits officer will begin again from the number one. In the example above, this means that "GRM1" is never used again in relation to this victim, but will be in relation to other victims. Each victim is unique as it has a different six-figure URN from any other victim because it has a different ACPO Body Recovery Booklet. The numbering of items such as those found in a wallet should be broken down at the time of the post mortem. The wallet and contents should be individually exhibited, packaged and entered into the exhibits register. Letters such as "a", "b", "c", "d" should *not* be used to address the contents; instead, sequential numbering should be used. So, the wallet would be "GRM1", the credit card with relevant details "GRM2 taken from GRM1" etc. Cash should be counted and recorded as one collective exhibit; again, this would be "GRM3 taken from GRM1".

12.7 STORAGE OF EXHIBITS IN THE MORTUARY

This will be the responsibility of the mortuary exhibits officer. All exhibits should be kept in a secure environment, away from the wet area. In some incidents it might be decided that clothing will be stored with the victim in the body bag. If this is the case, this should be recorded in the exhibits book.

Movements of exhibits must be recorded against signature on the exhibits register that refers to the particular victim.

12.8 REPATRIATION

Repatriation will take place once the presiding Coroner is satisfied that the identification of the deceased is positively proven, and authorises release.

Victims released to their families or their nominated undertakers will be done so against receipt of the appropriate documentation, which will be decided with the SIO or SIM and the Coroner at the time. This documentation may change, but must always be a permanent record which is disclosable in court and will become part of the incident documentation.

CHAPTER 13

Disaster Victim Photography

13.1 INTRODUCTION

The timely deployment of suitably qualified personnel to record both the scene and subsequent mortuary procedures at incidents involving mass fatalities is widely accepted as good practice. The importance of this part of the DVI process cannot be over-emphasised.

Photography plays a pivotal part in the evidential chain, and equally forms part of a permanent record of the event and may well be subject to continual review for decades to come.

Systematic and detailed photography not only assists in the identification of victims at such incidents but can, in some cases, aid specialists in establishing the cause of the disaster.

Because of the importance placed on photography, it has become standard policy to ensure that DVI-trained Scenes of Crime Officers (SOCOs) and police photographers are integral parts of both recovery and mortuary teams from the outset of deployments. These officers will carry out all scene, body recovery and mortuary photography, utilising the skills and specialist photographic techniques that they possess from years of extensive training. It is therefore unlikely that any mass fatality to which UK DVI is deployed will be without SOCOs or photographers in the team make-up. However, it should be borne in mind that because of circumstances beyond the control of UK DVI, "non-photographers" may have to carry out this crucial role, for example a foreign government restricting the number of DVI personnel permitted to enter their country, FCO requesting only two or three trained persons to confirm the identity of a few UK nationals. Both of these situations have been encountered on live overseas deployments, and with the ever-present risk of illness at disaster scenes, it is easy to see how, without warning, the resilience of key disciplines can be quickly depleted.

For these reasons, and in keeping with UK DVI's ethos of "omni-competence" all team members will be trained in DVI photography techniques. The rational being to ensure, as far as is practicable, that in a "worst case scenario" the victim identification process continues in an acceptable and professional manner until sick personnel return to their duties or replacement staff take up their post.

The aim of this chapter is to provide a good practice guide to DVI photography: it is not intended to be a technical manual of photography or to negate the requirement to have SOCOs/photographers as key members of UK DVI deployments. It is worth remembering at this juncture that basic crime scene photography skills are achieved following three weeks' intensive theoretical and practical training from NPIA (National Policing Improvement Agency). At the conclusion of this chapter and the residential training phase students are unlikely to be transformed into the next David Bailey or Annie Leibovitz: they will, however, possess the knowledge of what to do when a camera is thrust into their hands. Students will possess a level of competency which will ensure that at all times the dignity of the deceased is preserved. They will be aware of how to record all available physical evidence from the scene/mortuary in an acceptable professional manner and to a quality that can be presented at the highest forms of the judicial system.

There will be two distinct areas where students may find themselves being utilised in the role of photographer. The first is at the scene of the mass fatality disaster, and the second will be at the resilience mortuary following the recovery of fatalities from the disaster site. These two areas may initially seem to have little in common because of their diverse natures.

The scene will be crowded, noisy, bustling with numerous differing emergency services, hot, cold, wet or dry, with a sense of urgency and immediacy hanging over the recovery of each body part and cadaver. In contrast, at the mortuary, there will be only a handful of selected personnel, a calmer air of reverence towards the deceased, constant temperature, and a systematic and methodical approach to the recording and recovery of each individual piece of physical evidence. As different as these scenes may appear, they do in fact require that exactly the same ethos be applied. The photographic skills that students will learn are interchangeable: it is just the considerations for where they are being used that will differ.

Photographs presented at court, Coroners' inquests or fatal accident inquiries need to have the ability to convey the viewer into the scene, to allow an appreciation of the emotions involved and to show in detail, without bias, the results of the actions that took place.

As a disaster scene is effectively, until proved otherwise, a crime scene, the first step is to record the scene accurately prior to anything being removed or disturbed.

Remember: once disturbed, the scene can never be restored to its original state!

The significance of the location of items situated within the scene may turn out to be greater than is initially evident. While incidents such as natural disasters may, from the outset, have no obvious criminal element, it is prudent to tackle all such disasters as though they were crime scenes, and to follow the same basic principles of crime scene preservation throughout all aspects of the operation. No matter what the scene, therefore, a DVI photographer cannot take too many photographs and indeed it would be a very brave SIM or SIO who would criticise this being done. By recording the maximum amount of information available from an incident, an accurate pictorial record can be created. This record can ultimately be shown to Identification Commissions, Coroners, Procurators Fiscal or International Criminal Tribunals who, by viewing the position of every item of interest found, can better understand the collected evidence presented to them in order to confirm a victim's identity or as part of criminal proceedings. Always consider that the people who view the photographs in all likelihood will never have been anywhere near the scene or within the mortuary. It will be *your* methodical and sequential illustration of the sights, conditions, damage, injuries and identifying features that will convey all the facets of the incident and the diligence of the personnel who make up UK DVI.

Regardless of whether they are used at the scene or within the mortuary, any personnel who are deployed in the role as DVI photographer will always be regarded as "clean" team members. They *will not* handle any bodies, body fragments, productions/exhibits or other items of interest while engaged in this role.

Personal protective equipment (PPE) levels will be decreed by Safety Advisers (see Figure 13.1), but it should be noted that using a camera while wearing goggles or safety glasses can prove to be awkward. The wearing of gloves is another area where different schools of thought exist. It can be argued that by not wearing

Figure 13.1   Working in a mortuary environment

gloves a photographer is less likely to handle a contaminated item by mistake; on the other hand, it can be argued that by not wearing gloves a photographer can more easily sustain accidental contamination. While each argument has its own merits, realistically, it will depend on the type of incident, the hazards present, the Safety Advisor and SIO's policy decision and the individual's personal risk assessment as to whether gloves are worn while carrying out the role of DVI photographer.

Video recording both at the scene of a mass fatality incident and within the mortuary will probably be carried out in addition to, and in support of, the photographic element. This chapter does not cover videography *per se* but if for similar reasons of ill health or personnel restrictions, it is directed that non-trained staff carry out this function, then the basic principles outlined within this chapter should be applied. A relatively new recording technique which is becoming more commonplace within UK policing is the use of 360-degree spherical cameras at major incidents.[1] This equipment captures a scene in its entirety and has the facility for highlighting areas of interest and the inclusion of still photographic images and video imagery, thereby creating a concise overall picture of the incident that allows investigators, prosecution and jurors to be guided through a "virtual" walk through. This equipment is highly specialised, with only a small number of personnel usually found in each force who are trained to operate it. Because of the specialised nature of the equipment, and the degree of post-scene editing involved, this equipment will not be covered on the course or within this chapter. However, it is an advancement in technology of which all UK DVI personnel should be aware and be able to advise SIMs/SIOs on its existence and uses at an incident.

13.2 COMPOSITION AND PERSPECTIVE

Photography is purely a method of visual communication. Regardless of subject-matter, a photograph must possess good composition and perspective to ensure that the pictorial representation appears natural to the eye when viewed. Obscure camera angles, lack of scale labels and distracting backgrounds can produce distortions and unnatural appearances which can easily confuse. Composition of the photograph can be made easier by adopting the "rule of thirds", which should not be confused with the technical "thirding rule" associated with depth of field (see Figures 13.2 and 13.3). The "rule of thirds" has been seen as a valuable tool for composition since the early 19th century and is equally important today as it was then. It is quite simply an imaginary grid consisting of three rows of three boxes of equal size, creating four points where the horizontal and vertical lines intersect.

By imagining that the viewfinder is divided into these nine boxes, the subject-matter can be placed around any of the four points where the lines intersect. This avoids both the inclusion of natural obstructions or features which might give a

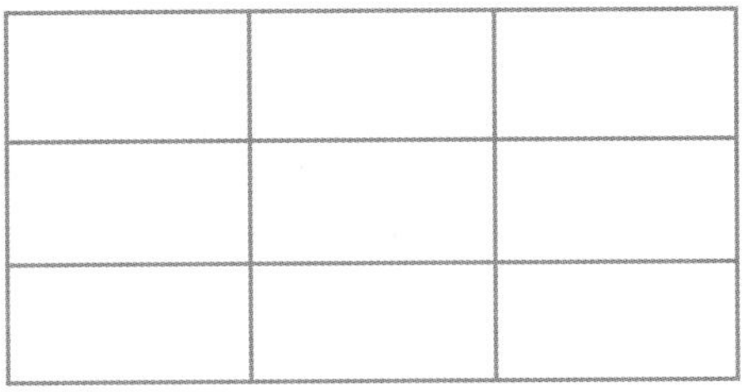

Figure 13.2   Example of the "rule of thirds" grid

false perspective to the final picture and other, background, activities that, when taken out of context, could be deemed to be disrespectful to the dignity of the deceased (remember that the viewer will *not* have been there when the images were captured). Usually associated with artists and painters, this simple rule can greatly assist in creating both an aesthetic quality and a professional end result, even in today's digital age.

Figure 13.3   Example of the "rule of thirds" grid on a photograph

Backgrounds are a very important factor to any evidential photograph, yet are frequently forgotten about or indeed simply not recognised for the important part they play.

A seemingly busy, crowded scene or cramped mortuary surroundings can be transformed quickly and easily into an almost photographic studio effect merely by utilising a standard green medical sheet, length of polythene/tarpaulin or indeed a neatly cut open brown paper evidence bag. Using any of these methods, it is possible to create a backdrop that is held up directly behind the subject- matter or used to place items of interest on so as to avoid incorporating unnecessary distractions or sensitive material in the composed photograph. It must be remembered that these images are disclosable and, as such, activities which are happening in the background and have been inadvertently caught in a photograph may both cause upset and result in an invasion of privacy for both families and victims.

13.3 GETTING STARTED

Currently, within UK policing, most photographers and scene examiners use Digital Single Lens Reflex (DSLR) cameras. In simple terms "Single Lens Reflex" means that the lens and the viewfinder share the same optical path, therefore the photographer sees exactly what the lens is focused upon.

Digital cameras utilise a removable storage medium in order to save the images. These "memory cards" come in various shapes and sizes but the four most commonly used in DSLR cameras are Compact Flash (CF), Secure Digital (SD), memory sticks and XD cards.

Prior to taking any photographs the memory card must first be formatted to ensure that no other images are present on the card.

Formatting the memory card is the ONLY way images will be removed from the card.

At no point, once the photography process has started, will any images ever be DELETED!

> One crucial aspect of the Procedure is that none of the images taken should be deleted without authority. Any deletion of images, intentionally or accidentally, may be the subject of a "challenge" or legal debate during any prosecution. Where such authority is given, deletions must be recorded in the audit trail and be subject to the requirements of the Criminal Procedure and Investigations Act 1996 and Attorney General Guidelines on Disclosure of Evidence.[2]

During the formatting process the operator will be given a number of default "YES/NO" options in order to avoid accidental erasing of images. If at any time you are handed a camera and are unsure whether the card contents have been saved, then it is prudent to download these images prior to carrying out the formatting procedure, or removing the memory card, lodging it as a production/ exhibit, and inserting a new unused/formatted card.

Once formatted, the camera is ready for use.

13.4 AUDIT TRAIL

As with all police and evidential procedures, the need for a comprehensive audit trail exists in DVI photography. The audit trail should ideally begin as soon as a photographer is requested to attend an incident. This is done by the creation of a work report or "job sheet". This form of written and/or electronic contemporaneous recording is common place with SOCOs and photographers in their daily duties. DVI assignments are no different regarding the need to record each individual action. This enables a full review of the process both during or after an investigation. At present there is no official UK DVI photographic work report,

DVI
Post Mortem Examination
Log

Incident. *Aircrash* - *Anyhtemowhere* Date. *13/06/2007*

Deceased particulars. *MK*

Body Label URN. *12345678* Search Grid Ref. *B4*

Time/date pronounced life extinct. *1313* by who. *Dr. No*

IB No.......................... FSL No................. Integrity No........................,

POST MORTEM EXAMINATION CHECK SHEET
MORTUARY LOCATION *Dundee*

S.I.O. /S.I.M.	Det.Ch.Supt. Dixon
Pathologists	Dr. Jones & Prof. White
DVI Team Leader	PC Smith
DVI Team Members	PC Orange, PC Blue, PC Red, PC Purple. SOCO John Doe
Start time	1000hrs 13/06/07
Finish	1300hrs 13/06/2007
Photographs y/n	No. of films/memory cards 2 X 128Mb CF cards
Productions y/n	No. of productions 24
Others Present	Dr McLean Forensic Odontologist Depute PF

Photographer *John Doe* Body Label URN *12345678*

PHOTOGRAPHS/VIDEO TAKEN
Mortuary Location *Dundee*

No	Subject	location	Taken by
1-4	body bag full length	mortuary	JD
5-7	close up body bag label	"	JD
8-11	bag opened label attached	"	JD
12-16	full length clothed	"	JD
17-21	sectional clothed	"	JD
22	close up body label		JD
23-25	views damages t-shirt	"	JD
26-30	close up views damage to t-shirt with scale		JD
123	resealed body bag bearing label 1234567		JD

Figure 13.4   An example of a photography log which could be used in a mass disaster situation

Figure 13.4 shows an example of the type of logs that could be utilised to record the required information for photography at the scene.

Each force throughout the UK will have its own style of recording process, and therefore it is advisable to make contact with your own scenes of crime section or photographic unit and familiarise yourself with the type of forms that would be used "in-house" in the event of a mass fatality incident. Minimum required information would be date, location, start time, finish time, photographer's name/force number and home force identifier. The exception would be terrorist-related incidents, at which only shoulder/collar/warrant numbers are listed as opposed to names. Each photograph should then be itemised as soon as is practicable to form a frame-by-frame account of every media card used. Within the mortuary environment the same information is recorded, as well as noting the unique reference number (URN) for each body or body part on the form.

It is worthy of note that good practice would dictate that each URN will require a unique photographic work report when working in the mortuary. This procedure is unlikely to be feasible within the field but it would be cognisant to consider carrying out a similar procedure within each search parameter sector/ grid where deployed. Here, instead of recording the body label URN the sector/ grid reference letter and number would be noted on the work report.

13.5   DISASTER SCENE PHOTOGRAPHY

Setting the scene is one of the important functions that photography carries out at any disaster scene. Scene photography takes time and all DVI practitioners, SIMs and SIOs must understand that while it may appear to be taking an excruciating amount of time to "take some photos", the photographer gets only one chance at capturing the scene before it changes forever. As previously noted, DVI photographers are classed as "clean" and at no time should a designated photographer handle any bodies, body parts or fragments.

Systematic views should be taken to enable the location, position and condition to be fully appreciated. Initially this will mean general views taken from the four corners of the cordon, although this should not be restricted to only four photographs. Due to the size or scale of an incident, numerous photographs may be required in order to encompass the cordon area fully.

The secret to achieving a pictorial overview of the scene is to take overlapping photographs by including a set point in each shot. Using this fixed point of reference, ie a section of damaged building, vehicle or something as simple as a tree, it is possible for the viewer to build up a panoramic view of the scene in their mind's eye.

All general photography should be taken with the camera positioned at standing-height eye level and, ideally, secured on a tripod. Not only will photographs taken at eye level help to replicate the view that witnesses would have had but this procedure also avoids the danger of producing obscure angles. The tripod not only creates a stable working platform, leaving the operator's hands free to use flash guns etc, but, importantly, it reduces the risk of camera shake, especially when working in lower light conditions.

While taking into account the requirement to photograph the scene "as is", and the purpose behind the taking of the photographs from a DVI perspective, it must also be recognised that views that are clumsy or confusing could be construed as undignified to the victims. Always be aware of the surroundings, and compose each photograph in order to maximise the amount of available information within your shot. Avoid, as far as is practicable, taking photographs that capture other personnel in the frame. Watch for obstructions, and obscure angles that could create distractions or confusion to those who will ultimately be viewing the photographs. If need be, create a "sterile" or neutral background using polythene sheeting/tarpaulins, or whatever appropriate means is at hand, in an attempt to produce a professional end product.

Within the scene itself the same procedure should be adopted for each search grid/sector that is entered. When recording the search grids it is vital that the identifying reference, usually alpha-numeric, is included in all the general shots, and that the same reference is incorporated in close-up shots showing scene labels and body fragments (see Figure 13.5).

Drawing attention to any particular point of interest can be accomplished by using markers during the scene examination. The URN labels incorporated

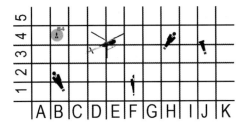

Figure 13.5   Example of search grid pattern with item of interest at grid B4

in the body labelling booklets, while robust and fit for purpose, do not always immediately stand out, especially when general overview photographs are taken. To assist in highlighting areas of interest it may be helpful to utilise such things as coloured plastic/metal numbered markers (normally used by SOCOs), or attaching high visibility tape to the top of marker pegs. As well as being used to indicate objects that are foreign to an area, markers might also be employed to show signs of disturbance, displacement of objects from their natural surroundings or to indicate a path or route of a particular energy source/catastrophic event.

Once the preliminary examination has been carried out, and all the relevant items have been found and marked, the scene should then be re-photographed. It is preferable that these "before" and "after" images should be taken from the same position, although this is more for the viewer's benefit than for evidential necessity. General views of the scene, incorporating the markers, allow the viewer to see the relationship between items (see Figure 13.6).

Figure 13.6   Showing the process of framing the area of interest. On the left, a wide establishing shot. In the middle is a closer, more detailed shot and the image on the right shows the individual marker

The next step in the procedure is to take full-length photographs of each identified item of interest. When dealing with a body part or fragment, good practice is to include a view of the front page of the body labelling booklet showing the URN.

Close-up views of the highlighted items can then be taken, removing any risk of ambiguity over their position prior to them being removed (see Figure 13.7). For close-up photography rigid scales, rulers and adhesive arrows can be incorporated to assist with gaining a perspective of size. Probably without doubt the most vital part of close-up photography is to ensure that the URN bar code label from the body labelling booklet is clearly visible in each and every close-up shot as well as the grid sector or building reference. Remember that while taking close up or macro views, any item that requires to be moved, rotated or turned should only be done by a "dirty" member of the recovery team.

At no point should the photographer ever handle any body parts or contaminated items.

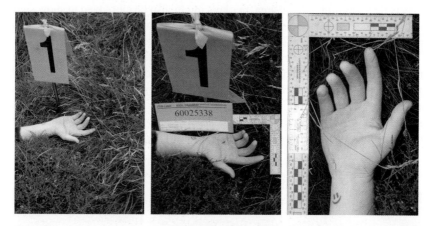

Figure 13.7   Photography of items of interest, showing the series of photographs incorporating the URN and scale

Once the body fragment/part is secured within an appropriate recovery bag, more views should be taken clearly showing scene marker, the URN and body labelling booklet prior to forward transportation to the body holding area and thereafter the mortuary (see Figure 13.8).

While it might be thought that once the items of interest have been removed from the scene the photography element also finishes, it should be borne in mind that closing shots of the scene can prove equally as important as the opening shots. Once all the activity has quietened at the scene it is often worthwhile to take closing general overview photographs of the area, showing all the scene markers *in situ*. Generally these closing shots are of benefit because of the distinct lack of personnel, vehicles and equipment, therefore giving a "clean" overview that can be presented anywhere without the fear of causing undue distress or suffering to the viewer or relatives of the deceased.

Figure 13.8   Showing the closed body bag with labels and completed body recovery book

Scene Safety Note: When taking photographs at any incident it is all too easy for the photographer to become completely absorbed in the act of taking photographs.

In recording the scene the photographer will be composing shots, concentrating on ensuring images are in focus, monitoring light levels to ensure suitable aperture settings, using close-up and macro photography and therefore can develop an almost "tunnel vision" and become unaware of what is happening around them. For these reasons it is vital that when taking photographs at any large-scale disaster, especially where damaged buildings/structures are present or recovery operations include the use of machinery and/or vehicles, the photographer is accompanied by a designated safety officer/buddy. It will be role of the designated safety officer to guide the photographer through buildings, identifying head and trip hazards, remaining alert for oncoming vehicles and generally being eyes and ears for the photographer during their time within the scene. If you are deployed at a scene, ensure you are not left to work solo, identify the hazards and inform the Team Leader of the requirement for a Safety Officer to accompany you.

Further reading on scene photography can be found online: Interpol, Disaster Victim Identification Guide – Victim identification.[3]

13.6   DISASTER MORTUARY PHOTOGRAPHY

Considerations and tactics for the mortuary photography phase should begin before any bodies or body parts arrive. The SIM, Coroner/Procurator Fiscal and SIO should have met and agreed the photographic forensic strategy in advance of post-mortem examinations taking place, and DVI mortuary teams identified. Depending on the circumstances and scale of the incident, it is likely that the mortuary teams will have had no contact with the scene in order to avoid the risk of cross-contamination.

The "setting" of the scene has already been referred to as one of the functions that photography performs at any disaster scene, and it is no different within the mortuary environment. Mortuary DVI photography can be a time-consuming task because all items of interest, clothing and injuries need to be fully recorded prior to their being packaged or further examinations taking place. Personnel involved within the mortuary must understand that, unlike many other police post-mortem examinations, DVI mortuary activities are driven by the speed of the scribe and the photographer and not merely by the pathologist. While team members may feel an urge to have the photographer speed up, it is vital to remember that the photographer gets only one chance at capturing the condition of the deceased, the clothing as worn, and any other physical evidence that is present before that cadaver's original state changes forever. Locard's theory of transference (every contact leaves a trace), which is usually associated with perpetrators leaving evidence at scenes, is equally applicable to DVI work, in that all the actions taken during recovery and examination alter the original conditions and transform them into something new and different.

The fatigue of personnel must also be taken into account in respect of the physical exertion that photographers undergo while carrying out their duty. DSLR cameras, with flashgun units attached, weigh more than might be realised and is a factor that has been commented on numerous times by UK DVI officers who have been assigned the photography role during the Advanced DVI course in Dundee. Mortuary managers and Team Leaders should take this fact into account when deployed at a live incident. Similar to the safety note for scene photography, the mortuary environment has numerous hazards of which the photographer can fall foul if precautions are not in place. As previously mentioned, there are various operations and considerations on which the photographer will be concentrating to ensure that the best possible images and available evidence are captured, and therefore can become less aware of their surroundings increasing their risks. A "clean" team member should be appointed to act as a safety officer for the photographer. This safety officer will be responsible for the photographer's general welfare, identifying slips, trips, head hazards and contaminated areas/items, as well as steadying them while on step ladders etc. Only "dirty" members of the mortuary team will handle bodies, body parts/fragments and any item removed from same for photography. At no point will the photographer compromise their "clean" status.

13.7   PHOTOGRAPHY WITHIN THE MORTUARY

Utilising the "rule of thirds" as previously explained, well-composed, sequential photographs must be taken to enable a full pictorial history of the actions and findings of the post-mortem examination. Setting up of a sterile working area in advance is advisable so that items of interest requiring close up photography can be dealt with easily away from the examination table. Think of how you will be taking the photographs and where possible create this sterile area in such a manner that avoids undue strain injuries. Ideally the camera will be set up on a tripod to allow the lens to be positioned at a 90-degree angle to the subject-matter for 1:1 reproduction. The luxury of a tripod may not always be available and where this is the case a small table, stool or even the floor can be adapted to allow items to be positioned in such a manner as to facilitate scaled photographs to be taken without causing undue strain both to the photographer and to the production/exhibit officers. Sterile areas can be created by taping down standard green medical sheets or if no medical supplies are available then consideration should be given to improvising with the use of polythene sheeting/tarpaulins or brown paper sacks cut open and taped together to form a working area (see Figure 13.1).

To ensure the continuity of each item brought into the mortuary it is essential that the URN and body labelling booklet front cover are photographed on the outer surface of the body bag prior to opening. Initial photography of the fragment/body bags should be full-length shots either taken from directly above or, if no platforms are available, then the bag should be held so that the camera is straight onto the subject. These initial photographs will require a background to mask out other activities within the mortuary and also to avoid "hotspots" from the flash bouncing back from stainless steel surfaces. Like the sterile areas, backgrounds can be created from standard green medical sheets held up behind the subject-matter and laid over the mortuary tables or improvising with the use of polythene sheeting/tarpaulins or brown paper sacks cut open and taped together, as previously stated.

On opening the body bag, further images should be taken, showing the body/ fragment label and the bag label in the same frame, thus supporting the integrity of the item to be examined.

With the body/fragment bag removed, the subject must then be photographed full length again, as before, showing the attached URN label.

As the pathologist carries out their initial external examination of the clothed subject, any areas of interest should be recorded as directed. In recording these it is vitally important that a URN bar code label is included. Obviously, the attached body/fragment label, although an ideal size to be visible in general shots, will be too large to be included completely when recording areas of interest during the visual examination. In order to ensure that a URN is in each and every shot, and taking into account composition of shots, and in particular the exclusion of unnecessary distractions, eg hands and fingers, a large, medium and small URN bar code should be taken from the rear of the body labelling booklet solely for the use of the photographer. Taking a medical or forensic swab, cotton bud, or similar small-type probe and attaching the URN bar code label, covered in clear tape (to waterproof), will create a perfect marker that can be held next to the area of interest without the inclusion of gloved hands. This simple tool will facilitate the inclusion of the URN in each and every image taken, regardless of the distance from the lens to subject-matter.

For all photographs where scale is important and/or the image will be required to be printed at actual size, then a rigid scale must be included, with URN, and the camera lens positioned at 90 degrees to the subject. Where possible, good practice would dictate that a tripod and angle finder should be used to ensure that the 90-degree angle is achieved. Where a tripod and angle finder are not available, the rigid scale can be positioned within the viewfinder and additionally a team member can be used to watch the angle of the lens and advise corrective movements as required.

Following the initial external examination, the clothing, possessions and jewellery will be removed systematically. It is advisable that photographs are taken of each layer of clothing and the position of personal effects and jewellery as they are disclosed and prior to their removal. These images both provide evidence of the positioning of items and enhance the continuity process throughout the examination. Once each item is removed and prior to them being packaged by the exhibit officer, general and close-up views should be taken on the created sterile area, with URN and scales in place (see Figure 13.9).

Once the body/body part has been fully stripped, full-length unclothed views should be taken, as previously stated, again ensuring that the URN is visible. Unique identifying marks such as medical scarring, tattoos, birth marks and piercings should then be recorded, with the URN bar code labels and, where appropriate, rigid scales within the frame, as directed by the pathologist.

Other views, such as dental work or anthropological features, may also be required, and the photographer will usually be directed by the relevant specialist or, if unavailable, the pathologist about which images are required. Where facial

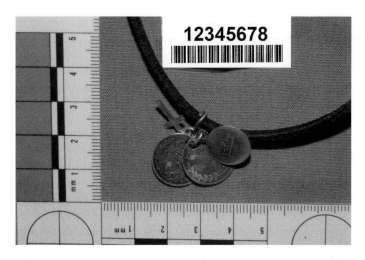

Figure 13.9   Personal items should be photographed on a neutral background, with a scale and the URN in the picture

reconstruction is likely to be a necessity then further detailed images will be required of the head and face.

The penultimate area of photography within the mortuary will generally be that of recording the ridge detail in the fingers, palms and soles of the feet in order to assist with identification.

Before attempts are made to take fingerprints, palmprints and/or foot impressions it is imperative that photographs of these areas of ridge detail are taken. This ensures that these details are recorded if destruction occurs during the printing process. Initially each hand should be recorded in its entirety, with URN, rigid scale and an identifier describing which hand is being photographed. Following the general views, the four finger sequence – fore, middle, ring and little fingers and thumb of each hand should be recorded as a single composition and thereafter each digit in turn individually photographed, with scale, URN and respective identifier (RT – right thumb, RF – right fore, RM – right middle, RR – right ring, RL – right little etc). These close up views should be of sufficient detail to allow the ridge detail to be clearly evident. Fingerprint officers will then powder or ink the areas of ridge detail and the photographic process should be repeated before any attempts are made to recover impressions. Following impressions having been recovered it might be prudent to take further general views of each hand/foot.

At this stage the full post-mortem examination will take place, depending on the set criteria.

On completion of the pathological and other associated specialist scientific examinations the subject will be placed into a body/fragment bag for storage pending the outcome of the identification commission and eventual repatriation.

Final "closing" photographs should be taken, showing the sealed bag with attached URN and body labelling booklet and other associated paperwork.

Before commencing with the photography of any other body or body part the memory card(s) from the camera *must* be downloaded onto a Master Compact Disc (CD) and entered as the last production/exhibit in the log relating to the URN that has just been processed.

13.8 DOWNLOADING DIGITAL IMAGES AND THEIR INTEGRITY

After concluding photographic duties at either the scene or the mortuary the captured images must be downloaded in order that they become a secure production/exhibit and to allow prints to be produced as required. Every force will have their own system of work pertaining to the downloading of digital images based on the Home Office guidance.[4]

The basic principle, however, is that the images from the removable "memory card" are copied directly onto a CD-R disk which is "Write Once, Read Many" (WORM) (in other words, it can be written to only once, as opposed to CD-RW (which are re-writeable and should never be used for evidential purposes). Alternatively, secure servers can be utilised, especially for long-term storage. Usually the first CD that is created is deemed to be the *master copy* and will be retained as the production/exhibit; at the same time or subsequent to producing the *master* a *working copy* will be created. The *master* will be stored securely pending any production at court, if required, and in the event of any question as to the integrity of the images will be removed from its packaging and viewed at this time. The *working copy* will be used as part of the investigation and will assist in preparing any Identification Commission submissions or criminal prosecution reports.

The HOSDB Digital Imaging Procedure v2.0 (2) also states that:

> "Where it is believed that images relate to any crime or incident pending civil or criminal proceedings they must be retained ensuring compliance with the Criminal Procedure and Investigations Act 1996, the Data Protection Act 1998 and ACPO (2006) Guidance on Management of Police Information."[4]

It is advisable to make contact with your force Scenes of Crime or Photographic Section to acquaint yourself with in-force procedures and equipment. As with all forms of technology there are various makes and types of system that are available and in use to download the memory cards onto Master and Working Copy CD.

Some machines produce one CD at a time; other equipment produces multiple CD copies.

Both of these types of systems are portable and run off mains, vehicle or battery power sources. Regardless of which system is in use in force, when deployed as part of UK DVI to any mass fatality incident in the United Kingdom it is prudent to suggest that the procedures adopted for the downloading of digital images will be those used by the host force where the incident has occurred. When deployed overseas it is at present uncertain exactly which type of system will be available for use. It might be the case that when acting as part of an International DVI response the DSLR cameras are plugged directly into a laptop or computer PC via a USB cable and the images are downloaded onto CD in this manner. Alternatively, systems similar to that in use in UK policing may be available for use both for scene and for mortuary work.

No matter where you are deployed and what equipment is available to you, the basic principles to which you should adhere to will be to burn two CDs, one of which should be labelled as the master copy, sealed and lodged as a production/ exhibit, and the second retained for the investigation team. Once the CDs have been checked and all the images are seen to be there (faults do happen with these machines, and it won't be the first time a blank CD has been bagged as a production), then the memory card can be formatted, by following the appropriate camera formatting procedure, all the images erased and the card left ready for use on the next shift.

13.9 CONCLUSION

Forensic photography, like any specialist skill, requires a great deal of training before the practitioner can be comfortable that they can capture images regardless of what conditions or environments they find themselves in. DVI photography is no different and at every opportunity suitably qualified SOCOs and/or photographers should be included as integral parts of any UK DVI deployment. If the general ethos outlined in this chapter is followed then, regardless of any previous levels of camera competency, any member of the UK DVI Team should, when it all goes horribly wrong, be able to pick up the SOCO/photographer's camera and, with confidence, compose, capture and present professional-quality photographs that can be produced at any Identification Commission or judicial court anywhere in the world.

In having the ability to carry out this function the identification process can carry on unhindered until such time as replacement staff are found or team members return to duty. Possibly, and more importantly, you will have enabled the body in question to be processed, and perhaps have allowed for a more timeous conclusion as to the identity of the deceased and thereby eased the suffering of the next-of-kin.

Things to remember:

- Make sure the memory card is formatted before starting.
- Fill out scene/mortuary photo log.
- Think about composition.

- Be aware of backgrounds.
- Utilise backdrops.
- Take as many photographs as you can.
- NEVER EVER DELETE!
- Overview.
- Take as many photographs as you can.
- Mid-view.
- Take as many photographs as you can.
- Close-up view.
- Take as many photographs as you can.
- NEVER EVER DELETE!
- Rigid Scales.
- URN.
- Safety Officer.
- Download to master and working copy CDs.
- Integrity.
- DISCLOSURE.
- YOU can do it, don't be afraid of the camera!

REFERENCES

1 R2S Crime website [online]. Available at: http://www.r2scrime.com/ [Accessed 10.12.2008.]
2 Home Office website. Digital Imaging Procedure 58-07 [online]. Available at: http://scienceandresearch.homeoffice.gov.uk/hosdb/publications/cctv-publications/DIP_2.1_16-Apr-08_v2.3_(Web).pdf?view=Standard&pubID=555512. [Accessed: 11.11.2008.]
3 Interpol website. Draft of the New DVI Guide [online]. Available at: http://www.interpol.int/Public/DisasterVictim/Guide.asp [Accessed: 12.11.2007.]
4 Home Office website. Storage, Replay and Disposal of Digital Evidential Images 53-07 [online]. Available at: http://scienceandresearch.homeoffice.gov.uk/hosdb/publications/cctv-publications/53_07_Storage_Replay_and_Di1.pdf?view=Standard&pubID=504030 [Accessed: 11.1.2008.]

CHAPTER 14

Fingerprints and DVI

The following chapter is intended as guidance and background on the taking of fingerprints/footprints from the deceased victims of disasters. Fingerprints are one of the three primary identifiers as outlined by Interpol in its DVI Guide.[1] In common with both DNA and odontology, the usefulness of this identification technique can vary with the disaster involved and the subsequent state of the cadavers. For a disaster such as September 11, identification was led by methodologies which allowed body parts to be reunited, such as DNA,[2] however during the identification of the victims of the Asian tsunami fingerprinting joined odontology as one of the two most important methods of identification.[3]

Suitably trained Scenes of Crime Officers, fingerprint experts and photographers should be an integral part of any DVI Team deployed to carry out the recovery and/or identification phases of any DVI deployment. In the vast majority of occasions these experts will carry out the functions of recording and recovering ridge detail evidence from cadavers for the purposes of identification.

This chapter is intended to give all personnel an insight into this particular function of DVI teamwork and furnish them with the basic ability to recover identifiable impressions from a cadaver to assist in the identification process should trained practitioners be unavailable.

While other techniques will be referred to in this document anything other than basic photography and powdering/inking of ridge detail should be avoided until the appropriate personnel are available to carry out this role.

Since before the judicial acceptance of fingerprints as a unique and conclusive means of identification, these marks have been used in a variety of ways including; authentication of art, as a signature for illiterates, for official seals on documents and as pre-historic decoration. As time has passed there have been many developments in the methods used to enhance and record prints and in the examination of marks, new technology for recording finger and palm prints is still being developed and put in place throughout the country.

14.1   THE SKIN AND THE DEVELOPMENT OF FINGERPRINTS

The skin is an organ system which covers the whole body, protecting the cells within by providing the essential fluid environment they need to both survive and be protected from the immediate environment. The skin itself is made up of two different layers; the epidermis, an outer layer of epithelial cells and an inner layer of dense connective tissue known as the dermis. Mostly the skin is thicker on the posterior area of a body part than it is on the anterior, but this is reversed on the hands and feet. The outer surface of the skin of the hands and feet also differs from the rest of the body in that it is arranged in a series of grooves (also known as furrows) and ridges. In life the main purpose of these ridges is to help to increase friction so that we can grip things. The patterns that these ridges form are recorded as a fingerprint or footprint. Fingerprint analysis is done by comparing the patterns of friction ridges found in the skin on the palm of the hand, the palm side of the fingers and thumb (the palmar surface) and the soles of the feet (the plantar surface). While the ridges and therefore the furrows lie parallel to each other they form a series of twists and turns as well as dead ends and starts. It is the pattern formed by the changes in direction of these ridges and furrows that is unique to each individual. The ridge patterns themselves are formed by the *dermal papillae*. These are a layer of cells which lie between the tough outer *epidermis* and the thicker, inner *dermis*. The pattern forms in the fetus and while growth occurs after this the pattern remains the same throughout life.[4] The ridge patterns which show on the epidermis are mirrored in the dermal layer (dermis), although if imaged the ridges show a tramline effect along their top, and the whole print can be slightly smaller than the same print made from the epidermis. Because of the mirroring of the pattern, identification can be made of prints taken from the dermis but those taking the prints should always record clearly which layer of skin has been used to enable those reading the images to take any differences into account.

Flexion ridges can also be seen where digits and hands bend. Unlike ridge patterns, flexion ridges are not always permanent and can change with age. They can help those reading the prints to orientate them but cannot be used as a means of identification due to their transitionary nature. Subsidiary ridge systems which may exist within the depths of the normal ridge system are permanent, however and can be used for identification purposes if they show up in the fingerprint image taken from the individual or the latent print.

On the summit of each of the ridges there are sweat glands, the moisture produced by these eccrine glands leaves an impression of the pattern of the ridges of that particular finger when it comes in contact with a surface – this is how finger marks can be recovered from handled items at crime scenes or within person's homes. These left behind fingerprint images are known as "latent prints".

The development of friction ridges begins in early fetal life.[5] They are fully formed around the 24th week and persist throughout life without changing. It is due to this unchanging nature of fingerprints that they have become so popular as an identifier. These ridges remain intact after death until they are lost when the body decomposes.

232

Around the sixth week of fetal life, volar pads form on the fingers, palms and interdigital areas: these are seen as bulges on the epidermal surface. The pads increase in size until around 13 weeks when they begin to regress. There has been a lot of research on the relationship between volar pads and friction ridge pattern. Studies have shown that there is a genetic influence on the physical aspects of volar pads and that these aspects, such as height, location, contour and inclination have an effect on the overall pattern of ridges. It has also been demonstrated that the regression of the volar pad and initiation of ridge formation have an effect on final overall ridge patterns. Thus when the volar pads begin to regress, around week 13, the cells which make up the ridges begin to form on the bottom of the epidermis, in the basal layer.[5] Early formation of ridges when the pads have yet to completely regress, are associated with whorls and late formation with arches. It is interesting to note that 60–65 per cent of the population has loops, 30–35 per cent whorls and around 5 per cent arches (see Figure 14.2). There are subdivisions within these three broad categories which give the basis of the 10-point classification system in current usage.

In most fingerprint patterns there are areas that are easily recognisable and can be used as points of reference within the ridge system. These fixed points are called "cores" and "deltas". The core is usually in the centre of the print while deltas are typically in the bottom half and can be offset to the right, left or both sides (see Figure 14.1).

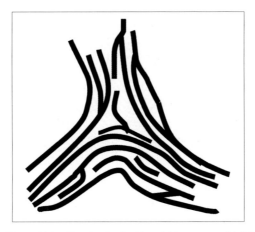

Figure 14.1   Showing the fixable point known as a "delta"

There has been no indication of hereditary control over the detail of individual ridges.

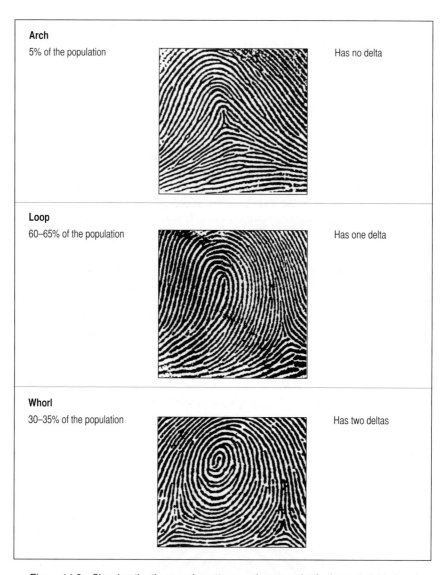

Figure 14.2 Showing the three main patterns – these can be further subdivided and combinations of the pattern types are also possible: these are called composites

14.2 THE HISTORY OF FINGERPRINTS

As a conclusive identification tool, fingerprints have been used successfully in the judicial system for over one hundred years. This is as a result of a great volume of work and research by a number of people, much of which went on for many years.[6,7] In order to have an identifier which is robust it is necessary to prove that it does not change throughout a person's life and that it is unique to them.

There are records from as early as 1684 which refer to fingerprints, concerning patterns upon the fingers and palms, sweat pores and epidermal ridges. Botanists, artists and physiologists all took a great interest in examining these marks but none suggested that they could be utilised for personal identification until a Scottish missionary, Dr Henry Faulds, became interested in fingerprints while working in Japan. In 1880 he published a paper in a British scientific journal outlining the potential of the use of fingerprints as a unique method of identification. He believed in this potential to the extent that he offered to work with Scotland Yard and set up a fingerprint identification process with them at his own expense, an offer which was rejected by the police. His paper raised some interest however, prompting an English civil servant working in India to write in to discuss his experiences of using fingerprints as contact signatures.[6,7]

Working as a British civil servant in India, Sir William Herschel (1833–1917), who reportedly had always been deeply interested in fingerprints, began using them as unique marks to check the identity of soldiers who were unable to sign for their allowances. He was responsible for paying the money to these soldiers and because they were not literate, needed to devise a system which prevented fraud. After carrying out experiments over a period of 60 years Herschel established the "Principle of Persistency" of papillary ridges – fingerprints are formed during early fetal life, they remain constant throughout life and are one of the last recognisable features to disappear after death. Ridges begin to form on the human fetus between the third and fifth month of pregnancy, the ridges, pattern and detail all grow simultaneously as the body grows, persisting, without change, throughout life. The ridges outlast most features of the body after death remaining intact and recordable until the flesh reaches advanced stages of decomposition.

Sir Francis Galton (1822–1911) was the first to investigate the uniqueness of the fingerprint, attempting to calculate the improbability of two people having the same fingerprints. Galton is also responsible for defining the basic patterns used in present-day methods to classify fingerprints. However, his most significant contribution to identification by fingerprints was perhaps the recognition of the minutiae of fingerprints which, ever since, have been referred to as Galton details or ridge characteristics.[6,7]

The Galton details are what make each fingerprint or palm print unique to an individual and are easily recognisable to a trained eye. Close examination of a fingerprint will reveal that the ridges are not just straight lines but instead contain many interruptions and breaks. These anomalies within the ridges are known as ridge characteristics – or Galton Details. The two main types used for identification purposes are the "ridge ending" and the "bifurcation". The other four characteristics are basically just variations of these details.[4,7]

Characteristic	Description	Image
Ridge Ending	This is where a ridge just ends abruptly. The ridges on either side usually just carry on, converging a little to take up the space created by the ending of the other ridge.	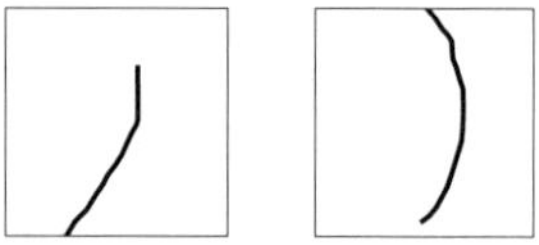
Lake	Formed when a single ridge divides into two and then rejoins almost immediately, forming a small circle or ellipse.	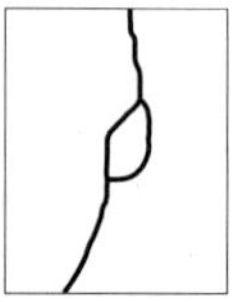
Bifurcation	A bifurcation is formed when a ridge splits into two, like a fork. In this instance the ridges on either side with diverge to make extra space.	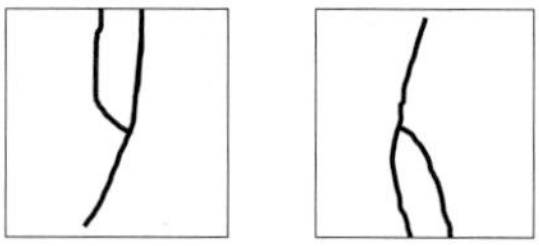
Independent Ridge	A small ridge which is completely separate from any other ridge.	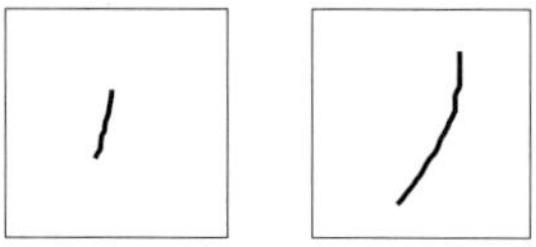
Spur	Can be described as a combination of a short independent ridge and a bifurcation.	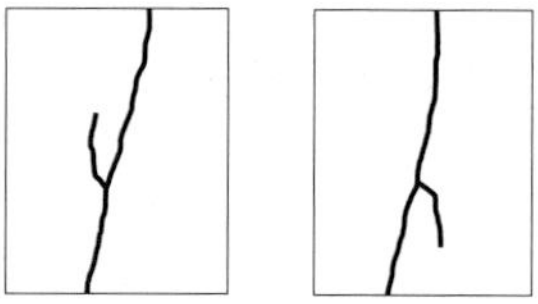
Crossover	As the name suggests, this is a crossover between two ridges. A small ridge is joined at either end to two ridges running parallel to one another.	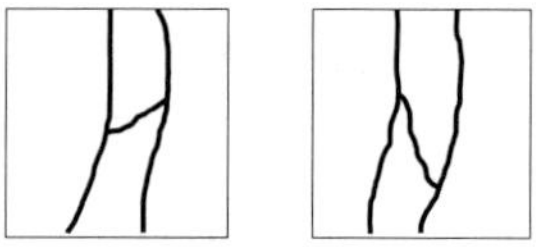

Figure 14.3   Showing the ridge patterns as described by Galton

In 1892 Galton published a textbook entitled *Fingerprints*. This book introduced the ideas of pattern types within the prints themselves as outlined above.

Once the ability to classify and compare prints was established it became possible to use them for identification. The use of fingerprint examination however was a cumbersome process, especially as banks of reference fingerprints began to be accumulated. A useable classification system had to be developed to make this new technology workable. This system was developed by Sir Edward Henry in 1897 and while it has undergone some refinements, it is still in use today in most English-speaking countries. In 1900 Henry published a book entitled *Classification and Uses of Fingerprints*. Shortly afterwards, in July 1901, the Fingerprint Bureau at New Scotland Yard was established.[6, 7]

The worth of fingerprinting for identification proved itself and it quickly became the main method of identification in criminal investigation. Every finger, thumb and palm print is unique due to the positioning and combination of Galton details – this goes for the toes and soles of the feet too! This makes prints taken from these areas clearly recognisable and hence identifiable.

When two fingerprint impressions are compared in order to establish identity there has to be an agreement in the sequence of ridge characteristics. This is called coincident sequence and means that the same characteristics must be; present, arranged in the same order and have the same relationship to each other, finally there must be enough of these characteristics within the impressions to ensure that the combination is unique to that print. Despite many years of use and the comparison of many millions of sets of ridge patterns, no two prints have ever been shown to be the same, even those from identical twins.[4, 5, 7]

The original method of identifying fingerprints was based on 12 points of agreement with no characteristics in disagreement. This was changed in 1924 by New Scotland Yard to the 16-point standard. The 16-point standard required 16 characteristics to be in agreement, again with none that were not in agreement. Therefore both the original 12 point and the subsequent 16-point standards relied purely upon ridge characteristics and the sequence that these details occurred in within any two impressions.[8] The 16-point standard was the "gold" standard for proof of identity in court, although there was provision for an identification to be made on less points of agreement, that this was being used had to be stated. While the 16-point standard was effective, it is also a higher number of points of agreement than is accepted in many courts around the world. A series of reviews concluded that it was not necessary for there to be this many areas of agreement and that it was enough that the fingerprint expert was able to show enough points of agreement between two prints for an identification to be made. This is known as the non-numeric standard.[9] The non-numerical standard, introduced in England and Wales in 2001 and to Scotland in 2006, allows the fingerprint expert to move away from completely relying on counting ridge characteristics within impressions. Now, it is possible for the expert to incorporate other information in their comparison including pattern type, general ridge flow, creases, scars and any other minute detail found within the ridges themselves.[8, 10]

14.3 FINGERPRINTS AND DVI

As noted fingerprints are one of the main identification criteria listed by Interpol,[1] although their use, as with any of the identification systems is limited by the type of disaster and the needs of those identifying victims. As in any DVI situation, however identification is about comparison. The identification team needs to compare the fingerprints taken from the deceased (post-mortem fingerprints), ideally taking in mortuary conditions and accurately recorded, with fingerprints which the individual has left behind in life, on personal possessions etc (ante-mortem fingerprints). A match between these two sets gives an identification which can then be taken to the Identification Commission.

14.4   ANTE-MORTEM FINGERPRINTS

Ante-mortem fingerprint collection in the UK is the remit of the Family Liaison Officer (FLO). Unless they themselves are an expert in fingerprint recovery they would work with an experienced SOCO (Scenes of Crime Officer) who would collect any prints identified. The skill is in identifying where an individual may have left a set of prints which can be attributed, without doubt, to them. This should be possible with a little ingenuity and creative thinking. With the increase in the use of biometrics for security reasons, it might be that the individual has their prints already on a database. As the aim of the fingerprinting is for identification it might be possible to make a direct comparison of the fingerprints of the deceased by taking the fingerprints obtained from the body to those collected from the home or work place. If the fingerprints match and all the other individuals who access the property are accounted for, then those which match give an identification, this saves the time involved in trying to narrow down an index set of latent prints. Footprints are also unique for the same reasons as fingerprints so if these can be found they should also be collected.

14.5   POST-MORTEM FINGERPRINTS

Post-mortem fingerprints, also known as reference prints are those prints which are taken from the body itself. When taking prints in a mass disaster situation it is advised that impressions are taken of all fingers, palms and feet, giving the greatest opportunity possible for a match to take place as an identification can come from any match between ridge patterns. It may be that as a result of the disaster, damage (trauma, decomposition etc) may have occurred to some of the areas from which prints can be taken, however all areas which contain patterning can be used and therefore, even if there is only a part of a finger which can be printed, this should still be done.

The inquiry into the identification of the victims of the *Marchioness* disaster[11] found that the hands of the deceased were removed by fingerprint officers to be sent to the Metropolitan Police Laboratory for printing. While this was not considered to be unusual practice at the time; no family members were informed that this had occurred. Additionally, of the 25 individuals who had hands removed only 4 were identified through fingerprints, the rest were identified through dental records, indeed some of the hands were removed after this positive identification had been made. Finally in a number of cases the hands were not returned to the body before the body was released to the family. Even before the Inquiry was published the practice of hand removal was reducing. The Interpol Guide to DVI states that "During PM (post mortem) examination of bodies it is essential to ensure that only unavoidable changes are made to the bodies examined".[1] This is recognised in the approach taken by fingerprint experts in the UK today.

Fingerprinting in the mortuary should follow the procedures laid out in the forensic strategy which has been decided upon by the SIM. Ideally two fingerprint officers/SOCOs would process each body. It is important that accurate records are kept throughout the process and all prints taken are accurately and clearly labelled as it might not be possible to return and take sets of prints at a later date due to deterioration of the body, indeed the process of taking the prints may cause damage.

It should be noted that suitably trained Scenes of Crime Officers, fingerprint experts and photographers should, in the vast majority of occasions, carry out the functions of recording and recovering ridge detail evidence from cadavers for the purposes of identification. As noted above, while this chapter gives an overview of the techniques involved in recovering identifiable impressions from a cadaver, anything other than basic photography and powdering/inking of ridge detail should be avoided until the appropriate personnel are available to carry out this role.

The method used to take prints from the bodies will depend upon the state of those bodies and what supplies are available.

14.6   PHOTOGRAPHY

The aim of the entire DVI process is ultimately the identification of the victim. By ensuring that the best quality of fingerprints is obtained from the deceased, the greater the likelihood that this will be achieved. Like many forensic applications the taking of ridge detail impressions from a victim may be a destructive process, if it is not recorded properly then these impressions may be lost forever and the identification process held up. It is vital therefore that photographs are taken of all fingers, palms and the soles of the feet before clothing is removed or any attempt is made to take prints. In this way, if the skin loses integrity and ridge detail is lost, the photographs can still be used for comparison purposes. Photography as a method of recording the prints is non-destructive, and gives a permanent record of the print. It may also aid the choice of technique used when printing is done. The lens MUST be at 90 degrees to the subject-matter to allow for actual size enlargements to be produced and oblique lighting will show the ridge and furrow detail in relief, although care should be taken that the image does not appear to reverse itself. If this occurs it can be corrected when the image is printed. Each finger should be photographed individually with a scale visible in the picture. An accurate written record should also be kept of each photograph taken.

In situations where there are a large number of bodies, such as happened after the Asian tsunami it is good practice to take a photograph after the fingerprinting techniques have been done and before washing the ink/powder off the hands. This gives a visual record that prints have been taken. It is also good practice to take photographs of any impressions which are taken. This ensures that there is a back-up record if paperwork goes missing.

14.7   CONDITION OF BODIES

The condition of the bodies of the victims of mass disaster is affected by the type of disaster in which they have been involved, ie natural occurrence, an accident or criminal acts. Many of the processes can cause damage to the epidermis. It should also be remembered that the body is not only affected by the event itself, but also by the conditions after the event. For example, the heat and humidity in Thailand, combined with the time it took to refrigerate remains after the Asian tsunami, were the cause of a great deal of damage to the bodies of those who had died during the event.

14.8   MACERATION

This is the term given to the changes undergone by soft tissue after it has been immersed in water for a long period of time. The skin begins to form deep wrinkles, which in turn affect the ridge structure and in time the epidermis separates from the dermis. In some situations the skin might slough off altogether. This results in what is known as an "epidermal glove". This resultant "glove" can be placed over the hand of the individual taking the fingerprint and powder or ink applied and the print taken.[12] Prints can also be taken from the dermis. If this is swollen and detail lost it may be necessary to place the hand in boiling water for a couple of seconds, being very careful not to cause damage to the dermal ridge detail. This causes the dermis to shrink and, once dried, impressions can be taken.

14.9 BURNING

Burning is associated with exposure to high temperatures but can also happen with exposure to some chemicals or extreme cold. Problems encountered are usually the clenched-fist position often referred to as "pugilistic", dehydration leading to shrinkage of the dermis, and the epidermis becoming very delicate and brittle. If the skin is hard but not too fragile, the skin can be placed into a 2 per cent sodium hydroxide solution. This softens the skin enough that it should then be possible to take fingerprints. As with the use of boiling water mentioned previously, great care should be taken when using this methodology to prevent damage to the ridge detail.

14.10 DECOMPOSITION

Once an individual dies the process of decomposition begins. The first effects of this process are seen in the soft tissue and are highly dependent on environmental conditions. In high heat and humidity soft tissue decomposes within days, in colder environments this can take longer. Decomposition results in the skin appearing to be slimy and discoloured, and sloughing of the skin can also occur with entire sections of the epidermis becoming loose or coming away altogether from the underlying dermis. In circumstances when the skin is beginning to disintegrate due to decomposition or the nature of the death, using powders or ink may be destructive and so after photography of the visible ridges, casting may be possible. If the epidermis is lost, it may be possible to take impressions from the dermis.

14.11 DESICCATION AND MUMMIFICATION

This occurs through long exposure to dry air and can happen in both cold and hot conditions.

During the process of mummification soft tissue becomes very hard and leathery. Softening of the skin can be undertaken using the 2 per cent sodium hydroxide solution in exactly the same way as would be done for burnt skin. Again, care has to be taken not to cause damage using this approach.[13, 14]

14.12 *RIGOR MORTIS*

Rigor mortis is the temporary stiffening of the muscles of the body after death.

Problems encountered during *rigor mortis* are generally in straightening fingers to facilitate the effective taking of an impression. An Anatomical Pathology Technologist (APT) can help deal with any problems involving *rigor mortis*, this usually entails a massage of the hand in order that the digits can be moved to an appropriate position for fingerprinting to take place. If there are wrinkles or creases in the skin then this can be overcome by stretching the skin or by inflating the bulb of the finger with glycerine or melted wax.

14.13   WRINKLING AND CREASING

One of the most common problems encountered when fingerprinting dead bodies is that the skin wrinkles and creases. Most times this can be overcome by gently massaging and stretching the skin until it tightens and becomes smoother.

There are two methods which can be used to reduce the creasing on fingertip skin. Winding thread or string as a ligature around the base of the finger and up to the joint below the tip will force fluids up to the tip of the finger causing it to swell and flatten out the creases. It is also possible to inject the tip of the finger with glycerol, embalming fluid, paraffin wax or Vaseline using a large bore needle and syringe. This is also facilitated by tying a piece of thread below the finger joint at the base of the fingertip preventing the fluid from moving down the finger. Once the finger has swollen, an impression can be taken.

14.14   MOISTURE AND SEEPAGE

It is common for the skin of the deceased to lose moisture through their pores. This moisture can interfere with the process of printing. As dead bodies naturally seep moisture through their pores and as they may be kept in a refrigerated area, it is important that digits are dried before any ink or powder is applied.

14.15   RETENTION OF IMPRESSIONS FROM THE DECEASED

There are many different techniques that can then be used to obtain the finger-prints, generally powders should be used before inking. It is good practice to ensure that as each impression is lifted a record is made of which finger, hand or foot it has been taken from. The process of decomposition means that fingerprints can be lost and it may not be possible to go back to the body for another chance. Accurate recording at the time will ensure that errors are limited. In addition to which digit the impression has been taken from it is also vital to record the methodology used to take the print and the URN for that body or body part MUST be recorded on every form completed.

Where lifting tape and adhesive labels have been used to obtain impressions they should be mounted on acetate sheets, preferably in the correct finger order to mirror a conventional fingerprint form, and annotated accordingly. A copy of this recording sheet can be found at the end of this chapter.

14.16 METHODOLOGY

There are a number of methods which exist for taking print impressions. They have all been tried and tested and any or a combination of them should enable the practitioner to take prints in most circumstances. These methods fall broadly into four categories, *photography*, *inking and printing*, *powder deposition* and *casting*, and they can all be used to recover prints from the epidermis and dermal layer of the skin. New methods of taking fingerprints are constantly being developed and many forces in the UK now have equipment which allows them to scan fingerprints. This technology has a number of limitations, not least of which is the need for the appropriate software and computer systems as well as power to keep it all running.[15] This chapter therefore has focused on those technologies which can be used in any disaster and in any situation: that is not to say that it is impossible that a more up-to-date technology might be used.

14.17 POWDER METHODS

Prior to any powders or inks being applied the ridge detail MUST be photographed with scale labels.

The area of ridge detail should be gently dried using paper towels.

Black fingerprint powder is liberally applied using a brush to the surface of the skin taking care not to overload the brush and clog the ridges. A white adhesive paper label is then pressed with the adhesive side down onto the powdered area and carefully peeled away. The paper label is then applied, adhesive side down, on to a clear acetate sheet and the finger position noted on the acetate. *A standard fingerprint form photocopied onto acetate provides the ideal medium for this.* If the epidermis or dermis to which the powder is being applied is too fragile for the use of adhesive tape or labels then the area can be photographed.

There are a number of different powders which can be used; aluminium fingerprinting powder and black fingerprint powder, both of which are applied using a brush. The use of magnesium strips and ammonium chloride have health and safety implications.

14.18 INK METHODS

In situations where the condition of the skin is good the use of ink to obtain impressions is quick and effective, as such it is a commonly used technique for fingerprinting. Using a roller, ink should be spread across the area to be printed, this ink is then transferred into a pre-prepared fingerprint card by wrapping the card around the digit. If using ink methods, these cards should be in a prepared

DVI fingerprint pack. Alternately, adhesive labels can be used as per the black powder technique. In each case accurate labelling is vital. In the case of the palms and soles of the feet, the prints can be obtained by pressing clean white paper firmly onto the inked areas of the skin. This should transfer the ink to the card or label giving an inked impression of the print. If adhesive labels are used they should be placed onto a clear acetate sheet and a record made of the finger and hand from which the impression was obtained.

It may be more appropriate for the "double-glove" technique to be used, especially if the epidermis is fragile or creased. In this method, ink is applied as above. Whoever is taking the prints then places a second latex glove over the pair which they are wearing. The inked finger is then rolled over this second glove in the area of the officer's hand known as the hypothenar area. This is the fleshy area at the base of the little finger. This impression can then be cut out of the glove and stuck onto a clear acetate sheet. Again, the finger and hand should be recorded for each of the impressions taken.

In some situations the epidermis can become detached from the underlying dermis. This may happen in the body bag or when the officer comes to take the prints. As mentioned previously, the epidermal glove can be taken, either whole or even as pieces of skin and placed over the glove of the officer taking the print and then inked and printed as described above in any of the inking methods. As in every method mentioned accurate recording is vital. Note should also be made that a careful search of the body bag should be done in every situation to locate any epidermal skin that might have become detached in the event that it might yield useable prints.

14.19   CASTING METHODS

There are a number of methods for casting fingerprints in existence. They involve applying a specially designed material to the surface with ridge detail.[16] Once this is set it is peeled off giving a reproduction of the ridges and furrows. This remains a permanent record which can be photographed or have an impression taken with ink or powder as described above. If done carefully and accurately casting can be extremely sensitive and will show up all necessary detail. It is important to note the method on the recording form.

14.20   CONDITION OF THE SKIN

The condition of the skin will be dependent both upon the disaster type and any exposure to the environment which might have occurred in the ensuing period. The condition of the skin can quickly deteriorate which in turn can cause difficulties in obtaining ridge impressions. Methods exist which can aid in optimizing ridge impressions and if problems are identified in the condition of the skin then fingerprinting should be delayed until appropriate practitioners are available.

All impressions should be marked with a unique reference number (URN), where on the body they have been taken from and the method used to take them. They are then passed to fingerprint experts who will undertake comparisons with ante-mortem prints which have been collected by the FLO teams.

14.21   DIRECTION AND COLOUR

The method used to take the prints affects the way in which they are read as some methods will highlight ridge detail and others will highlight furrow detail. Anyone taking prints should ensure that the method used is recorded accurately on the recording form and this can then be taken into account by those doing the matching of prints.

Method	Direction	Colour of ridge
Ink and printing	Correct	Correct
Adhesive labels	Correct when impression photographed through the back of the acetate sheet	Correct when impression photographed through the back of the acetate sheet
Lifts with adhesive tape	Correct	Correct
Powder	Incorrect-can be corrected by photographic methods	Correct
Cast	Correct	Incorrect
Impression of cast	Incorrect	Incorrect

Table 14.1   Listing the direction and colour associated with each method of fingerprinting

14.22   POINTS FOR CONSIDERATION

* Ideally a SOCO/Fingerprint Officer should be involved in the process of obtaining the prints and a SOCO/police photographer should be assigned to take any photographs, as this is a very specialised function.
* Each body should be assessed by a Fingerprint Officer, to determine the best method to be used for obtaining maximum results.
* Body bags should be searched and all epidermal skin, regardless of size, along with any body parts that contain friction ridge detail should be recovered and assessed for prints.
* Photographs should be taken of the skin before prints are taken, after prints are taken and of the prints themselves.

- Multiple prints of each finger should be considered to ensure the maximum amount of ridge detail is recorded to assist the identification process. Differing methods of recovery may be a consideration for practitioners.
- If the epidermal skin has become detached, prints should be taken from the dermis. This fact should be noted on the documentation.
- Each individual finger impression MUST be properly annotated with the correct finger position and from which hand it originates.
- Note the method used to obtain the impressions. This will inform fingerprint experts on the correct colour and direction of the ridges when they make comparisons with ante-mortem prints.
- The last set of prints should be a plain set consisting of printing all four fingers simultaneously if this is possible. This will enable the fingerprint expert to check that the prints taken have been annotated accurately.
- Prints should be obtained from the soles of the feet wherever possible.
- The appointed Fingerprint Officer will assess each form to determine the quality of the impressions. Where impressions fall below the required standard, further impressions may be required to be recovered.
- The correct unique body reference number (URN) MUST be affixed to each set of impressions taken.

HEALTH AND SAFETY – FINAL NOTE

Personal protective precautions should be taken whenever an officer takes prints of the deceased. Additionally, the resultant fingerprint impressions obtained should be packaged and clearly labelled as a **health hazard**. Where possible, they will eventually be either subjected to autoclaving or appropriate precautions will be taken if autoclaving is likely to destroy or damage the production. Equally, all equipment used in the process should either be destroyed in the appropriate manner or subjected to autoclaving.

REFERENCES

1 Interpol, *Draft of the New DVI Guide* (2009) [12.02.09] [online]. Available at: http://www.interpol.int/Public/DisasterVictim/Guide.asp#chap4.
2 G MacKinnon and A Z Mundorff, "The World Trade Centre – September 11, 2001" in T Thompson and S Black (eds), *Forensic Human Identification: An Introduction* (CRC Press, Oxford, 2007), pp 485–499.
3 O W Morgan, P Sribanditmongkol, P Perera, Y Sulasmi, D Van Alphen and E Sondorp, "Mass Fatality Management following the South Asian Tsunami Disaster: Case Studies in Thailand, Indonesia, and Sri Lanka" (2006) 3(6) *PLoS Medicine* 195.

4 D Maltoni, D Maio, A K Jain and S Prabhakar, *Handbook of Fingerprint Recognition* (Springer, New York, 2005).

5 M Kücken and A C Newell, "Fingerprint formation" (2005) 235(1) *Journal of Theoretical Biology* 71.

6 C Beavan, *Fingerprints* (1st edn, Hyperion, New York, 2001).

7 J Berry and D A Stoney, "History and Development of Fingerprinting" in H C Lee and R E Gaensslen (eds), *Advances in Fingerprint Technology* (2nd edn, CRC Press, Boca Raton, 2001), pp 1–40.

8 M Vatsa, R Singh, A Noore and S K Singh, "Combining pores and ridges with minutiae for improved fingerprint verification" (2009) 89(12) *Signal Processing* 2676.

9 R Knowles, "The new (non-numeric) fingerprint evidence standard – is it pointless?" (2000) 40(2) *Science & Justice* 120.

10 D T Stoney, "Measurement of Fingerprint Individuality" in H C Lee and R E Gaensslen (eds), *Advances in Fingerprint Technology* (CRC Press, Boca Raton, 2001).

11 L J Clarke, "Public Inquiry into the Identification of the Victims following Major Transport Accidents" (HMSO, London, 2001).

12 G J Knobel, "Taking Fingerprints from a Decomposed Body Using the 'Indirect Cadaver Hand Skin–Glove Method'" (2005) 95(9) *SAMJ* 665.

13 R Fields and D K Molina, "A Novel Approach for Fingerprinting Mummified Hands" (2008) 53(4) *Journal of Forensic Sciences* 952.

14 W D Haglund, "A Technique to Enhance Fingerprinting of Mummified Fingers" 1988 33(5) *Journal of Forensic Sciences* 1244.

15 G N Rutty, K Stringer and E E Turk, "Electronic fingerprinting of the dead" 2008 122 *International Journal of Legal Medicine* 77.

16 D Porta, M Maldarella, M Grandi and C Cattaneo, "A New Method of Reproduction of Fingerprints from Corpses in a Bad State of Preservation Using Latex" 2007 52(6) *Journal of Forensic Sciences* 1319.

URN_____

DVI   CADAVER FINGERPRINT FORM

Production No. _____   Date _____

Taken by _____   Witness _____   Mortuary _____

Location _____

1. Right Thumb	1. Right Fore	1. Right Middle	1. Right Ring	1. Right Little

6. Left Thumb	7. Left Fore	8. Left Middle	9. Left Ring	10. Left Little

Left Fingers	L Thumb	R Thumb	Right Fingers

Left Palm

Right Palm

URN _____

CHAPTER 15a

Regulation and Tissue Identification

15a.1 INTRODUCTION

Both the Human Tissue Act 2004[1] and the Human Tissue (Scotland) Act 2006[2] came about largely in response to the Alder Hey Inquiry[3] and the Bristol Royal Infirmary situation[4] where body parts were retained after post-mortem examination without either the consent or the knowledge of family members. Both Acts[1,2] centre on informed consent and place great emphasis on the need for such. The Acts[1,2] cover a number of activities involving human tissues including both their storage and transplantation. The Acts[1,2] are relevant to DVI situations within the UK due to the need to license premises within which post-mortem examinations and the retention of human tissues, both for evidential and identification purposes, take place. The differences between England, Wales and Northern Ireland, compared with Scotland will be addressed separately within this chapter but officers from all parts of the UK must be aware of the systems that are currently in place on both sides of the border. It is of note that the Acts[1,2] only apply to the UK and any international deployment must abide by the rules of the relevant country or conform to agreements between governments and governmental organisations.

15a.2 ENGLAND, WALES AND NORTHERN IRELAND: THE HUMAN TISSUE ACT 2004 AND THE HUMAN TISSUE AUTHORITY

The Human Tissue Authority[5] (HTA) is the body responsible for the governance of the Human Tissue Act 2004.[1] Currently there is a Bill being progressed through Parliament which may result in the HTA[5] being superseded by the Regulatory Authority for Tissue and Embryos.[6] Therefore it must be borne in mind that this section is only current at the time of writing and it is imperative that operators ensure the current status of legislation is understood.

15a.3 CONSENT

The Human Tissue Act 2004[1] underlines the need for consent when a post-mortem is to be performed. In a mass disaster situation the need for consent is

251

covered by the actions of the Coroner as consent is not required if a post mortem is ordered by the Coroner. This also applies to the removal of any body parts or tissues required by the Coroner for investigation (Coroners Rules 1984).[7] Despite this, the work of any pathologist undertaking a post-mortem remains under the auspices of the HTA[5] and both the pathologist and the mortuary must still comply with the relevant Codes of Practice.[5] The Home Office felt that among other things this would reduce the chances of any disfiguring processes being carried out either unnecessarily or without total transparency. It should be noted that a record must be kept of the processing and fate of any material removed from the remains during a post mortem under the Coroners Rules 1984 (rules 9A and 12A).[7]

15a.4   LICENSING

The HTA[5] issues and oversees the licensing of premises. All premises where post mortems are to be carried out must be licensed under the Human Tissue Act 2004.[1] The Act specifies that post mortems are to be carried out for the purposes of:

1. Providing information about or confirming the cause of death.
2. Investigating the effect and efficacy of any medical or surgical intervention carried out on the person.
3. Obtaining information which may be relevant to the health of any other person (including a future person).
4. Audit, education, training or research.

It can be seen from this list that post-mortem examinations for the purposes of identity are not listed. However it is the practice in the UK to perform post mortems after a DVI incident to establish/confirm the cause of death and the identity of the deceased forms an integral part of the subsequent judicial process.

The licensing process ensures that all establishments which currently undertake post mortems on a regular basis are licensed, so if an established, licensed premises are used in the event of a mass disaster the appropriate licence will already be in place. The licence covers any building which is attached to the mortuary in question or indeed which is on the same site as the licensed premises, for example on the same hospital site. However, in most mass disasters it is not appropriate to use existing facilities such as these and therefore a temporary or emergency mortuary is utilised. A temporary mortuary would not have a pre-existing licence in place, so whether NEMA or a local facility such as an aircraft hangar is used, the process of licensing the premises needs to be undertaken prior to the commencement of any post-mortem examination.

The licensing process is relatively time consuming and therefore the HTA[5] has undertaken to try to speed up this process to facilitate rapid response capabilities.

However at present, the actual process and the need for named individuals remains the same. The legal requirements before a licence can be issued are (taken from the HTA website):[5]

- The HTA must have received an application for a licence.
- The HTA must be satisfied that the proposed Designated Individual (DI) is a suitable person.
- The HTA must be satisfied that the proposed Licence Holder (LH) is a suitable person/entity.
- The HTA must be satisfied that the premises are suitable.
- The licence and any conditions must be acknowledged in writing by the DI and LH.

It should be noted that the need for a licence only applies to the place in which the bodies are stored and where they undergo post-mortem investigation. The pathologist can examine the deceased at the scene and the remains can be transported to the designated facilities without the involvement of the HTA as a licensing authority.[1]

The Human Tissue Act[1] names a number of statutory roles that must be filled by named personnel in order for a licence to be granted. These are;

- the licence holder;
- the designated individual;
- persons acting under the direction of the designated individual,
- persons designated by the designated individual.

15a.4.1 Licence Holder[1,5]

This is usually a corporate body, such as an NHS trust or a local authority, however, there must be a named contact, who is responsible for paying the licence fee. Before applying for a licence they must have the consent of the designated individual; however the licence holder can apply to vary the licence or to remove the designated individual without his or her consent. In the event of a mass disaster the local authority should have named this individual within its Mass Fatalities Plan.[8] The HTA will provide guidance to the local emergency planning team so that, whoever or whatever organisation this is, it knows how to begin the application procedure.

15a.4.2 Designated Individual (DI)[1,5]

This is a key role, as the Designated Individual is the person under whose supervision the licensed activities are authorised to be performed. They have specific responsibilities as set out in s 18 of the Human Tissue Act 2004.[1] They must consent to an application or make it themselves. Finally, they must undergo training provided by the HTA.[5]

The statutory duties as set out in s 18 of the 2004 Act[1] are:

- they must ensure that the other persons to whom the licence applies are suitable persons to participate in carrying out the licensed activity;
- to ensure that suitable practices are used in the course of carrying out that activity;
- to ensure full compliance with the conditions of the licence.

Who should be the Designated Individual?

"The person might be a head of department, a clinician, a scientist, or a manager. What is important is that it is a person who is in a position to secure that activities are conducted properly by people who are suitable to carry out those activities and that all the necessary requirements are complied with."

Lord Warner, House of Lords Grand Committee[8]

For the purposes of a mass disaster situation the HTA[5] has suggested that the local authority will have named an individual or number of individuals who can take on the role of DI. This does not have to be a police officer (the SIM) but could be either the lead pathologist or indeed the Coroner. This designated individual will have access to e-learning material on the HTA website[5] which will ensure that they are ready and able to submit the application for a licence without delay and that the HTA[5] is agreeable for them to do this, having undertaken the relevant checks beforehand, as the HTA[5] must be satisfied that the proposed DI is a suitable person to supervise the activity which is being authorised by the licence. They must be satisfied that the applicant is a suitable person to be the holder of the licence and that the premises are suitable for the activity to be authorised by the licence.

15a.5 AFTER GAINING THE LICENCE

The HTA[5] has proposed that within 72 hours of the mass disaster event the local Head of Regulation will be on hand to work with the Mass Fatalities Co-ordination Group.[9] Their presence on site would enable them to give appropriate advice enabling compliance with the Human Tissue Act 2004[1] in a dynamic situation.

15a.6 ABOUT THE LICENCE

Usually, only one activity can be carried out per licence. The authority recognised that establishments carrying out post-mortem examinations are likely to undertake more than one activity. Consequently, three potential licensable activities have been clustered together. These are:

- the undertaking of a post-mortem examination;
- storage of the body of a deceased person, or relevant material from a human body for a scheduled purpose (see below);
- removal of tissue from the body of a deceased person for a scheduled purpose (see below) other than post-mortem examination or transplantation.

Regarding post-mortem examinations, a scheduled purpose is as follows (the following is as written in the Human Tissue Act 2004):[1]

15a.6.1   Scheduled purpose requiring consent: general

- Anatomical examination.
- Determining the cause of death.
- Establishing after a person's death the efficacy of any drug or other treatment administered to him/her.
- Obtaining scientific or medical information about a living or deceased person which may be relevant to any other person (including a future person).
- Public display.
- Research in connection with disorders, or the functioning of the human body.
- Transplantation.

15a.6.2   Scheduled purpose requiring consent: deceased persons

- Clinical audit.
- Education or training relating to human health.
- Performance assessment.
- Public health monitoring.
- Quality assurance.

15a.6.3   Licence conditions

There are two sets of conditions that a licence may impose. They are, firstly the statutory conditions that apply to all licences of a particular type and secondly any additional conditions that may also be added to a licence. A copy of the conditions to be imposed by the licence must be acknowledged in writing by the applicant for the licence and, where different, the proposed Designated Individual.

15a.6.4 Statutory licence conditions[5]

- The licensed activity must only take place on the premises specified in the licence.
- Activities performed under a licence must be supervised.
- Information required by the HTA must be recorded.
- Records must be kept as specified by the HTA.
- Copies of records or extracts that may be requested by the HTA must be provided.
- HTA fees to cover the cost of "superintending compliance with the terms of licences" must be paid.

15a.6.5 Codes of Practice[5]

The HTA has produced codes of practices that give practical guidance and lay down the standards that the HTA expects to be applied when carrying out licensed activities.

15a.7 SCOTLAND: HUMAN TISSUE (SCOTLAND) ACT 2006[2]

The HTA[5] covers England, Wales and Northern Ireland; although there is some cross-over in that the HTA is involved in the licensing of establishments for the storage of tissues which are to be used in transplants etc. This does mean that there is no requirement for licensed premises in a mass disaster situation for post mortems or storing bodies re a temporary mortuary situation should this occur in Scotland.

REFERENCES

1 Human Tissue Act 2004 (c 30) (HMSO, London) [online]. Available at: http://www.opsi.gov.uk/ACTS/acts2004/ukpga_20040030_en_1. [Accessed: 10.06.08.]
2 Human Tissue (Scotland) Act 2006 (asp 4) (HMSO, London) [online]. Available at: http//www.opsi.gov.uk/legislation/scotland/acts2006/20060004.htm. [Accessed: 17.10.2007.]
3 M Redfern, J Keeling and E Powell, "Report of the Royal Liverpool Children's Inquiry" (2001) [online]. Available at: http//www.rlcinquiry.org.uk. [Accessed: 17.10.2007.]
4 "Learning from Bristol: the report of the public inquiry into children's heart surgery at the Bristol Royal Infirmary 1984–1995", presented in July 2001 [online]. Available at: http//www.bristol-inquiry.ord.uk. [Accessed: 17.10.2007.]
5 Human Tissue Authority website [online]. Available at: http//www.hta.gov.uk/abouthta.cfm. [Accessed: 17.10.2007.]

6 Regulatory Authority for Tissues and Embryos [online]. Available at: http//www.hta. gov.uk/about hta/how we work/rate.cfm. [Accessed 17.10.2007.]

7 King's College London, Coroners Rules 1984 (SI 1984/552) [online]. Available at: http://www.kcl.ac.uk/depsta/law/research/coroners/1984rules.html. [Accessed: 22.10.07.]

8 Department of Health, "Human Tissue Authority. A guide to licensing for Designated Individuals and Licence Holders" (2006) [online]. Available at: http://www.hta.gov. uk/_db/_documents/2006-03-01_Guide_to_licensing_for_DIs_and_LHs_final_PDF. pdf. [Accessed 17.10.2007.]

9 Department of Health, "Human Tissue Authority. Licensing of emergency mortuaries" (2007) [online]. Available at: http://www.hta.gov.uk/guidance/licensing_of_ emergency_mortuaries.cfm. [Accessed 17.10.2007.]

Stable Isotope Analysis in Support of Disaster Victim Identification

15b.1 INTRODUCTION: WHY WE ARE WHAT WE EAT AND DRINK

Our world and everything within it is made up from 92 naturally occurring chemical elements. If we focus solely on organic matter, be this a piece of wood, an apple, an animal or a human, the most common elements encountered are hydrogen, carbon, nitrogen, oxygen, sulphur and phosphorus. Of the 92 natural chemical elements,[1] almost all occur in more than one form.[2] The abundance of each element and its different forms was fixed when the earth was formed and has not changed since that time.

Since the differences between these forms are very subtle and because the vast majority of these different forms are stable (ie do not decay) we are usually unaware that they exist. In addition, these subtly different forms are not equally abundant. If we use carbon as an example, figures usually quoted for abundance of the two stable carbon forms refer to their abundance on a global scale, ie when considering the entire carbon mass of the earth system (organic and inorganic) the natural abundance of carbon-12 (^{12}C) and its heavier form carbon-13 (^{13}C) is 98.89 atom% and 1.11 atom%, respectively. However, the compartmental isotope abundance of light elements, that is the abundance of light elements within any given locality, is not fixed, but is in a continuous state of flux. The combination of biological, biochemical, chemical and physical processes and the unique way in which they are processed in different plants, animals and even entire ecosystems leads to variations in the abundance of these two carbon forms, eg comparing sweet corn (maize) with barley.

The abundance variations are generally quite small (0.0005 to 0.08 atom%) but can be detected readily with modern techniques, namely isotope ratio mass spectrometry (IRMS) named after the scientific term "isotope" used for an element that occurs in more than one form. Ultimately, the various chemical elements and their isotopes are taken up into the human body through food and drink and are used to build and rebuild body tissues such as bone, hair and muscle, which is why we truly are what we eat and drink (Figure 15.1). Because isotopic abundance varies with source (eg who or what made a particular compound) and origin (ie the geographical location where the compound was made) this means that by measuring the stable isotopic composition of hair or bone of a victim, we may be

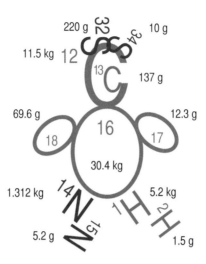

Figure 15.1   Isotopic composition for the major chemical elements comprising a Central European person with all weights given relative to an assumed body weight of 50 kg. Note: difference of sum total of the weights shown to 50 kg is due to the combined weight of all the other (minor) elements not represented here.

able to offer intelligence about dietary habits, geographical origin and possibly even recent movements (Figure 15.2).

15b.2   RATIONALE: WHY DO WE DO IT?

There is a need for quick screening tools to establish victim identity should natural or man-made disasters lead to a major loss of life. Because of its localised nature, the identification of victims in mass disaster scenarios resulting from a terrorist bomb attack can generally be established relatively quickly by circumstantial evidence, facial recognition, dental information, fingerprints and DNA analysis. However, a quite different scenario presented in the 9/11 and the 7/7 bombings because of the multi-cultural and ethnically diverse nature of cities such as New York and London (not to mention the tourist visitor element) and the potential for the inclusion of the remains of the suicide bombers. Similar situations were encountered in the Bali bombing and the 2004 tsunami where, in the case of the latter in particular, the heterogeneous tourist visitor element (plus environmental conditions) resulted in lengthy delays to the identification process, misidentification, mis-association and a significant proportion of unidentified. In these situations, a reliable verification of geographical home of the victim and/or their ethnicity would be of tremendous assistance as a preliminary sifting criterion prior to confirmation of personal identity.[3]

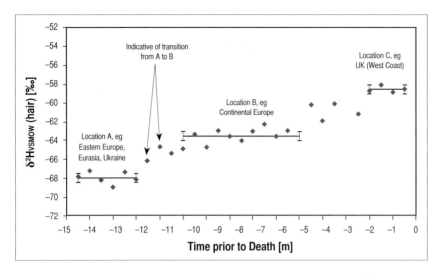

Figure 15.2 ^2H stable isotope analysis of scalp hair from a murder victim showing a history of "recent" geographic movement over a period of 15 months prior to death. The ^2H isotope data clearly indicate residence in three distinctly different locations and movement in between. Note: the named areas for locations B and C are putative locations and shown for illustrative purposes

15b.3 STABLE ISOTOPE ANALYSIS: WHY IT WORKS

These days almost everybody has at least heard of DNA and how powerful a technique DNA comparison (often referred to as "DNA fingerprinting") has become in combating crime and securing convictions for crimes that would otherwise have remained unsolved. However, very few people are aware of the natural variation in most of the chemical elements that make up their bodies that are as intimate a part of us as our genetic DNA. Unfortunately, on the odd occasion that other variants of chemical elements are mentioned in the media, the focus is generally on radioactive isotopes (or radioisotopes) and the fact that most elements are accompanied by stable and not radioactive variants tends to get overlooked or misunderstood. The stable variants are called isotopes because they are the norm while radioisotopes are the exception. To make this point more clearly, the scientific community is increasingly referring to these normal isotopes as "stable isotopes" to avoid confusion with the less common – but perceived as more sinister – radioactive or radioisotopes.

At this point the reader's attention is drawn to the remarkable similarities between the organic, life-defining material DNA and the more basic, inorganic chemical elements in their various isotopic forms when utilised within the context of forensic sciences. DNA comparison is at its most powerful when a DNA profile from a suspect can be matched against a comparative sample secured from the crime scene or against an entry in the national DNA register. In a way the same is

261

true for the information locked into the isotopic composition of a given material. Stable isotope comparison[4] (often referred to as "stable isotope fingerprinting") is at its most powerful when the sample in question and its isotopic composition can be compared to that of a sample of known provenance. Similarly, the specificity of a DNA match based on six *loci* and the theoretical specificity of a multivariate isotope "fingerprint" are equally matched. Consider two samples of hair from two different individuals and assume that they both may exist naturally in any one of the given isotopic states per element. In the units of stable isotope measurement (δ-notation where δ-values are reported as [‰]) the minor hydrogen isotope (^{2}H) can assume about 700 different δ-values while the minor carbon isotope (^{13}C) can assume about 110 different δ-values.[5] Analysing an organic material such as human hair for their isotopic composition with regards to hydrogen (H), carbon (C), nitrogen (N) and sulphur (S) would theoretically yield a combined specificity of 1 in 1.03 billion.

Whether this theoretical level of specificity, and hence discriminatory power, is actually realised in nature has not yet been fully explored, but thus far the discriminatory power inherent in the nature of multivariate data such as multi-isotope "fingerprints" has been successfully used to protect consumers from fraudulent substitution of low-quality products or ingredients masquerading for the high-quality real product.[6,7] For example, wine, certain spirits, high-quality single-seed vegetable oils, natural flavourings and honey are all subject to stable isotope analysis (sometimes in conjunction with other analytical techniques) to determine/verify authenticity or to detect fraudulent labelling and misrepresentation.[8,9,10,11,12,13] The British Food Standards Agency has applied stable isotope analytical techniques for food authentication since the mid-1990s. Similarly, the European Office for Wine, Alcohol and Spirit Drinks (BEVAPS) has been using stable isotope analytical techniques and data to combat major fraud in the beverage sector since 1997 although stable isotope analysis had been used as early as 1993.[14,15] BEVAPS was established by the European Union in 1993 and is now part of the Food Products Unit of the Institute for Health and Consumer Protection at the European Commission's Joint Research Centre (JRC) in Ispra.

In a way, stable isotope comparison of food and food ingredients to detect adulteration can be regarded as the first forensic application of this technology. It is therefore not surprising that stable isotope comparison is now being increasingly used to provide forensic intelligence for criminal investigations, and to determine if two materials such as two drug samples[16] seized from different persons and/or premises came from the same source.[17] Analytical methods traditionally applied in forensic science laboratories establish a degree of identity between one substance and another by identifying its constituent elements, functional groups and by elucidating its chemical structure. So, for two samples of sugar, all of the aforementioned data will correspond and it can be concluded that they are chemically indistinguishable, they are indeed both sugar. However, it can be argued that although two substances in question are chemically indistinguishable they may not be the same, for example they may have come from different sources or be of different origin. This assertion, which has already been made in defence of people standing trial for drug offences, can be contested by stable isotope analysis. Two chemically indistinguishable compounds will be isotopically distinguishable if they are of different geographical origin or are derived from a different source. In the case of sugar, traditionally the two main sources of sugar are sugar cane and sugar beet. With the help of stable isotope comparison it is perfectly straightforward to determine whether a sugar sample is either cane sugar or beet sugar. In addition, it is even possible to say where approximately in the world the sugar cane or sugar beet was grown and cultivated (see Table 15.1).

Food	$\delta^{13}C$ [‰]	δ^2H [‰]
Sugar (sugar beet; Poland)	−25.42	−71.0
Sugar (sugar beet; Sweden)	−26.84	−93.4
Sugar (sugar cane; Brazil	−11.76	−21.4
Sugar (sugar cane; South Africa)	−11.10	−6.7

Table 15.1   Isotopic abundance of ^{13}C and ^2H in sugar from different sources and origin

The same principle has been utilised in recent years in behavioural and ecological studies, for example feeding and migration patterns of animals and birds. In a similar way in which stable isotope analysis of food authenticity has moved on to forensic applications, stable isotope comparison for the purpose of studying animal behaviour has taken the logical step of being applied to aid human identification in cases where circumstances hamper the use of traditional methods such as DNA comparison, fingerprinting and odontology.

Variations in the isotopic abundance of chemical elements such as hydrogen (H), carbon (C), nitrogen (N), oxygen (O) and sulphur (S)[18,19,20] that are the building blocks of the compounds forming the human body reflect the isotopic make-up of food and water consumed and as such reflect the lifestyle and geographic origin of a person. In other words, diet and geo-location influence the isotopic signature of body tissues such as hair, nail, teeth and bone, and can hence be used to aid human identification in cases where no viable material is available for DNA comparison or where a DNA match cannot be found in a reasonable period of time because DNA databases have to be searched on a global scale (9/11; 2004 tsunami) or cannot be found at all.

The basic principle behind establishing lifestyle and geographic life history using stable isotope comparison is the fact that the body's only source of carbon and nitrogen is a person's staple diet. Similarly, the body's major source of hydrogen is water (H_2O), either from directly consumed water as liquid intake or from water indirectly consumed in foods such as fruit and vegetables.

Almost all chemical elements occur naturally in more than one form. Using the simplest element – hydrogen – as an example, one could say hydrogen, symbolised by ^1H, and its sibling deuterium, symbolised by ^2H, are identical twins but are of different weight and of different abundance. Deuterium (^2H) is the heavier twin whose weight differs from that of hydrogen (^1H) by one atomic mass unit (amu). Deuterium is also the less abundant of the two hydrogen isotopes. The same is true for the carbon twins. Here, sibling carbon-13 (^{13}C) is the heavier twin, weighing 1 amu more than its sibling carbon-12 (^{12}C); as for the two hydrogen isotopes, the heavier carbon-13 is the less abundant of the two carbon isotopes. Where the twin analogy has its limitations is the matter of abundance or occurrence but only for as long as we stay with the example of two complete twins. Obviously, the abundance ratio of any given pair of twins is 1:1 or 50 per cent : 50 per cent, ie when meeting any one twin in a crowd where both are known to be present one has an even chance of speaking to either twin A or twin B. However, if we consider a hypothetical case where both twins were victims of a major explosion the probability of any given body part belonging to either twin now becomes a function of the number of pieces into which each body has been divided. The same, in a way, is true for chemical elements and their "overweight" twins, the isotopes, the vast majority of which are stable isotopes, do not decay and hence are not radioactive. If one would take apart a lump of sugar to its molecular level one would find that, depending on circumstances (in this case which plant had produced the sugar), one would have a 98.9617 per cent or a 98.9015 per cent chance of finding carbon-12 if the sugar was beet sugar or cane sugar, respectively. Similarly, one would have a 1.0833 per cent and a 1.0985 per cent chance of finding carbon-13 in beet sugar and cane sugar, respectively. So, generally speaking, one always has a better chance of encountering carbon-12 than carbon-13, ie carbon-12 has a higher abundance than its isotope carbon-13. However, on a case-by-case basis one finds that chemically identical substances such as sugar can exhibit different isotopic compositions where a variation in carbon-12 abundance is accompanied by a proportional yet opposite variation in carbon-13. In this case, beet sugar contains more carbon-12 and less carbon-13 than cane sugar, while conversely cane sugar contains more carbon-13 and less carbon-12 than beet sugar.[21,22,23]

Minute yet significant differences as in the aforementioned example enable us to come to conclusions about a person's dietary habits and geographic origin when analysing various body tissues for their isotopic make-up. In other words, the isotopic composition of human tissues such as hair, nail, tooth and bone retain a record of a person's life history which is similar to the way in which tree rings keep a record of a tree's growth, and hence age, as well as growth rate and environment for each growth period.[18,24] Stable isotope analysis of the aforementioned tissues enables us to construct an isotopic "fingerprint" that may not necessarily permit direct identification of this person but will provide sufficient intelligence to construct a profile that will help to focus traditional identification techniques such as DNA, fingerprints and odontology.

An isotopic "fingerprint" of a white Caucasian male can tell us whether he came from the USA, the UK or Australia. Let's assume indications are that he came from the USA. In this case we may be able to determine whether he came from Florida or Oregon, and we may even be able to speculate on whether he was a vegetarian or a meat eater. So, from a vast pool of potential victims the search for the identity of this white Caucasian male has been reduced to a much smaller pool and, hence, focused on much more manageable numbers of potential victims, such as white male vegetarians from Oregon, USA.

15b.4   SAMPLING

15b.4.1   General considerations

In keeping with stringent "good laboratory practice" (GLP) regulations, fresh disposable gloves, hats and lab coats or hooded crime scene full-body suits should be worn at all times and sterile or new equipment (such as scalpel blades and tweezers) should be used to prevent contamination. Samples collected should be documented and logged using an established chain of custody procedure, and the signatures of the collecting officer and subsequent recipients of the samples collected. All descriptions and procedures should be documented contemporaneously, using documentation log sheets and examination sheets.

15b.4.2   Hair

Scalp hair should be collected as a "lock" of hair with an overall thickness of around 5 mm comprising approximately 100 individual hairs. The lock should be cut as close as possible to the scalp and from a place that will yield maximum length. This lock should be straightened out and held together by two pieces of Scotch tape at the cut and the tip (marked C and T respectively), or rolled up in a piece of tin or aluminium foil, folded tight at the cut end allowing the tips to protrude. The lock should then be placed in a self-seal evidence bag and the bag should be smoothed towards the seal before sealing it to remove most of the air from the bag. Since the bags are meant to be sent to the analysing laboratory as soon as possible, no particular storage requirements have to be observed other than keeping the bags and samples cool and dry.

15b.4.3   Nails

A fingernail sample should be collected by extracting one entire fingernail, ideally from the ring finger of the left hand if possible but any finger will do. Should the extraction leave traces of fleshy tissue still attached to the nail, do not remove them other than by physical means (scalpel). It is not crucial for traces of fleshy tissue to be removed, but in this case refrigeration of the sample is a must. The extracted nail should be double-bagged, ie placed in a self-seal or zip-lock bag before being put into the evidence bag. Please note that nail clippings are not sufficient.

15b.4.4 Bone

Collecting bone samples may not always be appropriate or even feasible under the circumstances of a DVI operation. However, a slice of femoral bone (Figure 15.3) cut from the mid-section of the femur (diaphysis) is a valuable resource of a person's long-term life history, and should be collected whenever this might be possible. If only one femur is present, it might be worth considering that this bone is used by the anthropologist to estimate the stature of the individual (see Chapter 19). Ideally, the slice of bone should be flesh free, though this may not be entirely possible to achieve in the field and largely depends on the state of decomposition. Any soft tissue and bone marrow should be removed as much as possible by means that will not compromise the isotopic composition of the sample, ie no chemical intervention. This means that excess tissue should be cut away using a scalpel, which may require changing scalpel blades quite often. If this should not be feasible under prevailing circumstances, it is better not to make any attempts at defleshing the bone sample. In other words, excess flesh, muscle, etc should not be removed and especially not by chemical means (eg oxidizing or alkaline digest). The bone sample must be double-bagged and kept frozen.

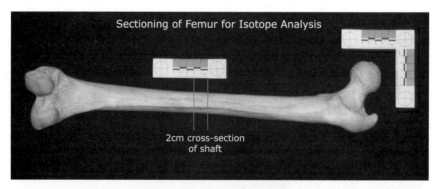

Figure 15.3   Sectioning the femur

REFERENCES

1   "Periodic table", *Wikipedia, The Free Encyclopedia* [online]. Available at: http://en.wikipedia.org/w/index.php?title=Periodic_table&oldid=244465339. [Accessed: 27.11.2007.]

2   "Isotopes", *Wikipedia, The Free Encyclopedia*. [online]. Available at: http://en.wikipedia.org/wiki/Isotope. [Accessed: 27.11.2007.]

3   E Rauch, S Rummel, C Lehn C and A Büttner, "Origin assignment of unidentified corpses by use of stable isotope ratios of light (bio-) and heavy (geo-) elements – A case report" (2007) 168(2) *Forensic Science International* 215.

4   S Benson, C Lennard, P Maynard and C Roux, "Forensic applications of isotope ratio mass spectrometry – A review" (2006) 157 *Forensic Science International* 1.

5   B Fry, *Stable Isotope Ecology* (Springer, New York, 2006).

6   W Meier-Augenstein, "Stable isotope analysis of fatty acids by gas chromatography–isotope ratio mass spectrometry" (2002) 465 *Analytica Chimica Acta* 63.

7   W Meier-Augenstein, "GC and IRMS Technology for 13C and 15N Analysis of Organic Compounds and Related Gases" in P A de Groot (ed), *Handbook of Stable Isotope Analytical Techniques* (Elsevier BV, Amsterdam, 2004) at 153.

8   F Angerosa, O Breas, S Contento, C Guillou, F Reniero and E Sada, "Application of stable isotope ratio analysis to the characterization of the geographical origin of olive oils" (1999) 47(3) *Journal of Agricultural and Food Chemistry* 1013.

9   F Angerosa, L Camera, S Cumitini, G Gleixner and F Reniero, "Carbon stable isotopes and olive oil adulteration with pomace oil" (1997) 45 J*ournal of Agricultural and Food Chemistry* 3044.

10 S Kelly, I Parker, M Sharman, J Dennis and I Goodall, "Assessing the authenticity of single seed vegetable oils using fatty acid stable carbon isotope ratios (C-13/C-12)" (1997) 59 *Food Chemistry* 181.

11 S D Kelly, C Rhodes, J H Lofthouse, D Anderson, C E Burwood, M J Dennis, and P Brereton, "Detection of sugar syrups in apple juice by delta H-2 parts per thousand and delta C-13 parts per thousand analysis of hexamethylenetetramine prepared from fructose" (2003) 51(7) *Journal of Agricultural and Food Chemistry* 1801.

12 A Rossmann, C Lullmann and H L Schmidt, "Mass-spectrometric determination of carbon and hydrogen isotope ratios for honey authenticity control" (1992) 195 *Zeitschrift fur Lebensmittel-untersuchung und -forschung* 307.

13 S E Woodbury, R P Evershed, J B Rossell, R E Griffith and P Farnell, "Detection of vegetable oil adulteration using gas-chromatography combustion isotope ratio mass-spectrometry" (1995) 67 *Analytical Chemistry* 2685.

14 G Calderone, C Guillou and N Naulet, "Official methods based on stable isotope techniques for analysis of food. Ten years of European experience" (2003) 8–9 *Actualité Chimique* 22.

15 A Rossmann, H L Schmidt, F Reniero, G Versini, I Moussa and M H Merle, "Stable carbon-isotope content in ethanol of EC data-bank wines from Italy, France and Germany" (1996) 203 *Zeitschrift fur Lebensmittel-untersuchung und -forschung* 293.

16 J R Ehleringer, D A Cooper, M J Lott and C S Cook, "Geo-location of heroin and cocaine by stable isotope ratios" (1999) 106 *Forensic Science International* 27

17 W Meier-Augenstein and R H Liu, "Forensic Applications of Isotope Ratio Mass Spectrometry" in J Yinon (ed), *Advances in Forensic Applications of Mass Spectrometry* (CRC Press, Boca Raton, 2004) at 149.

18 W Meier-Augenstein, "Stable Isotope Fingerprinting – Chemical Element 'DNA'?" in T J T Thomson and S M Black (eds), *Forensic Human Identification* (CRC Press, Boca Raton, 2006) at 29.

19 M P Richards, B T Fuller and R E M Hedges, "Sulphur isotopic variation in ancient bone collagen from Europe: implications for human palaeodiet, residence mobility, and modern pollutant studies" (2001) 191(3–4) *Earth and Planetary Science Letters* 185.

20 M P Richards and R E M Hedges, "Variations in bone collagen delta C-13 and delta N-15 values of fauna from Northwest Europe over the last 40 000 years" (2003) 193(2) *Palaeogeography Palaeoclimatology Palaeoecology* 261.

21 E A Hobbie and R A Werner, "Intramolecular, compound-specific, and bulk carbon isotope patterns in C-3 and C-4 plants: a review and synthesis" (2004) 161(2) *New Phytologist* 371.

22 W Meier-Augenstein, "Applied gas chromatography coupled to isotope ratio mass spectrometry" (1999) 842(1–2) *Journal of Chromatography A* 351.

23 A Rossmann, J Koziet, G J Martin and M J Dennis, "Determination of the carbon-13 content of sugars and pulp from fruit juices by isotope-ratio mass spectrometry (internal reference method) – A European interlaboratory comparison" (1997) 340 (1–3) *Analytica Chimica Acta* 21.

24 I Fraser, W Meier-Augenstein and R M Kalin, "The role of stable isotopes in human identification: a longitudinal study into the variability of isotopic signals in human hair and nails" (2006) 20(7) *Rapid Communications in Mass Spectrometry* 1109.

CHAPTER 15c

DNA Profiling and Identification

15c.1   INTRODUCTION

"In order to minimise the distress inevitably suffered by relatives and friends of victims of major disasters as a result of the identification process, the general aims of all concerned must be:

1. Provision of honest and, in so far as this is possible, accurate information at all times. In particular, it is of the utmost importance that relatives should be kept fully informed at every stage.
2. **The avoidance of mistaken identity at all costs.**
3. The adoption of the most sympathetic and caring approach possible."

Lord Justice Clarke[1]

It is a simple fact that mass fatality incidents, whether natural or man-made, accident or terrorist incident, are not rare events (see Table 15.2). It is also a fact that many such incidents may not be confined to a single country but often impact on the global community. Each incident may have its own particular characteristics, and may require a tailored response, but the main task of the Disaster Victim Identification Team will be to identify the deceased, reconcile fragmented bodies if necessary and to enable the return or repatriation of the victims' bodies to their families.

DNA profiling has become a major tool in the identification of the victims of such mass fatality incidents.[2-7] In some circumstances it is the only technique which will allow the reconciliation of fragmented bodies; having said that, the techniques of DNA profiling should be viewed as just one of the "tools" at the disposal of the DVI Commander or Senior Identification Manager (SIM). Forensic DNA scientists are not often involved in the first response to a mass-fatality incident but a strategy for DNA-based victim identification and the processes for post-mortem and ante-mortem DNA sample collection[6] must be part of the DVI commander's initial strategies.

This chapter will outline the science of DNA profiling but will concentrate on the strategic decisions and operational considerations that are required to integrate DNA profiling into the DVI processes.

Date	Incident	Type
1987	*Herald of Free Enterprise*	Marine accident
1988	Pan Am flight 103, Lockerbie, Scotland	Terrorist bombing of aircraft
1993	Waco, Texas, USA	Fire, Mount Carmel Complex
1995	Tokyo, Japan	Terrorist sarin gas attack
1999	Ladbroke Grove/Paddington, London, England	Rail accident
2000	Chinese illegal immigrants, Dover, England	Transport incident
2001	World Trade Center, New York, USA	Terrorist incident
2002	Night club and bar bombing, Bali	Terrorist incident
2002	Beltway sniper attacks, Washington	USA criminal act
2003	Housing complex Riyadh, Saudi Arabia	Truck bomb – terrorist incident
2003	Istanbul, Turkey – on two separate dates	Truck bombs – terrorist incidents
2004	Train bombings, Madrid, Spain,	Terrorist incidents
2004	Chinese "cockle pickers", Morecambe, England,	Marine accident
2004	South-east Asia tsunami,	Natural disaster
2005	Hurricanes Katrina and Rita, USA,	Natural disasters
2006	Djibouti, ferry accident	Marine accident

Table 15.2   Examples of mass fatality incidents over the last 30 years

15c.2   OVERVIEW

DNA profiling may be used as a primary tool for the re-unification and identification of victims of mass fatality incidents. DNA profiling techniques may be particularly useful if the victims' bodies are disrupted or in a state of putrefaction. In the latter case, DNA profiles can be successfully obtained from teeth or samples of bone.

DNA profiling, like many of the identification processes, is a comparative technique. The scientist needs a reference sample, or samples, with which to compare the DNA profile of the victim. These reference samples can be provided from the National DNA Database if the deceased had previously come to police attention; as surrogate reference samples from the deceased individuals themselves (preserved histology samples, hair brushes, tooth brushes, razors and worn clothing); or they can be samples provided by close genetic relatives.

The reader may have come across texts or papers relating to DNA profiling and may be confused by the terminology used. A short glossary is provided at the end of the book to clarify some of the specialist terms. The booklet "DNA Present and Correct" and the interactive CD-ROM "Dealing with DNA" provide a simple introduction to the topic for police officers.[8–9]

There are different types of DNA that can be extracted from cellular material and which can be used in differing circumstances to give the investigator useful information.

15c.3   CHROMOSOMAL DNA AND SHORT TANDEM REPEAT DNA PROFILING

"DNA" stands for *deoxyribonucleic acid*, which is a complex chemical found in virtually every cell in the body. The chromosomal, or nuclear, DNA carries genetic information from one generation to the next and is the chemical "blueprint" which determines our genetic makeup. *Nuclear DNA* is inherited from our parents such that a person's DNA profile contains half the characteristics from his/her biological father and half from his/her biological mother. Genetically identical twins have the same DNA profiles while non-identical siblings can share a considerable proportion of their genetic characteristics. The degree of genetic similarity diminishes as the degree of genetic relationship decreases (Table 15.3).

Relationship	Relatedness coefficient
Identical genetic twins	1 – same DNA profile
Siblings	0.625
Parent – child	0.5 – one allele at each locus
Grandparent/grandchild or half sibling	0.25
Uncle/nephew or aunt/niece	0.125
First cousin	0.0625

Table 15.3   The degree of genetic similarity diminishes as the degree of genetic relationship decreases

The techniques used by forensic scientists to visualise DNA profiles examine a specific set of DNA characteristics. Each of these components is known as a "locus" (plural *loci*) and they form only a tiny fraction of the total DNA molecule. The *loci* selected for the DNA profiling tests are known to be highly variable and can be highly discriminating between individuals. The variation between individuals is caused by short pieces of DNA being repeated end to end, over and over again. This gives a variation in length of the DNA fragment under scrutiny which gives us the discrimination between individuals and the name of this type of DNA profiling – *short tandem repeat or STR profiling*.

At every locus an individual displays two characteristics (known as *alleles*). The list of *loci* plus the allelic designations makes up the *DNA profile*. This is usually recorded as X, X (female) or X, Y (male) plus a string of numbers representing the allelic designations (see Figures 15.4 and 15.5).

15c.4   HOW IS DNA PROFILING DONE?

The main steps in STR DNA profiling are:

- Extraction: The DNA is isolated from other cellular material.
- Quantification: The amount of DNA extracted from the sample is measured to determine the optimal amount of DNA required for amplification.
- DNA amplification: (polymerase chain reaction or PCR): Specific areas of the DNA are targeted and multiple copies are produced.
- Electrophoresis: The amplified DNA "product" is separated according to size.
- Analysis and interpretation: The DNA profile is designated in such a way that it can be easily visualised, and stored in a computer for comparison with other DNA profiles or with profiles held on national DNA databases.

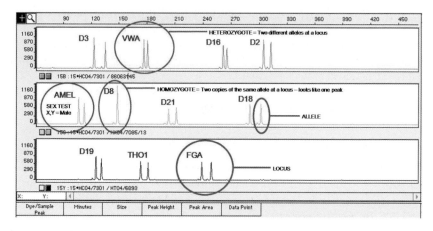

Figure 15.4   Computer visualisation of a DNA profile

15c.5   CASE EXAMPLES

The following case examples demonstrate how STR profiling is used to assist with disaster victim identification.

15c.5.1   Case example 1 – The identification of a recovered body

The wreck of a boat and some human remains were recovered from a freshwater lake where they had lain for more than 30 years. A DNA profile was obtained from bone tissue (femur) and compared with DNA profiles obtained from living relatives: an alleged sibling and an alleged child. The results are shown in Figure 15.5.

272

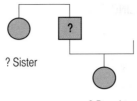

? Sister

? Daughter

	Amelo	D3	vWA	D16	D2	D8	D21	D18	D19	THO1	FGA
Child	X,X	14,16	18,18	12,13	17,24	9,13	27,31.2	17,18	14,16.2	7,9.3	21,26
Femur	X,Y	16,17	17,18	12,13	24,25	9,12	30,31.2	16,17	14,14	7,7	21,26
Sister	X,X	16,16	17,18	12,13	17,24	13,15	30,31.2	16,17	14,15.2	7,7	22,26

Shaded numbers in the child and sister samples denote alleles also present in the femur.

Figure 15.5   DNA profiling results for the identification of a marine accident victim

It can be seen in Figure 15.5 that half of the alleles or DNA characteristics in the child's DNA profile are present in the DNA profile obtained from the femur. This is the result expected if the femur were that of the child's biological father. It can also be seen that the DNA profile from the sister has 14 alleles in common with that obtained from the femur. This is the expected level of "band share" for siblings and strengthens the evidence of identification of the human remains found in the lake being those of the missing man.

15c.5.2   Case example 2 – The London bombings

In circumstances of an explosion, whether accidental or a terrorist event, bodies can become severly disrupted. DNA profiling can be used to reunify the remains of bodies disrupted in the blast and to identify the deceased. The results of one such test are shown in Figure 15.6.

These DNA profiling results are those expected if the tissue sample is that of the deceased "V". It can be seen that at each locus the DNA profile of the tissue sample contains one "allele" inherited from the mother and one inherited from the father. At two of the *loci*, vWA and D19, it is not possible to assign the maternal or paternal alleles. This does not affect the outcome of the identification process in this case, since they are identical in all three samples.

Y-chromosome DNA STR analysis and paternal inheritance

The Y-chromosome is the genetic differentiation of males from females – all males have X and Y chromosomes, whereas females have two copies of the X chromosome (designation X, X).

There are a special set of STR markers associated with the Y-chromosome that can be used to investigate paternal-line relationships. For many laboratories this is not a routine test but is one of the tools the DNA scientists and Senior Identification Manager (SIM) can consider in particular family circumstances.

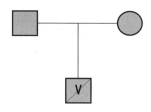

	Amelo	D3	vWA	D16	D2	D8	D21	D18	D19	THO1	FGA
Victim	X,Y	15,16	15,18	10,13	23,24	10,13	29,30	14,14	12,15	9,9	25,26
Mother	X,X	14,16	15,18	9,10	18,24	10,13	30,30	14,18	12,15	6,9	20,26
Father	X,Y	14,15	15,18	11,13	18,23	13,13	29,32.2	14,14	12,15	9,9.3	22,25

Shaded numbers in the tissue sample denote alleles present in the alleged mother.

Underlined numbers in the tissue sample denote alleles present in the alleged father.

Figure 15.6   DNA profiling

Mitochondrial DNA sequencing and maternal inheritance

In some circumstances, particularly if the tissues samples are heavily decomposed or compromised in some other way, the chromosomal DNA might be too degraded to allow the scientist to generate an STR profile. In this case it might be possible to utilise the mitochondrial DNA to give some useful information.

Mitochondrial DNA is also present in many cells of the body, and at much higher levels than chromosomal DNA. Mitochondrial DNA is a relatively short molecule and is resistant to degradation because of this. Mitochondrial DNA is inherited solely through the maternal line and can give only limited discrimination between individuals (approx 1 in 300 compared with 1 in 1,000 million for STR analysis).

Despite its shortcomings, mitochondrial DNA may give useful information under the right circumstances.

15c.5.3   Case example 3 – Anna Anderson: Russian princess or pauper?

In 1918 the Russian Royal family were executed by the Bolshevik regime and the bodies concealed in a forest near Yekaterinburg in the Urals. In July 1991 nine skeletons were found in a shallow grave approximately 20 miles from Yekaterinburg – were these the bones of the Russian Royals?

Mitochondrial sequencing was chosen as an appropriate method of DNA profiling given the age and condition of the bones tested.[10] The reference sample was provided by His Royal Highness, Philip the Duke of Edinburgh. This sample was chosen as the Duke was a direct maternal relative of the Tsarina Alexandra, as can be seen in Figure 15.8. Identical matches between the mDNA from Prince Philip and the samples developed from the putative Tsarina and the three children showed that they were directly related, supporting the identification of the remains.

Figure 15.7   Tsar Nicholas II, the Tsarina and their family

In Berlin in 1922 a woman, who later took the name Anna Anderson, claimed that she was the Royal Duchess Anastasia. She convinced a number of people of her claim, apparently speaking knowledgeably of the Royal Family and life in the Russian Court.

After her death, a tissue sample taken during an operation in 1979 was retrieved from a hospital pathology department and, having been certified as that belonging to Anna Anderson, was subjected to mitochondrial DNA sequencing.

Mitochondrial DNA sequences were determined from the pathology sample of Anna Anderson and the reference sample provided by HRH the Duke of Edinburgh. These sequences were shown to be different and therefore Anna Anderson could not be maternally related to him and by definition could not be the Royal Duchess Anastasia.

Anna Anderson was believed to have been a woman called Franziska Schankowska, born in Pomerania in about 1896. Subsequently, the mitochondrial DNA sequence from the pathology sample of Anna Anderson was matched to a sample of a Mr Carl Maucher, the great nephew of Franziska Schankowska, and a direct maternal descendent from her.

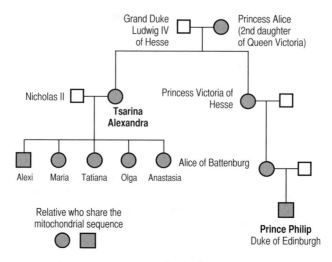

Figure 15.8   The maternal relationship between HRH Prince Philip and the Tsarina Alexandra

These results confirmed that Anna Anderson could not have been the Royal Duchess Anastasia and was likely to have been Franziska Schankowska.[11]

15c.6   DNA PROFILING TO IDENTIFY VICTIMS OF MASS FATALITY INCIDENTS[12]

In managing the DNA identification process for a major mass fatality incident it may be appropriate to appoint a Lead Scientist to support the SIM. The Lead Scientist will then create the DNA Identification Team. This team will manage all

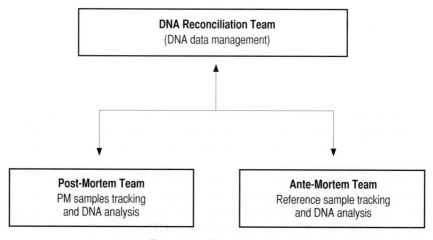

Figure 15.9   Team interactions

aspects of the DNA profiling process; sample tracking, DNA laboratory analysis, re-work policies (if samples prove intractable), production of the DNA profiles and management and reporting of the DNA identifications.

This team has three distinct functions:

- post-mortem sample profiling;
- ante-mortem (reference) sample profiling;
- DNA data reconciliation and data matching.

The interactions of these teams are shown in Figure 15.9.

The scientists in each section will also be responsible for liaising with, or providing advice to, the relevant investigative teams. So, the DNA PM Team leader will be responsible for advising the pathologist and other PM specialists of the best samples to obtain, and the DNA AM team leader will have the responsibility of advising the Family Liaison Officers (FLOs) and Family Assistance Centre staff of the best reference samples to obtain in the particular family circumstances.

The DNA data generated by these teams will be collated, matched and reported by the DNA Reconciliation Team. The DNA Lead Scientist should head this team and report to the Coroner or SIM at least once a day.

15c.7   THE DNA ANTE-MORTEM TEAM

The purpose of collecting ante-mortem samples is to provide the reference DNA profile(s) against which the DNA scientist will compare the post-mortem DNA results.

Ante-mortem samples can take the form of:

- personal effects from the missing person (toothbrush, hairbrush, razors or unwashed items of clothing or underwear);
- medical samples from the missing person (cervical smear samples, newborn's bloodspots from hospitals; preserved tissue biopsies etc);
- reference samples from close genetic relatives – see below.

Any samples being accepted as personal effects of a missing person *must* have evidence of provenance in the form of documented witness accounts or medical records. These samples should not have been shared (eg toothbrushes or razors) as this can cause issues in the collation of DNA data.

The continuity of the sample from collection to laboratory examination needs to be carefully recorded and a method of sample labelling needs to be established. For a UK-based incident it is recommended that the National DNA Database crime stain kits (*8-series bar codes*) should be used. This ensures that each sample is labelled with a unique bar code.

277

The reference sample kits should be submitted to the laboratory as soon as possible. If there is to be any delay in submission, the kits and DNA samples should be frozen.

A fuller description of potential personal (direct or surrogate) reference samples is shown in Table 15.4.[13]

15c.8   FAMILY RELATIONSHIP ANALYSIS

DNA-based identifications can also be carried out by comparing the DNA profile of a post-mortem tissue sample with the DNA profiles of close family members (see above). It is necessary for the FLO to determine the most appropriate samples for any given case. The DNA Lead Scientist should be able to provide DNA scientists to support the FLOs and advise on the collection of ante-mortem samples.

Family samples may include (in order of preference):

- *Identical twin siblings*: will provide an identical DNA profile to their twin sibling.
- *Parents*: mother and father should each share half of their DNA profile with their children. It is important that issues of non-paternity and adoption (no genetic similarity) are considered sensitively.
- *Spouse and child*: again, issues of non-paternity and adoption need to be considered.

Quality of recovered DNA	Common samples	Samples to consider
Good sources of DNA	Toothbrush Razor Hair brushes/combs	National DNA database Clinical blood/semen/ bone marrow samples Pathology/histology samples
Fair sources of DNA	Lipsticks/deodorant sticks Pillowcases Used drinking vessels Used underwear	Cervical smears Cigarette butts Ear plugs/ear phones Mouthguard/mouthpiece Motorcycle helmets Spectacles
Poor sources of DNA	Jewellery/watches Outer clothing Towels Shoes Hair bands/ear muffs	Baby Hair Trimmers/scissors Nail files Dentures

Table 15.4   Classification of direct reference samples. Reproduced from M Prinz et al (2007)[13]

- *Siblings*: at least two, though more siblings provide a better chance of identification. Avoid taking samples from "half-siblings" if possible.
- *Grandparents*: where possible, samples should be taken from both maternal grandparents and both paternal grandparents.

If there is any doubt as to the best combination of family samples to collect, the FLO should contact a forensic biologist or geneticist from the DNA identification team. A useful resource in this area is the ACPO Family Liaison Strategy Manual (2003).[14]

Any samples being accepted as a reference sample from a relative of a missing person must have evidence of provenance, and the continuity of the sample from collection to laboratory examination must be carefully recorded. It is recommended that the Figure 5-series DNA Volunteer kits are used to collect such samples. In this way, each reference sample is given a unique bar code number and the *consent* to the taking of the sample is also recorded. If a number of relatives offer to provide samples to support the identification process; take them. It is better to have too many reference samples than too few.

One issue that may have to be explored with sensitivity by the FLOs is the *issue of non-paternity*. In the UK, approximately 15 per cent of the questioned paternity tests carried out show that the alleged father of a child is not the genetic father. So, it would not be unusual for the father of a deceased victim to volunteer to provide a reference sample, but he may be unaware that he is not the victim's biological father. The FLO has a vital role in helping to elicit such information from the family.

If an issue of non-paternity were to be uncovered in the DNA testing, this would not be disclosed to the sample donor or wider family. The primary aim of the DNA Identification team is to assist with the identification of the victim – it is in no one's interest to create additional issues for a family at a time of great distress.

Similarly, if a spouse and child are available to provide samples to identify a missing parent, it is important to establish that the child has not been adopted, as there could be no genetic relation to the missing parent.

15c.9   THE DNA POST MORTEM TEAM

The type of sample required for DNA profiling of victims' remains will depend on the nature of the incident, the speed of recovery of the bodies and the state of decomposition (or preservation).

If the bodies are largely whole and in reasonable states of preservation, it might be possible to recover blood samples, pulled hair samples (hair roots), buccal (cheek cell) scrapes or good quality muscle samples. As the body stars to decay, the probability of recovering such samples diminishes and deep muscle, teeth and bone samples should be considered.

In some circumstances the forensic pathologist may seek advice about sample selection from the forensic DNA specialist. The PM team has the responsibility to ensure that the best samples are selected for DNA analysis in the particular circumstances of the incident. It may be advantageous to select multiple samples for analysis at the initial post-mortem examination.

The selection of post-mortem samples will be incident-specific, but a guide is shown in Table 15.5.

State of decomposition of body	Suggested samples
Body in good condition, largely whole	Blood sample, buccal swab, pulled hair (root) samples, muscle tissue
Little decomposition, fragmented	Blood samples, deep muscle tissue
Decomposed	Teeth without fillings (pref. molars)
	5–10cm sample long bones (femur/tibia/humerus)
	Any bone sample available (~10g)
Burned bodies	Any of the samples above if available
Co-mingled remains	Multiple samples as above

Table 15.5   Sample collection at post-mortem examination

It is imperative that the continuity of the victims' samples from collection to laboratory examination needs to be carefully recorded and a method of sample labelling needs to be established. Interpol have devised a set of forms which is often used for this purpose.[9]

Within the UK, the ACPO Emergency Procedures Group has devised a Victim Identification procedure and has designed a specific Body Recovery Booklet and post-mortem forms which should be used for any mass fatality incident.[15] All of the booklets are coded with a unique reference number (URN) and bar code. The booklet contains forms to record details of the body (or body part) recovery; location, description, recovery personnel involved and scene notes etc and it covers the recovery and movement log between the recovery site and the mortuary. The booklet also contains a set of URN and bar coded labels so that subsequent PM forms can be immediately identified to that particular body.

The Victim Identification Booklet (see Figure 15.9) also contains a set of bar code labels which are specifically designed for the DNA team. The labels are made of a material which will stand up to the rigours of the laboratory process. The DNA label set contains alphanumeric bar codes so that the DNA profiling results obtained from multiple samples taken from the same body can be tracked to that particular PM examination (ACPO Victim Label Booklet).

All of these bar codes have been generated with the co-operation of the Custodian of the National DNA database. The DNA profiles obtained from the

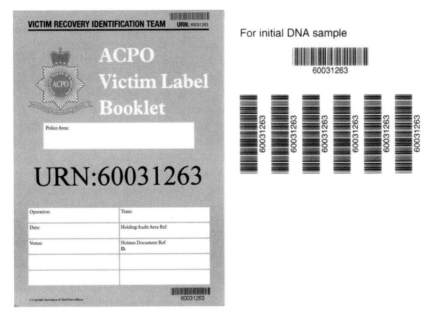

Figure 15.9   ACPO Victim Recovery Booklet and an example of the DNA labels contained within it. Note that the booklet and labels carry the same bar code

victims' body samples can be compared with those held on the National DNA database to assist with identification. The DNA database legislation was changed following the South East Asia tsunami incident to allow DNA profiles from victims of natural disasters to be compared with those held on the National DNA database. Prior to this legislation the National DNA database could only be used for the investigation of criminal acts.

15c.10   THE DNA RECONCILIATION TEAM AND MANAGEMENT OF DNA DATA

The DNA Reconciliation Team has the task of managing the DNA Identification Process; matching the data from the DNA Ante Mortem Team with that from the DNA Post Mortem Team and declaring the "identifications" to the Identification Commission.

For the DNA Team, the data will be compiled into three sets of DNA profiles – the victims' surrogate or direct reference samples (obtained from toothbrushes, hair brushes etc); family reference or kinship samples; and that from the post mortem (victims' remains) samples.

The DNA Team will hold all of this data in a centralised database – this is important even if the DNA profiles have been generated by multiple agencies or testing laboratories. There should be a data transfer process which allows tracking of all samples and minimises the amount of manual data entry. Wherever possible the data transfer should be electronic, to avoid manual data entry errors.

If the mass fatality incident involves the disruption of the victims' bodies the DNA Reconciliation team will have the additional responsibility of associating body parts with matching DNA profiles.

In the event of a major mass fatality incident, the number of DNA profiles generated can run into thousands or even tens of thousands. In the aftermath of the September 11 attack on the World Trade Center in 2001, over 20,000 body parts and 10,000 reference samples were processed by the New York DNA teams. The scale of such a DNA matching exercise should not be underestimated. To date, 1,602 of the 2,749 World Trade Center victims have been identified, mostly through DNA testing that matched victims' remains to a personal reference sample or through kinship analysis.

The Home Office purchased a software application called M-FISys (Mass Fatality Identification System) to assist in the management of the DNA data that could be generated within a major incident.[16–18]

The M-FISys application was created in response to the data management issues of the World Trade Center disaster in September 2001. This application will allow the DNA team to:

- match profiles from different body parts for the reconciliation of disrupted remains;
- match DNA profiles from bodies or body parts to direct reference samples;
- match DNA profiles from bodies or body parts to kinship (family) samples;
- utilise STR or mitochondrial analysis;
- screen samples against exclusion samples (police or scientific staff) – a QA check;
- calculate likelihood ratios or posterior probabilities (strength of evidence calculations);
- create management reports.

15c.11   STATISTICAL CONSIDERATIONS

Many police officers looking at scientific publications or reports concerning DNA profiling are immediately alarmed by the apparent concentration on statistical issues. It is a fact that the mathematics of individual statistical calculations involved can often be daunting, but this is the realm of the specialist scientist. It should not be a concern to the Coroner, SIM or any other officer. What you want to know is simply: "What does the statistic mean?".

Let's start with some basic concepts.

Allele frequency

The genetic components (or alleles) which make up a DNA profile occur with known frequencies in a given population. There are simple formulae which allow the scientist to calculate the probability for a given combination of alleles. This can simply be extended to calculate the probability of a particular DNA profile occurring. It is important to use allele frequency (population) databases that reflect the ethnic origins of the missing persons.

Direct profile matches

In this instance we are considering a "match" between a DNA profile from a victim's sample and a DNA profile obtained from a personal (direct) reference sample. The question we are asking is: "What is the probability that this individual, effectively picked at random from the population, will match this particular profile?"

The answer is: the probability of the particular combination of alleles that make up that DNA profile. This is usually stated as ... "1 in a billion" from STR profiling in the UK.

Kinship or family relationship matches

This is a little more complicated in that the scientist has to consider two explanations for a given result. Either the evidence (DNA profile) occurs because of the claimed family relationship or there is no family relationship and the evidence occurs by chance. In a family relationship case the DNA statement will state the alternatives being tested.

For example, consider the case where a DNA profile is obtained from a sample and this is thought to be from Charlie, the son of Fred and Mabel. The statistic issues section of the statement might read:

"In carrying out this statistical analysis I have considered the probability of obtaining this DNA profile given the following alternatives:

a) Fred and Mabel are the natural parents of the victim.
b) An unrelated couple are the natural parents of this victim.

Such an analysis of these results shows that the DNA profile from the body believed to be that of Charlie is 1 billion times more likely if Fred and Mabel are the natural parents of Charlie."

What this result is saying is that, *given the DNA result obtained*, the alternative (a) is a billion times more probable than alternative (b). The figure quoted is the ratio of the probabilities, ie probability of (a) divided by probability of (b). This is often called a *likelihood ratio*.

Prior and posterior odds

One of the decisions the Coroner and the SIM will have to make is to set the criteria for identification. If the primary identification technique is to be DNA profiling this can be a numerical value or threshold.

The Coroner may decide that he or she wants to be 99.99 per cent sure that every "identification" is correct. This means that he or she is prepared to accept an incorrect identification in 0.01 per cent of cases! Let's take an example of a mass fatality incident involving a thousand victims.

Given a particular DNA profile generated from *one* of the samples, what is the probability of choosing the correct individual from the pool of 1,000 deceased individuals? The answer is 1 in 1,000 (or 1,000 to 1 against). This is known as the *prior odds*.

The Coroner has decided that he or she wants to be 99.99 per cent sure that he has identified the correct body, but this is a statement of *posterior probability*. To convert a probability to odds we use the simple expression:

$$\text{Probability} = \frac{\text{Odds}}{\text{Odds} + 1}$$

So, to achieve the Coroner's required probability of 0.9999 (99.99 per cent) the *posterior odds* have to be 10,000 to 1 on (10,000/10,001 = 0.9999).

Prior and posterior odds are related as follows:

$$\text{Posterior odds} = \text{likelihood ratio} \times \text{prior odds}$$

In other words, the prior odds multiplied by the likelihood ratio (or weight of DNA evidence) gives us the posterior odds. We can now ask the question "What does the DNA likelihood ratio have to be to give the Coroner the required posterior odds of 10,000 to 1 on?".

Rearranging the equation and adding the values in a scientific notation:

$$\text{Likelihood ratio} = \frac{\text{posterior odds}}{\text{prior odds}} \qquad \text{ie likelihood ratio} = \frac{1 \times 10^4}{1 \times 10^{-3}}$$

Or $\qquad$ Likelihood ratio = 1×10^7 (or 10,000,000)

In this case, to meet the Coroner's identification threshold the likelihood ratio the DNA team would have to achieve is 10 million.

15c.12 STRATEGIC CONSIDERATIONS FOR THE INVESTIGATING OFFICER

Criteria for confirmation of identity

DNA profiling is viewed by the public as a "magic bullet" that will always lead to the identification of an individual. While DNA profiling is a powerful technique, there are circumstances where its use might be limited.

Given the circumstances of a particular incident, one of the first strategic decisions that the Coroner and the SIM need to make is what level of confidence they require to determine an "identification" which meets the appropriate legal requirements. They must then decide how they might reach, and demonstrate, that level of confidence. It is in this process that the Coroner and the SIM decide which forensic techniques will be deployed in a given set of circumstances.

For instance, it may be considered that evidence from two primary identification processes are required to confirm the "identity" of the victim.

Primary identification processes

- Fingerprints.
- Odontology (dental comparison).
- DNA analysis (direct or through family relationship analysis).
- Unique medical condition (comparison of AM medical procedures with PM findings).

Alternatively, it may be deemed sufficient to utilise one primary technique, with the results being supported by one or more secondary identifiers.

Secondary identification processes

- Personal documentation – wallets, purses, driving licences, ID cards etc.
- Personal effects – jewellery, mobile phones, PDAs etc.
- Medical – scars etc.
- Tattoos and other body modifications.

Examples

In the case of the Sarin gas attack on the Tokyo Underground (1999), where the victims' bodies were undamaged, it could be argued that sufficient evidence of identification could be obtained from a fingerprint match with documentation and personal effects.

Conversely, in the September 11, 2001 attacks on the World Trade Center, USA, where many of the victims' bodies were severely disrupted and the tissue samples decomposing, DNA profiling techniques provided the key information leading to the identification of the victims: 50 per cent of the identifications reached in this incident were as a result of DNA profiling tests.

Under UK law, the legal acceptance of the identification of a victim is the prerogative of the Coroner/Procurator Fiscal. The SIM has to work with the Coroner/Fiscal to establish the identification criteria and make a strategic decision about which identification methods will be used to meet these criteria given the nature of the particular incident. DNA profiling may be one of the primary identifiers selected.

15c.13   INTERNATIONAL CONSIDERATIONS

A UK-based mass fatality incident may well involve victims from a number of different countries, or victims with a variety of cultural or faith backgrounds, particularly if the incident occurs in a major city. The SIM should be aware of the logistical issues involved in collecting DNA reference samples from victims' personal effects or close genetic relatives.

If it is a possibility that some of the victims are overseas visitors, the SIM has to make the decision whether:

(a) to involve overseas police forces in the collection of DNA samples;
(b) to deploy Family Liaison Officers overseas to collect samples;
(c) to staff a Family Assistance Centre with the appropriate personnel who can create family trees and take appropriate samples.

The Lead Scientist should be able to provide the appropriate information to support the decision-making process. DNA scientists should also be available to work with the FLOs and in the Family Assistance Centre if necessary.

15c.14   WHAT CONSTITUTES A "BODY PART"? HOW FAR DOES THE DNA ANALYSIS GO?

One further issue for the Coroner/Fiscal to decide is how far the DNA analysis should go?' Current DNA profiling techniques are extremely sensitive and can generate a DNA profile from a very small amount of tissue or bone.

There is also a perception that DNA profiling is expensive compared to other primary identification techniques – let's be clear on this: all of the strategic decisions taken by the Coroner/Fiscal or SIM will have cost implications and may impact on the families of the victims. It is better to make a strategic decision, record it in the policy book and communicate that decision, honestly and openly, to the families, than to make decisions "on the hoof" and try to manage the subsequent fall-out.

For example, in the investigation of the London bombings in July 2005 the SIM and the Coroner made the following decision: all *recognisable* body parts, however small, would be subjected to DNA profiling to ensure that, wherever possible, the disrupted bodies of the victims were reunited before return to their families. It was also decided that unrecognisable body parts or tissue samples under 5cm^3 in size would not be subjected to DNA profiling. This tissue, classified as "residual human tissue", was collected together and given a dignified disposal as unidentified human remains (see Figure 15.10).

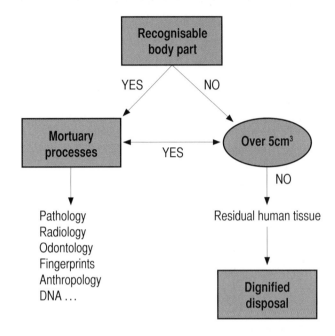

Figure 15.10   Strategic "decision tree" – how far do you take the DNA profiling?

15c.15   SAMPLE AUTHORISATION

In some circumstances the Coroner/Fiscal may feel compelled to limit the authorisation for taking tissue samples; particularly in the case of the bodies of babies and very small children. If this is the case the policy should be recorded in the incident policy book.

15c.16   RESOURCING A MAJOR MASS FATALITY INCIDENT

In the UK there are three major suppliers of forensic DNA testing: the Forensic Science Service Ltd, LGC-Forensics and Orchid Cellmark. All of the forensic suppliers have the capability to analyse both reference samples and body tissue samples for DNA profiling.

The forensic science suppliers have differing levels of capability to handle a mass fatality incident or indeed multiple, contemporary incidents – some suppliers might have an almost infinite capacity to analyse reference samples but a limited capacity to handle tissue samples. Some of the suppliers may have a particular expertise in the analysis of badly degraded tissue samples or in the analysis of bone or teeth samples. All of the forensic science suppliers have routine caseloads which may impact on their ability to deliver DNA profiling services in the event of a mass fatality incident. It will be for the forensic science suppliers to inform the SIM if they have any particular resourcing issues.

This is a potential source of difficulty for the SIM. In the event of a large-scale mass fatality incident or an incident involving foreign nationals it is probable that more than one forensic science supplier will be involved. DNA profiling data might also be supplied from overseas laboratories. It is strongly advised that the DNA profiling Identification Team is managed through a single Lead Scientist. He or she can ensure that maximum resources are made available to the Incident Commander while minimising the impact on the routine delivery of DNA profiling services to the police and National DNA database.

It is also strongly advised that the forensic science supplier appoints a Lead Scientist to work with the SIM on the implementation of the strategic plans for the DNA identification process. One of Lord Justice Clarke's[1] suggested recommendations from the *Marchioness/Bowbelle* inquiry was:

"Consideration should be given to the inclusion of a member of the Forensic Science Service or other forensic adviser on the Identification Commission in order to advise as to the use of DNA profiling and the taking of samples."

15c.17   ANTE-MORTEM SAMPLES

The Lead Scientist and the SIM should develop a policy to ensure that sufficient ante-mortem DNA samples are collected when there is an opportunity. This requirement should be collated with those of the other identification teams (fingerprints, odontology, radiology etc) and the FLOs tasked with interviewing and collecting all the required data and samples in one family visit if possible.

The DNA laboratory should not be processing ante-mortem DNA samples from missing people that are not needed for identification in that specific disaster unless this will aid the identification of other victims. This leads to a waste of resources, and may cause exhibit storage and data management issues.

15c.18   POST-MORTEM SAMPLES

Similarly, the Lead Scientist and SIM should develop a policy to ensure that sufficient post-mortem DNA samples are collected when there is an opportunity. This requirement should be communicated to the pathologist and other PM specialists. The PM DNA team should be available to advise the pathology teams about DNA samples in particular case circumstances.

There is a debate about taking DNA samples from bodies of victims which have been identified by other means. In some circumstances this may be advisable. If the incident contains multiple victims of the same family then DNA samples should be taken from all the bodies or body parts.

15c.19   ETHICAL CONSIDERATIONS

In the light of recent sensitivities about the removal and retention of tissues and organs at post mortem for scientific purposes and the public concerns at the creation of a National DNA database and the retention of genetic information, it is right to consider the ethical issues surrounding the collection of samples for DNA profiling and the use of these DNA profiles in the identification of the victims of a mass fatality incident.[19]

15c.20   CONSENT

It is essential to obtain informed consent for the purposes of DNA testing from each of the victim's relatives when samples are taken. The National DNA database Volunteer Kits (5-series bar codes) are ideal for this as the paperwork contains a consent statement. The relatives should be informed that by nature the DNA techniques are comparative; that samples taken from them will be processed and the DNA profiles compared with those generated from the tissue, bone or teeth samples recovered from the victim's bodies. The relatives should also understand that small samples of tissue, bone and teeth may be taken from each of the bodies and that these samples will be destroyed as a result of the DNA testing processes.

At the end of the DNA identification exercise the participating laboratories should return any remaining tissue samples to the charge of the Coroner/Fiscal who should arrange an appropriately dignified method of disposal.

15c.21   DATA PROTECTION

The participating DNA laboratories need to be registered with the data protection authorities so that a database containing the personal details of the victims and relatives can be held legally. All of the forensic science suppliers in the UK have this appropriate registration.

15c.22   DESTRUCTION OF DNA SAMPLE EXTRACTS

The participating laboratories should hold DNA sample extracts pertaining to the victims and their family members until the Identification Commission has accepted a declared identification. The laboratory may then destroy any remaining DNA extracts.

15c.23   ISSUES OF NON-PATERNITY

The express aim of the DNA identification process is to identify the deceased persons from whom the post-mortem samples have been collected. In a minority of cases it may become apparent that a victim's body can be identified by comparison with their mother's DNA profile, but the man who presented the reference sample as the deceased's father is shown not to be the biological parent. Under these circumstances the Identification Commission may declare the identification and release the body to the family. If the DNA profiling tests are later challenged in court, the Identification Commission may have to reveal the true situation to the relatives if so directed by the court.

15c.24   CONCLUSIONS

While it may not be pleasant to contemplate future mass fatality incidents experience has shown that these incidents are not uncommon. We are all too familiar; perhaps even blasé, about world events. It is important that as professionals in the Disaster Victim Identification field we continue to learn about specialist techniques and participate actively in training and planning exercises.[20]

As has been stressed throughout this chapter, DNA profiling is but one of the tools the Coroner/Fiscal and the SIM may choose to deploy in the investigation of a particular mass fatality incident. DNA profiling is not always the "magic bullet" the public perceives it to be, but it can be extremely powerful when used in appropriate circumstances.

Using DNA profiling in combination with other identification techniques will improve the confidence with which a particular identification is viewed. An interdisciplinary approach to the Identification of victims of mass fatality incidents is to be encouraged and it is important to stress that such an approach should be one of the primary strategic decisions made by the Coroner/Fiscal and the SIM.

REFERENCES

1 Report of Lord Justice Clarke, *Public Inquiry into the Identification of Victims following Major Transport Accidents* (The Stationery Office, Norwich, 2001) [online]. Available at: http://www.marchioness-nsi.org.uk/index.htm. [Accessed: 14.11.2007.]

2 C N Maguire and V E Tate, "The use of DNA profiling in the identification of victims of an aircrash" (1993) 5 *Advances in Forensic Haemogenetics* 282.

3 T M Clayton, J P Whitaker and C N Maguire, "Identifications of bodies from the scene of a mass disaster using DNA amplification of short tandem repeat (STR) loci" (1995) 76 *Forensic Science International* 7.

4 T M Clayton, J P Whitaker, D L Fisher, D A Lee, M M Holland, V W Weedn, C N Maguire, J A DiZinno, C P Kimpton and P Gill, "Further validation of a quadruplex STR DNA typing system: a collaborative effort to identify the victims of a mass disaster" (1995) 76 *Forensic Science International* 17.

5 R Clarke, *The Trawler Gaul: The search for the bodies of the crew in Northern Russia* (Dept of the Environment, Transport and the Regions, London, 2000).

6 C N Maguire, "Submission to Part II of the Non-statutory Inquiry into the identification of the victims of the collision between the *Bowbelle* and the *Marchioness*" [online]. Available at: http://www.marchioness-nsi.org.uk.submissions>Forensic Science Service>S2_00180.500–519. [Accessed: 14.11.2007.]

7 D Barry, "At Morgue, Ceaselessly sifting 9/11 traces", *New York Times*, 14 July 2002 [online]. Available at: http://www.werismyki.com/artcls/ceaselessly_sifting.html. [Accessed: 14.11.2007.]

8 *DNA – Present and Correct: A Guide to DNA Profiling* (The Forensic Science Service, Birmingham, 2000).

9 *Dealing with DNA – An interactive Guide to DNA Profiling* (Ver 1.1) (The Forensic Science Service, Birmingham, 2006).

10 P Gill, P L Ivanov, C Kimpton, R Piercy, N Benson, G Tully, E Evett, E Hagelberg and K Sullivan, "Identification of the remains of the Romanov family by DNA analysis" (1994) 6(2) *Nature Genetics* 130. Available at: http://nature.com/ng/journal/v6/n2/pdf/ng0294-130.pdf. [Accessed: 14.11.2007.]

11 P Gill, C Kimpton, R Aliston-Greiner, K Sullivan, M Stoneking, T Melton, J Nott, S Barritt, R Roby, M Holland and V Weedn, "Establishing the identity of Anna Anderson Manahan" (1995) 9(1) *Nature Genetics* 9. Available at: http://nature.com/ng/journal/v9/n1/pdf/ng0195-9.pdf. [Accessed: 14.11.2007.]

12 Disaster Victim Identification – Interpol website [online]. Available at: http://www.interpol. int/Public/DisasterVictim/Guide/Default.asp. [Accessed: 14.11.2007.]

13 M Prinz, A Carracedo, W R Mayr, N Morling, T J Parsons, A Sajantila, R Scheithauer, H Schmitter and P M Schneider, "DNA Commission of the International Society for Forensic Genetics (IFSG): Recommendations regarding the role of forensic genetics for disaster victim identification (DVI)" (2007) 1 *Forensic Science International: Genetics* 3.

14 *ACPO Family Liaison Strategy Manual* (National Crime and Operations Faculty, Bramshill, 2003) [online]. Available at: http://www.acpo.police.uk/asp/policies/Data/Family_Liaison_2003.pdf. [Accessed: 28.11.2007.]

15 Victim Recovery Identification Team, "ACPO Victim Label Booklet" (National Crime and Operations Faculty, Bramshill).

16 H D Cash and M J Hennessey, "Human Identification software for missing persons, scaleable for a Mass Fatality Incident: Building on lessons learned over the course of a major Disaster Victim Identification Project" 15th International Symposium on Human Identification (2004).

17 H D Cash, J W Hoyle and A J Sutton, "Development Under Extreme Conditions: Forensic Bioinformatics in the Wake of the World Trade Center Disaster", Pacific Symposium of Biocomputing (2003), p 638.

18 Gene Code Forensics, Inc website [online]. Available at: www.genecodeforensics.com/software. [Accessed: 14.11.2007.]

19 B M Knoppers, M Saginur and H Cash, "Ethical Issues in Secondary Uses of Human Biological Materials from Mass Disasters" (2006) *American Journal of Law, Medicine and Ethics Symposium* 352.

20 "Lessons learned from 9/11: DNA Identification in Mass Fatality Incidents (2006)" [online]. Available at: http://www.ncjrs.gov/pdffiles1/nij/214781.pdf. [Accessed: 14.11.2007.]

GLOSSARY

allele(s)   Alternative forms of DNA structure at a given locus – accounts for the recordable differences between individuals.

autosome   Any chromosome other than the X and Y (sex) chromosomes.

amplification   A part of the DNA profiling technique where specific DNA regions are targeted and copied millions of times (*see* **PCR**).

cell   The smallest component of an organism capable of independent reproduction and from which DNA can be extracted for forensic analysis.

chromosome   The biological structure present in the nucleus of a cell containing DNA which act as the vehicles of inheritance, transmitting genetic information from one generation to the next.

degradation   The physical break-up of a biological molecule such as DNA because of adverse environmental or chemical conditions.

deoxyribonucleic acid (DNA)   The molecule that codes the genetic information within its structure.

DNA profile   The pattern of DNA characteristics (alleles) used to identify an individual. A DNA profile can be visualised as a pattern of bands on a computer screen; as a graphical representation known as an electropherogram; or as a numeric code.

DNA profiling   The laboratory techniques used to determine a DNA profile.

double helix   The shape of the DNA molecule.

electropherogram   A graphical representation of a DNA profile.

electrophoresis   A method of separating large molecules, such as DNA, using an electric current.

gene   The basic unit of heredity.

genetic code   The chemical structure (or sequence of nucleotide bases in the DNA molecule, designated "A", "C", "T" and "G") which carries the genetic "message".

genotype   The alleles present at one locus.

heterozygote   An individual with two different alleles at one locus (seen as two bands in a DNA profile).

homozygote   An individual with a pair of identical alleles at a locus (seen as a single band in a DNA profile).

identical twins   Identical twins develop because a fertilised ovum splits into two early in its development. As each growing fetus has originated from the same genetic material, their DNA profiles will be identical.

locus/loci   The specific location of a gene on a chromosome.

mitochondrial DNA   A type of DNA present in the mitochondria in a cell. Mitochondrial DNA is inherited through the maternal line.

mitochondrion   A component of the cell which contains its own DNA inherited through the maternal line.

mutation   A change in the structure of the DNA.

nucleus   The component of the cell which contains the chromosomes.

PCR   Polymerase chain reaction (*see* **amplification**).

reference sample   A sample taken from a known person, for comparison purposes.

SGMplus™   The DNA profiling system in current use in the UK and most of Europe. In this system, 10 informative loci and a sex test are analysed in order to give the DNA profile.

short tandem repeat (STR)   Describes the physical make-up of the alleles analysed in the current DNA profiling tests – multiple copies of short DNA fragments arranged in sequence, eg "CGAT-CGAT-CGAT-CGAT- CGAT-CGAT-CGAT".

Y-STR profiling   DNA analysis of the Y chromosome – inherited through the paternal line.

CHAPTER 16

Forensic Radiography

16.1 INTRODUCTION

The value of radiography to forensic analysis was recognised very shortly after the discovery of the X-ray by Wilhelm Roentgen in 1895. He took the very first picture using X-rays of the hand of his wife (Anna Bertha). The technology was utilised shortly after this to locate a bullet lodged in the leg of a gunshot victim. These images were subsequently used in the successful prosecution case for attempted murder.[1]

Since Roentgen's discovery of X-rays, radiography has been used as a diagnostic medical tool: but X-rays can also cause cancer and subsequent death, this being one of the medical dichotomies of today.[1] Increasing knowledge, evolving technology and skills have led radiology departments to offer a wider range of radiographic examinations which seek to investigate an ever-widening range of pathologies, and have extended the medical possibilities of this discipline. The biological effects of ionising radiation can result in numerous different effects on the human body and examples are summarised:

- Damage to the skin due to low photon energy.
- Sterility or the production of mutations.
- Gastrointestinal or central nervous system syndromes.
- Radiation-induced cancer, for example leukaemia, breast cancer and genetic damage.

Justification in exposing humans to X-radiation is one of the basic principles of radiation protection.[2] This concept was described in the 1977 recommendations of the International Commission on Radiological Protection.[3] However, the benefits to humans undergoing X-ray examinations should, and in most cases do, "outweigh the small risks to them or their descendants from the radiation received".[4]

Despite the huge advances in medical imaging technology, the control of patient radiation exposure is left to the individual operator. Recent studies of the application of dose reference levels (DRLs) within radiology departments for each examination have concluded that there is a difference between minimum and maximum individual patient dose values that can vary up to a factor of 75. The reasons given for this were multi-factorial. The list included exposure factors, variable focal film distances and radiographic technique.[5,6] Watson *et al* are quoted as saying: "Medical radiation is the largest artificial source of radiation exposure and the contribution from this source has increased by approximately 10 per cent in recent years."[7] Recent publications on UK population doses have found that the average annual dose from artificial radiation is approximately 0.42 mSv, mainly derived from the use of X-rays in medical procedures. The overall average annual dose is suggested to be almost 2.7 mSv and the collective population dose in 2001/2002 from diagnostic radiology was 22,700 man.Sv, resulting in an average annnual dose of 0.38mSv.[8,9,10] These figures are less than the average dose in similarly developed countries – the figure being 0.73mSv. This is thought to be due to the UK having lower frequencies of examinations and lower doses per examination.[11]

In the past, the use of ionising radiation has resulted in harmful effects due to the absence of standard radiation safety regulations. The equipment tended to be used for somewhat frivolous purposes, for example the shoe-fitting fluoroscope used by shoe shops throughout the 1930s to 1950s.

Today, the Medical Exposures Directive requires that every medical exposure should be justified. In the UK, the majority of the provisions of Council Directive 97/43/Euratom of 30 June 1997 (the "Medical Exposures Directive")[12] set out the basic measures for the protection of persons undergoing medical exposures. The regulations and guidance apply to the NHS and the private sector. The Ionising Radiation Regulations (IRR 1999)[12] detail the regulations for the implementation which were derived from and reflect the 1990 recommendations of the International Commission on Radiological Protection (ICRP). The IRR 1999[12] are aimed at employers, radiation protection advisers, health and safety officers, radiation protection supervisors and safety representatives. The publication "Work with ionising radiation: IRR 1999: Approved code of practice and guidance" is extensive and includes the general principles and procedures for the safe delivery of ionising radiation, arrangements for the management of radiation protection, designated areas, classification and monitoring of persons, arrangements for the control of radioactive substances and equipment and the duties of employees.

The National Radiological Protection Board (NRPB) joined the Health Protection Agency (HPA) in April 2005. The HPA's role is to provide an integrated approach to protecting UK public health through the provision of support and advice to the National Health Service (NHS), local authorities, emergency services, other "arm's length" bodies, the Department of Health (DoH) and the Devolved Administrations. The Agency was established as a special health authority (SpHA) in 2003 and part of its remit is radiation protection. The Centre for Infections at Colindale is the base for communicable disease surveillance and specialist microbiology. The Centre for Radiation, Chemical and Environmental

Hazards is based at Chilton and the Centre for Emergency Preparedness and Response, focusing on applied microbiological research and emergency response, is based at Porton.

Practitioners and operators who deliver *medical* exposures must have successfully completed a training programme. Schedule 2 to the Ionising Radiation (Medical Exposure) Regulations 2000 (IR (ME)R 2000)[12] details the relevant functions and specific areas of practice for practitioners and operators. "Operators" refers to anyone who performs "a range of functions covered by the term 'practical aspect'". The range is extensive and includes "supporting functions prior to exposure". In addition to delivering a radiation exposure which, for example, could be a general X-ray examination or fluoroscopy, these functions can include the calibration and testing of X-ray imaging equipment and the preparation and administration of radiopharmaceuticals. While it is true that radiographic examination of cadaveric material does not have to be restricted to qualified radiographers, it is strongly advised that personnel be appropriately trained to uphold health and safety requirements and meet judicial demands. In many situations, forensic odontologists will take the responsibility for producing their own dental images but this is not likely to be a path followed by either the forensic pathologists or the anthropologists.

One of the most common difficulties that people have is a clear understanding of the distinction between radiography and radiology. Radiography is the use of a specific range of electromagnetic radiation (usually ionising) to view objects, animals or humans. Radiology is a medical specialty that utilises an image to diagnose trauma and pathological conditions and can be applied in some instances to treat patients. On a very basic level of understanding, radiologists are medically qualified personnel who report the radiological findings from the images produced by a radiographer. Presently, in a mass fatality situation it is not common for radiologists to be actively involved in diagnosing the resultant images.

A medical radiographer normally produces the images for analysis by a forensic specialist, ie forensic pathologist, forensic odontologist or forensic anthropologist. Radiological investigations are used to confirm the identity of the living and deceased subjects, to identify suspected non-accidental injury (NAI) and to determine and confirm the cause of death[13] and the location of foreign bodies.[14]

In some instances, particularly overseas, it may not be feasible to utilise a UK radiographer and in these situations the specialists will instruct local clinical personnel with regard to the type of images that they require. In forensic medicine, radiography is said to be "one of the most commonly used methodologies in the collection of forensic evidence".[15] The range of investigations can include Computed Tomography (CT), Magnetic Resonance Imaging (MRI), Radionuclide Imaging (RNI) and occasionally angiography, venography and ultrasound (US). It is mainly plain film radiography, however, that is requested, which is usually for anterior-posterior (AP) and lateral (LAT) projections.

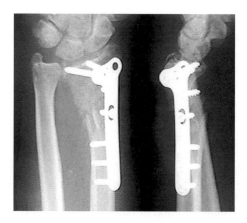

Figure 16.1   Radiograph showing fractured radius and plate

A specialised field of radiography has developed in recent years: forensic radiography.[16] Radiographers are trained in the production of the types of images required for interpretation by forensic specialists. It is generally recognised that the UK is ahead of most other countries in the recognition of the value of forensic radiography to mass fatality scenarios. The Association of Forensic Radiographers[17] defines this discipline as: the application of the science of diagnostic imaging to questions of law.[15] With reference to the medico–legal aspects of law and the evidence and authentication required to be produced, prior to being accepted in a court of law, information must be judged to be admissible as evidence and therefore must be properly authenticated and the continuity of evidence must be demonstrated. Only primary evidence is admissible in court therefore the original hard copy images (radiographs) can be submitted. The latter may not be possible, however, especially when using digital equipment that results in digitally stored images. The Society of Radiographers (SoR) therefore has taken legal advice and recommends that a hard copy image is created at the same time as the digitally stored image.[15]

The ability to image what cannot be readily viewed by the naked eye is a valuable resource to many aspects of a forensic investigation. This aids in:

1. the detection of injuries;
2. identification of pathological conditions;
3. identification of foreign objects that may be:
   - hazardous to the practitioners;
   - of evidential value;
   - useful for identification purposes;
     a. surgical implants (Figure 16.1);
     b. dental artefacts;

    c. personal effects;

    d. immediate awareness of the number of individuals represented;

4. immediate awareness of contents of a body bag;

5. comparison of ante-mortem and post-mortem information. This is most commonly undertaken for dental analysis, although comparison of skeletal images can occur.[18] Check this link[19] and test your ability to compare ante-mortem and post-mortem dental cases.

The following section will consider the range of radiographic approaches utilised in mass fatality incidents for the purposes of establishing identification. The interpretation of the images will be considered in the appropriate sections of the chapters on forensic pathology, odontology and anthropology.[20]

16.2   UK DVI

Xograph Imaging Systems Ltd is under contract to the Home Office to supply specialist radiographic equipment[21] to the National Emergency Mortuary Arrangements (NEMA) when it is established anywhere in the United Kingdom.

At present, two sets of equipment have been retained in order to provide sufficient resilience to supply NEMA, whether deployed as a single mortuary facility or two smaller facilities. These include:

- two mobile image intensifiers (C-Arms) – fluoroscopic examinations;
- two mobile imaging tables;
- one direct digital mobile X-ray unit;
- one mobile imaging table (with cassette tray); and
- two mobile direct digital dental imaging systems.

If radiographic equipment is required then there will be direct liaison with Xograph for deployment. An Xograph field service technician is on permanent callout and will install and power up the equipment ready for use.

All equipment is lightweight and easily assembled/disassembled. It will be transported to and from the site by Xograph in suitable transportation vehicles. The equipment can be expected to operate in "field hospital" conditions, in temperatures between 10 and 35°C and humidity of up to 75 per cent. The imaging requirements for a CBRN (chemical, biological, radiological and nuclear) deployment will be co-ordinated through Alliance Medical and will likely be restricted to Multiple-slice Computed Tomography (MSCT) equipment. This service will be provided through a mobile CT scanner and specialised technicians. It is possible that in time MSCT may well replace all other forms of radiographic imaging for mass fatality incidents.[22]

16.3 FLUOROSCOPY

Fluoroscopy is an imaging technique commonly used to obtain "real-time" images of the objects of interest through the use of a fluoroscope (Figure 16.2). In its simplest form, a fluoroscope consists of an X-ray source and fluorescent screen but, when these are coupled to an X-ray image intensifier and image analysis system, the images can be both played and recorded on a monitor with an option for a thermal paper printout of the image.

Fluoroscopy imaging modalities can be used to screen for:

1. unexploded ordinance and other hazardous material;
2. rapid charting of fragmentary remains;
3. location of personal effects;
4. location and documentation of projectiles and fragments *in situ*;
5. location and documentation of other items of evidence.

Each fluoroscopy unit has the following specifications:

- Ziehm Surgical C-Arm Image intensifier with large (23cm) field size.
- Single or dual 100Hz display monitor C-Arms are each supplied with a mobile monitor cart with dual image display on flat panel LCD display technology.

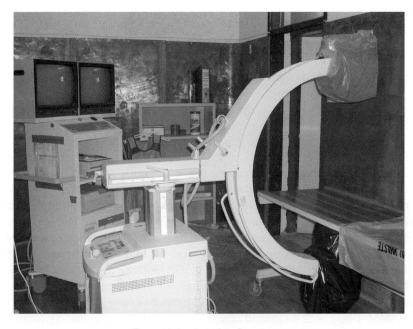

Figure 16.2   A modern fluoroscope

- Supplied with a Sony UP 980CE thermal video printer (for use with both Sony roll thermal film and roll thermal paper).
- Last image hold.
- DAP meter.
- Laser targeting device on intensifier (integrated laser cross-hair Localiser).
- Security key switch: the key switch can be configured either to inhibit switch-on/power-up when removed or can allow power-up but will inhibit X-ray production.
- Facility for radiographic exposures: the source image distance is fixed at 90cm.
- CDR writer: images can be exported to the drive in either TIFF or DICOM formats. Approximately 1,000 TIFF images can be stored on one CD.
- 1,000-image memory; and
- Image output primary capture to Dicom 3.0. The images can also be exported on CD in TIFF format for use in most Windows applications such as MS Word, MS PowerPoint etc.

16.4 DIGITAL RADIOGRAPHY

Digital X-ray imaging systems use X-radiation but the sensors record digital images instead of requiring exposure to photographic film and subsequent wet developing as used in the more traditional approach. The advantages for digital radiography are that they are faster (no developing needed) and as a digital output the images can be e-mailed, compared, enhanced etc, resulting in greater flexibility. Other advantages include the ability to gain wider exposure latitude which can dramatically reduce exposure errors and therefore radiation dose to subjects.[23,24] This is due to the higher quantum detection efficiency of the image plate phosphors.[25] Disadvantages include an increase in subject positioning faults.[26]

In the early stages there was some debate as to the admissibility of these digital images in the courtroom but this has now been overcome, as previously indicated. Image chain-of-custody is secured by preserving the original image on unalterable archive media, such as read-only CDs or WORM (Write Once, Read Many) drives in the same way as the photographer will secure images when using digital cameras. Some imaging programs use secure tagged block file extensions which cannot be changed so that, if the image is modified, it can only be saved as a different file extension. Digital radiographic images can be enhanced for optimal viewing, enlarged by a mouse click to aid visualisation and be displayed side by side for ante-mortem and post-mortem comparison. The digital nature of the image also makes them amenable to computer comparison via systems such as Plassdata.

In the mass fatality situation, digital radiography will largely be used for:

1. examination of the skeleton;
2. establishing projectile pathways;
3. evaluating a preliminary age at death;
4. investigating and recording ante-mortem trauma;
5. establishing and identifying features.

The direct digital X-ray machine is robust, portable and easily transported. One unit is available in each set of UK DVI equipment and has the following specifications:

- High Frequency 4kW + Mobile X-ray unit.
- Focal spot of 0.6 and 1.4mm (nominal).
- Supporting mechanism; integral mobile stand.
- System can be operated with the Direct Digital system de-selected for conventional or dental radiography as required.
- Integrated Direct Digital Flat Panel X-ray plate 35×43 cm in size.
- Image size approx 6 million pixels.
- Carbon Fibre Secondary Radiation Grid.
- Integrated Control PC and Monitor; with colour touch-screen control.
- Rapid X-ray to Preview Image Time (less than 5 seconds);
- 1,000+ image memory.
- Key switch.
- Halogen light beam diaphragm for X-ray beam alignment and sizing.
- Image export to remote PC.
- Networked DICOM Viewing workstation with CD-Writer and suitable CD-writing software, ie non-integrated CDR Writer.
- Image output to Dicom 3.0 Standards and JPEG format.
- Facility for rapid print-out via networked printer or similar.
- Transportation case.
- Requires a continuous Single-Phase Line.
- Automatic Regulation from 110 to 230 VAC ± 10 per cent, 50/60 Hz.

Digital dental radiography produces images of both the teeth and the immediate bones that house them. These can show cavities, hidden dental structures (such as wisdom teeth), artefacts associated with dental intervention, developmental anomalies and bone loss that cannot be seen during a visual examination. Teeth are particularly robust and so tend to survive traumatic events that can see the rest of the body highly fragmented. As many individuals in the Western world attend a dental surgeon at some point throughout their life, there is a high probability that ante-mortem information will be available for comparison with the post-mortem data.

Mass disasters[27] such as the World Trade Center and the 1995 Oklahoma City bombing[28] demonstrated that when the victims number in the hundreds or thousands, the traditional plain film method of exposing radiographs and manually comparing dental records to determine identities is complicated, time-consuming and sometimes even careless. Digital dental radiography dramatically increases the quality and speed of these evaluations, particularly when combined with computer-based dental chart matching software,

Direct dental radiography will be used for age estimation and identification through comparison of ante-mortem and post-mortem data evaluation. Xograph will provide four intra-oral dental digital radiography systems complete with a laptop and appropriate software. In order to access the stored images for viewing and remote radiographic reporting, a central workstation will be supplied. In addition, CIFA (Centre for International Forensic Assistance) has two portable nomad systems that can be deployed overseas by the odontologists. These will facilitate dental imaging in the absence of local support capabilities.

16.5 DIRECT DIGITAL DENTAL X-RAY SYSTEM

The construction of each system and all accessory components is portable, lightweight (maximum 2.5kg), robust and durable. Storage facilities are compact and robust to tolerate frequent mobility and transit. The system and all components are easy to clean and disinfect and comprise the following elements:

- System memory of 512 MB.
- System able to operate at exposures of up to 70kV.
- Internal DVD/RW drive with at least two USB ports.
- System operating temperature range minimum: 5° to 35° C.
- The system has operating capabilities at humidity up to 75 per cent.
- Enhanced security measures to restrict access to the system; and
- Peripherals: mouse pad; video/TV output; minimum two USB; IEEE 1394 connectivity; infrared; and secure wireless networking capability.

16.5.1 Display

- 19" TFT/LCD Display XVGA with 1280 × 1024 resolution with embedded DICOM curve.
- Wide angle of vision (178°).

16.5.2 Image acquisition

- Direct Digital imaging capability using sensor/CCD.
- Sensor/CCD operation range: 2.2m to 10m from the system.

- Sensor/CCD types and dimensions: Size 1 (20×32 mm effective area); and Size 2 (26×34mm effective area); 4mm thickness.
- Sensor/CCD compatible with Rinn® dental positioning aids.

16.5.3 Image manipulation

- Contrast enhancement.
- Window width/level.
- Negative enhancement.
- Image filtration.
- Zoom/Magnification.
- Rotation/Mirroring.
- Distance and angulations measurements.
- Text and symbol annotations.
- Comparison of multiple images.

16.5.4 Image and data storage/export

- Images can be exported in TIFF, JPEG and BMP file formats.
- DICOM conformant.
- Printing and scanning compatibility. (The system supports TWAIN and importing of images from Intraoral cameras and scanners.)

16.6   DENTAL X-RAY TUBE

This is an ultra-lightweight portable dental tube (4.5kg) of rugged construction with stand and protective transportation case.

- **Output**: selectable anode voltages (kVs) 50 to 70kV (±2kV); The anode current range is 2 to 8mA. Exposure timer range is 0.01s to 3.2s (in 26 steps).
- **Voltage** is 220–240VAC 50/60Hz switchable.
- Focal spot size of the X-ray tube is 0.7mm. Focus-to-cone tip distance is 20 cm.

The tube is suitable for film; Computed Radiography (CR); and Direct Digital Radiography applications.

16.7   COMPUTED TOMOGRAPHY (CT)

CT imaging uses X-rays in conjunction with computing algorithms to image the body. In CT, an X-ray generating tube opposite an X-ray detector (or detectors) housed in a ring-shaped apparatus rotates around the object in a spiral fashion, producing a computer-generated cross-sectional series of images (tomogram). Spiral multi-detector CT utilises 8, 16 or 64 detectors during continuous motion of the object through the radiation beam to obtain much finer detailed images in a shorter exam time. With computer manipulation, these images can be reconstructed into 3D images and this is particularly useful for evaluation of trauma to the skeleton.

A team of researchers led by Professor Guy Rutty of the University of Leicester Forensic Pathology Unit used a mobile MSCT scanner at the mortuary for the examination of the victims of a vehicle mass fatality incident.[29]

This approach provided superior information to two-dimensional plain film (anterior–posterior (AP) and lateral), providing on-site soft tissue and bony reconstruction. The system proved faster than traditional temporary mortuary radiography, yielding greater information related to identification, health and safety, autopsy planning and cause of death.

Professor Rutty said:

"The demonstration of the ability to utilise mobile MSCT technology under these circumstances may result in a complete rethinking of the type of radiology to be used in temporary mortuaries or mass fatalities scenes. The work presently being undertaken by my research team within the Forensic Pathology Unit at the University of Leicester in this area is hoped to develop new approaches to mass fatality radiological investigation which may be adopted throughout the world."

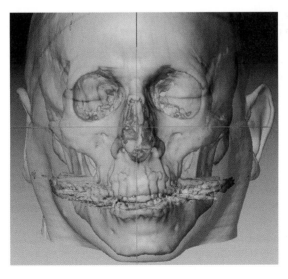

Figure 16.3   3D shaded surface display of a CT scan of a head

This approach has been labelled by some as a "virtopsy"[30] as there is no cutting into the remains and the specialists can "view" the remains without disturbing them. This has obvious benefits for CBRN situations where health and safety are paramount but it also serves as a valuable tool when cultural or religious requirements may request/require non-physical intervention. It is possible that the mass fatality mortuary[31] of the future will be run by APTs and MSCT radiographers with the images being beamed directly to the experts who can analyse them from their desks.

16.7.1   Other examples of the use of CT

With spiral CT and MRI examinations and now the production of subsequent 2D multi-planar reformation (MPR) and 3D shaded surface display (SSD) (Figure 16.3) reconstruction visualisation of, for example, an entire gunshot wound[32] can be created to display complex skull fractures and subsequent brain injuries (such as wound channels and deeply driven bone splinters). This can be documented, complete with graphic detail. CT and MRI can also document vital reaction to the gunshot by demonstrating air emboli in the heart and blood vessels and image the classic pattern of blood aspiration to the lung; gunshot residues deposited within and under the skin are therefore visible on viewing the resultant images.

REFERENCES

1   A R Bleich, *The Story of X-Rays from Rontgen to Isotopes* (Dover Publications Ltd, New York, 1960).

2   R H Corbett and K Faulkner, "Justification in Radiation Protection" (1998) 71 *British Journal of Radiology* 905.

3   International Commission on Radiological Protection, *Recommendation of the ICRP*, Publication 26 (Pergamon Press, Oxford, 1977).

4   P C Shrimpton and S Edyveen, "CT Scanner Dosimetry" (1998) 71 (841) *British Journal of Radiology* Jan 1.

5   D Johnston and P C Brennan, "Reference dose levels for patients undergoing common diagnostic x-ray examinations in Irish hospitals" (2000) 72 *British Journal of Radiology* 396.

6   P C Brennan and D Johnston, "Irish X-ray Departments demonstrate varying levels of adherence to European Guidelines on good radiographic technique" (2002) 75 *British Journal of Radiology* 243.

7   S J Watson, A L Jones, W B Oatway and J S Hughes, "Ionising Radiation exposure of the UK population: 2005 review".

8   D Hart, M C Hillier and B F Wall, "Doses to patients from medical x-ray examinations: 2000 review" (NRPB Chilton, Didcot, 2002).

9   D Hart and B F Wall, "Radiation exposure of the UK population from medical and dental examinations" (NRPB-W4 Chilton, Didcot, 2002).

10 D Hart and B F Wall, "UK population dose from medical x-ray examinations" (2004) 50 *European Journal of Radiology* 285.

11 United Nations Scientific Committee, "UNSC on the effects of atomic radiation sources and effects of ionising radiation", *UN Report to the General Assembly with Scientific Annexes*, vol 1 *Sources* (UN, New York, 2000).

12 European Commission, Council Directive 97/43/Euratom of 30th June 1997 on health protection of individuals against the dangers of ionising radiation in relation to medical exposure, and repealing Directive 84/466/Euratom [1997] *Official Journal of the European Communities* L180, 40, 22.

13 J M Messmer and M F Fierro, "Radiologic Forensic Investigation of Fatal Gunshot Wounds" (1986) *Radiographics* 6(3).

14. R P Bixler, C R Ahrens, R P Rossi and D T Thickman, "Bullet identification with Radiography" (1991) 178 *Radiology* 563.

15 College of Radiographers, "Guidance for the Provision of Forensic Radiography" (College of Radiographers, London, 1999).

16 T Kahana and J Hiss, "Forensic Radiology" (1999) 72 *British Journal of* Radiology 129.

17 Association of Forensic Radiographers [online]. Available at: http://www.afr.org.uk/. [Accessed: 06.11.07.]

18 J Crane, "Forensic Radiology: from Belfast to Bosnia" (2000) 12 *Imaging* 284.

19 Follow this link to test your comparison abilities [online]. Available at: http://images. google.co.uk/imgres?imgurl=http://www.bobble.uklinux.net/images/case.10b. jpg&imgrefurl=http://www.forensicdentistryonline.org/Fire_Folder/case1.htm&h=7 48&w=1484&sz=32&hl=en&start=41&tbnid=iX9LSvWSYslWbM:&tbnh=76&tbn w=150&prev=/images%3Fq%3Dradiographs%2Bantemortem%2Bpostmortem%26s tart%3D40%26gbv%3D2%26ndsp%3D20%26svnum%3D10%26hl%3Den%26ie% 3DUTF-8%26oe%3DISO-8859-1%26sa%3DN. [Accessed: 06.11.07.]

20 I Sanders, M E Woesner, R A Ferguson and T T Noguchi, "A new application of forensic radiology: Identification of deceased from a single clavicle" (1972) 115(3) *American Journal of Roentgenology* 619.

21 Radiographic equipment, Xograph Healthcare Ltd [online]. Available at: http://www. xograph.com/index.php. [Accessed: 06.11.07.]

22 T Kahana, J A Ravioli, C L Urroz and J Hiss, "Radiographic Identification of Fragmentary Human Remains from a Mass Disaster" (1997) *American Journal of Forensic Medicine and Pathology* March 18(1) 40.

23 M D Murphey, "Computed Radiography in musculoskeletal imaging" (1997) *Seminars in Roentgenology* 32(1) 64.

24 A P Hufton, S M Doyle and H M L Cary, "Digital Radiography in paediatrics: radiation dose considerations and magnitude of possible dose reduction" (1998) 71 *British Journal of Radiology* 185.

25 J Papp, "Digital Radiography" (1999) 7 *Seminars in Radiologic Technology* 121.

26 A Alman, A Tingberg, S Mattsson, J Besjakov, S Kheddache, B Lanhede, L G Mansson and M Zankl, "The influence of different technique factors on image quality of lumbar spine radiographs as evaluated by established CEC image criteria" (2000) 73 *British Journal of Radiology* 192.

27 M E Mulligan, M J McCarthy, F J Wippold, J E Lichtenstein and G N Wagner, "Radiologic evaluation of mass casualty victims: lessons from the Gander, Newfoundland, Accident" (1988) *Radiology* 168(1) 229.

28 P J Nye, T L Tytle, R N Jarman and B G Eaton, "The role of radiology in the Oklahoma City Bombing" (1996) 200 *Radiology* 541.

29 G N Rutty, C E Robinson, R BouHaidar, A J Jeffrey and B Morgan, "The role of mobile computed tomography in mass fatality incidents" (2007) 52(6) *Journal of Forensic Sciences* 1343.

30 M Thali, K Yen, W Schweitzer, P Vock, C Boesch, C Ozdoba, M Ith, M Sonnenschein, T Doernhoefer, E Scheurer, T Plattner and R Dirnhofer, "Virtopsy, a New Imaging Horizon in Forensic Pathology: Virtual Autopsy by Postmortem Multislice Computed Tomography (MSCT) and Magnetic Resonance Imaging (MRI) – a Feasibility Study" (2003) 48(2) *Journal of Forensic Science*.

31 M Sidler, C Jackowski, R Dirnhofer, P Vock and M Thali, "Use of multislice computed tomography in disaster victim identification – Advantages and limitations" (2006) *Forensic Science International*.

32 M J Thali, W Schweitzer, K Yen, P Vock, C Ozdoba, E Spielvogel and R Dirnhofer, "The 60-Second 'Digital Autopsy – Full-Body Examination of a Gunshot Victim by Multislice Computed Tomography" (2003) 24(1) *American Journal of Forensic Medicine and Pathology* 22.

CHAPTER 17

Forensic Pathology

17.1 INTRODUCTION

Disasters are unique and usually strike suddenly and without warning. There are many definitions of a disaster, but the most useful working definition is that it is an event that causes or threatens death or injury, damage to property or the environment or disruption to the community which, because of its scale, cannot be dealt with by the local resilience services as part of their day-to-day activities. Disasters demand a co-ordinated response, linking the resources and expertise of many organisations. It is essential that all the agencies who may be involved in a disaster co-operate in planning, training and exercising for the event. Similarly, co-operation is essential at the time of a disaster. As disasters are rare, it is likely that some people involved will have had no experience of similar events and, if there has been no effective planning and training, chaos and mistakes may result.

17.2 LEGAL BACKGROUND

Disasters with fatalities come under the jurisdiction of the Coroner in whose area the incident occurs. Fatalities from disasters overseas come under the jurisdiction of the Coroner in whose area "the body lies". In most cases this will be the area covering the point of arrival in England or Wales. The Coroner will appoint an appropriately qualified pathologist to perform the autopsies on his or her behalf (Coroners Rules 1984).[1] In Scotland, the judicial office of Coroner does not exist and the equivalent role is performed by the Procurator Fiscal[2] who is a member of the Lord Advocate's department.[3] The Procurator Fiscal applies to the appropriate sheriff court for permission to order an autopsy. A disaster would be such a case. In continental Europe the law in most countries is based on the Napoleonic Code.[4] The role of the investigating magistrate or chief of police is similar to that of the Coroner in that they are mainly concerned with finding out who has died and ensuring that there are no criminal aspects to the case.

17.3   AT THE SCENE OF THE DISASTER

The police and emergency services will be the first at the scene of a disaster. Their immediate concern will be the saving of life. If this is impossible, effective investigation[5] aimed at saving lives in the future assumes major importance. Planning and training ensure that the emergency services are aware of their contribution to successful investigation. However, there is usually public pressure for a speedy retrieval of human remains and restoration to their next-of-kin. Investigation can impede this process, and co-operation between the police and the accident investigators is essential. At the scene the main contributions of the police to the investigation are the maintenance of the security of the area and the preservation of evidence, particularly the distribution of the bodies and any wreckage. "Security" also includes security from both bystanders and well-intentioned officials.

It is important to ascertain whether any hazardous materials are involved before further action is taken. Photographs should be taken as soon as possible after the incident occurs, before the wreckage is moved or disturbed. Efforts should be made to preserve or record evidence of an ephemeral nature, such as ice and soot deposits. Photographs must be taken of the bodies before removal. Aerial photographs of the site are also routinely taken and satellite imaging of the scene is usually made available. However, there is considerable public pressure to remove the dead bodies as soon as possible and, in general, the lack of such photographs should not impede the investigation, provided the location of each body in the wreckage is known. Mapping the locations of the fatalities is more important. This is best achieved with a system of staking, labelling and recording GPS co-ordinates, and is normally the responsibility of the police. However, it is important that the body recovery team are made aware of any potential hazards and matters of health and safety that they might encounter. They may need to obtain advice from environmental health officers and consultants in communicable disease control (see Chapter 21). All the personnel involved in the recovery procedures should be provided with appropriate protective clothing.

Once death has been confirmed, a uniquely numbered label will be securely attached to the body, as per protocol. With disasters occurring in the United Kingdom the label will have been obtained from the ACPO DVI label booklet. Labels are attached to the upper areas of the body whenever possible. For body parts where this is not possible, it is enough to place the label in the bag with the fragment and ensure that the bag is also labelled. Disaster kits will contain pre-printed labels in triplicate for this purpose. The bodies should not be undressed or searched at the scene, nor should any property be removed from them or from their clothing. The recovery teams will then place the body or remains into a body bag and fix identically numbered labels to both the bag and the location from which it was removed. The location markers could be stakes or freestanding markers. It is sometimes useful for the pathologist to view the bodies *in situ* but this may not be possible. Parts of bodies (body parts) should be treated in a similar manner to whole bodies (see Chapter 4 for definition of what constitutes a body or body part; this might also be a decision which is made on the day). Once the Coroner/Fiscal has given permission to remove the bodies or body parts, they may be moved from the site, but great care must be taken to avoid cross-contamination and preserve the evidence. If evidential cross-contamination is a concern, all body parts should be placed in separate bags before being placed in the same carrier.

The bodies should then be taken to a holding area close to the accident site, before being taken to the temporary mortuary. Ideally, this holding area should be under cover and out of public view. It should be secure and accessible to vehicles. This holding area serves as a collection point and as a checking point to ensure that labelling of body bags is complete and correct. Refrigerated vehicles may also attend the holding area to allow appropriate storage, and phased and orderly transfer of the bodies to the temporary mortuary. The body bags must remain sealed throughout their time in the holding area. Alternatively, the holding area may be associated with the temporary mortuary site rather than the accident site.

17.4 THE MORTUARY

In England and Wales the responsibility for providing support to Coroners lies with the county council in shire areas, or borough council in metropolitan areas. They also have emergency planning responsibilities under the Civil Contingencies Act 2004.[6] Although these do not specify detailed requirements to plan for temporary mortuaries, the regulations and Home Office guidance promote the concept of integrated emergency management. These councils should therefore identify suitable, licensed, premises for use as a temporary mortuary in an emergency, or if they are unable to do this should have a contract with a firm that can supply a temporary mortuary, which must also be licensed. Ideally, one would be identified for each Coroner's district. Each site identified as suitable for a temporary mortuary should be capable of being equipped and fully operational within 24 hours. The costs incurred fall on the local authority responsible for funding the Coroner's service.

All the bodies from a major disaster should be taken to a single mortuary. This facilitates the difficult task of identification, avoids the unnecessary duplication of personnel and minimises the burden on the communications system, which would inevitably be under great strain. In major disasters the use of a hospital mortuary is not appropriate. If there are also live casualties as well as fatalities, the hospital approach roads should not be encumbered by vehicles bringing the dead to the mortuary. Additionally, the arrival of a large number of bodies at a hospital mortuary would overwhelm capacity, necessitating the use of a second or third mortuary. Many of the bodies from a major disaster may be severely burned or mutilated and a hospital mortuary is not suitable for large numbers of such cases. A public mortuary is similarly unsuitable because the capacity is likely to be overwhelmed by the arrival of a large number of bodies. A specifically

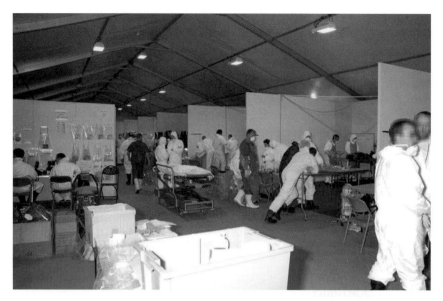

Figure 17.1   Tented mortuary used after the London bombings of 2005

designated temporary mortuary is the best solution for such a disaster. Ideally, buildings for use as a temporary mortuary should have been selected before the disaster or arrangements should be in place for the construction of a rapid construction tented solution (see Figure 17.1). In overseas locations the choice of a suitable temporary mortuary may be very restricted (Figure 17.2).

Figure 17.2   A mortuary in Kosovo

The fundamental requirement for a temporary mortuary is a large floor space at ground level in a sheltered building. It should be of sufficient size to allow all the investigations to be carried out efficiently on an open-plan design. Tents have been used successfully when such a building was not available. The key requirements are security and privacy. Easy road access is essential to facilitate the transport of bodies to and from the mortuary.

Adequate space and facilities for clerical work will be needed. The mortuary will need to be in constant and direct contact with the police, particularly their casualty bureau. Telephones and facsimile machines should be included in the communication system. Adequate light, heat, ventilation, water supply, drainage and sewerage will be needed together with power for electric saws and radiological equipment. However, it is frequently possible to improvise. As far as is practicable the recommendations of the Health Services Advisory Committee (1991) on safe practice in the mortuary and post-mortem room should be followed. The responsibility for the health and safety aspects of the operation of the temporary mortuary rests with the designated supervising pathologist who will liaise with the environmental health officer, consultants in communicable disease control and others who may give useful advice.

Many personnel from a variety of backgrounds may be required during the investigation: pathologists, mortuary technicians, clerks, photographers, police, forensic odontologists, anthropologists and, perhaps most important of all, personnel need to be available to move bodies within the mortuary. The mortuary should be divided into a reception area for bodies as they are received where the documentation may be initiated. The provision of another area for external examination, unclothing and photography will depend on the way in which the mortuary is set up, it may be that this becomes part of the processing of the body and therefore would not involve a separate area. Dental examination may take place here as well. Autopsy facilities will be required, as will areas for special investigations such as radiology, anthropology and fingerprinting. Finally, an area should be set aside for the embalming and encoffining of the bodies. It is useful to have a secure room for the storage of both specimens and property removed from the fatalities. There are many publications listing the equipment that should be available in the temporary mortuary.[7] If possible, trolleys should be provided; these can act as autopsy tables and also be used to move bodies within the mortuary area. Every person in the mortuary must wear appropriate protective clothing. In many accidents, particularly those in which sabotage or explosions are thought to play a part, radiography will be required. Special facilities will be needed for this purpose (see Chapter 16).

In addition to the facilities that will be needed at the temporary mortuary, additional remote facilities will be required to complete the investigations. These will include a DNA analysis laboratory and other more advanced scientific facilities as may be required.

In major disasters the provision of refrigeration is a great advantage in that this removes the need for haste in the investigation that may lead to evidence being overlooked or destroyed. Portable refrigeration in the form of containers which can be used as either refrigerators or freezers may well provide an answer to this problem and should be sourced as early as possible.

As part of the disaster plan the Coroner or Procurator Fiscal in conjunction with the police will have nominated a pathologist with appropriate experience to act as the supervising pathologist. He or she will be responsible for the planning of the mortuary facilities, identifying the equipment needed and the organisation of the mortuary once it has been activated. The mortuary will be commissioned when it is known that any disaster is of such a size as to require special arrangements. To maintain security it is important that all personnel who may need access to the mortuary have some readily identifiable security pass or badge. Security passes will be coded to ensure that access to sensitive areas is strictly controlled.

Before commencing the examinations a meeting should be held to discuss what is needed and how this is to be achieved. The Coroner or Procurator Fiscal will be present along with the SIM, the supervising pathologist and the odontologist. Depending on the nature of the accident, other attendees may be SO 15, the Air Accidents Investigation Branch (AAIB),[7] the Marine Accident Investigation Branch (MAIB)[8] and the Rail Accident Investigation Branch (RAIB).[9]

On arrival each body or part of a body will be logged in a register. A document case containing appropriate documents is allocated to each body or body part. It is helpful if this is transparent and waterproof. It should have a checklist of procedures to be followed that can be signed or initialled by the appropriate person once the action is complete. Every document should bear the body number. Contained in the case will be the International Criminal Police Organization (Interpol)[11] disaster victim identification form that is now used in disasters with fatalities of differing nationalities. All information is entered into Plassdata, a computer system based on the Interpol forms, which assists the comparison of post-mortem data against ante-mortem data, as part of the identification process.

17.5 POST-MORTEM EXAMINATION

Acts of terrorism or crime involving the use of firearms or improvised explosive devices may be the cause of a disaster and so each victim should undergo radiological examination to detect the presence of bullets or fragments of shrapnel (see Figure 17.3).

X-ray examination may also aid identification by demonstrating radio-opaque implants used in dentistry and implants (Figure 17.4) used in orthopaedics together with old fracture sites. The determination of radiological age can be useful when there are children and young adults involved (see Chapters 18 and 19). The hands and jaws are particularly valuable in this respect. The configuration of the frontal sinuses is often characteristic; but is only of any value if there are ante-mortem radiographs available for comparison. If pacemakers or defibrillators are discovered they should be identified before any attempt is made to remove them.

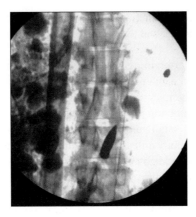

Figure 17.3   Radiograph showing a bullet lodged in the spine

These have unique identifying numbers which are recorded when they are placed *in situ* (see Figure 17.4).

Figure 17.4   Unique identifying number on shaft of metal femoral head implant

Before the external examination can begin the victim must be undressed and detailed descriptions made of clothing, possessions and jewellery. Photographs should be taken of all possessions and clothing. While these are unlikely to be used as a primary method of identification, they may provide useful clues as to the likely identification of the body.

Some police forces believe that the removal of property from accident victims is solely their responsibility. While the restoration of personal possessions to the next-of-kin is clearly the duty of the police, its removal from the deceased should be a joint effort. Ideally, the victim should be undressed and searched by a team consisting of the pathologist and the police. In this way vital clues are unlikely to be overlooked.

A passport or wallet containing a driving licence and credit cards discovered in the jacket pocket of a male victim is likely to belong to that individual. However, such documentary evidence must still be treated with caution: for example, it is not uncommon for one individual to carry all the family's passports. It is clearly vital that rescuers should be instructed that nothing should be placed with a body unless it is definitely associated with it. Contacting individuals named in an address book may give the name of someone who was a passenger on the crashed aircraft – and this is the responsibility of the FLO. Airlines can usually say to whom a boarding card has been issued. In common with all documentary evidence, this needs to be treated with caution, as the interchange of tickets, boarding cards and seats is not uncommon.

Jewellery can be distinctive in design and has the advantage of resisting mechanical damage or fire. Inscriptions are frequently found on wedding and signet rings and these usually remain on the hands. Unfortunately, the amputations that frequently occur in accidents can limit the value of rings in identification. A ring discovered on an amputated limb may give proof of death and it may be possible to relate the limb to the remainder of the body. Other possessions, such as keys, may give useful confirmatory clues to identity, as they may be shown by the police to fit the car or house of one of the passengers, but only after that person has been confirmed as one of the missing.

As transport passengers are frequently seen off at the departure point, and few clothes are carried in aircraft or trains, relatives may be able to describe accurately the clothing worn by the casualties. It may be very difficult for the pathologist or police to describe clothing, as this is often severely damaged or burnt. It is useful to remove samples of distinctive clothing and clip unsoiled pieces to a card bearing the body number. If required, the card can be placed in a transparent envelope and shown to the relatives of the victim, who may be able to identify it. Even after incineration, it may be possible to find fragments of clothing which assist the identification. Some clothing, particularly that of children, may have labels bearing the owner's name. Other labels may be useful; the manufacturer's label may help. The common use of chain stores limits their value, but the size inscribed upon the labels may indicate the wearer's physique.

Once the body has been undressed it should be subject to a detailed external examination for physical or medical clues to aid identification. The differentiation between physical and medical methods of identification is somewhat artificial. Medical methods include the external and internal evidence of previous operations or disease (Figure 17.5), while physical methods include such characteristics as race,[12] gender,[13] scars, tattoos, birthmarks[14] and facial and head hair.[15] Such evidence may be used to limit the general classification of the victims by dividing them into groups by race, gender, age, general height and weight and other such characteristics and may prove of value as confirmatory evidence of identity. While

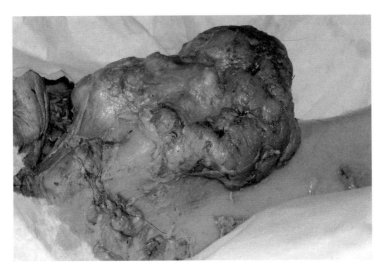

Figure 17.5   Femoral tumour

an absent gall bladder could never be proof of identity, it may be valuable when only a few unidentified bodies remain.

Occasionally, separate body parts may be contained in a body bag with another body. If this occurs, the part should be treated as if it were a new body found in the mortuary and given a new ACPO DVI number. It can then be examined at a later time.

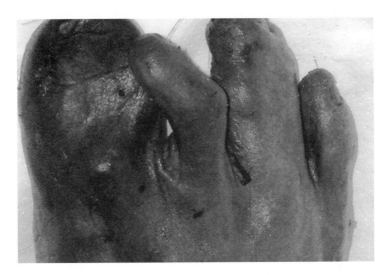

Figure 17.6   Syndactyly of the right foot

Some medical and physical characteristics may be so distinctive as to provide primary evidence of identification. Examples include physical deformities, such as webbed fingers or syndactyly (Figure 17.6); uncommon operative procedures such as limb amputation or major heart operations; and the retention of orthopaedic implants such as artificial joints and plates used for the treatment of fractures.[16] It may be necessary to compare post-mortem radiographs with those taken in life in order positively to confirm identity. Many of the larger orthopaedic implants have serial numbers (Figure 17.4) and it may be possible to obtain evidence of these from the hospital that implanted the device in the patient, although they can be difficult to remove.

Tattoos frequently bear the names of a loved one or their design may be so distinctive as to permit positive identification. However, it is important to note that coincidences do occur and identification based solely on tattoos should be made with extreme caution. The reasons for tattooing are many and varied, and they can represent a significant event or membership of a group, meaning that the tattoo is not unique. Tattoos can be compared with photographs of the deceased taken in life or photographs taken from the victim could be shown to their next-of-kin. Body piercing is now common in both sexes, and it is important to note the presence or absence of piercing and to retain any jewellery inserted.

Samples for DNA analysis[17] will be taken. Bone or a tooth may be used: if tooth is used, a molar from the back of the mouth should be selected rather than incisors or canines so that potential facial comparison is not impaired. In the UK it is important that the provisions of the Coroners (Amendment) Rules 2005[18] are observed. In particular, a pathologist shall make provision, so far as possible, for the preservation of material which, in his or her opinion, bears upon the cause of death or the identification of the deceased. Where he or she preserves material he or she must notify the Coroner of that fact in writing (this includes electronic communication). The Act also indicates how long such material may be kept and how it is to be disposed of once it is no longer needed. DNA collection does not come under the Human Tissue Act 2004,[19] however the guidelines according to PACE should still be observed.

A problem that arises both at the start and the end of the identification process is that of how many bodies have been recovered. With the gross destruction that frequently accompanies a disaster, this may be difficult. If there has been significant disintegration, the larger portions of tissue, such as limbs, should be dealt with in the same way as intact bodies. Those that are potentially identifiable should be examined at the mortuary after all the whole-body autopsies have been completed. Each portion should be described and examined and the detailed contents of each bag should be recorded. Anatomically trained forensic anthropologists can be of considerable assistance in this situation (see Chapter 19). If disintegrated fragments can be matched with a particular body, their combined disposal may eventually take place. With major parts such as whole limbs it may be possible to match them by skin and hair colour and by comparing that anatomical point of separation. Smaller body parts will require DNA analysis to allocate the parts to the appropriate torso. If no such identification is possible, the unidentified remains should be disposed of at the end of the investigation, after consultation with the Coroner or Procurator Fiscal.

17.6 THE IDENTIFICATION COMMISSION

No sudden or unnatural death can be properly investigated until the victim has been identified. Coroners are required to ascertain who the deceased was (Coroners Rules 1984).[1] The need for identification has been justified on many grounds ranging from the purely sociological to the right of every individual to an identity after death, as interpreted from Article 6 of the United Nations Universal Declaration of Human Rights.[20] This states: "Everyone has the right to recognition everywhere as a person before the law." The absence of identification can seriously delay the administration of the estates of the dead and the granting of probate. However, in a disaster the most compelling reason for identification is the investigation of the cause of the incident. The identification of the dead is not an end in itself but an essential element of the investigation into the cause and events of the incident.

In all but accidents with a small number of casualties, a secretariat to co-ordinate the identification process will be needed. This has been called an identification commission. The Coroner or Procurator Fiscal, or the police acting on his or her behalf, institutes the identification commission. Its role is to:

- liaise with the Coroner or Procurator Fiscal;
- control the running of the mortuary;
- confirm the appointment of the supervising forensic pathologist;
- evaluate the ante- and post-mortem data;
- formally evaluate individual identifications;
- compile evidence of identification for submission to the legal authorities.

All the information about those who are thought to have perished is correlated with the information obtained from the victims of the accident. The collection of personal information from the bereaved families and other sources is a task that requires tact and diplomacy and is the responsibility of the Family Liaison Officer.

The information coming into the identification commission must be recorded in a logical manner. Two sets of documents are needed, namely documents containing details on each unidentified person and documents with observations on each unidentified body. The International Criminal Police Organization (Interpol)[8] has devised a set of forms for use in the identification of unknown bodies. In disasters with large numbers of victims, Interpol may use the Plassdata program to compare ante-mortem with post-mortem data.

The function of the commission is to search the two sets of documents for common factors. For example, if an individual is reported as wearing a particular item of jewellery and a similar item is found on one of the deceased, a preliminary identification may be made and the folders regarded as "engaged". A search is then made for confirmatory methods of identification. Ideally, all the information on the deceased should match the information on the missing person. Most legal authorities require confirmation to be with either dental, fingerprint or DNA evidence. Less commonly, medical or physical methods may be accepted. When corroborative evidence of the identification is found, the two folders (ante-mortem and post-mortem) are regarded as "married". Final release of the victims should not take place until all possible identifications have been made.

The methods used in ascribing the right name to the right body are largely a matter of common sense, provided there is sufficient information in each of the folders. The relative values of the various methods employed vary according to the nature of the accident and the likelihood of coincidences. In the Asian tsunami of December 2004 the primary method of identification in Thailand was dental in 51.8 per cent of cases; fingerprints in 34.8 per cent; DNA in 13.0 per cent; and physical/medical in 0.2 per cent.[15] However, as ideally more than one method would be used, the frequency of their use was dental 55.5 per cent; fingerprints in 34.8 per cent; DNA in 14.2 per cent; and physical/medical in 22.9 per cent.[21]

It must be noted that the value of the various methods of identification depends upon the circumstances of the incident and the nationalities of the passengers. Some countries, such as the United States and Japan, hold extensive fingerprint records; therefore this is of value in nationals of those countries. In the Lockerbie disaster of 1988[22] there were a large number of American citizens on board and fingerprints proved valuable in 40 per cent of the identifications. Dental records are less readily obtained or indeed available in less developed countries which may also have a problem with processing DNA samples.

17.7 SUMMARY

Most legal authorities require identification to be made using dental, fingerprint or DNA evidence. Occasionally, physical or medical evidence may be used. Clothing, possessions and jewellery are used as initial clues to identification. Pathologists are an essential part of the team responsible for the identification of the dead in mass disasters. Identification should not be seen as an end in itself, but as a vital tool in the investigation of the disaster.

REFERENCES

1 King's College London. Coroners Rules 1984 (SI 1984/552) [online]. Available at: http://www.kcl.ac.uk/depsta/law/research/coroners/1984rules.html. [Accessed: 22.10.07.]

2 "Procurator Fiscal", *Wikipedia* [online]. Available at: http://en.wikipedia.org/wiki/ Procurator_fiscal. [Accessed 22.10.2007.]

3 "Crown Office and Procurator Fiscal Service" [online]. Available at: http://www. crownoffice.gov.uk/About. [Accessed: 22.10.2007.]

4 *The Napoleon Series: Code Napoleon; or, The French Civil Code. Literally Translated from the Original and Official Edition* (published by a Barrister of the Inner Temple, Paris, 1804) (tr attributed to George Spence) (cf *Cushing's Anonyms: A Dictionary of Revealed Authorship* and *Halkett & Laing's Dictionary of Anonymous and Pseudonymous English Literature* and in the *Dictionary of National Biography*) (William Benning, Law Bookseller, London, 1827). [online]. Available at: http://www. napoleon-series.org/research/government/c_code.html. [Accessed: 22.10.2007.]

5 "King's Cross fire", *Wikipedia* [online]. Available at: http://en.wikipedia.org/wiki/ King's_Cross_fire. [Accessed: 22.10.2007.]

6 Civil Contingencies Act 2004 (c 36) (HMSO, London) [online]. Available at: http:// www.opsi.gov.uk/Acts/acts2004/ukpga_20040036_en_1. [Accessed: 22.10.2007.]

7 A Busuttil, J S P Jones and M A Green, *Deaths in Major Disasters: The Pathologist's Role* (2nd edn, 2000, Royal College of Pathologists) [online]. Available at: http:// www.rcpath.org/resources/pdf/majordisasters.pdf. [Accessed: 23.10.2007.]

8 Air Accidents Investigation Branch website [online]. Available at: http://www.aaib. dft.gov.uk/home/index.cfm. [Accessed: 14.11.2007.]

9 Marine Accident Investigation Branch website [online]. Available at: http://www. maib.gov.uk/home/index.cfm. [Accessed: 29.11.2007.]

10 Rail Accident Investigation Branch website [online]. Available at: http://www.raib. gov.uk/home/index.cfm. [Accessed: 14.11.2007.]

11 Interpol DVI Forms [online]. Available at: http://www.interpol.int/Public/ DisasterVictim/Forms/Default.asp. [Accessed: 22.10.2007.]

12 "Race", *Wikipedia* [online]. Available at: http://en.wikipedia.org/wiki/Race. [Accessed: 22.10.2007.]

13 "Gender", *Wikipedia* [online]. Available at: http://en.wikipedia.org/wiki/Gender. [Accessed: 22.10.2007.]

14 "Birthmarks", *Wikipedia* [online]. Available at: http://en.wikipedia.org/wiki/ Birthmarks. [Accessed: 22.10.2007.]

15 "Facial and Head Hair", *Wikipedia* [online]. Available at: http://en.wikipedia.org/ wiki/List_of_types_of_facial_hair#C. [Accessed: 22.10.2007.]

16 E K Simpson, D A Eitzen and R W Byard, "Role of Orthopedic implants and bone morphology in the identification of human remains" (2007) 52(2) *Journal of Forensic Sciences* 442.

17 Prinz *et al*, DNA Commission of the International Society for Forensic Genetics (ISFG), "Recommendations regarding the role of forensic genetics for disaster victim identification" (2007) (1) *Forensic Science International: Genetics* 3.

18 Coroners (Amendment) Rules 2005 (SI 2005/40) (HMSO, London) [online]. Available at: http://www.opsi.gov.uk/SI/si2005/20050420.htm. [Accessed: 10.06.08.]

19 Human Tissue Act 2004 (c 30) (HMSO, London) [online]. Available at: http://www.opsi.gov.uk/ACTS/acts2004/ukpga_20040030_en_1. [Accessed: 10.06.08.]

20 Universal Declaration of Human Rights, Art 6 [online]. Available at: http://www.un.org/Overview/rights.html. [Accessed: 22.10.2007.]

21 O W Morgan, P Sribanditmongkol, C Perera, Y Sulasmi, D Van Alphen and E Sondorp, "Mass Fatality Management following the South Asian Tsunami Disaster: Case Studies in Thailand, Indonesia, and Sri Lanka" (2006) 3(6) *PLoS Medicine* 95.

22 Dumfries and Galloway Police, "Lockerbie Air Disaster" [online]. Available at: http://www.dumfriesandgalloway.police.uk/foi/class_cat/pub_int/lbie_kvz.htm. [Accessed 09.06.08.]

CHAPTER 18

Forensic Odontology

18.1   INTRODUCTION

Historically, forensic dentistry (odontology) has played a major role in identification methods. As far back as AD 50, in the time of the Emperor Nero, records
show that his mistress's battered body was identified by her teeth. Other important
historical incidents such as the Paris Bazaar fire (1898),[1] the pyjama girl case
(1934),[2] Dr Buck Ruxton murder (1935)[3] and the Haigh acid bath case (1949)[4]
illustrate the long history of association between forensic investigation and dental
evidence. But this is not just a process relegated to the past: forensic odontology
continues to play a pivotal role in not only the identification of the deceased but
also the prosecution of the perpetrators, for example Ted Bundy (1974)[5] and
Rosemary and Fred West (1994).[6]

Teeth are the hardest tissue in the human body and therefore are the most
resistant to trauma, decomposition, water immersion and fire. Dentistry is
therefore of immense value in the identification procedures in mass disasters[7]
where body disruption may be extensive. Recent examples where this discipline
has proved to be of significant value include the Lockerbie air disaster (1988),[8]
the Asian tsunami tragedy (2004),[9] the London bombings (2005)[10] and the Dhow
boat disaster (2006).[11] Despite the advent of DNA profiling and recent advances
in DNA science, dental identification still provides a quick, economic and reliable
way to identify the deceased, providing comparable ante-mortem records are
available.

Some interesting recent statistics from the tsunami disaster in Thailand as of
December 2005 show:

*   1,248 positive identifications had been made on dental information alone;
*   727 on fingerprints alone;
*   32 on DNA alone.

Other identifications were achieved using a combination of methods.[9]

Visual identification of the deceased is not recommended – in fact it must be
positively avoided as, even with a complete body with relatively little external
trauma or decomposition, mistakes have occurred and will often occur. In the

emotive state suffered by the next-of-kin and in their urgency to find their loved ones, misidentifications happen. The consequences of a misidentification can be widespread – if the wrong body is returned to the wrong relative, then somewhere else another body may also have been identified (and returned) incorrectly. This has important social and psychological implications and legal ramifications such as insurance, inheritance and remarriage, to name but a few. Identification mistakes have occurred following many mass fatality incidents including Lockerbie,[8] the Asian tsunami both in Sri Lanka and Thailand[9] and the Luxor terrorist attacks[12] (when one family went through the entire funeral process only to be informed later that the wrong body had been returned to them).

The reliability of visual identification is affected by a number of factors: these can include post-mortem trauma or decomposition related alterations, for example bloating after water immersion, fire damage and body fragmentation. The photograph in Figure 18.1 was placed outside the mortuary in Colombo in the hope that victims could be visually identified!

However, despite this unreliability, in some situations visual identification is the only method available due to a lack of retrievable or verifiable AM fingerprints, DNA material and dental information.

It must be acknowledged that relatives and friends of the deceased may be so determined to find their loved one that they will unconsciously misidentify, in order to alleviate the stress and unhappiness caused by "not knowing", thereby achieving the goal of claiming some remains upon which to focus their grief. Alternatively, they may express complete denial during which they refuse to

Figure 18.1   Photograph of bodies placed outside the mortuary in Colombo

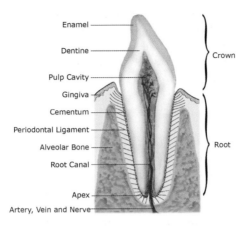

Figure 18.2   Cross-section through a tooth, showing the layers of tissue

accept the reality of the situation and will reject the body as being that of their next-of-kin in an attempt to protect their belief of survival of their loved one. Grief is a particularly unpredictable emotion that is unique to each situation.

Visual identification may become confused if a significant period of time has elapsed since the person was last seen. Obviously the circumstances are different but also many of the physical attributes of identity may have changed, reflecting the effects of ageing, hair loss, weight gain or loss, physical infirmities etc.

18.2   ANATOMY OF THE TEETH

The human tooth basically comprises three layers (Figure 18.2):

1. **enamel**: this is the outermost layer of the tooth and is the hardest and most resistant tissue in the human body, being approximately 97 per cent mineral;
2. **dentine**: this layer lies directly under the enamel and creates the form of the tooth;
3. **pulp cavity**: this is in the centre of the tooth and contains blood vessels, nerves and connective tissue. As the pulp cavity is more or less sealed (there is only the small connection through the apex or root end to the outside), it is a useful source for DNA sampling.

The tooth itself is divided up into the crown, neck and root areas and articulates with either the maxilla (upper jaw) or mandible (lower jaw) (Figure 18.3). The anterior teeth (incisors and canines) are single-rooted teeth while the posterior teeth (premolars and molars) are multi-rooted (Figure 18.4). For this reason the anterior

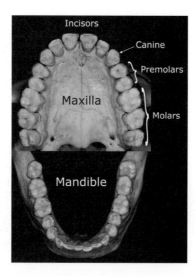

Figure 18.3   Dentition in situ *in the maxilla and mandible*

teeth are easier to remove from the jaws and following trauma can be easily lost. These should be looked for and reinserted into the jaws for photographic purposes should a superimposition of the skull onto a photograph be required at a later date. These anterior teeth should not be destroyed for DNA or isotope purposes.

The human dentition is recorded when examined, in relation to four quadrants: the upper and lower quadrants and right and left sides. For example, the first molar on the left-hand side of the top jaw would be designated as "upper left". The human adult dentition (Figure 18.4) has a possible 32 teeth, consisting of:

- 4 upper incisors (large cutting teeth in the front of the mouth);
- 4 lower incisors (smaller cutting teeth in the front of the mouth);
- 2 upper and 2 lower canine teeth (dog-like "fang" teeth);
- 8 premolars (double-pointed teeth, 2 behind each canine);
- 12 molars (multi-pointed chewing teeth, 3 in each quarter behind the premolars).

The deciduous (child's) dentition has 20 teeth which are obviously smaller in size than their adult counterparts but nonetheless do have some corresponding features and comparable nomenclature:

- 4 upper incisors;
- 4 lower incisors;
- 2 upper canines and 2 lower canines;
- 8 molars.

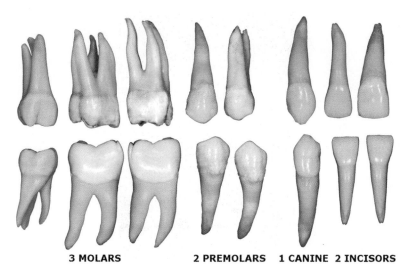

3 MOLARS   2 PREMOLARS   1 CANINE 2 INCISORS

Figure 18.4   Right upper and lower dentition

From the age of 6 months post-partum (after birth), the deciduous (milk or baby) teeth erupt through the gum in a well-documented sequence. However, even before eruption they can be detected by radiographs (X-rays) (Figure 18.5) in the bone of the jaws, and the age of the child can be estimated with a fair degree of accuracy.

At about 6 years of age the adult dentition begins to erupt, again in sequence, and this process continues until the final molars (wisdom teeth) erupt in the early 20s. The anterior adult teeth form deep in the bone below the juvenile dentition, and push against the deciduous teeth as they grow. This pushing combines with resorption of the root (this is where the root of the tooth gradually disappears, allowing the next tooth to come through) to cause the tooth to become loose and, eventually, the baby teeth are shed from the mouth. Therefore children between

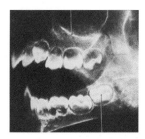

Figure 18.5   Teeth can be detected by X-ray in the bone of the jaws before eruption

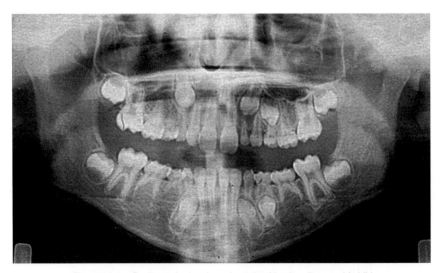

Figure 18.6   Radiograph showing mixed dentition in a 7-year-old child

6 and 12 years of age tend to display a "mixed dentition" stage, having a mixture of both permanent (adult) and deciduous (baby) teeth (Figure 18.6). Again, this regularity of development, eruption and loss enables the odontologist to age children and young adults reasonably accurately and this can be a vital tool in the identification process.

In adulthood, dental ageing becomes less precise. However, more recently, methods have been devised to age a tooth to within approximately 5 years. These methods are laboratory based and therefore are more complex, expensive and time consuming. The most tried and tested is Gustafson's method. Here, the tooth is removed and ground down to be wafer thin and a cross-section of the tooth from tip to root is produced. The specimen is examined with a light source behind and a measurement is made of the translucency of the root. The more translucent the root is (ie the more light can shine through it), the older the tooth is and therefore the older the individual to whom the tooth belonged.

Another method of ageing adult teeth measures the change in amino acids in the enamel and dentine. Through life, the amino acid molecule changes from being right handed to left handed, and by measuring the ratio of one to the other, a good age estimation can be obtained.

18.3   SEARCH AND RECOVERY

In this vital initial stage of operations it is essential that all available information is retrieved and documented. Anterior teeth are often lost from the body due to

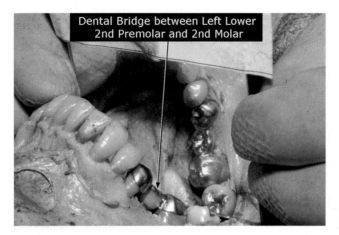

Figure 18.7   Dental bridge

trauma and this is particularly true of the lower front teeth, which is unfortunate as these may be of particular value to the odontologist. It is therefore vital that officers have a basic knowledge of the morphology of human teeth and associated structures such as dental crowns,[13] bridges (Figure 18.7), dentures, fillings etc. and are able to differentiate these from other artefacts.

18.4   PROCEDURES INVOLVED IN A DENTAL IDENTIFICATION

These can be summarised as:

1. collection of ante-mortem data;
2. collection of post-mortem data;
3. reconciliation (or comparison) of this data;
4. presentation to identification commission, identification board, Coroner/ Procurator Fiscal or appropriate authoritative body;
5. release of remains and (if abroad) repatriation.

18.4.1   Collection of ante-mortem data

Scientific methods of identification (ie fingerprints, DNA and dental) almost always involve the comparison of ante-mortem and post-mortem data and thus rely on the quality and quantity of both sets of data. Dental data is usually collected by the Family Liaison Officers and can be available from a variety of sources:

- dental practitioners;
- dental clinics;
- orthodontic and other specialists;
- doctors;
- family and friends;
- workplace colleagues;
- hospitals.

It is important to ask for documents, invoices, letters etc relating to dentists, doctors, health care workers, hospitals, dental clinics, health care businesses etc. Also ask for any dental items such as:

- old dentures;
- models (or casts);
- teeth;
- toothbrushes (DNA source);
- mouthguards (including bleaching trays) etc.

It is also important to remember to ask for any suitable photographs, for example:

- person smiling and/or showing their teeth;
- person standing;
- person from the side and from the front;
- any other pictures that may seem relevant and are recent.

The correct documentation of photographs is vital and the following should be recorded on the back of a duplicate of each photo:

- name of missing person;
- last known address;
- when the photograph was taken;
- how old the person was when they went missing;
- name and contact details of photograph provider;
- if there is more than one person on the photograph, make it clear to whom the details refer.

From professional medical and dental sources it is important to ask for:

- dental charts and *ALL* dental records;
- all correspondence;
- X-rays;
- models (casts);

- specialist records;
- medical and dental clinical photographs etc.

In reviewing the AM data, an assessment is made of:

- how accurate and relevant the information is to the current date;
- whether the information was guessed or was known;
- how reliable the interviewees are.

There is one overriding consideration here: *too much* AM data is better than *too little*, provided it is accurate and reliable.

In practice, and unless the disaster is small in scale, all ante-mortem dental data is assessed, interpreted and collated by a team of odontologists working as the "home team" (which, paradoxically, may not be at home!). This is a vital part of the process, as dental records are sometimes out of sequence, written in another language or system and use different abbreviations and notation. These are then collated and, if necessary, a final composite AM record constructed. Occasionally it is necessary for an odontologist to contact the missing person's dentist personally to clarify matters. Once collated and assembled, the records are copied and retained at the home base. The originals and collated records are forwarded to the field site, mortuary or information centre both in electronic and in hard format. There are now computer systems, eg Plassdata, which aid the comparison of ante-mortem and post-mortem dental data and the home team may also be responsible for entering this data directly onto the computerised system.

18.4.2 Collection of post-mortem data and dental post-mortem procedures

In the mortuary the bodies and body parts will be examined by the odontological team and as much information as possible recorded, even if at the time it does not always appear to be significant. One must bear in mind that sometimes the body will only be able to be examined once and a second chance to gain information will not be forthcoming!

In the mortuary there is usually a "flow" system where the body is examined in turn by the many disciplines involved.

In the dental section the dentists usually work in teams of two – one "clean" (doing the recording and assisting) and one "dirty" (undertaking the actual examination). The dental PM procedure can take the following format, although variation to this routine may occur, depending upon the situation:

1. Checking all URNs, ensuring that there are no discrepancies.
2. Photography of facial structures, frontal and profile (with URN, time and date clearly visible).
3. Exposure of mandible (disarticulate only if necessary).

4. Cleaning teeth (using a toothbrush and water and/or alcohol) and replace any loose teeth.

5. Photography of teeth (with URN, time and date clearly visible).

6. Photography of any dentures, tongue piercing, braces and any other relevant material that may be either intra-oral or peri-oral.

7. X-rays should be taken of all teeth, in accordance with the dental protocol.

8. Undertaking of a detailed full mouth examination and charting (both dentists will sign the chart).

9. An age assessment may be made at this stage, based on the clinical appearance of the tooth and periodontal regions.

10. The extraction of a tooth (usually a large molar) for DNA analysis.

11. The correct handling, labelling and packing of any specimens should be ensured. These should be handled as little as possible, especially in the region of the root tip. The tooth should be extracted using surgically clean instruments and placed it into a sterile container. The container should be labelled with the URN, place, date and time of removal and signed by the operator.

12. At the completion of the examination, the replacement of any tissue, dentures, bridges etc and restoration to a dignified appearance should be undertaken.

If a computer matching program is to be used, all the post-mortem details are now entered onto the system. This includes the information pertaining to charting, photographs, noted anomalies, X-rays, age evaluation etc.

18.4.3 Reconciliation

This is the process of comparison of dental ante-mortem and dental post-mortem information. The AM form is written conventionally on a yellow background while the PM form is on a pink background.[14]

In a small-scale disaster, the reconciliation can often be done using just paper. However, in a major disaster with a large number of casualties, computer programs are of great value and save much time. In Thailand, following the Asian tsunami, where there were approximately 4,000 bodies awaiting identification, the Plassdata program[15] was used and, despite some initial problems, proved exceptionally valuable. But, as with any computer program, its success depends upon the quantity and particularly the quality of the input information. Suggested matches between AM and PM information are identified by the program and must then be examined in detail by the odontologists and any discrepancies must be explained before a tentative match can be accepted.

The dental comparison can be based on actual conservations (fillings, crowns, bridges etc), radiographic information concerning the shape and form of the tooth

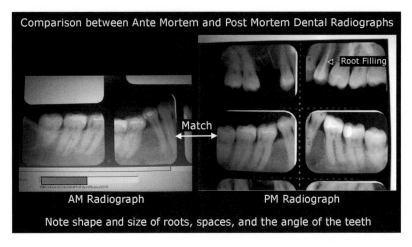

Figure 18.8 Radiographic comparison between ante-mortem and post-mortem images

and its roots, and even the comparison of AM and PM photographs of the teeth. Radiographs (see Figure 18.8) can also reveal crowns, root fillings, apicectomies (root surgery), root abscesses and cysts etc which would not have been seen in the visual mouth examination. Superimposition photography techniques have also been used very successfully to confirm comparisons. Radiographs (X-rays) are essential for finding "hidden dentistry".

An identification is then categorised in one of five ways:

1. established (beyond doubt);
2. probable (very likely);
3. possible (no discrepancies but insufficient unique information to confirm identity beyond doubt);
4. excluded (the information precludes a match);
5. insufficient information comfortably to establish any of the above conclusions.

Although on first sight all except "established" (Group 1) could be perceived as being of limited value, this is in fact not the case. "Probable" and "possible" matches are useful in that they can be used to focus other disciplines (fingerprints and DNA) to prioritise checks. "Excluded" means that the particular match can be removed from the system and not used again. With an "established" identification the AM and PM hard copies are checked and compared again and, if all is in order, the files are sent to the identification commission for further processing. The comparison details are recorded in such a way that each tooth can be compared, the result detailed and discrepancies explained.

18.4.4   Presentation and the identification commission

One of the prime functions of the identification commission is to review all the evidence available and decide whether the identification is established. The constitution of this official body depends on the location and jurisdiction of the legal authority. In England and Wales the Coroner has complete control and decides who is to be present. It is usually recommended that the team leader from each discipline be present, allowing any discrepancies to be discussed, explained and further explored. This means that the senior fingerprint expert, senior DNA expert, senior odontologist, a senior investigating police officer (to present the physical evidence) and the pathologist should be present. However, this is at the discretion of the Coroner.

In some countries and situations the identification commission meets and reaches a conclusion and then one representative (depending upon the primary identification method) will present the evidence to the Coroner in a court of law. This was the procedure adopted in Sri Lanka for the tsunami victims.

Before a body can be released to relatives and if necessary repatriated, the Coroner must be satisfied regarding the identification and ensure that all the necessary paperwork is in order. Repatriation can be complicated and usually involves the use of specially sealed coffins and sealed body bags, numerous tags and export and import licences. In an ideal world it is better to make all the identifications before any bodies are released – however, in practice, especially in large disasters, this rarely happens due to the many conflicting pressures.

18.4.5   Summary

Forensic odontology is a valuable tool in the identification of unknown bodies. It is important that experienced and forensically qualified dentists are used for this work. They usually work in pairs and are quite familiar with AM, PM, reconciliation and mortuary procedures, health and safety considerations and working protocols and are prepared to write legal reports for later use in any court proceedings.

All members of the DVI team must be prepared to work together and be familiar with the basic processes involved in the work of each member of the team and their particular discipline. In this way we attain our final goal of returning the deceased to their relatives and loved ones with dignity and respect, and secure in the knowledge that the correct identification has been achieved.

18.5   DENTAL CHARTING

There are well over 100 different methods of tooth charting and although attempts have been made for many years to come to an international universal system, this has not been successful. Listed below are some of the more common systems used and an example in each method of how the upper left first premolar tooth is written. (To avoid confusion, only adult teeth have been noted.)

18.5.1 Palmer's/Szigmondy

8 7 6 5 4 3 2 1 / 1 2 3 4 5 6 7 8   /4
8 7 6 5 4 3 2 1 / 1 2 3 4 5 6 7 8

18.5.2 FDI

18 17 16 15 14 13 12 11 / 21 22 23 24 25 26 27 28   24
48 47 46 45 44 43 42 41 / 31 32 33 34 35 36 37 38

18.5.3 Haderup

8+ 7+ 6+ 5+ 4+ 3+2+ 1+/ +1 +2 +3 +4 +5 +6 +7 +8   +4
8– 7– 6– 5– 4– 3– 2– 1–/ –1 –2 –3 –4 –5 –6 –7 –8

18.5.4 Some European

D8 D7 D6 D5 D4 D3 D2 D1/ G1 G2 G3 G4 G5 G6 G7 G8   G4
d8 d7 d6 d5 d4 d3 d2 d1/ g1 g2 g3 g4 g5 g6 g7 g8

18.5.5 In papers

UR8 UR7 UR6 UR5 UR4 UR3 UR2   UR1 / UL1 UL2 UL3   etc UL4
LR8 LR7 LR6 LR5 LR4 LR3 LR2   LR1 / LL1 LL2 LL3 etc

18.5.6 Universal

1 2 3 4 5 6 7 8 / 9 10 11 12 13 14 15 16   12
32 31 30 29 28 27 26 25 / 24 23 22 21 20 19 18 17

18.5.7 Holland

sdM3 sdM2 sdM1 sdP2 sdP1 sdC sdI2 sdI1 / sgI1 sgI2 sgC   etc sgP1
diM3 diM2 diM1 diP2 diP1 diC diI2 diI1 / giI1 giI2 giC   etc

18.5.8 Other USA

16 15 14 13 12 11 10 9 / 8 7 6 5 4 3 2 1   5
32 31 30 29 28 27 26 25 / 24 23 22 21 20 19 18 17

18.6 DENTAL PROTOCOLS

18.6.1 Ante-mortem protocol

1. Check all identifying details on records.
2. If records suggest that other records may be available, contact relevant dentist.
3. Copies of all records and radiographs (hard copy or digital).
4. Compile composite dental charting from information from all records available.
5. Fill in all available details onto F1 and F2 Interpol forms.[14]
6. Quality assure with another forensic dentist and both sign F1, F2 and copies of radiographs.
7. Copies will stay in exhibits office and originals will be available for reconciliation process.
8. Ensure that part A0 is also completed with duration of treatment and relevant dates.

18.6.2 Post-mortem dental protcol in temporary mortuary

The dignity of the deceased must be respected at all times. Assume that you have only one attempt to get all the information that may be helpful for a dental identification. See also section 18.4.2.

18.6.3 Equipment

- Mirror.
- Probe.
- Light source ± magnifying lens.
- Alcohol in squeezable bottle.
- Toothbrush.
- Disclosing fluid/etching fluid.
- Canisters of compressed air to clean teeth.
- Mouth prop.
- Camera with macro lens and ring flash.
- Portable dental X-ray machine.
- Dental X-ray films.
- Dental X-ray processing facility if not digital.
- Lead aprons.
- X-ray mounts.
- Processing fluids.

- Extraction forceps (lower premolar extraction forceps should be suitable for all teeth if have nothing else).
- Scalpel and spare blades.
- Periostial elevators.
- Ageing charts.
- Universal containers.
- Pens and paper.
- PM forms.
- Paint pot for sterilising equipment.
- Sterilising tablets.
- Visors.
- Gloves.
- Masks.
- Appropriate footwear, eg Wellington boots.
- Appropriate protective clothing for mortuary, eg mortuary scrubs, white suits with hoods.
- Risk assessment should be in place for health and safety issues.

18.6.4 Examination process

- Two dental examiners – one "clean", one "dirty" – working together.

"Dirty" dentist:

- Check unique PM identifying numbers on body bag and body.
- Photograph facial structures (AP and both laterals), retract lips for comparison with "smiling" photographs.
- Examine facial skeleton.
- Facial flap to expose mandible, maxilla and associated teeth: never make direct cuts into facial soft tissues.
- Disarticulate mandible (only if necessary) but always keep with body.
- Clean teeth with tooth brush and alcohol to remove debris.
- If avulsed teeth with body, replace in correct anatomical position. Make a note of this.
- Photograph jaws and teeth: AP in and out of occlusion, both laterals in and out of occlusion, mandibular and maxiliary occlusals. Photograph dentures/ orthodontic appliances if present, in and out of the mouth. Remember to include unique PM number, time and date.
- X-ray jaws and teeth of *all* victims: full mouth periapical including roots of developing teeth, right and left bitewings, occlusals if clinical or radiographic

evidence of, eg, impacted canines or premolars or pathology. Minimum ×2 bitewings (right and left) and ×10 periapicals.

- Check radiographs prior to further examination.
- Full dental examination of teeth, noting teeth present, missing, restorations occlusion, orthodontic appliances, arch shape, anomalies of tooth position, congenital abnormalities, trauma and pathology.
- If orthodontic appliance present, take silicon dental impressions. These will need to be sterilised and cast off site. Photographs may also be taken off site with unique identifying number, time and date and added to PM files.
- Extract tooth for DNA. Preferably sound fully developed (closed apices) first molar tooth; if this is unavailable, then extract another molar or premolar tooth. *Avoid* extracting anterior teeth and using teeth avulsed post-mortem found in body bag with body.

"Clean" dentist

- Process radiographs.
- Mount radiographs in correct orientation. Label with unique identifying number, time and date. Both dentists should sign as being correct.
- Compile composite dental chart using information from clinical examination and radiographs in consultation with "dirty" dentist.
- Place tooth extracted for DNA into appropriate container, secure container and label with unique PM identifying number date, time and place of examination.
- Ensure that *all* relevant dental information is entered onto PM charts, particularly Fl and F2 sheets.
- The odontogram should be filled with an accurate representation of the position, size and shape of any restorations present.
- Check radiographs.

18.6.5 Quality assurance

- Change dentists between one case and another (ie "dirty" becomes "clean" and "clean" becomes "dirty") and repeat dental examination and check composite charting and information on Fl and F2 are correct.
- Make sure disarticulated mandible is retained *in situ* if possible when body bag closed at end of examination. If necessary, label mandible with unique PM identifying number.
- Do age estimation from clinical and radiographic examination.
- Both dentists should sign the mounted radiographs with time and dates.
- Both dentists should sign tooth exhibit for DNA analysis and Fl and F2 as being correct.

- Make sure Fl and F2 forms are reunited with rest of PM forms relating to body with same unique PM identifying number, if for some reason they have become separated. Both dentists should check that *all* details are correct on PM forms, dental photographs, dental radiographs and dental DNA sample.

As a sign of respect, make the body as presentable as possible, even if it will not be viewed.

REFERENCES

1 C Duvall, "Notre Dame-De-Consolation – The Charity Sale Bazaar – Commemoration Site" [online]. Available at: http://www.parissweethome.com/parisrentals/art_uk.php?id=38. [Accessed: 01.11.07.]

2 "Pyjama Girl", *Wikipedia* [online]. Available at: http://en.wikipedia.org/wiki/Pyjama_Girl. [Accessed: 01.11.07.]

3 University of Glasgow. Forensic Medicine Archives Project [online.] Available at: http://www.fmap.archives.gla.ac.uk/Case%20Files/Ruxton/Case_File9.htm. [Accessed: 01.11.07.]

4 J Villanueva, "John Haig – Acid Bath Murderer" (2005) [online]. Available at: http://foros.cotija.com/archive/index.php?t-18361.html. [Accessed: 01.11.07.]

5 R Bell, "The Ted Bundy Story" [online]. Available at: http://www.trutv.com/library/crime/serial_killers/notorious/bundy/index 1.html. [Accessed: 01.11.07.]

6 M Bardsley, "Fred and Rose West" [online]. Available at: http://www.bbc.co.uk/crime/caseclosed/fredwest1.shtml. [Accessed: 01.11.07.]

7 D Page, "Forensic Disaster Response: The Crash of Comair 5191" *Forensic Magazine* (Feb/March 2007) [online]. Available at: http://forensic.texterity.com/forensic/20070203/?pg=10. [Accessed 01.11.07.]

8 Dumfries and Galloway Police, "Lockerbie Air Disaster" [online]. Available at: http://www.dumfriesandgalloway.police.uk/foi/class_cat/pub_int/lbie_kvz.htm. [Accessed 09.06.08.]

9 O W Morgan, P Sribanditmongkol, C Perera, Y Sulasmi, D Van Alphen and E Sondorp, "Mass Fatality Management following the South Asian Tsunami Disaster: Case Studies in Thailand, Indonesia, and Sri Lanka" (2006) 3(6) *PLoS Medicine* 95.

10 J Bennetto, "Terror in London: Officer identifying victims of Asian tsunami", *The Independent* [online]. Available at: http://findarticles.com/p/articles/mi_qn4158/is_20050712/ai_n14719308. [Accessed: 14.06.08.]

11 M Theodoulou, "Britons among Bahrain boat disaster dead", *Times Online (2006)* [online]. Available at: http://www.timesonline.co.uk/tol/news/world/article700355.ece. [Accessed: 09.06.08.]

12 BBC News, *On this Day*, "Egyptian militants kill tourists at Luxor" [online]. Available at: http://www.timesonline.co.uk/tol/news/world/article700355.ece. [Accessed: 09.06.08.]

13 Oral Health Centre, "Dental crowns" [online]. Available at: http://www.webmd.com/oral-health/dental-crowns. [Accessed: 01.11.07.]

14 Interpol DVI forms [online]. Available at: http://www.interpol.int/Public/DisasterVictim/Forms/Default.asp. [Accessed: 15.05.08.]

15 Plassdata DVI System International [online]. Available at: http://www.dvisystem.com. [Accessed: 14.11.07.]

CHAPTER 19

Forensic Anthropology

19.1 WHAT IS FORENSIC ANTHROPOLOGY?

Forensic anthropology involves the application of scientific techniques to aid in the identification of the human, or what remains of the human, for medico–legal purposes. This holds true whether the material presented for analysis is intact, fragmented, skeletonised or burned. The primary role[1] of the forensic anthropologist (FA), therefore, is to analyse indicators of biological and personal identity to assist in the process of assigning a name to the deceased individual or to provide information pertaining to the manner of their death.

The traditional role of the FA is to create an identity profile for the deceased. In the absence of recognisable soft tissue they may have to rely solely on hard tissue skeletal and dental indicators. In all cases the FA will attempt to establish the following four major biological identity parameters for the deceased:

- sex (and/or gender);[2]
- age at death;
- height (stature);
- ancestral origin (race).

Additional skills will assist with:

- determination of the minimum number of individuals present (MNI);
- separation of human from non-human remains;
- interpretation of pathologies, trauma and surgical intervention;
- identification of fragmented, disrupted and burned remains and their reconstruction;
- comparison of ante-mortem and post-mortem data (such as radiographs);
- identification of body modifications (tattoos, piercings etc);
- facial identification, superimposition and reconstruction.

Anthropologists also have an increasing caseload in identification of the living and may be involved in issues pertaining to people trafficking, immigration and image identification, perhaps through vein pattern recognition analysis, facial recognition from CCTV footage or by establishing the current age of the individual by non-invasive techniques.

19.2   WHO IS THE FORENSIC ANTHROPOLOGIST?

In the UK, the forensic anthropologist is generally an academic trained to a high level in the disciplines of human anatomy[3], osteology[4] and/or human identification. Few are employed full time within their role as a forensic anthropologist and most are employed by higher educational institutions (HEIs) as lecturers in related disciplines.

While the discipline of forensic anthropology has a long and traditional association with departments of anatomy, in the UK it has also developed within departments of archaeological sciences. Therefore the academic leading the forensic anthropology team may arise from either a medical or an archaeological background but they will all be registered practitioners with the Council for the Registration of Forensic Practitioners (CRFP).[5] Forensic anthropology has been a recognised discipline within this register since 2001 and currently has eight registered practitioners in this discipline.

All lead forensic anthropologists are also team members for the Centre for International Forensic Assistance (CIFA),[6] having evidenced their investment in continued professional development through registration with the CRFP, and most are members of their adopted professional association – the British Association for Human Identification (BAHID).[7]

Humanitarian and mass disaster scenarios such as Kosovo, Iraq, World Trade Center, the London bombings, the Bali bombings, the Indian tsunami etc saw an increase in the call for the skills provided by this profession. This increased involvement in mass disaster scenarios, criminal casework and humanitarian assistance has also resulted in a demand for academic courses to teach this subject.

19.3   WHERE DOES THE FORENSIC ANTHROPOLOGIST BELONG IN THE DVI SCENARIO?

The wide remit of this discipline requires that its expertise be made available in three distinct areas:

- the crime scene;
- triage;
- with the other identification sciences in the mortuary facility.

19.4   FORENSIC ANTHROPOLOGY AND THE CRIME SCENE/DISASTER SITE

At the crime scene the forensic anthropologist can assist in the accurate preliminary identification of a number of issues including:

* evidence of commingling;
* identification of body parts;
* identification of fragments;
* advice on how best to retrieve body parts.

In many disaster situations there may be no role for the forensic anthropologist at the disaster site but in some instances, particularly overseas, their insight may prove invaluable, especially where remains must be exhumed for identification purposes. Under these circumstances, anthropologists who are also experienced in archaeological techniques will prove to be of considerable assistance.

19.5   FORENSIC ANTHROPOLOGY AND TRIAGE

The identity of human remains is not always immediately apparent, particularly when there is extensive rubble to be cleared from a site following an incident. Having the experienced eyes of a forensic anthropologist to assist will ensure that fewer fragments are overlooked and less non-human material is included. It should be borne in mind that it is not always immediately obvious even to the trained eye what is human and what is not. The recovery process following the World Trade Center incident relied heavily on anthropologists in the triage situation.[8] Separating fragments of bone and body from the detritus of building and aeroplane rubble at the Fresh Kills site yielded a significant volume of additional human remains. Disasters that involve restaurant facilities or impact on non-human fauna will necessitate separation of human from non-human remains (Figure 19.1). Restaurants, for example, contain the remains and bones of pigs, chickens, cow, sheep, fish, deer and many other potentially more exotic animal species. Similarly, the incident that occurs in a subway tunnel may result in the presence of non-human remains including those of pets travelling on the train, the remnants of animal products that passengers may have been carrying as grocery shopping, mice, rats and many other environment-specific species. It is therefore vital that the FA is competent not only in the identification of human remains but also in those of all vertebrate species.

Triage can also involve the need to identify what is recent and what is not. Following Hurricane Katrina, the flood waters eroded the ground in local cemeteries[9] so that the remains of the long deceased were recovered along with those who perished in the incident. The degree and extent of decomposition of the remains enabled the examining forensic anthropologists readily to separate the two groups. The way in which a body decomposes[10] under different circumstances

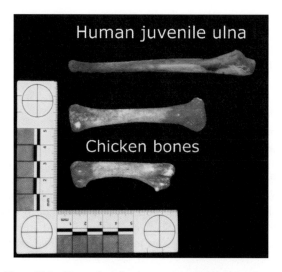

Figure 19.1   Human juvenile ulna compared with chicken bones

is known as taphonomy and it can provide important information in relation to the identification of the remains.

19.6   FORENSIC ANTHROPOLOGY AND THE MORTUARY

The most common and arguably most valuable location for this discipline is within the mortuary environment. In this setting, the FA undertakes a number of roles:

1. to assist in the identification of body parts and fragments;
2. to assist in the accumulation of evidence for identification purposes;
3. to assist the other identification disciplines;
4. to reconstruct areas of the body following fragmentation.

19.7   EQUIPMENT

The equipment that a forensic anthropologist will require may look relatively sparse and unimpressive. The discipline is not highly technical and relies more on the experience of the practitioner and reference to published research.

Access to radiographs is generally essential although if the remains are completely skeletonised then this may not be so vital. However, in the presence of soft tissue then radiography (whether fluoroscopy, flat plate or CT) will allow evaluation of the skeletal components of the individual without recourse to maceration (see below). Radiographs are particularly useful for the diagnosis of fracture, identification of surgical procedures or evaluation of the age of the individual.

Maceration[11] is the removal of soft tissue from the underlying bones and is usually achieved by prolonged immersion of the body part in hot water, microwaving, steam removal or the introduction of biological agents that dissolve the soft tissue. Each approach is time consuming, noxious and unpleasant and should be avoided if at all possible. Commercial macerators can be purchased but if this process is likely to be required in the mortuary then it is usually to view a small and specific part of the body and the use of a microwave may suffice although steam cleaners have been found to be highly effective depending upon the degree of decomposition of the remains. The use of Dermestid beetle colonies[12] is recommended for delicate specimens but this is very time consuming.

Calipers and an osteometric board are the principal measuring devices employed by the FA. Calipers come in all shapes and sizes to best serve the function and fit the specimen that needs to be measured. There are many kinds of calipers – needle point, craniometric and digital – but in the mortuary situation it is likely that simple flat plate, non-metallic calipers will suffice. These could be used to measure ends of bones to determine sex or measure the lengths of juvenile long bones to determine age among a variety of other requirements.

The osteometric board is designed to measure the lengths of long bones primarily to establish the height of the deceased. For archaeological purposes these may be made from wood but for DVI and mortuary practice they should be constructed from washable materials.

Recourse to reference charts will be a common occurrence for the forensic anthropologist. Most will carry their own personal and preferred reference material but a basic and regularly updated folder of ready reference material is included with the UK DVI equipment pod. These charts will relay information on:

- measurements of bone particular to males and females to allow determination of sex;
- closure time for growth plates to assist in the determination of the age of death;
- mathematical regression formulae to allow evaluation of stature from the lengths of long bones;
- indicators of ancestry from the skeleton.

Charts are also commercially available and so these may be pinned up on the walls of the mortuary for easier reference.

Included in the UK DVI equipment pod is a set of plastic replica hand and foot bones that are strung into their anatomical position. These are vital for rapid identification and sideing of these difficult skeletal elements. For example, it can be quite difficult to separate right and left carpal bones in the wrist and to separate lateral from intermediate cuneiforms in the foot.

19.8 HUMAN VERSUS NON-HUMAN MATERIAL

Whether the FA is located at the scene, in triage or within the mortuary the ability to identify human from non-human material is an important primary step in the analysis and documentation of any remains.

Humans share a common form with many animals and the science of taxonomy relies on classification according to certain common traits.[13] For example, man lies within the *subphylum* Vertebrata[14] which includes all faunal forms that have a central segmented axis (ie a vertebral column or spine). This includes fish, reptiles and all mammals. Man also resides within the *class* Mammalia which is characterised by fauna that have hair/fur, give birth to live young, suckle them and are warm blooded. This includes cats, rabbits, elephants and all primates.[15] Man also resides within the *order* of Primates which is characterised by fauna that have forward-facing stereoscopic eyes, flat nail beds and opposable thumbs. Animals that are closest to the human in terms of this taxonomic pedigree are more difficult to separate from human remains. For example, primate remains are closer to those of man than are the remains of dogs but they in turn compare more favourably with the human than do the bones of the average cod!

The location of the incident (UK, overseas, rural, urban etc) will dictate which faunal species are likely to be present and therefore the FA has an element of forewarning for what might be expected. There are several known specimens that can cause confusion: for example, the tail bones of a horse are very similar to human finger bones; the ribs of a pig are very similar to human ribs; and the bones within the flipper of a seal can be confused with the human hand (Figure

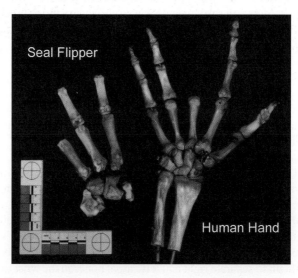

Figure 19.2   The bones of a seal flipper can easily be confused with those of the human hand

19.2). The unexpected does always have to be anticipated, though, as non-native species can be introduced by man into an unnatural habitat.[16]

Confirmation of animal remains will largely reside in identification of a particular series of body characteristics. For example, the presence of feathers or fur will be a clear indication, as will the presence of claws as opposed to flat nailbeds. Equally, the teeth and the shape and size of the bones (Figure 19.3) will give a clear indication of human versus non-human origin, thereby avoiding unnecessary inclusion of non-human material.

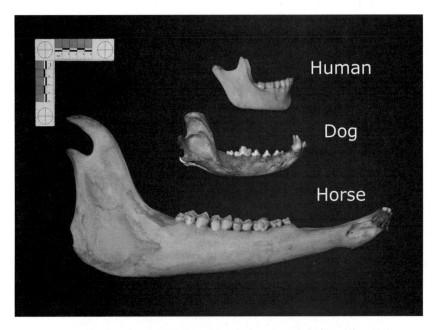

Figure 19.3   Comparison of human, canine and equine mandibles and teeth

19.9   FRAGMENTED BODY PARTS

When faced with traumatic intervention, the human body can fragment, and reconstruction of the parts can prove quite a challenge. Incidents of explosion generally result in corporeal fragmentation, and a basic understanding of the anatomical construction of the human body facilitates identification of body parts.

The human is a complex organism that is constructed from a series of interconnecting body systems that serve particular functions. There are at least 10 recognised systems within the body:[17]

1. **integumentary**: skin, hair and nails;
2. **cardiovascular**: heart and blood vessels (veins and arteries);
3. **respiratory**: larynx, trachea, lungs and other ancillary structures;
4. **neurological**: brain, spinal cord and nerves;
5. **digestive**: oesophagus, stomach, intestine and associated organs, eg liver, gall bladder and pancreas;
6. **urinary**: kidneys, ureters, bladder and urethra;
7. **genital**: ovaries, uterus, vagina, testes, penis and associated glands and ducts;
8. **lymphoid**: spleen, tonsil etc;
9. **endocrine**: thyroid, salivary glands, pancreas, suprarenal glands etc;
10. **musculoskeletal**: all muscles and bones.

Each of these systems comprises organs and these have a specific shape or form and are composed of a specific type of tissue which reflects its function. Therefore a liver can never be confused with a stomach. This symbiosis between form and function permits identification of fragmented body parts. However, the body is not organised according to systems but rather via the topographical alignment that represents the integration of each of these systems.

A cross-section through the thorax (chest) will show representative structures from the respiratory, cardiovascular, musculoskeletal, integumentary, neurological and digestive systems. But this is the only place in the body where such a combination will occur and therefore the pattern and location of each of these structures allows identification of a body region. For this reason, an anatomically trained forensic anthropologist is particularly useful when disrupted human remains are to be examined.

A cross-section of a limb will show the skin and hairs of the integumentary system (hair form will assist in determining whether this is axillary hair, pubic hair or limb hair), muscles, bone, fat, blood vessels and nerves. The form of the bone will indicate which part of a limb is represented (single bone in the upper arm and thigh but two bones side by side in the forearm and lower leg). The muscles groups that are present will inform as to whether this is the upper part of that limb section or the lower. The position of the nerves and blood vessels as well as the muscle groupings will assist in the determination of whether it is from the right- or the left-hand side of the body.

19.10   IDENTIFICATION OF SKELETAL ELEMENTS

The hard tissues of the human body are of particular value in disaster victim identification. They tend to survive most insults, including: trauma, decomposition and burning. The hard tissues are defined as the bones and the teeth of the body. The teeth are described elsewhere in this text via the specialty of forensic odontology and therefore this chapter will consider only identification from the skeleton.

The adult human skeleton comprises approximately 206 bones, all of which the FA must be able to identify not only when intact but also when fragmented. Some of these bones are of greater value in establishing identity than others and some will survive insult more readily than others. But as the FA does not have any control either over which parts of the body will be presented, or what condition they will be in, they must be able to extract as much information as possible from any skeletal element that is presented for analysis.

In its most simple form, the human skeleton is divided into two quite distinct parts: the axial and the appendicular skeleton (Figure 19.4).

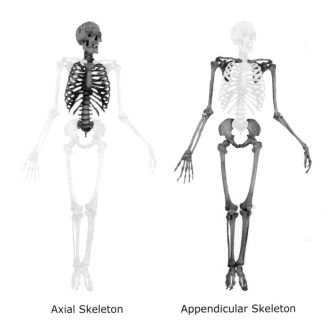

Axial Skeleton   Appendicular Skeleton

Figure 19.4   The adult skeleton divided into axial and appendicular portions

The axial skeleton comprises those structures that are present in the midline of the body. This includes the skull (27 bones), the vertebral column (29 bones) and the bones of the thorax (27 bones).

The appendicular skeleton comprises paired right and left appendages (upper and lower limbs) and their attachments to the axial skeleton (pectoral and pelvic girdles respectively). These represent a total of around 134 bones – 68 in the pectoral girdle and upper limb and 66 in the pelvic girdle and lower limb.

Where any two bones meet there is an articulation or a joint. So, for example, between the lower part of the thigh and the upper part of the lower leg there is the knee joint. The presence of joints allows bones to move and these joint areas are particularly useful for identification of skeletal elements. Therefore when a FA is attempting to identify a bone they will look at the overall shape (morphology) of the bone and the shape and size of its joint surfaces.

19.11   FRAGMENTED AND BURNED REMAINS

Once the morphology of the skeleton is understood, then the identification of fragmented or burned sections relies on the ability to visualise the bone in three dimensions, looking for patterns and recognisable landmarks that allow it to be matched to the parent bone in the same way that we fit together pieces in a jigsaw puzzle.

Realignment of bone fragments and subsequent reconstruction of the parent bone will facilitate identification of biological indicators and may even assist in the determination of the cause of death (Figure 19.5). Under extreme circumstances reconstruction of the parent bone may prove impossible but identification of fragments will still allow an evaluation of the minimum number of individuals (MNI) present when presented with commingled remains.

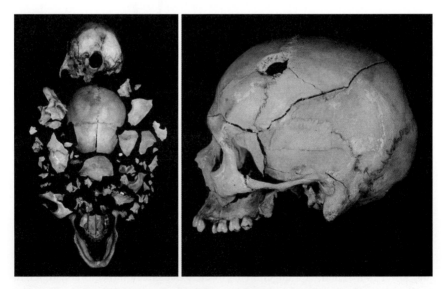

Figure 19.5   Fragmented skull reassembled to show cause of death
(Courtesy of M Warren)

19.12 IDENTITY

The human presents with at least two definable identities – biological and personal identity. Biological identity is based on features which allow an individual to be placed within a defined group within in any given society and are a broad brush approach to identification. Personal identity refers to those aspects of identification that allow a person to be recognised by others as a named individual.[18]

19.12.1 Biological identity

There are four principal factors that pertain to biological identity and all of these can be determined with some degree of accuracy from evaluation of remains:

- sex and gender;[2]
- age at death;
- stature;
- ancestry (race).

These four features typify a statement that might be released by the police to the public following an event where a suspect has been witnessed – "the suspect is a male, aged between 25 and 30 years, between 5 ft 6 ins and 5 ft 8 ins in height and of oriental race". These factors therefore achieve a broad vision of who the individual might be and the same principle applies to disaster victim identification approaches.

19.13 Sex and gender

Sex and gender[2] are of course strongly linked, but they are not one and the same thing. Sex refers to the genetic sex of the individual and the ways in which this manifests itself in the body. Gender refers to the sexual presentation under which the individual chooses to live and present themselves to society. In the majority of cases sex and gender equate but they will not always.[19] Individuals who choose to dress as the opposite sex (transvestites), choose to live as the opposite sex (transgender) or choose legally and surgically to change to the opposite sex (transsexuals) must be borne in mind. The presence of stereotypical clothing, breast implants, absence of a penis etc are not always indicative of genetic sex and may be a manifestation of gender choice. Under these circumstances, such modifications are in fact indicators of personal identity as well as biological identity. Regular doses of sex steroids will both change the external appearance of the individual and have an effect on skeletal structure.[19]

The presence of a uterus or ovaries is definitively indicative of sex but their absence is not, as these structures can be surgically removed. However, the presence of a penis may be indicative of sex but it may also be an indication of gender reassignment through surgical reconstruction. It is very tempting to assume that the external and therefore circumstantial indications of gender do indeed represent the biological and genetic sex of the individual but this is not always so. Sometimes individuals at one point or another during their lives will present as a gender that does not equate to their birth (genetic) sex. A very small proportion of individuals are of true indeterminate genetic sex through clinical conditions including Kleinfelter syndrome (XXY), Turner syndrome (XO) and other truly hermaphroditic conditions which are extremely rare. Therefore while sex is generally a dichotomous variable (ie male or female), this is not always as clearly delineated as it may first appear.[20]

In the majority of instances, circumstantial personal effects and the external and internal anatomy of the individual will be in accordance with their genetic sex but any disharmony will likely be realised following the internal post-mortem examination. Therefore sex determination from soft tissue evidence can preclude the requirement for this biological factor to be established by the FA. However, when remains are fragmented, burned or skeletonised then the sex of the individual may not be immediately obvious and the FA must turn to the hard tissue elements for evidence.

Sexual dimorphism refers to the differences that exist between the sexes and the FA will target those areas of the skeleton that exhibit the greatest degree of dimorphism as they will represent the areas where accuracy of sex prediction will be greatest. Differences between the sexes exist throughout the body tissues and systems and it is a well-recognised fact that, even from birth,[21] boys are heavier and taller than girls although the level of dimorphism[22] is not great and

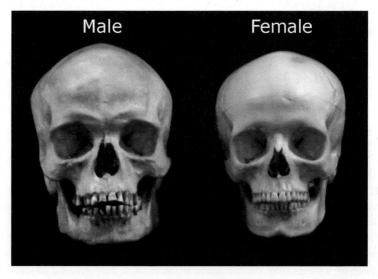

Figure 19.6   Sexual dimorphism in the skull

determination of sex from juvenile skeletal remains is therefore not reliable. This changes during puberty when there are significant secondary sexual changes that result in differences that become large enough to discriminate sex.

There are two principal ways in which sex will manifest itself in the post-pubertal skeleton: increased muscle mass and alteration to the pelvis in preparation for the development of a birth canal.

During puberty, the male starts to produce larger quantities of the male hormone testosterone. This stimulates male pattern secondary sexual development and also increases muscle mass. The larger and more powerful muscles show more pronounced sites of attachment to the bones and result in bones that are stronger and larger. Therefore for most measurements of any bone in the skeleton, the male is either proportionally or absolutely larger than the female. The supra-orbital region tends to be more rugged in males, often exhibiting marked brow ridges (Figure 19.6). The sites of muscle attachment and their effects on bone appearance are particularly obvious in the following regions of the skull (Figure 19.7):

- mastoid process;
- nuchal region;
- orbital region;
- mandible.

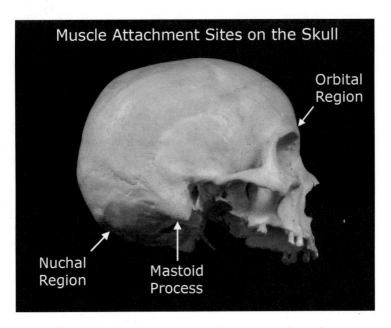

Figure 19.7   Some major muscle attachment sites on the cranium

The biggest changes to occur in the skeleton as a result of sexual maturity occur in the pelvis which alters dramatically in shape around the time of puberty in preparation for its role as a birth canal and is the most sexually dimorphic region of the adult human skeleton. In principle, the opening into the pelvis and the exit from the pelvis must become sufficiently large to be able to allow a fetal head to pass through. This requirement does not exist for the male and so only the female shows these biomechanical alterations, thereby setting up a functional difference between the sexes.

The areas of the pelvis (Figure 19.8) that show the most sexual dimorphism are:

• the greater sciatic notch;
• the sub-pubic angle;
• the shape of the pubic body;
• the shape of the sacrum.

There are other areas of the skeleton that display sexual dimorphism, including the way in which bone is laid down in the costal cartilages of the chest (the area between the ribs and the breast bone). With advancing age, the male costal

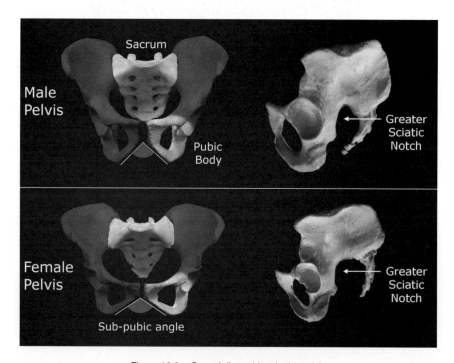

Figure 19.8   Sexual dimorphism in the pelvis

cartilages form fine trabecular bone (that looks a bit like honeycomb) while the female costal cartilages lay bone down in dense nodules (Figure 19.9). The bone is laid down in a different way because of the different circulating levels of sex hormones – oestrogens in the female and testosterone in the male.

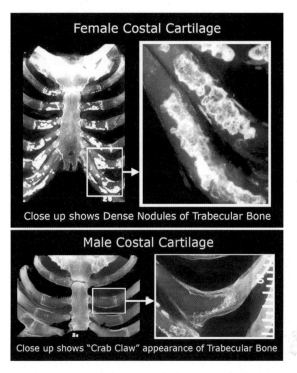

Figure 19.9   Sexually dimorphic costal cartilage ossification

19.14   PREDICTION OF AGE

The prediction of age at death from human remains can prove problematic, particularly in the adult years. The human passes through three basic stages, assuming that they live to a normal life expectancy. The first stage is developmental, as the individual grows and matures. The second stage is largely static, where there is a small amount of continued maturation but largely the skeleton remains in stable homeostasis. The third stage is degenerative, where the body starts to deteriorate and break down. In many instances circumstantial evidence of the age of the individual, for example clothing, hair colour, skin appearance, personal effects etc, may prove to be of limited value and can indeed be highly misleading.

Therefore, a more reliable approach to the evaluation of the age of the individual requires recourse to internal examination of the body.

19.14.1 Stage 1: Developmental

The regular pattern by which teeth form, erupt and are replaced is extremely valuable in age prediction and this is considered in the chapter on odontology. This section will only consider skeletal indicators of the age of the individual.

The events that occur in this phase of life are generally predictable and, as such, form a very reliable indicator of the age of the individual. For example, growth is so predictable that up until puberty you can buy clothes specific to the age of the child, such as a sleep-suit for a 3-month-old baby or a shirt for a 10-year-old child. Within this period, it is a general rule that the younger the individual, the more reliable and accurate will be the estimation of their age, because the growth-related factors are more predictable in the younger years. This reliability is lost as the individual ages. With fetal remains, age can be predicted to within weeks; in the young child to within 1–2 years; in the adolescent to within 2–4 years; in the young adult to within 5 years; and in the mature adult to within 5–10 years. The developmental phase therefore covers the life span from the fetus to the end of puberty and the attainment of adult status.[23]

Within the skeleton, the FA will examine which of the bones have formed, what they look like and their size. These three factors will help to establish the age of the individual.

Radiographs are particularly useful at identifying which bones have commenced formation in the young child. Figure 19.10 shows a radiograph of a child of approximately 2 years of age. Only two bones can be seen in the wrist – the capitate and the hamate – both of which begin to develop in the first year.

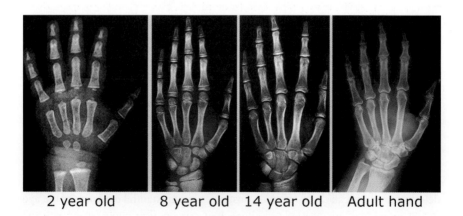

2 year old   8 year old   14 year old   Adult hand

Figure 19.10   Skeletal development in the hand

No other bones of the wrist can be seen at this stage as they are still cartilage and have not yet begun to develop bone. Equally, the bone that will form the wrist end of the radius has begun to develop but the bone that will form the wrist end of the ulna has not because this will not appear until about 5–7 years of age. By 8 years of age all the bones have developed but when this is compared with the adult X-ray it can be seen that there are clearly a larger number of "bones" present in the child which are not represented in the adult. The radiograph of the hand of the 14 year old is closer to the final appearance of the adult form (Figure 19.10). This is an indication of how the bones form and grow in the skeleton. For example, look at the bones as they develop in the index finger and at the proximal phalanx in particular. In the radiograph of the 2 year old it is clear that the central shaft of the bone is separate from a little sliver of bone down at its base – this is known as the epiphysis or secondary centre of ossification and is the site of bone growth. As the individual gets older (8y and then 14y) the shaft of the bones get both longer and wider and so does the base but eventually the two will fuse together to form the complete adult bone. Therefore in the proximal phalanx of the index finger we talk about appearance of the primary ossification centre (shaft) occurring between 9 and 11 fetal weeks of age and the appearance for the secondary centre (base) occurring between 1 and 2 years of age. Epiphyseal fusion (when the shaft fuses with the base) occurs between 14 and 15 years in females and 15 and 16 years of age in males.[23]

Thus for every bone of the human skeleton the FA must know the sequence of when each part of a bone forms and when it eventually fuses to attain its adult form. This provides a tremendous wealth of information pertaining to the developing individual and therefore gives reliable indicators of the age of the individual up to and including changes associated with adolescence and puberty.

With increasing age, all the long bones of the skeleton (particularly those in the limbs) increase in size. Using calipers for a very young child, but an osteometric board for the older child, the FA will be able to measure the length of the bones and be able to predict the age range of the child. Obviously this is very dependent upon the ancestry of the individual and their personal health status. Children who are small for their age, perhaps through issues of illness or malnourishment, will be predicted as younger if this is the only route adopted for age determination and similarly two children of a similar age are quite likely to display very different bone lengths if they originate perhaps from a Mongoloid ancestry compared with a Caucasian background. It is for this reason that the FA will look not only to indicators of size but also to indicators of maturity through recourse to their stage of dental and skeletal development as evidenced through radiography and gross inspection.[24]

19.14.2   Stage 2: Stasis

This stage of human development largely covers the period from the end of puberty until the early to middle 30s. Within this period there are still some areas of development of the skeleton but there are few signs of degeneration. This could be classified as the early adult years.

Specific areas of the skeleton can be of some value in the prediction of age in this stage although it must be borne in mind that a larger range of ages will be assigned utilising these approaches.

- **Skull sutures**: the joints between the flat bones of the skull vault can be used in age prediction. In the young individual these sutures are wide open and large fontanelles (soft spots) are present on the top and at the sides of the skull. While the fontanelles fuse very early in life (by the end of the second year) the other sutures remain relatively open and well defined until the third decade when they will start to close over and eventually obliterate. There is great variability in the timings of this event but it can be utilised with some caution to provide a very broad indication of age.[25] In many ways this is a last resort approach and not one upon which the FA would base any great reliance.
- **Joint surfaces**: these show some changes with age and those that are utilised in this static period of development are the pubic symphysis and the auricular surface of the sacro-iliac joint of the pelvis, the medial end of the clavicle and the sternal end of the rib.
- The articular surface of the **pubic symphysis** shows age-related changes that can prove to be of value in the prediction of age in the under-40s. In principle, the young surface displays deep ridges and furrows but with increasing age

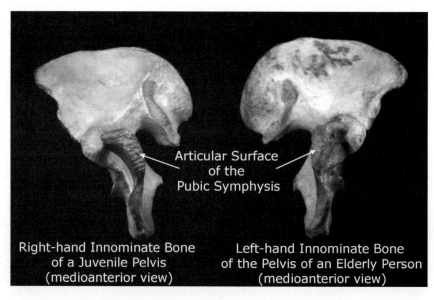

Figure 19.11   Age-related smoothing of the articular surface of the pubic symphysis

this surface smoothes over to produce a well-defined articular surface before it eventually commences breakdown (Figure 19.11).[26] The auricular surface of the sacro-iliac joint shows similar changes to those found in the pubic symphysis and tends to survive inhumation more readily.[26]

- The medial end of the **clavicle** is the last bone to show union of a growth centre. The epiphysis appears in the centre of the medial end of the bone between 16 and 20 years and fusion is often not complete until the late 20s.[23] Throughout the 1980s and 1990s, forensic anthropologists paid a lot of attention to changes in the sternal end of the rib surfaces and developed a series of standards to which a specimen could be compared. The changes adopt a different appearance in males and females and therefore necessitate an evaluation of sex before age can be attempted and there is an indication that ancestry should also be known before any reliance is placed on this approach.[26]

19.14.3 Stage 3: Degenerative

This stage is characterised by deterioration of the bone and joint structures. Diseases and afflictions of old age leave their markers on the skeleton and can therefore be utilised as proxy indicators of advancing age. However, many of these factors, for example evidence of arthritis, surgical joint replacement, tooth loss, presence of dentures and trabecular bone loss, may also be influenced by diet, lifestyle, exercise, medication, sex, weight, ancestry and many other factors. Therefore age evaluation in this stage of life can be complicated by a variety of influences of which the investigator may be unaware. Consequently, age evaluation in the post-40s carries a broad range of possible ages. It must be noted that as well as removing bone, advancing age can see bone being laid down in some areas of the skeleton, for example the xiphoid process, the costal cartilages, the walls of the trachea and the thyroid and cricoid cartilages of the larynx.[26]

19.15 EVALUATION OF RACE, ETHNICITY, ANCESTRY OR CULTURAL AFFILIATION

Through a genuine desire not to offend, in conjunction with an admixture of groups, the biological classification of race or ancestral origin no longer carries a precise definition. Many will feel uncomfortable with the use of the word "race" largely as it has connotations of subservience, abuse, domination and collective shame. However, the honest fact is that we do make day-to-day assessments of people's origins through the way that they look, whether it is pale skin, red hair or some other obvious trait that we associate with the four broad "races" of man.[27] Our classifications have largely been based on skin colour, hair colour, hair texture or facial characteristics (nose, mouth, eyes etc) but may now include DNA analysis. Many believe that the concept of "race" is outdated and unrealistic but unfortunately it is a major indicator of classification in the event of a mass fatality in most of our cosmopolitan cities.[28]

For example, the assessment of race or ancestry was pivotal in the processing of the deceased in Thailand following the Indian Ocean tsunami. Those who were considered to be "Western", ie not indigenous to the area, were separated from those who were considered to be local Thais, to ensure a more speedy identification process of foreign nationals. Inevitably, this led to conflict with many countries that did not hold that a visual assessment of racial origin was sufficient to be able to separate indigenous Thais from South Koreans, Japanese or of course those of ancestral oriental origin who were national citizens from other countries. The issue of race or ancestry is unquestionably fundamentally flawed in our mobile modern society but it is one that must be addressed. Many are also uncomfortable with the terms used for classifications of the four historical principal races "Negroid, Mongoloid, Australoid and Caucasoid" but all are both phenotypically and genotypically structured. Recent genetic studies have shown that only some 3–5 per cent of the variations seen in man are at the populational level and any truly specific genetic attributes are rare. However, when allele frequencies are clustered they do unquestionably form five wide groups that correspond loosely with global geography:

- Africa;
- Eurasia (Europe and west, central and south Asia);
- East Asia;
- Oceania;
- the Americas.

The FA must look for indicators of this genetic expression in the bones that are presented to them and may not have the benefit of additional information pertaining to skin colour, hair type, facial soft tissue features, etc.

Perhaps not surprisingly, the skull is the most informative of the skeletal regions for the assessment of race or ancestry but it should be borne in mind that not every variable is expressed in every skull and this is the most difficult of the biological indicators of identity for the FA to determine in the absence of soft tissue indicators.[27]

In the absence of cranial remains the FA may attempt a race/ethnicity evaluation on bones such as the femur (thigh) or look at the ratio of different limb bone lengths. However, neither of these is considered to have the discriminatory capacity of the skull.

19.16   STATURE OR HEIGHT

Our evaluation of the height of other individuals is largely gained by comparison with our own perceived height. If we believe ourselves to be approximately 6ft then we will compare others to that standard. However, if the difference is more than approximately 6 inches then we rarely achieve reliable accuracy. We also have a tendency to overstate our own stature as there is a social perception that it is more desirable to be tall and we exacerbate this by the wearing of artificially high footwear. In addition to this, our height fluctuates by over an inch throughout the course of a normal day and we lose height with advancing age. Further, the way in which we measure height can also lead to inaccuracies, usually as a result of errors attributable to the untrained person recording the height and the variation in the measuring equipment utilised.

Our height is therefore a variable characteristic that is open to error of interpretation and measurement. For this reason, it is usually extremes of height that are particularly useful for identification. If the individual under investigation is over 6 ft tall and we are looking for an individual of 5 ft 1 inch then they are unlikely to be the same individual. However, the closer the range then the less value this characteristic will have for the purposes of achieving identification.

Obviously, the most reliable estimation of stature is likely to arise from a direct measurement of the intact body, however, the equipment for measuring such a dimension tends to involve a significant amount of approximation and a metal tape measure!

Not surprisingly, fragmentation of the body complicates the evaluation of stature. Most parts of our body are largely in proportion and so it is appropriate, although not always reliable, for the FA to be able to "predict" the length of the body based on different parts that are represented. Obviously, the parts of the body that will give the greatest accuracy are those that take part in the overall length of the body, for example leg length or back length, but stature can even be estimated from foot length or hand length.

Stature can also be predicted from bone length and, as stated before, those bones that actively take part in the length of the body are more reliable indicators of height than those that do not, eg the bones of the leg (femur, tibia and fibula) are more indicative of height than the bones of the arm (humerus, radius or ulna). These measurements can be calculated into specific regression mathematical formulae that allow stature to be predicted with acceptable levels of reliability (eg *stature* (cm) $\pm$ 3.417 = [2.26] [*femur length*] + 66.379). It is important that both the sex and race of the individual be determined before stature is calculated as different tables are required for males and females and for each of the racial groups. Stature can also be predicted from fragmentary bones but the error rate for calculation is high.

19.17   PERSONAL IDENTIFICATION

Establishing the personal identity of the deceased can be assisted through markers left by certain lifestyles and life history events. Traits of personal identity have been discussed in other chapters, including those on DNA, fingerprints, odontology etc.

In a role to assist the pathologist, the FA may identify scars, birth marks, tattoos, piercings and other surface modifications. They may also assist in the identification of surgical intervention through prostheses (joint replacement hardware) and other foreign objects placed within the body, for example contraceptive devices, pacemakers etc. This is not a role that is specific to the FA but it is one where they can assist. In the absence of an odontologist, the FA may assume the role of charting and identifying teeth but in most mass disaster situations where an odontologist is present, the FA will provide a supportive role.

19.18   CAUSE OF DEATH

The FA does not provide any direct evidence of cause or manner of death. However, they can assist the pathologist in the reconstruction of remains that may elucidate some information pertaining to the trajectory of a projectile, eg pathway of a bullet or perhaps for the identification of the implement that caused the fragmentation (see Figure 19.5).

19.19   INDICATORS OF PREVIOUS TRAUMA/PATHOLOGY [29]

By recourse to the skeleton as a diary of previous events in the life history of the individual, the FA can provide information that might tally with evidence from medical records. Although healed fractures may leave no external indication of their presence, the bone does not tend to heal in such a perfect format that its presence can be concealed when looking at the human skeleton. Areas of callous formation, misalignment of broken ends and episodes of infection around the fracture site all leave indications of its occurrence. Common conditions such as arthritis or osteoporosis can be detected as well as the less common and therefore more valuable indicators such as Paget's disease or bone cancers. Any alteration to the bone through either trauma or disease can lead to a potential marker of identity.

19.20   FACIAL ANTHROPOLOGY

Facial analysis falls within the remit of the subject of forensic anthropology but requires an additional level of practitioner expertise for effective evaluation.

19.20.1   Environmental effects on facial appearance

Disaster victims may be exposed to a wide variety of environmental conditions. With disasters involving water, such as floods, storms or accidents involving aquatic vessels, the bodies may be totally or partially submerged or exposed to periods of drenching. Disasters involving fire, such as explosions, lightning strikes or chemical spillage, may lead to a range of burn, heat and smoke damage. Human remains may suffer from post-mortem trauma to the soft tissues, such as avulsions (tears), bruising, lacerations, puncture wounds, scrapes and distortion; or to the skeleton, such as fractures, fragmentation and compression injuries. There may be insect or animal activity, such as feeding, scattering of body parts, infiltration or burial.

Some environments may lead to preservation of the soft tissues, such as peat bogs (acidic tanning of the skin), deserts (mummification) or warm, moist wrappings (adipocere formation). In addition, the position of the body may lead to tissue distortion and discolouration.

There are a series of post-mortem stages relating to human bodies, usually noted as *algor mortis*, *rigor mortis*, *livor mortis* and decomposition, but there is a high variability to the timing of these stages, depending upon the climate and conditions of the body. Some climates may lead to rapid deterioration of the body, so that the individual is unrecognisable in a matter of days, whereas other climates will preserve a body for many centuries.

The post-mortem effects on facial appearance are as follows:

- When the heart activity and blood flow stop, the face will become pale (death pallor) and the loss of muscle tone and skin elasticity will create a flaccid appearance to the cheeks, mouth and neck.

- *Rigor mortis* is a recognisable sign of death, caused by a chemical change in the muscles, causing the limbs of the corpse to become stiff and impossible to move or manipulate. The onset of *rigor mortis* does not follow a constant or symmetrical order; however, it will typically develop in smaller muscles first – in the eyelids, face, lower jaw and neck.

- When circulation ceases with death, blood will tend to settle to low-lying areas of the body under the influence of gravity and will accumulate in vessels in those parts underneath the body. This shows as a purple or reddish-purple skin discolouration, known as lividity (*livor mortis*). Lividity may be observed on the ear lobes of a face that has been laid on its back, initially appearing as a patchy mottling of the skin and subsequently spreading to produce extensive discolouration. Sometimes the distended blood vessels within intense areas of lividity may rupture to produce a scatter of purple–black haemorrhages.

- Even before decomposition begins, the face may be unrecognisable. Skin colour may be unreliable due to pallor and lividity, eye colour may be obliterated as putrefaction of the eyeballs will be almost immediate, and hair pattern may be unreliable due to hair loss at the roots. The jaw of the cadaver becomes slack, giving an unusual facial expression, and the outer angle of the eye will appear up-turned due to the effects of gravity and *rigor mortis* of the ligaments of the eye.

- Decomposition or putrefaction is the final post-mortem stage, and is the gradual deterioration of the tissues. The first visible sign of decomposition is a green or greenish-red discolouration of the skin, where haemoglobin, from burst red blood cells, stains the surrounding tissues. The face may acquire a marble vein-like pattern. The skin surface becomes translucent and shiny and is a dusky reddish-green to purple–black colour.

- Fermentation within the body cavities will then occur, and gas production will bloat the body. The eyelids become swollen and tightly closed; the lips swollen and pouting; the cheeks puffed out' and the distended tongue protrudes between the lips. Hair may become loose at the roots, and may be easily pulled out. Decomposition will eventually lead to skeletonisation.

- Sometimes decomposition of a corpse does not lead to skeletonisation and the body fat remains as adipocere, a yellow/white, waxy material. Formation of adipocere is rare, but appears frequently at the cheeks.

- Desiccation of the soft tissues after death may occur in conditions of dry heat and air currents. In these cases the soft tissues shrivel onto the skeleton. This is known as natural mummification.

- Where a body is thrown from place to place or compressed, prominent features, such as the ears and nose, may be distorted. Even mild pressure, such as the weight of a body bag, may alter facial features.

All these post-mortem effects will affect the facial appearance of a cadaver, to the extent that the person may no longer be visually recognisable.

19.20.2 Facial recognition by relatives

The face of a dead body does not necessarily resemble the person in life. Even initial post-mortem changes can cause confusion and doubt in the mind of a relative when viewing the body. Without a recognisable hairstyle, facial expression or skin colour, the face may appear very different, and the family member may respond with uncertainty or misidentification.

Records from disaster victim investigations have shown many cases of incorrect recognition. The desire to identify a loved one may cause the relative to imagine facial details that are not visible. Alternatively, hope for the return of the missing person may preclude recognition where the face is not well preserved.

In some circumstances it may not be appropriate to exhibit the body in its existing condition. Trauma and decomposition of the face may be distressing to the relative and any emotional reaction to the state of the body may obscure visual evaluation and recognition.

19.20.3   Techniques to enhance recognition

Post-mortem depiction

A forensic artist may be able to alter an image of the face of the cadaver to eliminate trauma and discolouration, to reduce the effects of decomposition and to recreate the facial appearance of a victim.

This may be achieved by manual sketch or painting techniques or by employing Adobe Photoshop or other illustrative software to create a photograph-like image.

The artist will use knowledge of anatomy and the effects of decomposition to produce a realistic and reliable interpretation of facial appearance.

Multiple views of the face of the cadaver will be optimal material for the forensic artist even though a single frontal view is usually produced.

Facial reconstruction from the skull

Where the remains are skeletonised and unidentified, it may be possible to utilise facial reconstruction in an attempt to enhance recognition.

Facial reconstruction (otherwise known as facial approximation) is the process used to reproduce the facial appearance of an individual by relating the skeletal structure to the overlying soft tissue. Essentially, a facial reconstruction estimates the facial appearance of the individual in life.

Facial reconstruction has been used to provoke recognition in forensic identification investigations worldwide, and is a powerful forensic tool that significantly enhances the chances of identification of the deceased.

Two-dimensional facial reconstruction involves the production of a frontal image of the face from a frontal image of the skull. This can be created manually by an artist, as a sketch or painting, or by computer software as a facial composite.

Three-dimensional facial reconstruction involves the production of a facial model as a sculpture or a movie. This can be created manually with clay or digitally using computerised systems.

19.20.4   Facial identification from skeletal remains

Where the victim has a suspected identity, without available positive identification by DNA or dental analysis, craniofacial superimposition may be utilised.

In disasters affecting Third World or highly populated countries this may be one of the few techniques available for identification. DNA analysis is not useful in identification when whole families or large numbers of family members are victims, and dental records may not exist or be accessible for large sections of the community. Craniofacial superimposition can provide an alternative legally accepted method of identification.

Craniofacial superimposition involves the comparison of the skull with images of the individual in life. The skull is aligned to match the angle of view of the face of the individual and an image of the skull is taken using similar camera settings and position. The image of the skull and the image of the suspect can then be superimposed in an attempt to assess similarities and differences (Figure 19.12). The images can be scaled using teeth or external objects in the image of the suspect (such as jewellery or furniture).

In this way the proportions and feature positions can be compared between skull and face to evaluate the suspected identity. Characteristic features to the face and the skull, such as a hooked nose, cleft chin or dental anomaly, will improve the chances of positive identification.

Craniofacial superimposition has been utilised to identify the remains of Joseph Mengele and the victims of the Cromwell Street serial murders.

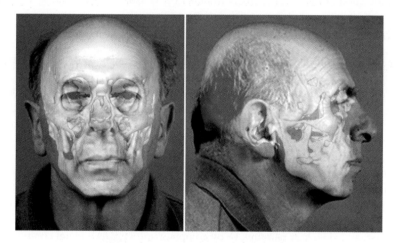

Figure 19.12   Craniofacial superimposition

19.21   CASE STUDIES

19.21.1   The body in the suitcase

The body of a young oriental female was found curled up in a suitcase at the side of a country road. Skin slippage had commenced and she had only been there for a few days. The cause of death was established as asphyxiation but her identity was unknown. She was wearing only a bra and there were no circumstantial indicators of identity. All indicators agreed with her being genetically and morphologically female. She was of oriental racial ancestry (which could be determined from soft tissue, hair and DNA) and she was of relatively short stature. It was necessary to establish her age at death to complete the biological profile before ante-mortem and post-mortem data comparisons could commence.

Age determination

- All of her long bones had completed growth.
- All of her permanent teeth had erupted.
- The sutures of her skull suggested she was a young adult.
- Her pubic symphysis suggested that she was between 20 and 30 years.
- Her sacrum indicated that she may have been less than 25 years.
- Her sternum indicated that she was between 20 and 25 years of age.

When she was finally identified, it was confirmed that she had been 22 years of age when she died.

The small flakes of bone that can be seen at the side of the sternum (indicated by the black arrows) are epiphyses that are forming at the margins of the costal surface (Figure 19.13). The upper ones have completed fusion and this pattern is consistent with an age of between 20 and 25 years.

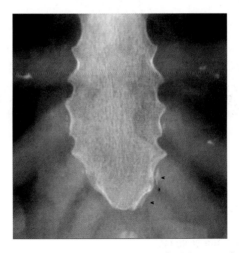

Figure 19.13   Age indicated by the presence of epiphyses at the sternum

19.21.2   The lone skull

A fragmented skull was found on a harbour wall. There was no indication of who had placed it there. Indicators suggested that it had been in the sea for quite some time. The forehead, vault and back of the head were present but no face.

Figure 19.14   Top view of skull, showing frontal part to the left and occipital part to the right

Only one missing person was known to police in that area. She had gone missing nearly 10 years previously and was 40 years of age when she disappeared. The question is: can this skull belong to a 40-year-old female?

Answer

This cannot be the missing 40-year-old female.

- The sutures are clearly visible and open – indicating a juvenile or a young adult.
- The junction between the sphenoid and occipital bones is still open and this closes by 18 years of age. It is not damaged – just unfused. This person must be younger than 18 but size suggests older than 12.

Who is it?

- Clearly a juvenile between the ages of 12 and 18 years.
- Sex cannot be determined with any reliability in the juvenile.
- Race cannot be assigned with any reliability.
- Stature cannot be estimated.
- No other indicators of personal identity.
- Stable isotopes indicated that death occurred between 10 and 15 years before the present date, ie it is of forensic concern.

Conclusion

Anthropology has been central in confirming who this individual is *not* but has not secured any evidence of who it *was*.

Figure 19.15
Lateral view of skull, showing face to the left, occipital region to the right and top of the skull is face down. Area with arrow is where the spinal cord exits from the skull.

Figure 19.16
Front of skull, showing the forehead region. The tops of the orbits are visible although the rest of the face is missing.

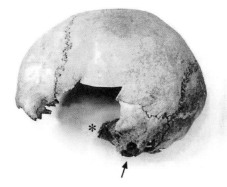

Figure 19.17
Lateral view of skull. Face is to the left and occipital region is to the right.
The straight cut was the result of a sample being taken for isotope analysis.
The mastoid process is marked with an arrow.

369

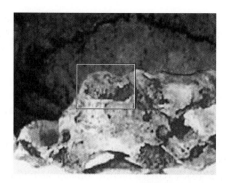

Figure 19.18   [Close-up of Figure 19.16] The junction between the sphenoid and occipital bones. It is still unfused. The position of this region is marked with an asterisk in the other images.

REFERENCES

1   American Board of Forensic Anthropology, Inc (ABFA) [online]. Available at: http://www.csuchico.edu/anth/ABFA/. [Accessed: 07.11.07.]

2   World Health Organization (WHO), "What do we mean by 'Sex' and 'Gender'?" [online]. Available at: http://www.who.int/gender/whatisgender/en/index.html. [Accessed: 07.11.07.]

3   "Human anatomy", *Wikipedia* [online]. Available at: http://en.wikipedia.org/w/index.php?title=Human_anatomy&oldid=245296916. [Accessed: 07.11.07.]

4   "Osteology", *Wikipedia* [online]. Available at: http://en.wikipedia.org/w/index.php?title=Osteology&oldid=233532657. [Accessed: 07.11.07.]

5   Council for the Registration of Forensic Practitioners (CRFP) [online]. Available at: http://www.crfp.org.uk/about/. [Accessed: 07.11.07.]

6   Centre for International Forensic Assistance (CIFA) [online]. Available at: http://www.cifa.ac/login.html. [Accessed: 07.11.07.]

7   British Association for Human Identification (BAHID) [online]. Available at: http://www.bahid.org/. [Accessed: 07.11.07.]

8   G MacKinnon and A Z Mundorff, "The World Trade Center – September 11, 2001" in T Thompson and S Black (eds), *Forensic Human Identification. An Introduction* (CRC Press, London, 2006) at 485.

9   L Koppel, "In Louisiana, dead were also displaced by Katrina", *San Francisco Chronicle*, 25 October 2005 [online]. Available at: http://www.sfgate.com/cgi-bin/article.cgi?f=/c/a/2005/10/25/MNGTFFDK6Q1.DTL. [Accessed: 28.11.07.]

10 Australian Museum Online, "Decomposition. What happens to the body after death?" [online]. Available at: http://www.deathonline.net/decomposition/decomposition/index.htm. [Accessed: 28.11.07.]

11 D W Steadman *et al*, "The effects of chemical and heat maceration techniques on the recovery of nuclear and mitochondrial DNA from bone" (2006) 51(1) *Journal of Forensic Sciences* 11.

12 "Dermestidae", *Wikipedia*. Available at: http://en.wikipedia.org/w/index.php?title=Dermestidae&oldid=239367527. [Accessed: 28.11.07.]

13 "The D'Arcy Thompson Zoology Museum", University of Dundee [online]. Available at: http://www.dundee.ac.uk/museum/zoology/welcome.htm. [Accessed: 28.11.07.]

14 K V Kardong, *Vertebrates: Comparative Anatomy, Function, Evolution* (McGraw-Hill Professional, 2004).

15 R M Nowak, *Walker's Mammals of the World* (6th edn, Johns Hopkins University Press, Maryland, 1999).

16 BBC News, "Big cat search in hospital grounds", 3 July 2002 [online]. Available at: http://news.bbc.co.uk/1/hi/scotland/2091250.stm. [Accessed: 28.11.07.]

17 A M R Agur and A F Dalley, *Grant's Atlas of Anatomy* (11th edn, Lipincott Williams and Wilkins, Maryland, 2005).

18 T Thompson and S Black (eds), *Forensic Human Identification. An Introduction* (CRC Press, London, 2006), pp 485–500.

19 G Herdt (ed), *Third Sex, Third Gender: Beyond Sexual Dimorphism in Culture and History* (Zone Books, New York, 1996).

20 P Gilbert, *A–Z of Syndromes and Inherited Disorders: A Manual for Health, Social, and Education Workers* (Nelson Thornes, Cheltenham, 2000).

21 N Cameron, *Human Growth and Development* (Academic Press, Elsevier, 2002).

22 D Franklin *et al*, "Sexual Dimorphism in the Subadult Mandible: Quantification Using Geometric Morphometrics" (2007) 52(1) *Journal of Forensic Sciences* 6.

23 L Scheuer and S Black, *Developmental Juvenile Osteology* (Academic Press, London, 2000).

24 J M Tanner, *Growth at Adolescence* (Blackwell Scientific, 1955).

25 R S Meindl and C O Lovejoy, "Ectocranial suture closure: a revised method for the determination of skeletal age at death based on the lateral-anterior sutures" (1985) 68(1) *American Journal of Physical Anthropology* 57.

26 W M Krogman and M Y Iscan, *The Human Skeleton in Forensic Medicine* (2nd edn, Charles C Thomas. Illinois, 1986).

27 G W Gill and S Rhine, *Skeletal Attribution of Race: Methods for Forensic Anthropology* (Maxwell Museum of Anthropology, University of New Mexico, 2004).

28 N J Sauer, "Forensic Anthropology and the concept of race: if races don't exist, why are forensic anthropologists so good at identifying them?" (1992) 34(2) *Social Science and Medicine* 107.

29 S M Black, "Bone pathology and ante-mortem trauma in forensic cases" in R Byard, T Corey, C Henderson and J Payne-James (eds), *Encyclopaedia of Forensic and Legal Medicine* (Elsevier, London, 2005).

SUGGESTED READING

Bachman, R B and Pickering, C, *The Use of Forensic Anthropology* (1996).
Brickley, M B and Ferllini, R, *Forensic Anthropology: Case studies from Europe* (2007).
Clement, J G and Ranson, D L, *Craniofacial Identification in Forensic Medicine* (1998).
Freedman, A D, *Death and Dying Grolier Multimedia Encyclopaedia* (1996).
Galloway, A, *Broken Bones* (1999).

Gordon, I and Shapiro, H A, *Forensic Medicine: A guide to the principles* (1975).

Iscan, M Y and Helmer, R P, *Forensic Analysis of the Skull* (1993).

Klepinger, L L, *Fundamentals of Forensic Anthropology* (2006).

Polson, C J, Gee, D J and Knight, B, *The Essentials of Forensic Medicine (4th eds, 1985).*

Prag, J and Neave, R A H, *Making Faces* (1997).

Scheuer, L and Black, S, *Developmental Juvenile Osteology* (2000).

Taylor, K, *Forensic Art and Illustration* (2001).

Vanezis, P, Vanezis, M, McCombe, G and Niblett, T, "Facial reconstruction using 3-D computer graphics" in (2000) 108 *Forensic Science International* at 81–95.

White, T D and Folkens, P A, *The Human Bone Manual* (2005).

Wilkinson, C M, *Forensic Facial Reconstruction* (2004).

CHAPTER 20

Reconciliation Investigation, Identification and Repatriation

20.1   INTRODUCTION

The initial investigation phases of a Disaster Victim Identification (DVI) operation occur from the point of recovery of the victim's body from the disaster scene, through the mortuary post-mortem examination.

Running parallel to this is the initial investigation at casualty bureau and the major incident room, which concentrates on establishing details of missing persons who are feared to be involved in the disaster.

Information relating to a missing person when they were known to be alive is referred to as "ante-mortem data" or "AM data".

Information gathered after death from the body of a disaster victim is referred to as "post-mortem data" or "PM data".

The secondary investigation phase begins with the analysis of evidence gathered and recorded during the initial investigation at the scene and at the mortuary (PM data), followed by the comparison of this evidence against details of missing persons (AM data). This matching of AM and PM data is referred to as "reconciliation investigation".

The objective of the investigation is the reliable identification of deceased disaster victims and the subsequent repatriation of their remains.

The reconciliation investigation is solely focused on identification of disaster victims. Any investigation pertaining to criminal cause, culpability, or negligence in relation to a disaster will be a separate investigation by the appropriate police command or other investigating authority. Close co-operation between the relevant investigation teams is required throughout the operation.

This chapter aims to provide a guide to the minimum standards of investigation expected in relation to reconciliation investigation.

20.2   STRUCTURE

The structure of the investigation process which aims to identify the deceased will depend on the scale of the disaster. For most DVI operations there will be a casualty bureau that collates information on persons who are reported as feared missing in the disaster. The number of persons initially reported missing may far exceed the number of casualties, often by thousands. The casualty bureau supplies information to a major incident room that collates the missing person information and issues actions. For larger DVI operations in the UK the actions may be recorded on the Home Office Large Major Enquiry System (HOLMES).[1]

We rely on the casualty bureau and major incident room personnel to filter out the missing person reports which relate to those who are later accounted for as safe and well, or found to be alive in hospital. The remaining missing person reports should then relate to those who are still unaccounted for, suggesting there is a strong probability that they have been caught up in the disaster. These are referred to as "Grade 1 missing persons". There may also be victims who, because of lifestyle or other factors, are not reported missing.

For smaller DVI operations the major incident room team may liaise directly with a mortuary-based pathologist and forensic team in order to identify victims. This may be appropriate in a situation such as a vehicle crash or vessel mishap, where the numbers of deceased are manageable and the names of all those on board are known at an early stage in the investigation (ie a "closed incident").

For larger disasters, a wider "Identification Centre" structure will be required as there will be more information to manage, increasing the risk of error; the title "Forensic Matching Centre" is also used. In addition to a major incident room that collates AM data and a mortuary-based operation that collects PM data, larger-scale DVI operations have further key elements. These elements include: AM and PM Data Management and Reconciliation Investigation and Repatriation. Large operations will also need to consider: Finance and Resources, Media Liaison and Diplomatic Liaison. The aspects of a larger DVI operation are described in this chapter, although the same principles should be considered for smaller DVI operations as appropriate and in proportion to the scale of the investigation.

20.3 MANAGEMENT OF ANTE-MORTEM AND POST-MORTEM DATA

It is quite likely that larger disasters will have an international component. The internationally accepted standard for recording information, relating to missing persons and deceased disaster victims, is by use of Interpol DVI forms.[2]

These forms are easily available to download from the Interpol website[3] along with instructions on their completion; the forms are available in English, Spanish, French and Arabic versions.

Information gathered during the recovery of the victim's body and during the post-mortem examination process is recorded on the pink Interpol Post-mortem (PM) DVI form – PM data.[2]

Missing person information or information about a person's life gathered via the casualty bureau and Family Liaison Officers (FLOs) is recorded on the yellow Interpol Ante-mortem (AM) form – AM data.[2]

The Interpol AM and PM DVI forms[2] mirror each other, in that the information for comparison is found at precisely the same location on each form. For example, information regarding height, jewellery or surgical scars is on the same page and in the same location on each form, regardless of which language version of the forms is used.

There are also similar ACPO Victim Profile forms in existence in the United Kingdom: these are simpler in layout than the Interpol forms, but follow the same principles. While these might be used locally, the National DVI Team will always use the Interpol forms. If the ACPO forms are used by local resilience and a victim is found to be from overseas, the information on these forms can later be transferred onto Interpol DVI forms.

In the early management of a major incident affecting the UK, "CASWEB" forms provide casualty bureau with the basic descriptive details of missing persons, survivors, injured and deceased victims. This provides the authorities with early information regarding the numbers of victims potentially involved in a disaster. The forms do not record sufficient details for scientific identification, but the names and basic descriptions of potential victims can provide early leads or clues as to identity.

The information supplied and filtered by casualty bureau and the major incident room will relate to Grade 1 missing persons: those likely to have been involved in the disaster. Where the standard and integrity of this data are high it will greatly progress the investigation to identify deceased disaster victims.

An investigator, ideally the FLO assigned to the case, will complete the yellow AM DVI form.[2] The investigator will record as much accurate information as possible about the physical characteristics of the missing person. The dental records relating to the missing person are obtained where available. A forensic examination of the missing person's home or workplace may take place, to obtain fingerprint or DNA information. If the missing person has a criminal record their fingerprints or DNA should be on file. Military or international identity records may hold similar information.

In addition to the AM data, there will also be a significant volume of PM data to manage for each unidentified disaster victim's body, including:

- The unique reference number (URN) allocated to the disaster victim's body or body parts, which should remain the same throughout the process. It must be remembered that in the situation of fragmented remains, which are reconciled, a series of URNs might have to be incorporated.
- Information and photographs, relating to the location where the victim's body was recovered.
- Pathology and other information obtained during the mortuary-based post-mortem examination, including the victim's sex, height, hair, physical features, marks and scars.
- Odontology information, including a dental assessment of the victim's age. It must be remembered that much of this information can also be gained via the forensic anthropologist.
- X-ray and Computed Tomography (CT) scan images.

- Fingerprint information.
- DNA samples and profiles.
- Information, exhibits and photographs in relation to clothing, jewellery and other property recovered with the victim.

Careful management and storage of this data are essential. Interpol DVI forms can be downloaded from the Interpol website and completed on paper by hand, or completed electronically before being printed.

The Interpol DVI forms can also be completed and stored electronically using the licensed Danish IT system "Plassdata DVI System International".[4] This system can also store scans and images attached to AM or PM forms. Significantly, this system also allows searches of AM and PM data which has been recorded on the Interpol DVI forms and entered as electronic data.[2] It can be used to search thousands of AM or PM files to locate matching features. It can search on dental features, DNA profiles and various descriptive features in relation to the disaster victim's body or clothing etc. Through the Plassdata DVI System,[4] versions of the Interpol DVI forms[2] are currently available in English, French, Spanish, Norwegian, Dutch, Swedish, German, Icelandic and Danish. Further information is available on the Plassdata DVI System International[4] website.

ACPO/UK DVI and Interpol are currently licensed to use Plassdata DVI System International.[4]

Plassdata DVI System International[4] does not search for fingerprint matches; however, it can store scans or images of fingerprints. Fingerprint information is stored and searched separately using the Automated Fingerprint Identification System (AFIS).[5]

A high standard of data management is essential throughout the identification process. For disasters that involve catastrophic numbers of deceased, a separate unit to manage AM and PM data should be considered. The AM/PM Data Management Unit should be led by a police manager who co-ordinates the activities of a team of police officers, police staff and forensic specialists. The accurate interpretation and inputting of data by this team is important to the effectiveness of the DVI operation. Great care should be taken if handwritten details on DVI forms are transferred onto electronic versions. A single number misread and wrongly recorded can cause serious problems to the investigation and lead to unsuccessful, or indeed incorrect, identifications. Similarly, extra care should be taken if cutting and pasting information between IT-based documents. A sample or serial number entered in error on the wrong document could have serious consequences to the integrity of the entire DVI operation. Where possible, to minimise the risk of error, the writer of any handwritten details should enter the information themselves onto an electronic version, or at least check that information has been transferred correctly.

Where an operation involves large numbers of hard-copy paper AM and PM files, consideration should be given to using an electronic bar code system to manage and log the movement of files between different units or investigators.

Odontology, fingerprint and DNA specialists will be present with the AM/PM Unit to receive, quality check and input AM and PM data relevant to their specialist area and to ensure that standards are maintained. Protocols may vary internationally for certain aspects: for example, the recording of dental data can vary throughout the world, so odontologists will be required to interpret this data and where necessary translate it, to ensure standardisation of data and facilitate the search for identity.

As fingerprint information is entered and searches are performed on the stand-alone AFIS system,[5] this facility may have to be housed at a separate location to the identification centre, for practical and technical reasons.

20.4 RECONCILIATION INVESTIGATION UNIT

The matching of PM data to AM data leading to identification is referred to as the "reconciliation process". The team carrying out this work will normally consist of:

- Police Reconciliation Co-ordinator;
- forensic odontologists;
- fingerprint specialists;
- DNA specialists;
- police investigators;
- administrative and analytical staff;
- a pathologist or anthropologist would also be consulted where required.

In a larger operation each specialist area should have its own team leader. Each team will have the responsibility to initiate searches of AM and PM data in relation to their relevant specialist area. Positive matches will be passed to the police reconciliation investigators, who will have a manager who co-ordinates this process. The Reconciliation Co-ordinator will report to the Senior Identification Manager (SIM).

A flow chart example of reconciliation investigation within the DVI process is included with this chapter (Figure 20.1). This example is based around a larger DVI operation; the model can be scaled down and adapted as appropriate to the circumstances.

Large-scale DVI operations may be subject to international observers or mutual aid, in the form of additional resources. They may be staffed by police and forensic specialists from international DVI teams in addition to the home nation. Interpol guidelines promote this co-operation, particularly if many of the disaster victims are likely to be from another nation, or from several other nations.

Computer-based technology such as the Plassdata DVI System[4] can greatly speed up the reconciliation process. For the majority of smaller DVI operations,

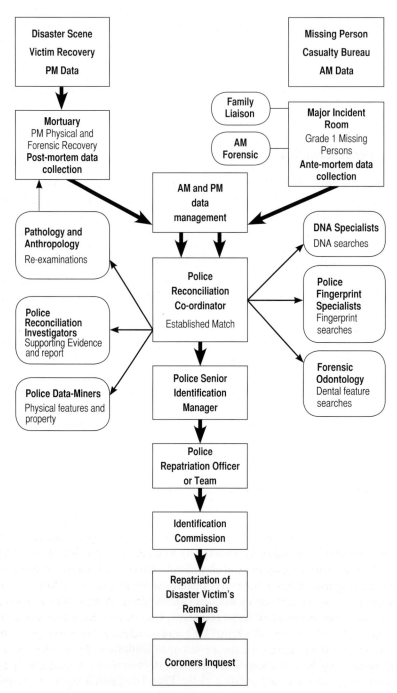

Figure 20.1   Reconciliation Investigation within the Disaster Victim Identification process

the reconciliation process can be done on paper. PM files can be split up into categories based on, for example sex, height and dental age assessment. The files can then be systematically compared against broadly matching AM files until matches are found. Obviously, this can be a significantly time-consuming process, but it is a feasible option for DVI operations involving smaller numbers of victims. Some examples of elimination tables for a paper-based reconciliation process are illustrated on the Interpol website.[3]

20.5 IDENTIFICATION STANDARDS

The identification standards will be set by the Coroner/Fiscal or identification commission in consultation with the Senior Identification Manager (SIM). Visual identification is not acceptable in mass disasters, as it has proved unreliable on many occasions in the past. The standards set, ideally, aim to identify each victim scientifically using at least one of the "primary identifiers" which are: odontology, fingerprints or DNA. In some circumstances a unique physical/medical feature or medical conditions may be acceptable as a primary identifier, such as a surgical implant with a unique serial number, for example a pacemaker device.

The identification should, where possible, be supported by other evidence: "secondary identifiers" such as marks, scars, tattoos, or physical features such as an amputation or physical peculiarity. Property such as jewellery and clothing can also assist in supporting identification. In the absence of a primary identifier, a variable number of secondary identifiers can be used as evidence of identification. Jewellery still firmly attached to the victim at the point of recovery, such as a ring with an inscribed message or significant date, is a good example of an accepted secondary identifier.

20.6 RECONCILIATION PROCESS

The practical workings of the Reconciliation Unit will include the use of the specialists who are present. An odontology team may be tasked by the Reconciliation Co-ordinator systematically to examine a specific batch of AM data. An odontologist examines each individual case and notes, for example, that a missing person has a distinctive dental feature recorded as AM data, such as a specific missing tooth or a particular type of filling. After initiating a search of PM data, the odontology team then makes a positive match between two particular files of AM and PM data. If the dental features recorded during the post-mortem examination process are found to match the dental records of a missing person, the forensic odontologist would then describe and certify the match between the AM and PM forms on a DVI comparison report. For larger DVI operations, best practice would be for a second forensic odontologist to assess, agree and counter-sign the match. The DVI comparison report links the two files. This information would then be passed along with the two files (AM and PM) via the Reconciliation Co-ordinator to the police investigators within the Reconciliation Investigation Unit. Similar arrangements will be in place for fingerprint specialists. PM fingerprints searched on a database may be found to match AM data from criminal or military records, or AM data from a nation where all citizens routinely supply fingerprints for identity documents. They may also match fingerprints recovered as a result of forensic examination of the missing person's home address or workplace, as part of the AM data collection process. The fingerprint specialist will then examine, describe and certify the match on a DVI comparison report, which should ideally be assessed, agreed and counter-signed by a second fingerprint specialist, before passing the information in a file to the police investigators via the Reconciliation Co-ordinator.

DNA specialists will also seek to make matches between DNA profiles that have been obtained from the victim's body (PM samples), and DNA profiles from AM data or samples. A DNA profile from a PM sample may match DNA held on a national database, or medical samples taken from the missing person at birth or during medical treatment. It may also match the profile of DNA samples recovered during forensic examination of the missing person's home address, from an item such as a toothbrush. Reference DNA samples may have been taken from the missing person's mother and other close relatives, with which a match has been made. The samples taken from relatives may include PM samples from other relatives who have died in the same disaster and who have already been identified. A second DNA specialist should ideally assess, agree and counter-sign any match before passing the information in a file to the police reconciliation investigators via the Reconciliation Co-ordinator.

In addition to taking forward the scientific matches made by the relevant specialists, police reconciliation investigators will proactively seek matches between AM and PM data on physical features, such as marks, scars and tattoos. Suitably skilled police staff such as crime analysts can play an important role in this particular area. Skilled staff with analytical skills may be tasked to carry out extensive searches of AM and PM data, or "data mining".

Police reconciliation investigators will also initiate searches to find matches of clothing and jewellery etc. The investigator should be aware, when carrying out such enquiries and searches, that clothes and shoe sizes vary among different regions of the world: for example, a male with UK size 8 shoes would wear size 9 in the USA, 27 in Japan or 42 in Europe. If a proportion of disaster victims is from a particular world region, a chart showing clothes and shoe sizes will be useful when inspecting photographs of clothing labels, to help narrow down the searches for victims.

The police reconciliation investigator will also act on intelligence received from the scene and mortuary. This information may create a positive lead: for example, a victim may have had identification documents on their person. This information can then form the basis of a lead from which to begin the gathering of AM information.

Caution must be taken when attributing documents and property to disaster victims. Such items are sometimes mistakenly placed with the victim's body by well-meaning people at the disaster scene. Items may also be placed by people with dishonest or malicious intentions.

It must also be acknowledged that families of disaster victims often find it difficult to comprehend that, even when a victim has identification documents or other strong clues to identity on their person, prompt identification does not occur. Strong leads can be acted upon; however, minimum standards of investigation and identification must be maintained and this may take some time.

Any match found by a police investigator is more likely to be a secondary identifier or a positive lead, unless it pertains to a unique physical feature that meets the standard of a primary identifier, such as a unique numbered implant. Having made a match, the investigator should seek primary scientific evidence of identification from one or more of the relevant specialists.

20.7 MINIMUM STANDARDS OF INVESTIGATION

The police reconciliation investigator must be very thorough, while respecting the skills and experience of specialist colleagues. The investigator has a duty to test the accuracy and integrity of evidence. The investigator must have a basic understanding of the relevant scientific identification areas, be aware of the strength of the evidence and ensure that there are no other wider factors that weaken it.

A positive or "established" match will be based upon the opinion of a relevant specialist, or ideally, the opinion of two specialists. After an established match has been passed to the police reconciliation investigators, they will then note the scientific evidence and seek to find further evidence and factors to support the identification.

The investigators will also specifically seek to verify that the records or samples checked by the specialists have not been mistakenly attributed to the wrong body earlier in the DVI process, during AM or PM collection or during data entry.

Odontologists, fingerprint, DNA specialists or police investigators should report matches as "identification possible", "identification probable" or "identification established". Probable or possible matches should be used as positive leads or lines of enquiry, although they may, along with sufficient other evidence, be considered as a contributing factor to support more robust indicators of identity.

Where there is only possible or probable identification achieved, the investigator can consider requesting the re-examination of a particular body. This would allow a pathologist to search for evidence of surgery, or a medical condition that the possible matching missing person had. This information may not have been recorded during the first post-mortem examination. A targeted X-ray to search for evidence of an old fracture may assist in establishing identification.

While the scientific evidence of identification may be overwhelming, all this is meaningless if the fingerprints, dental charts, DNA samples or other records relating to a victim's body were misplaced or replaced by those of another victim during the process. The investigator must check the continuity of samples used, as well as seek to back up the scientific evidence of identification with additional supporting evidence.

Start with basic facts: does the sex match that of the missing person? If it doesn't match, something may have potentially gone very wrong with the recording and management of data. Bear in mind that sex can sometimes be wrongly attributed or not assigned at all, particularly when dealing with decomposed bodies of pre-pubescent juveniles. The evidence of sex should, where possible, be supported by the relevant sexual physical features which are observed and recorded as present during PM examination by a pathologist. Ideally, sexual physical features should be clearly visible in PM photographs. Evidence of sex ideally should not rely only on the DNA profile obtained from a disaster victim; although it is accepted that, in cases where victim's remains are fragmented, there may be no alternative.

The investigator should also be aware that victims who have had gender reassignment surgery may have conflicting data recorded about them, during both AM and PM evidence gathering. Visible sexual features may differ from the sex attributed to the victim from a DNA profile. Family or friends providing missing person information recorded as AM data, could be unaware of some intimate, personal details of a disaster victim.

A victim's race is recorded using one of three categories on AM and PM DVI forms. These categories correspond to anthropological terms "Caucasoid", "Mongoloid" and "Negroid". Extreme caution should be exercised when assigning a category, for a number of reasons. First, race can easily be attributed incorrectly, particularly post-mortem and after decomposition has begun. Second, the three categories are used in physical anthropology to describe typical examples of perceived groups, which do not exist as distinct categories in reality: most people throughout the world are of ambiguous or mixed ancestry, whose backgrounds are a combination of the three types described. Therefore, the "race" of a disaster victim should be assigned only by a pathologist or forensic anthropologist.

- It should be noted that the term "Caucasoid" refers to persons of Asian or Arabic appearance, as well as white or dark-skinned European appearance. If comparing with the UK police codes used to record persons' descriptions, these fall into the category of race or identity codes 1, 2, 4 and 6.
- The term "Mongoloid" covers people of south-east Asian appearance, such as people of typically Chinese and Japanese appearance, but also applies to Native Americans, Inuits and several groups in Russia. This equates with the UK police race or identity code 5.

- The term "Negroid" includes persons of African or Caribbean appearance. The term is originally derived from the Latin for "black", but applies more to the shape of the skull than the tone of the skin, in an anthropological context (see Chapter 19). This equates with the UK police race or identity code 3.

These are anthropological terms, and the investigator should be aware that they are likely to cause offence to the relatives of disaster victims if used insensitively.

If the victim's remains are largely intact, the investigator should confirm that the AM and PM height matches, although it must be remembered that height can also be estimated from fragmented remains by a forensic anthropologist. It can be accepted that there may be some degree of discrepancy in height within a couple of centimetres, particularly if the AM height has been estimated, as opposed to information from official or medical records.

The investigator must check that the photographs from the recovery and post-mortem examination stages show the same unique number on labels as the PM file submitted. If victim recovery labels were not used and numbers were handwritten on body bags or DVI forms, have the numbers been interpreted correctly? Handwritten numbers can easily be misread, for example a figure "1" could be mistaken for a "7", a figure "4" mistaken for a "9", or a figure "6" mistaken for an "8". Simple mistakes potentially result in the identification being attributed to the wrong body.

When deciding whether a match of AM and PM data is robust, the reconciliation team needs to take into account the validity of the matches made. Where identification is established by fingerprints, does the fingerprint match that has been reported relate to perhaps twelve matching characteristics or just four? If the number of factors is low, should this just be listed as a probable or possible match rather than an established one, and therefore treated as a positive lead? The routine assessment by a second fingerprint specialist as part of the process should help eliminate such issues.

Where identification is made by odontology, does the match relate to one unique dental feature, or are there several matching factors? Similarly, should this just be listed as a probable or possible match rather than an established one and treated as a positive lead? Again, a second odontologist should help negate this issue.

If DNA or fingerprints were recovered from the missing person's home address, are they the only person from that address who is reported as missing? It is important that AM forensic recovery statements clearly state whether this is the case. If they do not, a further statement clarifying this issue should be requested and passed on to the team.

Additional supporting evidence provided by the police reconciliation investigator to support primary identification can be as simple as the missing person being the same sex and height as the disaster victim in question, or that the assessed dental age is a close match. Dental age assessment can be very accurate for infants and children, but becomes less accurate in adults. Marks, scars or distinctive physical features may also match. Clothing or jewellery which reinforces the identification evidence may also be present.

A family photograph obtained as part of the AM data collection may show the victim wearing particular clothing or jewellery, or show distinctive scars or features that match PM photographs. This can provide additional evidence to support the scientific identification. If the photograph of the missing person shows them smiling, a dental profile may be visible. A forensic odontologist may be able to match the profile of the missing person's teeth with the PM photographs to provide additional evidence. If a profile is very distinctive it may be the opinion of the odontologist that this should be considered as an established match, meeting primary identification standards.

In cases of probable or possible identification, the investigator should deal with this as a positive lead. For example, a forensic odontologist may report a probable or possible dental match between an AM and PM dental records, but it may be their opinion that the data is insufficient to allow an established match. In a case such as this, the fingerprint specialist can be tasked specifically to examine the relevant AM and PM fingerprint records for comparison, if available. DNA investigation could also be specifically focused around the AM and PM files in question.

The investigator should be careful not to influence a specialist's opinion by, for example, pointing out that an unrelated feature or clothing possibly matches. The specialist should have the chance first to independently and scientifically assess the AM and PM data in question, without the influence of other information which may prove later to be irrelevant. AM data relating to clothing may prove to be inaccurate due to a number of factors: the victim may have changed their clothes after the last sighting of them alive, or the person reporting them missing could simply be mistaken about what was worn.

Dental, fingerprint and DNA established matches should be based on the scientific evidence alone; factors such as clothing or jewellery should not be considered as a factor contributing to the scientific match by the relevant specialist. Such factors will be considered and documented by the police investigator as separate evidence to support or not support the identification.

20.8   DVI COMPARISON REPORT

When the reconciliation investigator has gathered enough evidence to support the scientific identification the DVI Comparison Report should be completed. A one-page DVI Comparison Report form is included in the Interpol set of DVI forms. This will summarise details of each match, whether probable, possible or established. The relevant AM and PM files that have been found to match should be linked together with this form. The evidence summary should include one or more of the following, depending on the identification criteria set for the DVI operation:

- the conclusion of the odontologist;
- the conclusion of the pathologist;
- the evidence of the fingerprint specialist;
- the evidence of the DNA specialist;
- the evidence of the police officer (reconciliation investigator) should be included in every report.

The investigator will require evidential statements from the relevant specialists to certify the matches, in addition to the DVI Comparison Report.

It is important that next-of-kin or other interested parties are kept informed of the progress of investigations through Family Liaison Officers. However, false hopes and unrealistic expectations can be raised where interested parties are made aware of possible, probable or even established identification matches at an early stage. It can take some time, especially in difficult cases, to meet an acceptable evidential standard. There may be pressure from the highest levels to prioritise certain cases, but families of victims deserve to be treated equally whatever their perceived status in society. Cases must meet the required evidential standard expected by the SIM.

There are some occasions where there may be justification for cases to be prioritised. For example, early identification of a driver or pilot involved in a crash may be requested for early toxicology tests. Identification of a suspect may be needed if the disaster is suspected to be the result of a serious crime.

If a victim's body has been fragmented and dispersed at the disaster scene then more than one PM file may relate to the same victim. The body parts will have been recovered separately and gone through separate examinations at the mortuary. The investigator should seek to ensure, as far as possible, that these are linked scientifically. This should all be completed, if possible, before presentation to the Coroner or identification commission, to avoid causing distress to any surviving family members where other fragments are later produced.

20.9   EVIDENTIAL REPORT/POLICE COMPARISON REPORT

To complete the investigation, the reconciliation investigator will also complete a more detailed evidential report or "Police Comparison Report" on the outcome of the reconciliation investigation. This report will confirm the details of the missing person and, if known, brief details of how they came to be involved in the disaster and, significantly, the evidence of identification.

The main body of the report should be written as an evidential report to the Coroner/Fiscal or identification commission. It should specifically state the evidence of scientific identification by the primary identifiers of odontology, fingerprints, DNA or a unique physical feature. The report should refer to the relevant forensic specialist or investigator who made the established match and, where appropriate, the second specialist who agreed and counter-signed the match.

The report should then detail the evidence of the police reconciliation investigator, describing as many factors as possible that support the scientific identification. It should state that the AM and PM data has been compared and matches were found on the following factors. The report should begin with a statement that the sex matches. If the victim's body was recovered largely intact, the report should state that the height matches. If the AM height was estimated, then there may be some slight differential in the height which should be commented on in the report. Other factors such as matching marks, scars, tattoos, clothing and jewellery, if available, should be included. Photographs may be included to illustrate the evidence.

If there is more than one primary identifier, then this makes the identification evidence particularly strong. However, supporting evidence should still be included in all cases.

Investigators should be aware that families of disaster victims may see the complete report. It should be written in terms that can, in general, be understood by persons without any specialist knowledge of disaster victim identification. A photograph showing a matching physical feature in AM and PM photographs may need to be included in the report to illustrate the evidence. In many cases it is possible to display this feature with sensitivity: for example, a tattoo on an arm could be photographed without showing the victim's face. It is accepted, though, that in some cases graphic photographs may need to be included to emphasise matches. A high standard of evidential content is the priority.

A DNA specialist's identification report may refer to comparison of PM samples with reference samples from the "alleged mother" or "alleged father" of a victim. If the victim's family are unfamiliar with forensic terminology, they could easily take offence at such a phrase. The DNA specialist's evidence should be summarised in the report in easily understood language, and the term "alleged" in relation to a parent or other close family member should be avoided.

A fetus still attached to its mother would be considered part of the mother's body, and therefore will form a single case to be presented to the Coroner/Fiscal or identification commission. However, in such circumstances the investigator should report the facts with the utmost respect, referring throughout the evidential report to both the mother and her unborn child.

Several members of the same family may be reported missing in the same disaster, whether related genetically, by marriage or other non-genetic association. This creates a situation where the identities of people from the same home or family could be confused, leading to misidentification, as the fingerprints or DNA recovered from a home address could be from any of the individuals. Similarly, where identification is through DNA comparison, two brothers or sisters could be confused with each other if the reference DNA samples were provided by their parents. In some cases, there will be significant differences in physical size or height which will make the correct identification more obvious and easier to confirm evidentially.

Where more than one person is missing from a family in the same disaster or where the primary identification is through DNA comparison, it is good practice to include a family tree diagram (Figure 20.2). The information to complete this is best obtained via a Family Liaison Officer (FLO) or the liaison officer representing the relevant home nation of the victim. The family tree diagram can illustrate factors such as which other family members are still missing, and illustrate who has provided reference DNA samples. If a family member is confirmed as deceased and identified, the diagram should include which primary identifier confirmed the identification of the particular victim.

The investigator's report should clearly explain why the victim in question cannot be confused with one of the other family members. This can be as simple as sex or significant height differences, or the fact that the other family members have already been reliably identified by scientific means.

When the investigator has completed their report it should be assessed and counter-signed by the Reconciliation Co-ordinator. If the Reconciliation Co-ordinator is satisfied with the accuracy, standard and presentation of the evidence it should be passed to the SIM for endorsement. The report as well as the AM and PM files should then be passed to the Repatriation Officer or Repatriation Team.

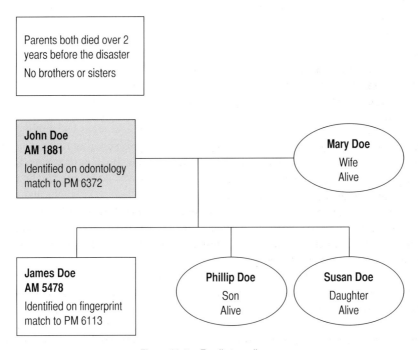

Figure 20.2   Family tree diagram

20.10   REPATRIATION OFFICER

The Repatriation Officer or Team will co-ordinate the presentation of evidence to the Coroner/Fiscal or identification commission. They will liaise with Family Liaison Officers or liaison officers representing other nations, to inform them that their relevant case is going to be presented to the Coroner/Fiscal or identification commission. They will co-ordinate the relevant specialists and investigators attending the hearing in order to present evidence.

They will also manage the retention and security of the files of repatriated victims and supply suitable copies of files to the authority representing the victim, and the police service or embassy that managed the original collection of AM data. They will ensure that after the hearing original AM photographs, particularly unique family photographs, are returned to next-of-kin via the FLO. However, high-quality colour copies of such photographs should remain with the original file for any future reference.

20.11   REPATRIATION OR RELEASE OF DISASTER VICTIM REMAINS

When the Coroner/Fiscal or identification commission has officially approved identification as established, the victim's body may be released to the next-of-kin or representatives of the next-of-kin. This activity will occur after identification has been established but normally before the actual Coroner's inquest into the circumstances of the death. Often, the release of remains may simply be through a local undertaker.

Officials representing another nation may decide to carry out some additional checks upon receipt of a victim's remains for repatriation from the UK. Similarly, UK DVI officers may be asked to travel abroad to retrieve the remains of a victim from an overseas DVI operation in which the UK team had limited or no involvement. Officers retrieving victims' bodies in these circumstances must be as certain as possible that they have the correct body. The receiving DVI officer should check that numbers on labels match records, and then visually and physically inspect the victim's body. Basic factors such as sex, height and any easily identifiable distinctive physical features should be checked where possible. For a higher level of confidence, a forensic odontologist would be required physically to examine the victim, to establish a match to any available AM dental records of the missing person.

If the receiving officer is not satisfied that the victim's body is the correct one, it should not be accepted. Further examination may be requested, with relevant specialists representing the UK present at the re-examination. If a victim's body is accepted, then some further investigation may be necessary, depending on the standard of the DVI operation and confidence in the process. This activity may take place abroad, or at the receiving mortuary in the UK. The activity could be limited to simply checking documentation and that unique seal or body numbers match. Where an increased level of confidence is required, a total re-examination of the victim's remains may be necessary. The victim's body may also need to be washed, as well as the washing and photographing of clothing and jewellery, etc. This is so that photographs can be produced at an inquest if required. Clothing, jewellery and other property may need to be cleaned, if the victim's family agree, before being passed on to the family by the FLO, preferably before they are shown photographs of such items.

If the victim is suspected to have died as a result of a criminal act, it may be that a special post-mortem examination or other forensic procedures are planned to take place in the UK. If this is the case, then the victim's body should be preserved as much as possible as a forensic exhibit, with minimal disturbance.

Some families may request that the remains of disaster victims are cremated or buried in the country where the disaster occurred. Families may also request that the disaster victim's remains are repatriated to a third country in which the victim has family or other links.

Where victim's remains are to be shipped from overseas to the UK or another nominated country, the DVI officer must be aware that there are strict international rules in relation to the carriage of human remains. Documentation including a "*Laissez-Passer* for a corpse" must be completed.

Under international agreements, specific standards of inner and outer coffin packaging and sealing are required. Where possible, the services of an undertaker should be secured abroad to assist the UK DVI officer, facilitate the repatriation process and ensure that international rules are followed.

Detailed rules in relation to the international carriage of human remains can be found on the Interpol website in the DVI section.

It is expected that the UK DVI officer will be working closely with UK Foreign and Commonwealth Office staff on any overseas DVI operation. UK DVI officers may be requested to deal with a disaster victim on behalf of another nation, such as a European Union or Commonwealth nation. In these circumstances, the same standards and procedures will be applied as if dealing with a UK case.

If a disaster victim has dual nationality it must be clearly established that any DVI activity, including repatriation, is carried out with the agreement of the other country involved and in line with the wishes of any next-of-kin. It must not be assumed that the UK should be the main responder in this situation.

If PM data is collected overseas, such as PM DVI forms or photographs on compact disc, a copy of this data should accompany the body. Standard procedure should be that data should be packaged hygienically, outside the main coffin and inside the lid of an outer coffin, protected by a unique seal number to facilitate checking back in the UK. If the disaster victim's remains are not escorted back to the UK, there must be close liaison between the DVI officer abroad and the receiving officer in the UK. Unique tamperproof seals should be used, such as the marked solder seals used by police counter-terrorist search teams, with the integrity checked on reception in the UK. The policing of UK airports includes contingency planning around large numbers of disaster victims being repatriated to the UK.

When an international disaster occurs with the loss of life of UK citizens, one designated UK Coroner/Fiscal will normally take responsibility for UK-based inquests into the deaths. This may be in addition to any identification commission or inquest that has taken place overseas in the relevant jurisdiction. UK DVI officers or the UK DVI SIM may be required to give evidence on individual cases, or the wider DVI process relevant to the particular disaster.

It is the responsibility of all involved in the disaster victim identification process to work towards establishing reliable identification to a high evidential standard. All activity, from investigation through to the final release of the disaster victim's remains, must be dealt with thoroughly and with integrity and dignity.

REFERENCES

1 Home Office Large Major Enquiry System (HOLMES) [online]. Available at: http://www.holmes2.com/holmes2/whatish2/. [Accessed: 06.06.08.]

2 Interpol DVI Forms [online]. Available at: http://www.interpol.int/Public/DisasterVictim/Forms/Default.asp. [Accessed: 15.5.2008.]

3 Interpol website [online]. Available at: http://www.interpol.int/. [Accessed: 15.05.2008.]

4 Plassdata DVI System International [online]. Available at: www.dvisystem.com. [Accessed: 14.11.2007.]

5 Automated Fingerprint Identification System (AFIS) [online]. Available at: http://en.wikipedia.org/w/index.php?title=Automated_Fingerprint_Identification_System&oldid=213517418. [Accessed 09.06.2008.]

CHAPTER 21

Health Risks and Welfare Issues Associated with DVI Work

21.1 INTRODUCTION

This chapter aims to prepare DVI personnel to practise in unfamiliar and stressful working conditions. It is directed towards officers and staff who are already committed to working in hostile, extreme and remote environments, where healthcare facilities may be limited.

The first section describes how the human body interacts with the environment and deals with the effects of extreme conditions on health. The second section provides a more detailed account of the physical health risks specific to DVI work and the final section considers psychological and emotional hazards associated with the work of disaster victim identification.

21.2 PHYSICAL HAZARDS

21.2.1 Heat

In normal circumstances, the ideal temperature for sedentary work is about 20°C (Celsius) and for heavy work it is 13°C.

In extremely hot (or cold) conditions, such as those experienced by DVI officers and staff during the tsunami DVI operation in 2004–05, the body's metabolism has to work much harder to maintain the body at its normal temperature of 37°C. The strain on the heart caused by excessive heat is accentuated by the need for the DVI officers to wear full personal protective equipment (PPE).

The World Health Organization recommends 24°C as the maximum temperature for working in comfort. However, due to the nature of DVI work, by definition performed in emergency situations, staff are frequently required to work at temperatures that far exceed these values. This, coupled with the need to wear full PPE, can cause a variety of physical problems.

Health problems associated with working in extreme heat

Sunburn

Exposure to the sun for any length of time can cause painful sunburn[1] which may have future consequences such as skin cancer. Precautions[2] against this include covering up against the rays (wearing long sleeves, for example), wearing a wide brimmed hat and using an appropriate factor sun cream (SPF 25+ is recommended).

Prickly heat

Prickly heat is a rash of red dots on the skin. It is common in DVI officers working in PPE in hot conditions and occurs due to blockage of sweat glands in the skin. It causes discomfort and itching.

Heat oedema (swelling)

DVI officers often experience swelling in the hands and feet when they are required to stand or sit for long periods in intense heat. It resolves with rest and elevation of the affected limb(s).

Heat exhaustion

Dehydration and loss of body salts (through sweat) leads to extreme fatigue or weakness, feeling faint or dizzy, muscle cramps, nausea, vomiting and diarrhoea.

Prevention

DVI officers and staff working in extreme heat need to ensure that they constantly replace the fluid and body salts lost through sweating. Officers doing heavy physical work, particularly in outdoor conditions, need to drink at least 4–5 litres of fluid per day and to replace lost body salts with oral rehydration solutions such as, for example, Rapolyte, Dioralyte etc.

It is vitally important for officers doing physical work to take frequent and regular rest breaks in order to allow the body to cool down. Regular rest breaks are particularly important if the conditions are humid as well as hot, since heat exhaustion is more likely to occur in these conditions.

Officers deployed in office-based roles still need to drink at least 3 litres of water each day.

It is important to prevent heat exhaustion and to deal with it early if it occurs, since, if untreated, it can progress to heat stroke which can be fatal.

Heat stroke

Heat stroke occurs when the body is no longer able to regulate its own temperature. The body temperature continues to rise, often up to 40°C or higher. Heat stroke is a medical emergency: if untreated it can damage the vital organs and lead to death.

Symptoms of heat stroke include mental changes, such as inability to concentrate, confusion, delirium or unconsciousness. Heat stroke is a particular hazard for DVI officers as the PPE essentially blocks the body's natural ability to sweat and lose heat.

Treatment

Symptoms of heat stroke require immediate medical attention. While awaiting medical attention the following measures can assist:

- remove PPE and outer clothing;
- take the person out of the heat, into a cooler environment, preferably an air-conditioned area;
- moisten the skin with tepid water;
- use a fan or towel to blow cool air across the skin;
- give cool fluids by mouth if the person is able to drink.

Heat stroke is characterised by an absence of sweating, so the skin will look red and flushed but will feel dry to the touch.

Hypothermia (cold exposure)

Hypothermia, also known as cold exposure, is characterised by dangerously low body temperatures, below 35°C.

It occurs when more heat is lost from the body than the body can generate, due to prolonged exposure to the cold.

Common causes include:

- wearing wet clothing in windy or cold weather;
- heavy exertion, not drinking enough fluids or not eating enough in cold weather.

Early symptoms

- Shivering.
- Cold, pale or blue/grey skin.
- Lack of concern or interest; poor judgement.
- Difficulty performing simple tasks.
- Slurred speech.

Late symptoms

- Trunk of body feels cold to the touch.
- Stiff muscles.
- Slow shallow breathing.
- Slow pulse.
- Confusion or loss of consciousness.

Note: Shivering may stop if body temperature drops below 32°.

Treatment of mild hypothermia

Hypothermia is a medical emergency and can rapidly lead to unconsciousness and death.

Treatment of mild hypothermia includes:

- getting the person out of the cold and wet environment;
- replacing wet clothing with dry clothing, including socks, gloves and hat;
- insulating the whole body, including the head and neck, from cold;
- using warm blankets or tinfoil to reheat the body slowly;
- giving warm, sweet drinks (non-alcoholic) and high-calorie snacks.

Treatment of severe hypothermia (body temperature less than 32°C)

Usually requires hospital admission and treatment with intravenous fluids.

21.2.2 Altitude sickness

Altitude sickness refers to the symptoms associated with travelling to high altitude (over 8,000 feet above sea level). DVI officers may be required to work in high-altitude locations at short notice.

The main health concerns associated with working at high altitude include:

- **Decreased availability of oxygen**. In high altitude, the air pressure decreases and it becomes harder for the lungs to take in sufficient oxygen. The body compensates by increasing the breathing rate, the breathing depth and the heart rate.
- **Dehydration**. Lower humidity and an increased breathing rate at high altitude cause the body to lose fluid.

Health risks

In ideal circumstances, the body would be given time to adapt slowly to the decreased availability of oxygen in the air.

The main health risks associated with doing physical work at high altitude are exacerbated by the fact that, in an emergency situation, DVI officers may not have sufficient time to acclimatise their bodies to the high altitude gradually.

The risk of altitude sickness is directly proportional to the rate of ascent, the height attained and the individual's level of physical exertion.

Individuals vary in their susceptibility to altitude sickness but, as a general rule, approximately 50 per cent of people ascending from sea level to 14,000 feet will experience symptoms. Onset of symptoms can occur any time from 8 hours to 4 days after arrival at an altitude of 8,000 feet.

Early symptoms

- Headache (commonest).
- Nausea and vomiting.
- Difficulty sleeping.
- Worsening headache.

Late symptoms

- Staggering.
- Confusion or change in behaviour.
- Difficulty breathing.
- Loss of consciousness.

Treatment

The first rule of treatment of altitude sickness is to stop ascending until the symptoms have disappeared. If the individual shows late signs or severe altitude sickness, it is advisable to move him or her to a lower altitude and to seek medical attention.

The best way to prevent altitude sickness is to make a slow, gradual ascent in order to give the body time to acclimatise to the reduced level of oxygen in the air. It is also advisable to limit the body's physical exertion and to drink plenty of fluids during the first few days following the ascent to altitude.

21.2.3   Infectious diseases

This section deals with the risks of contracting infections from the handling of dead bodies, specific to the work of DVI officers and staff (see Table 21.1).

Tropical diseases such as malaria are not covered as they are country specific and sometimes season specific, so it is always advisable to obtain up-to-date information regarding local conditions prior to departure.

How infectious are dead bodies?

Transmission[3] of infection requires:

- the presence of an infectious agent;
- exposure to that agent;
- a susceptible host.

When the human body dies, the infectious agents living within it will also die. However, this does not happen immediately after death and transmission of infectious viruses and bacteria from a cadaver to a living person may occur.[4]

395

Blood-borne
Hepatitis B
Hepatitis C
HIV
Gastrointestinal
Salmonellosis
E coli
Enteric fevers (typhoid and paratyphoid)
Cholera
Respiratory
Tuberculosis

Table 21.1   Specific infectious hazards associated with handling dead bodies
(Adapted from Morgan, 2004)[4]

The principal infectious risk to DVI personnel is likely to be blood-borne viruses such as Hepatitis B, Hepatitis C, HIV and possibly TB.

Blood-borne viral infections

Exposure to blood-borne viruses can occur due to direct contact with body fluids through broken skin, accidental penetration of the skin from bone fragments or needles, or from splashes of blood or body fluids to the eyes, nose and mouth. Use of PPE reduces this risk (see Figure 21.1).

Hepatitis B

Hepatitis B is a serious infection of the liver. It results from the transfer of the virus in blood or body fluids from an infected person. Hepatitis B is highly contagious – it is thought to be about one hundred times as contagious as HIV. Following one needle stick injury from an infected individual, the risk of infection is believed to be between 6 per cent and 30 per cent in those who have had no prior Hepatitis B vaccination.

In many developing countries, especially in sub-Saharan Africa, South East Asia, the Middle East, the Pacific and in some countries in Latin America, the prevalence of Hepatitis B infection is between 8 per cent and 10 per cent. Hepatitis B vaccination will prevent infection and will also be helpful for post-exposure protection.

Hepatitis C

Hepatitis C is estimated to affect about 3 per cent of the world population with prevalence being particularly high in Africa and the Eastern Mediterranean. There

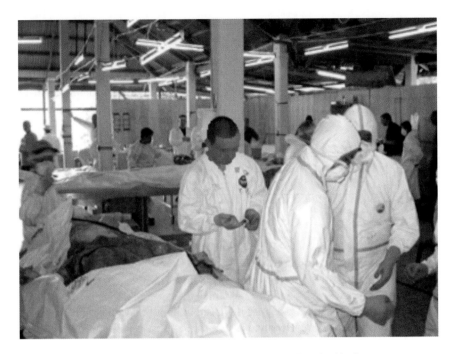

Figure 21.1   Use of PPE is required when handling dead bodies

is no vaccination against Hepatitis C, this is where the importance of PPE cannot be stressed enough. The wearing of PPE (body suit, boots, double gloving and face mask and goggles) acts as a second barrier to blood- and air-borne viruses.

HIV

The prevalence of HIV infection in individuals aged 14–45 years old is as high as 30–40 per cent in some African countries and about 0.1 per cent in Asia, Eastern Europe and Western Europe.

Importantly, infectious HIV can survive in cadavers for a considerable period of time (up to 16 days after death if stored at 2°C) and viable HIV has also been isolated from bone fragments, spleen, brain and lymph nodes at autopsy, six days post mortem. If a DVI officer is accidentally exposed to body fluids of a cadavar known, or strongly suspected, to be carrying HIV, post-exposure prophylaxis (PEP),[6] a combination of different medications, can be used to prevent HIV infection occurring in the officer. Only a consultant virologist can prescribe this medication, and its efficacy in preventing sero conversion,[7] which is the point at which an individual's HIV status changes from negative to positive, is directly related to the speed with which the treatment programme is commenced.

397

Gastrointestinal infections

Because corpses will commonly leak faeces, DVI personnel are likely to be exposed to infections from the victims' gastrointestinal tract. However, as the common gastrointestinal organisms do not survive for long periods following death of the body, there is relatively little risk of transmission of infection in comparison to blood-borne viruses.

Tuberculosis (TB)

There is evidence to suggest that handling cadavers, even intact cadavers, presents an increased risk of contracting tuberculosis. Those with prior BCG vaccination may have some protection against TB (see Table 21.2).

Universal precautions

Universal precautions for blood and body fluids should be followed.

When handling bodies, DVI officers should wear gloves and protective clothing appropriate to the conditions in which they are operating, ie full PPE. To avoid cross-contamination, personal items should not be handled while officers are wearing the full gloves, protective eye wear, suits, masks and boots which should be worn in situations where large quantities of body fluids or splashes of blood are anticipated. Hands must be washed thoroughly after handling cadavers and torn gloves must be replaced immediately and hands cleaned (see Table 21.3).

Diphtheria/tetanus/polio (every 10 years)

Typhoid (every 3 years)

Hepatitis A (2 "lifetime" doses)

Hepatitis B (choice of rapid or standard course followed by blood test)

TB / BCG – in defined circumstances, not necessarily travel-related

Rabies (3 doses, then 3-yearly booster)

Meningitis – 5-yearly

Cholera – 2-yearly

Flu – annually (note year-round risk in tropics)

Plus for those at "geographical" risk:

Yellow fever – for anyone who might need to travel to Africa/South America at less than 10 days' notice

Japanese encephalitis – for anyone who might need to travel to *rural* Asia at less than 14 days' notice

Tick encephalitis – for anyone who might need to spend time outdoors in rural central Europe at less than 14 days' notice

---

Table 21.2   Reducing the risk of infection: recommended vaccinations[5] for DVI workers

- Universal precautions for blood and body fluids
- Disposal or disinfection of used gloves
- Avoiding cross-contamination of personal items
- Thorough and frequent washing of hands after handling cadavers, using anti-bacterial products and always before eating and smoking
- Disinfection of vehicles and equipment
- Use of body bags
- Hepatitis B vaccination

Table 21.3   Reduction of risk of infection from dead bodies
(Adapted from Morgan, 2004)

21.3   PSYCHOLOGICAL WELLBEING

The nature of the work carried out by officers and staff in DVI situations poses unique emotional and psychological challenges.

DVI operations, by definition, expose personnel to busy, intense and emotionally demanding workloads, usually over a sustained period of time. Officers are exposed to scenes of death and destruction that they may not have witnessed previously. DVI work frequently involves prolonged contact with, or sight of, decaying or disrupted bodies. The working environment and working conditions are often challenging and hazardous, for example some victim identification work may need to be carried out in confined spaces, in extreme temperatures or even in the open air.

In addition to the challenges described above, DVI officers may have to work long hours with consequent lack of sleep and short meal or rest breaks. Finally, of course, DVI officers and staff are separated from family and friends for prolonged periods. At the same time, there is also intense pressure on DVI and staff to deliver results, requiring the DVI officer to remain focused on the job while simultaneously remaining alert to constantly changing environmental hazards.

The impact of cumulative stress in this type of work is well recognised. It is therefore *essential* that DVI personnel have an understanding of the normal emotional responses to a DVI operation and equally important that they are aware of the warning signs of negative stress or "burnout" in themselves and their colleagues.

21.3.1   Emotional reactions to traumatic situations

Exposure to traumatic situations can produce unusually strong emotional reactions that may interfere with an individual's ability to function at the scene or later.

Some people experience emotional aftershocks weeks or months after they have been involved in a disaster situation or a traumatic event. Man-made incidents usually tend to cause longer-lasting and more severe emotional reactions than natural disasters.

As stated above, strong emotions are *normal* reactions to an abnormal situation.

These feelings may include:

- feeling overwhelmed and pressurised due to demands from a variety of sources;
- sadness;
- anger may be felt about the injustice or senseless nature of the incident, particularly if the disaster is man made rather than natural;
- feelings of detachment, numbing or blocking of feelings;
- signs of emotional reactions to traumatic situations in others.

21.3.2   Warning signs

- Feeling overwhelmed by the situation to the point that it is difficult to continue.
- Feeling isolated and/or behaving unusually withdrawn.
- Behaving in a more aggressive, angry, irritable or confrontational way than normal, for example arguing with colleagues, friends or loved ones.
- Feeling in a low mood.
- Depressed or tearful most, but not necessarily all, of the time.
- Persistent feelings of intense anger.
- Feeling disoriented or experiencing difficulty in making simple decisions.
- Poor concentration or memory problems, for example difficulty recalling simple things or recent events.
- Difficulty identifying familiar people or familiar objects.

The list of warning signs and symptoms described above is neither exhaustive nor complete. If a DVI officer experiences any of these feelings or symptoms it is very important to seek medical help.

21.3.3   Post-Traumatic Stress Disorder (PTSD)

Post-Traumatic Stress Disorder (PTSD) may occur when a person has experienced, witnessed or been confronted with an event, which entailed actual or threatened death or injury or a threat to the physical integrity of themselves or others.

By the very nature of their work, DVI personnel are more likely than most other workers to encounter incidents of an emotional or shocking nature and to be exposed to traumatic experiences beyond the norm.

Symptoms

The main symptoms of PTSD are repeated and unwanted re-experience of the event, hyperarousal, emotional numbing and avoidance of stimuli that act as a reminder of the event.

Risk factors

Research on other emergency service workers has shown that certain specific factors increase the likelihood of an individual developing PTSD. For example, injuries or deaths in infants and children, exposure to gruesome injuries or deaths, and facing dangers or unpredictable situations all have greater impact. Previous personal traumatic experiences can influence the development and the degree of symptoms of PTSD. For example, firefighters with PTSD are likely to have experienced more negative life events prior to the trauma which caused their PTSD than those who have not developed PTSD.

Treatment

Most people who develop symptoms of PTSD recover without treatment over the next few months but in approximately 30–40 per cent the symptoms can persist for years. PTSD can be successfully treated with counselling and/or psychotherapy. DVI officers experiencing the symptoms of PTSD should *always* seek medical help.

Minimisation of psychological trauma: guidance for DVI supervisors

As a DVI supervisor, you can significantly minimise the risk of psychological trauma to your staff if you are able to anticipate, recognise and deal with the effects of stress in your staff. As a manager, you must be:

- aware of the potential stress risks;
- able to spot signs of fatigue or "burnout" at an early stage;
- able to help your staff through a period of sustained intense demand.

In any crisis situation there are four potential sources of psychological hazard:

- the event itself;
- the job that the officer is doing;
- the environment in which the officer is operating;
- the way in which the officer is managed.

21.3.4   Event stress

Event stress may be caused by emotional reaction to:

- trauma;
- witnessing death and suffering;
- interacting with distressed survivors or family members;
- working in physically dangerous or psychologically challenging conditions.

Event stress may also be associated with perceived mission failure, specifically loss of life and/or a perceived failure to resolve incidents or to find immediate solutions. This may be accentuated by media coverage. Sometimes, inaccurate reporting of a DVI operation, criticism or pressure to "deliver" may accentuate event stress.

21.3.5   Job stress

Job stress may be caused by:

- long working hours, often in a state of fatigue or jet lag;
- responsibility for life and death decisions;
- needing to find solutions urgently;
- heavy workload with difficult and often unfamiliar tasks.

Management issues that may be associated with job stress include:

- the need for recognition: If staff perceive that their extra effort is not being acknowledged, morale may suffer;
- the need for constant, clear communication;
- responsibilities and lines of authority must be clearly defined by the team leader.

21.3.6   How can DVI supervisors minimise stress in their staff?

It is important that DVI supervisors are aware of the symptoms of stress or exhaustion in their staff.

DVI supervisors need to be particularly observant of individual reactions and behaviours during periods of intense or sustained demand, since staff working under sustained pressure in a crisis situation are typically not the best judges of their own performance.

21.3.7   Physical symptoms of stress or exhaustion

- Nausea, upset stomach.
- Diarrhoea, loss of appetite.
- Exaggerated startle reaction.

- Headaches – aching muscles, particularly neck and shoulders.
- Disturbed sleep.

21.3.8 Behavioural symptoms of stress

- Mood swings.
- Irritability, aggression.
- Inability to prioritise.
- Diminished ability to cope with normal tasks and situations.
- Reduced confidence, making mistakes, forgetfulness.
- Poor decision-making.
- Increasing reliance on alcohol, caffeine or cigarettes.

If an individual displays many of the symptoms mentioned above, it is likely that his or her emotional reserves are becoming depleted and that their resistance is diminishing. Once fatigue or "burnout" sets in, efficiency, performance and effectiveness all suffer.

As stated above, because of the effects of stress or fatigue on thought processes, the person experiencing these symptoms may not be aware of their declining work performance and their reduced ability to cope. In this situation, it is vitally important that the manager spots the symptoms early.

If, as a team leader, you become aware that a member of your staff has become over-stressed, you must encourage him or her to leave the scene temporarily. Be aware of the techniques and facilities available for staff who become exhausted and over-stressed. Arrange for the officer to take some "time out" and if possible, provide support by arranging for the officer to talk to a trusted friend or a counsellor.

It is important that you demonstrate your concern and support. Generally, staff will cope better and longer in difficult situations if they feel that their manager cares about their welfare. Encourage and support staff with positive comments on their work, avoiding criticism where possible. Give staff permission to take care of themselves, for example encourage them to take adequate rest breaks, meal breaks etc. Remind your staff that it is not selfish to take a break – it is about self-preservation.

The "buddy" system has often proved valuable in the past, giving the officers someone to whom they can chat and who will remind them to take care of themselves while they also have responsibility to help their "buddy" in turn.

Finally, it is important that DVI supervisors set a good example. As team leaders, DVI supervisors can set an example by the way in which they handle their own personal stress. If, as a DVI supervisor, you feel that your own coping mechanisms are becoming exhausted or depleted, arrange for a replacement, temporarily withdraw yourself from the work situation and get some rest.

REFERENCES

1 "Sunburn", *Wikipedia* [online]. Available at: http://en.wikipedia.org/wiki/Sun_burn. [Accessed: 05.11.07.]

2 World Health Organization (WHO), "Ultraviolet radiation and the INTERSUN programme" [online]. Available at: http://www.who.int/uv/sun_protection/en/. [Accessed: 05.11.07.]

3 Pan American Health Organization, "Management of Cadavers following Natural Disasters" [online]. Available at: http://www.paho.org/English/DD/PED/te_cada. htm. [Accessed: 05.11.07.]

4 O Morgan, "Infectious disease risks from dead bodies following natural disasters" (2004) 15(5) *Rev Panam Salud Publica* [online]. Available at: http://www.scielosp. org/scielo.php?pid=S1020-49892004000500004&script=sci_arttext&tlng=en. [Accessed: 06.11.07.]

5 "Travel Vaccinations", *Netdoctor* [online]. Available at: http://www.netdoctor.co.uk/ travel/vaccines_index.shtml. [Accessed: 06.11.07.]

6 Department of Health, "Guidance from UK Chief Medical Officers' Expert Advisory Group on AIDS. 'HIV Post Exposure Prophylaxis'" (2004) [online]. Available at: http://www.dh.gov.uk/assetRoot/04/08/36/40/04083640.pdf. [Accessed: 06.11.07.]

7 "HIV/Aids – Symptoms & Diseases associated", *Health 24* [online]. Available at: http://www.health24.com/medical/Condition_centres/777-792-814-1756,22216.asp. [Accessed: 06.11.07.].

FURTHER READING

Auerbach, P S, *Wilderness Medicine* (4th edn, 2001).

Beaton, R and Murphy, S, "Secondary traumatic stress in crisis workers: research implications" in Figley, C, ed, *Compassion Fatigue* (1995) at 51–81.

Demiryürek, D, Bayramoglu, A and Ustacelebi, S, "Infective agents in fixed human cadavers: a brief review and suggested guidelines" (2002) 269 *Anat Rec* 194–197.

Gershon, R R, Vlahov, D, Escamilla Cejudo, J A, Badawi, M, McDiarmid, M, Karkashian, C *et al*, "Tuberculosis risk in funeral home employees" (1998) 40(5) *J Occup Environ Med* at 497–503.

Gershon, R R, Vlahov, D, Farzadegan, H and Alter, M J P H, "Occupational risk of human immunodeficiency virus, hepatitis B virus, and hepatitis C virus infections among funeral service practitioners in Maryland" (1995) 16(4) *Infect Control Hosp Epidemiol* at 194–197.

Healing, T D, Hoffman, P N and Young, S E, "The infections hazards of human cadavers" (1995) 5(5) *Commun Dis Rep CDR Rev* at R61–68.

Marx, J A, Hockberg, R S and Walls, R M (eds), *Rosen's Emergency Medicine: Concepts and Clinical Practice* (5th edn, 2001), pp 1979–1996.

Morgan, O, "Infectious disease risks from dead bodies following natural disasters" (2004) 15(5) *Rev Panam Salud Publica* at 307.

Noji, E K P H, "The public health consequences of disasters" (2000) 15(4) *Prehospital Disaster Med* at 147–157.

Pan American Health Organization, *Natural disasters. Protecting the public's health* (2000).

Persaud, R, "Post traumatic stress disorder in Doctors" (2005) 13 *studentBMJ* at 133–176.

Rischetelli, G, Harris, J, McCauley, L, Gershon, R R and Guidotti, T, "The risk of acquiring hepatitis B or C among public safety workers" (2001) 20(4) *Am J Prev Med* at 299–306.

United States of America, Centers for Disease Control and Prevention, "Hepatitis C virus infection among firefighters, emergency medical technicians, and paramedics" (2000) 49(29) *MMWR Morb Mortal Wkly Rep* at 660–665.

United States, Centers for Disease Control and Prevention, "Guidelines for prevention of transmission of human immunodeficiency virus and hepatitis B virus to health-care and public safety workers" (1989) 38(S–6) *MMWR Morb Mortal Wkly Rep* at 3–37.

United States, Centers for Disease Control and Prevention, "Guidelines for preventing the transmission of Mycobacterium tuberculosis in health-care facilities" (1994) 43(RR–13) *MMWR Recomm Rep* at 1–132.

Wagner, D, Meanricks, M and Ehlert, U, "Prevalence of Symptoms of PTSD in German Professional Firefighters" (1998) December 155 *American Journal of Psychiatry* at 1727–1732.

World Health Organization, "Hepatitis B" (Fact Sheet No 204) (2000).

World Health Organization, "Hepatitis C" (Fact Sheet No 164) (2000).

ACKNOWLEDGEMENTS

Jean Thomas and Nicky Jones – much of this chapter draws upon their work.

Dr Richard Dawood, Fleet Street Clinic, London, for advice regarding the DVI immunisation schedule.

Debbie Gilbert, for the photographs.

Richard Morris, for administrative support.

Grazia McCarthy, for typing.

Paul Madge, for consistent support and encouragement.

Index